Theatrical Milton

Edinburgh Critical Studies in Renaissance Culture

Series Editor: Lorna Hutson

Titles available in the series:

Open Subjects: English Renaissance Republicans, Modern Selfhoods and the Virtue of Vulnerability
James Kuzner

The Phantom of Chance: From Fortune to Randomness in Seventeenth-Century French Literature
John D. Lyons

Don Quixote in the Archives: Madness and Literature in Early Modern Spain
Dale Shuger

Untutored Lines: The Making of the English Epyllion
William P. Weaver

The Girlhood of Shakespeare's Sisters: Gender, Transgression, Adolescence
Jennifer Higginbotham

Friendship's Shadows: Women's Friendship and the Politics of Betrayal in England, 1640–1705
Penelope Anderson

Inventions of the Skin: The Painted Body in Early English Drama, 1400–1642
Andrea Ria Stevens

Performing Economic Thought: English Drama and Mercantile Writing, 1600–1642
Bradley D. Ryner

Forgetting Differences: Tragedy, Historiography, and the French Wars of Religion
Andrea Frisch

Listening for Theatrical Form in Early Modern England
Allison K. Deutermann

Theatrical Milton: Politics and Poetics of the Staged Body
Brendan Prawdzik

Forthcoming titles:

Perfecting the Law: Literature and Legal Reform in Shakespeare's England
Virginia Lee Strain

Visit the Edinburgh Critical Studies in Renaissance Culture website at edinburghuniversitypress.com/series/ecsrc

Theatrical Milton

Politics and Poetics of the Staged Body

Brendan Prawdzik

EDINBURGH
University Press

Edinburgh University Press is one of the leading university presses in the UK. We publish academic books and journals in our selected subject areas across the humanities and social sciences, combining cutting-edge scholarship with high editorial and production values to produce academic works of lasting importance. For more information visit our website: edinburghuniversitypress.com

© Brendan Prawdzik, 2017

Edinburgh University Press Ltd
The Tun – Holyrood Road
12(2f) Jackson's Entry
Edinburgh EH8 8PJ

Typeset in 10.5/13 Adobe Sabon by
Servis Filmsetting Ltd, Stockport, Cheshire

A CIP record for this book is available from the British Library

ISBN 978 1 4744 2101 0 (hardback)
ISBN 978 1 4744 2102 7 (webready PDF)
ISBN 978 1 4744 2103 4 (epub)

The right of Brendan Prawdzik to be identified as the author of this work has been asserted in accordance with the Copyright, Designs and Patents Act 1988, and the Copyright and Related Rights Regulations 2003 (SI No. 2498).

Published with the support of the University of Edinburgh Scholarly Publishing Initiatives Fund.

Contents

Acknowledgements	vi
Series Editor's Preface	viii
Introduction: Theatrical Milton	1
1. Speaking Body: The *Vacation Exercise* and *Paradise Lost*	14
2. Printless Feet: Early Lyrics and the *Maske*	50
3. Bending the Fool: *Animadversions* and the Early Prose	86
4. Theatre of Vegetable Love: *Paradise Lost*	130
5. Passion's Looking-Glass: *Samson Agonistes*	170
Epilogue: A Systemic Corpus	218
Works Cited	224
Index	240

Acknowledgements

This book could not have been completed without the encouragement of many people whom I admire, who intuited and nourished a potential often unknown to me. At the University of California, Berkeley, I was blessed to have a group of the finest advisors. Somehow, a dissertation titled 'Milton on Stage: Drama, Sin, and the Holy Script' allowed me to receive the PhD in 2009. For this, I am ever grateful to Victoria Kahn, James Grantham Turner and Jeffrey Knapp. Many years earlier, Ann Baines Coiro and Michael McKeon believed it worth their time to advise my undergraduate thesis – as it happened, on *Paradise Lost* – at Rutgers University. I give additional thanks to Kevis Goodman for her encouragement and mentoring, and to Janet Adelman, whose wisdom and care made better all whom she knew. David Loewenstein, Victoria Kahn and Lorna Hutson were instrumental to the publication of this project in their advice and direction. For bringing this project so smoothly to its conclusion, I am grateful to the staff of Edinburgh University Press, especially Adela Rauchova and James Dale, and for the careful eye and diligence of Patrick Davies.

Catherine Gallagher's confidence in my early work helped me to attain a Mabelle McLeod Lewis Memorial Fellowship, which provided a year of funded dissertation research. I received grants from the UC-Berkeley Department of English and the University that provided the time and clearness of mind for learning. 2009 was a difficult time to graduate, and I owe scholarly survival, in part, to UCLA's Center for 17th- and 18th-Century Studies, which granted an Ahmanson-Getty Postdoctoral Fellowship enabling a year of research in the jewel box of the William Andrews Clark Memorial Library, for whose expert and friendly staff I am ever grateful. Dorothy Hale and the UC-Berkeley's Department of English provided an additional year of postdoctoral study through a Roberta Holloway Postdoctoral Fellowship. Two weeks of research funding was granted by the Marco Institute for Medieval and Renaissance Studies at the University of Tennessee. I could not have become a UC-Berkeley graduate student without a Rotary International Ambassadorial Scholarship, which allowed me to enjoy language study at the University of St Andrews in 2001–2.

Other generous mentors along the way include Roger Easson, Ann Marie Wranovix, Nigel Smith and the members of the Marvell Society. Like all Miltonists, I am grateful for the generosity and efforts of Kristin Pruitt, Charlie Durham and Kevin Donovan, who made the biennial Conference on John Milton a haven for young scholars and a treasure of knowledge for the best and brightest in the field – and for David Ainsworth, who has led the way in keeping this beloved conference going. Alex Garganigo provided helpful commentary on Chapter 3, and the expert readers for Edinburgh University Press did the same for Chapters 3 and 5. My wife, Amy Sattler, whose patience and wisdom is inexhaustible, offered regular guidance, assistance and encouragement. Reid Barbour helped to work me through my first journal publication, and I owe thanks to *Studies in Philology* for permitting me to publish much of that article in Chapter 2. The same can be said for Louis Schwartz and the Duquesne University Press, which permitted publication of a part of Chapter 1. I owe an immeasurable debt to other peers and colleagues: Jesse Costantino, Sarah Townsend, Audrey Wu Clark, Thomas Lolis, Jordana Rosenberg, Matt Augustine, Neal Palmer, Blaine Greteman, Daniel Shore and Thomas Heron, among so many others.

To these all I owe the best of this book, and I accept any shortcomings as my own.

Brendan Prawdzik, Pennsylvania State University

Series Editor's Preface

Edinburgh Critical Studies in Renaissance Culture may, as a series title, provoke some surprise. On the one hand, the choice of the word 'culture' (rather than, say, 'literature') suggests that writers in this series subscribe to the now widespread assumption that the 'literary' is not isolable, as a mode of signifying, from other signifying practices that make up what we call 'culture'. On the other hand, most of the critical work in English literary studies of the period 1500–1700 which endorses this idea has rejected the older identification of the period as 'the Renaissance', with its implicit homage to the myth of essential and universal Man coming to stand (in all his sovereign individuality) at the centre of a new world picture. In other words, the term 'culture' in the place of 'literature' leads us to expect the words 'early modern' in the place of 'Renaissance'. Why, then, 'Edinburgh Critical Studies in *Renaissance Culture*'?

The answer to that question lies at the heart of what distinguishes this critical series and defines its parameters. As Terence Cave has argued, the term 'early modern', though admirably egalitarian in conception, has had the unfortunate effect of essentialising the modern – that is, of positing 'the advent of a once-and-for-all modernity' which is the deictic 'here and now' from which we look back.[1] The phrase 'early modern', that is to say, forecloses the possibility of other modernities, other futures that might have arisen, narrowing the scope of what we may learn from the past by construing it as a narrative leading inevitably to Western modernity, to 'us'. Edinburgh Critical Studies in Renaissance Culture aims rather to shift the emphasis from a story of progress – early modern to modern – to series of critical encounters and conversations with the past, which may reveal to us some surprising alternatives buried within texts familiarly construed as episodes on the way to certain identifying features of our endlessly fascinating modernity. In keeping

---

[1] T. Cave, 'Locating the Early Modern', *Paragraph*, 29: 1 (2006), 12–26, p. 14.

with one aspect of the etymology of 'Renaissance' or 'Rinascimento' as 'rebirth', moreover, this series features books that explore and interpret anew elements of the critical encounter between writers of the period 1500–1700 and texts of Greco-Roman literature, rhetoric, politics, law, oeconomics, *eros* and friendship.

The term 'culture', then, indicates a license to study and scrutinise objects other than literary ones, and to be more inclusive about both the forms and the material and political stakes of making meaning both in the past and in the present. 'Culture' permits a realisation of the benefits to be reaped after two decades of interdisciplinary enrichment in the arts. No longer are historians naïve about textual criticism, about rhetoric, literary theory or about readerships; likewise, literary critics trained in close reading now also turn easily to court archives, to legal texts and to the historians' debates about the languages of political and religious thought. Social historians look at printed pamphlets with an eye for narrative structure; literary critics look at court records with awareness of the problems of authority, mediation and institutional procedure. Within these developments, modes of research that became unfashionable and discredited in the 1980s – for example, studies in classical or vernacular 'source texts', or studies of literary 'influence' across linguistic, confessional and geographical boundaries – have acquired a new critical edge and relevance as the convergence of the disciplines enables the unfolding of new cultural histories (that is to say, what was once studied merely as 'literary influence' may now be studied as a fraught cultural encounter). The term 'Renaissance' thus retains the relevance of the idea of consciousness and critique within these textual engagements of past and present, and, while it foregrounds the Western European experience, is intended to provoke comparativist study of wider global perspectives rather than to promote the 'universality' of a local, if far-reaching, historical phenomenon. Finally, as traditional pedagogic boundaries between 'Medieval' and 'Renaissance' are being called into question by cross-disciplinary work emphasising the 'reformation' of social and cultural forms, so this series, while foregrounding the encounter with the classical past, is self-conscious about the ways in which that past is assimilated to the projects of Reformation and Counter-Reformation, spiritual, political and domestic, that finally transformed Christendom into Europe.

Individual books in this series vary in methodology and approach, sometimes blending the sensitivity of close literary analysis with incisive, informed and urgent theoretical argument, at other times offering critiques of grand narratives of the period by their work in manuscript transmission, or in the archives of legal, social and architectural history, or by social histories of gender and childhood. What all these books have in common, however, is the capacity to offer compelling, well-documented and lucidly written critical accounts of how writers and thinkers in the period 1500–1700 reshaped, transformed and critiqued the texts and practices of their world, prompting new perspectives on what we think we have learnt from them.

Lorna Hutson

for Amy

Introduction: Theatrical Milton

When the poet Andrew Marvell wrote the earliest piece of criticism on *Paradise Lost*, he imagined John Milton as a staged body: 'When I beheld the poet blind [...]'.[1] Marvell's Milton appears as the Biblical revenger Samson, whom *Samson Agonistes*, published three years prior, places on stage in the theatre of a false God. 'On Mr. Milton's *Paradise Lost*', published in the prefatory material for the 1674 second edition of the epic, presents a theatrical Milton, an embodiment shaped by audience, politics and scripture – in short, by what he would and did himself shape. He is his own preface, emerging from the conditions of writing. Were we to read the sinews of this body closely, we would, in the process, construct a new model of a poetic career. We would see the precise contours of Milton's interest in theatre and discover how it afforded him resources for poetic and polemical representation, as well as means to know, to transform and to re-present himself.

At the core of Milton's works is a contradictory relation to theatre that has neither been explained nor properly explored. Typically, scholars have linked Milton to theatre through his interest in genres.[2] In 1628, he wrote and performed in a comedic interlude as part of a Cambridge initiation ceremony. In 1632, he wrote a provincial aristocratic progress loosely related to the masque. In 1634, he wrote the Ludlow *Maske* ('Comus'). In the early 1640s, he drafted scores of sketches for possible Old Testament, Christian and British historical dramas. Two of the most developed of these sketches are for a drama about the Fall. In 1671, he added to *Paradise Regained* and the closet drama *Samson Agonistes*. And yet this evidence tells less than half of the story of Milton's relation to the dramatic medium in its various forms and discourses. Taken alone, it tells a misleading story.

Scholarly discussion of a 'dramatic' presence in Milton is fragmented and contradictory, largely because Milton's application of theatrical structures and engagement with dramatic forms cannot be reduced, at any point in his career, to an unqualified pro- or anti-theatrical stance. Milton returns to the idea of theatre so frequently not because he was an aspiring playwright or an avid playgoer but, rather, because theatre was for him a problem – neither something to abjure nor to embrace uncritically – that helped him to set up the terms of negotiation for ethical, spiritual and poetic action. The early lyrics flirt with popular drama in ways that are intriguing yet equivocal. Significant threads of anti-theatrical discourse appear in the early poetry, the epic, the brief epic and even texts that are generically dramatic. These are, furthermore, distinct from the popular dramas of Shakespeare, Jonson, Middleton, Beaumont, Fletcher and Shirley. If the popular dramatic tradition is how we measure Milton, then Milton is not a dramatist.[3]

Theatrical Milton brings coherence to the presence of theatre in Milton through the concept of theatricality. In this study, 'theatricality' comes to mean several interrelated things. To begin with, it identifies a discursive field entailing the rhetorical strategies and effects of framing a given human action, including speech and writing, as an act of theatre. Seventeenth-century theatricality overwhelmingly served the ends of polemic. Political and theological cultures in seventeenth-century England developed a treasury of representational resources in order to stage – to satirise and, above all, to de-legitimate – rhetors of politics, religion and print. The semiotics of theatricality drew upon the physical structures of the theatre, the characters or character types of the stage, the presence of spectators, and a rhetoric of the theatrical body derived from classical traditions. Once 'published', the rhetor can be claimed *as* a theatrical subject through the imposition of theatrical structures – including props, costumes, architectural elements, and spectators – and through the representation of the body. The agent forfeits control over the signification of her body, as this materialised ethos is made to speak to new audiences and to new contexts, almost always to the purposes of satire or in order to render the rhetor illegitimate or inauthentic.

How are 'theatricality' and 'drama' distinct? To begin with, theatricality is unbound by genre; as we will see, it permeates Milton's prose, lyrics, epic and brief epic. It is also never far from his self-representations, in all of their variety. Drama, on the other hand, is a genre, yet it becomes theatrical when framed, within the text or performance, as a drama that is being seen. Theatricality always inhabits metadrama, and metadrama is always theatrical. Dramas-within-dramas and dramatic set-pieces in poetry or prose do occur, and in these moments the dramatic and the theatrical overlap, because the scene is being represented as a drama being seen. For instance, in Thomas Kyd's *The Spanish Tragedy*, *Soliman and Perseda* is a drama being staged within the play that we are seeing. Yet we cannot deny the theatricality of, say, Bel-Imperia, because we accept that she is a human being, with her own feelings and motives, who is, nonetheless, playing a dramatic part. When Shakespeare's Hamlet recognises himself as a dramatic character, we are seeing, as an epiphenomenon of the drama that we are seeing, his theatricality. When, in the *Apology Against a Pamphlet* (1642), Milton refers to Bishop Joseph Hall as a 'boasting *Thraso*', he is using this reference to Plautus's *Miles Gloriosus* in order to mark Hall as theatrical.[4] He is not, of course, staging the drama of *Miles Gloriosus*. On the whole, drama is much less mobile than theatricality; this is, in part, because it requires a more complete set of framing features, and, in part, because it requires narrative temporality. Paradoxically, despite the framing that drama requires, its narrative temporality makes it, as a construct, tend toward dissolution. In scholarly practice, the word 'drama', as denoting a quasi-theoretical concept, has often meant little more, or nothing more, than narrative.[5] The non-dramatic use of the word 'drama' is superabundant in both scholarly and lay discourses. In short, the construct of theatricality has the benefit of being, at once, more mobile and more precise.

Rhetorical Delivery

The theatrical Milton develops around the rhetorical tradition of *actio*. This tradition of bodily rhetoric begins with Demosthenes (384–322 BC) and was developed among Cicero – in *De oratore* (55 BC), *Brutus* (46 BC) and *Orator* (46 BC) – and his contemporaries. It was augmented by Quintilian in the *Institutio oratoria* (AD 95) and memorialised in Plutarch's accounts of Demosthenes and Cicero in *Parallel Lives* (c. 100 AD).

Actio – translated as 'delivery' and alternately termed *pronuntiatio* – refers to the discipline of the body in oratory. Teaching of rhetoric by Cicero and Quintilian focuses on gestures of the arms, facial expression, general carriage of the body, and voice. *Actio* destabilises what might generally be termed the rhetorical body because it originates in theatrical practice. Demosthenes, explains Plutarch, was a failed orator until he became acquainted with the tragedian Andronicus, who demonstrated the degree to which the skills of the actor could enhance the power of oratory. Andronicus drilled Demosthenes, helping to strengthen the orator's weak voice by having him declaim while running uphill, while facing the ocean waves, and with stones in his mouth. Demosthenes learnt gesture by practising in front of a mirror.[6] If rhetoric involved a disciplining of logical and written forms, it always involved a disciplining of the body. In the intensely competitive political environments in which Demosthenes and Cicero operated, excesses of voice and, particularly, of bodily gesture rendered the orator vulnerable to association with the feminine and the comedic; the orator's body was, essentially, open to queering by spectators and competing rhetors.[7] Oratory became further associated with comedy through the story of Cicero's training in *actio* by the famed comedian Roscius, as also recounted by Plutarch.[8]

There are several places where Milton addresses the tradition of *actio* directly. For instance, in *Paradise Lost* (1667), he describes Satan, who is preparing to commence the temptation, as an ancient Greek or Roman orator whose gestures win over the audience before his speech begins.[9] When, in *Of Education* (1644), Milton discusses the place of declamation in his pedagogy, he suggests that students read speeches by Demosthenes and Cicero, as well as tragedies by Sophocles and Euripides, in order to 'memor[ise]' and 'solemnly pronounc[e]' them 'with right accent', in order to attain the 'spirit and vigor' of these authors.[10]

The association of gesture with the feminine and the comedic continues in Milton, as it would in a wide variety of contemporary rhetorical, religious and political texts. Milton also applies these associations to himself. As Chapters 1 and 2 discuss, in his early works, Milton considers the feminisation of his own rhetorical self, the feminised theatrical body being a font of inspired poetic power. But the association of the gesturing body with the comedic would prove more troublesome for Milton the politician. The way that Milton treats the proximity of the body's gesture to the comedic depends, largely, on his view of and relation to the public, which, as Paul Hammond argues, remained an abstraction that could flex to meet the rhetorical situation, and from which Milton would increasingly distance himself.[11] Milton embraces a comedic aspect to his authorial identity in *Animadversions upon the Remonstrants Defence Against Smectymnuus* (1641), where his polemical style is at its least restrained. Not coincidentally, in this tract he dons an authorial persona related to the stage fool, speaking with a satirical voice that is attuned to the satirical pamphlets published by opponents of the Church in 1641–2. However, his troubled embrace of foolery was short-lived. Subsequent texts show him working to distance himself from, and finally to disavow, the figure of the stage fool.[12]

Religious Culture and the Holy Script

The rhetoric of *actio* is by no means the only influence on Milton's theatricality. He was, of course, well familiar with the social and architectural structures of theatre, as well as with the use of costumes and stage properties. We see hissing spectators in the *Vacation Exercise* (1628), *Animadversions*, the *Apology*, *Eikonoklastes* (1649) and *Paradise Lost*; costumes and stage properties in *Of Reformation* (1641), *Animadversions*, the *Apology*, *Reason of Church Government* (1642), *Paradise Lost* and *Paradise Regained* (1671); active theatre spectators in a wider range of texts; and detailed descriptions of theatre spaces in *Paradise Lost, Paradise Regained* and *Samson Agonistes* (1671). Milton might easily have attended plays, whether at Cambridge or after his return from the Continent in 1639, and might have as easily absorbed his knowledge from conversations, pamphlets and quarto and folio editions of plays. After all, his first published poem in English was 'On Shakespear', an equivocal meditation on the playwright that, somehow, made it into the Second Folio of Shakespeare's works in 1632.[13]

The print culture of the 1640s was suffused with theatricality, despite the closing of the theatres in 1642. Milton's anti-prelatical tracts focus on Anglican ritual as theatrical, in part, in its rigid formalism. In this analysis, ritual becomes scripted performance, the *Book of Common Prayer* itself becomes script, and the speech of priest and congregation becomes a lifeless rehearsal of script. For Milton, Anglican formalism is so troubling because it hardens the Spirit into a 'crust of Formalitie' and, thus, impedes the Christian's and the community's spiritual connection with God and scripture.[14] This stifling of the Spirit serves the ends of Laudian reform, the consolidation of prelatical wealth, and the powers of the Caroline regime. The Milton that wrote *Of Reformation*, *Of Prelaticall Episcopacy*, and *Reason* sees Anglican forms as supplanting the script, as it were, of the Bible, though even in these early tracts the language of direct scriptural access, or of a type of scriptural literalism, is in conflict with emergent poetic sensibilities.

Brief satirical tracts from 1641–2 placed the time's antagonists within mini 'dramas' of exposure and punishment. They played a vital role in theatricalising the religious and political scene. These 'playlets' were informed by the Marprelate tracts that troubled, during the late 1580s, Elizabeth I's efforts to consolidate Church and State. The Marprelate tracts attempted to absorb the populist spirit of the amphitheatres into a ludic, seemingly improvising prose style. Soon after the death of the beloved stage fool Richard Tarlton, the pseudonymous Martin Marprelate appeared in print, embracing the persona and voice of the stage fool to make a mockery of the bishops, rather than to develop and to perpetuate serious arguments against the Church establishment.[15] From the beginning, the Martinist strategy invited the persona to be de-legitimated as a grotesque comic figure; the mantra, from Proverbs 26:5, of 'Answer[ing] a fool according to his folly', could be practised reiteratively, *ad infinitum*.[16] The Elizabethan regime promoted numerous works, including satires, poems and interludes, that aimed to turn Marprelate's target audience against him.[17] The longer that Marprelate remained in the public eye, the less credible and less amusing he became. Ultimately, the authors and printers of the Marprelate conspiracy were captured and died in prison or on the scaffold – with the exception of Job Throckmorton, a gentleman and MP.[18]

This story anticipates a crucial period in the development of Milton's theatricality and authorial identity. Adopting something like the figure of the stage fool in *Animadversions*, Milton assails Anglican hypocrisy and deadness of spirit. At the same time, he taunts the prelates – particularly Joseph Hall, to whose *Humble Remonstrance* (1641) he responds – and represents them as surrounded by a menacing popular audience that is constricting around them. In 1641, the polis was, for Milton, a public of active readers and writers capable both of *recta ratio* and of toppling the Anglican establishment with aggression, if need be. In a remarkable visionary passage of *Animadversions*, Milton transfuses the energies of the stage fool into millennial prophecy; the spirit of inspired foolishness leads to a direct assertion of the Spirit's power to 'renovat[e] and reingend[er]' scripture.[19] If the rigid formalism of the Anglican Church reduced scripture to a dead letter, the lithe, spirited improvisation of the stage fool could help to galvanise it.

But when Milton was first attacked in print, and effectively so, in the 1642 *Modest Confutation of a Slanderous and Scurrilous Libell*, he realised how vulnerable the foolish persona was to charges of indecorum, and to the satirical use of the rhetoric of *actio*. The Modest Confuter styles Milton as a buffoon who outrageously disrupts a serious religious and political scene. Moreover, this buffoon is a 'Ringleader' of the 'very beasts of the people'.[20] The Confuter identifies Milton with Marprelate's populism and heirs – such as Martin Mar-Priest, Martin Claw-Clergie and Bartholomew Bang-Priest – of the late 1630s and early 1640s. As we have already seen, the rhetoric of *actio* associated unrestrained gesture with an undisciplined populism. In subsequent tracts, Milton works to distance himself from the stage fool at the same time that he was becoming increasingly wary of populism. The rhetoric of *actio* – of wild gestures, gaping mouths, contorted faces and overly voluminous declamation – was an effective but unstable resource in religious and political satire. In the *Apology*, Milton is quick to turn the language of 'antick and dishonest gestures' against the Anglicans.[21] By the time that he attacked, in *Eikonoklastes*, the King's self-representation as a martyr, he was able to organise several resources of theatrical rhetoric to pulverise the King's image.[22]

As Chapter 5 details, by the early 1650s, the anti-theatrical rhetorical palette had become more colourful. The available representational resources responded to the extravagant behaviours of emergent sectarians – particularly, the early Quakers, against whom this satirical language was used to de-legitimate claims to direct spiritual illumination. Words such as 'gesture', 'action', 'motion', 'mimic' and 'antic' could readily connote madness, Satanic possession or simply the playacting of spiritual presence driven by self-interest.

Theatrical Milton does not add to the list of work about the influence of Shakespeare on Milton's sense of literary authority or on his poetics of the imagination.[23] Nonetheless, *Hamlet* – the most richly theatrical of Shakespeare's plays – offers insight into Milton's sense of the relationship between the theatrical body and script. Hamlet's instructions to the visiting players before the staging of *The Murder of Gonzago* are particularly illuminating.

> Speak the speech, I pray you, as I pronounced it to you – trippingly on the tongue; but if you mouth it, as many of your players do, I had as lief the town-crier had spoke my lines. Nor do not saw the air too much with your hand, thus, but use all gently; for in the very torrent, tempest, and as I may say the whirlwind of your passion, you must acquire and beget a temperance that may give it smoothness. O, it offends me to the soul to hear a robustious, periwig-pated fellow tear a passion to tatters, to very rags, to split the ears of the groundlings, who for the most part are capable of nothing but inexplicable dumb shows and noise [. . .] And let those that play your clowns speak no more than is set down for them; for there be of them that will themselves laugh to set on some quantity of barren spectators to laugh too, though in the mean time some necessary question of the play be then to be considered: that's villainous, and shows a most pitiful ambition in the fool that uses it.[24]

Hamlet's grievances belong to the Ciceronian tradition that views the action of the body as a type of speech that must be carefully managed in order to maintain its eloquence: '*Est enim actio quasi corporis quaedam eloquentia, cum constet e voce atque motu*' ('In fact, action is like a type of eloquence, with corresponding voice and motion').[25] Shakespeare is applying a formal understanding of *actio* rather than a merely generic notion of propriety or decorum in Elizabethan theatre.[26] Common features include the wild gesturing of the hands and exaggerated pronunciation that corresponds with the facial gesture of 'mouthing'.[27] These gestures fail to represent the 'passion' or emotional state of the character inherent to the script, but, rather, 'tear' it 'to tatters' in their excess.

Moreover, these actions are directed toward the 'groundlings', the often uneducated ('barren') and relatively poorest of the spectators who took their standing position on the ground before the stage. These are the spectators who cared less about the art of theatre than about the banter, acrobatics and jigs of the fool at play's end. In Milton, these spectators would, after 1642, be relegated to the comedic and its negative, discrediting associations. Shakespeare applies the rhetoric of *actio* to the same ends during Volumnia's precise instructions to Coriolanus as to how he should act in order to secure the favour of the polis:

> Go to them with this bonnet in thy hand,
> And thus far having stretch'd it – here be with them –
> Thy knee bussing the stones – for in such business
> Action is eloquence, and the eyes of the ignorant
> More learnèd than the ears.[28]

So Milton would associate the 'silly gazers' who gaped with admiration at the postures of Charles I in the *Eikon Basilike* with the 'inconstant, irrational, and image-doting rabble'.[29]

In Hamlet's speech, the structures and language of theatre and *actio* are not bound to anti-theatrical values. Of course, Hamlet does not abjure playacting – only a certain kind. In a play that so often foregrounds correspondences between theatre and the play's reality; in which the revenger's dilemma depends on the alignment and measure of timing, emotion and action appropriate to the execution of revenge; and in which the revenger seeks a way to mediate between the 'script' provided by his father and improvisation, the key question is not whether to act but, rather, *how* to act. In addition to demanding that the actors speak 'trippingly', that they speak and gesture 'gently', and that they convey even tempestuous passions with 'temperance' and 'smoothness', Hamlet again implies the Ciceronian correspondence of speech and action: 'let your own discretion be your tutor. Suit the action to the word, the word to the action, with this special observance: that you o'erstep not the modesty of nature'.[30] In playacting, to 'suit the action to the word' implies an appropriate enacting of 'the word' of the script. Such is precisely what play troupes, from the Renaissance to the present, negotiate in the blocking of lines and in rehearsals – as materially and spatially situated individual bodies and as a collective, interacting body.

The tension between rigorous obedience to script and wild improvisation that contorts or defies the script furthermore played out in the theological conflicts of the mid-seventeenth century, particularly in debate over styles of prayer and exegesis. Milton applies the language of costume and stage properties while assailing the imposed forms of the *Book of Common Prayer*. Indeed, an oppositional readership familiar with strategies of anti-theatrical rhetoric could see the *Book* itself as a play-script permitting no improvisation: not only words, but even actions and feeling, are scripted and compelled. On the other hand, the anti-theatrical use of *actio* identified extemporary prayer and exegesis with extra-Biblical fantasies that violated the dominant decorum of solemnity. This strategy was particularly effective in anti-Quaker satire, which often foregrounded the correspondence between the quaking of the body – which signified, for the Quakers, the unmediated presence of the Spirit – and an erroneously extemporary relationship to scripture. Thus, improvisation was integral to any responsible Christian poetics, even as it tended toward extra-scriptural error.

As Dayton Haskin has argued, Milton's relationship to scripture underwent a transformation during the first half of the 1640s.[31] In *Of Reformation*, Milton professes scripture's clarity and direct accessibility. Certainly no later than the Divorce Tracts, we see an embrace of scriptural ambiguities, obscurities, aporia and potential contradictions that need to be resolved through comparisons of scriptural passages and through *recta ratio*. Thus, in *Tetrachordon* (1645), Milton achieves a justification of divorce on the grounds of incompatibility by generating a harmonious truth from four scriptural passages. Likewise, the Jesus of *Paradise Regained* seeks understanding of his Messianic identity by 'revolv[ing] / The Law and Prophets'.[32]

As I argue in Chapter 3, Milton's absorption of the stage fool into his authorial persona initiates an extraordinary prophetic passage that synthesises Leviticus and Revelation into a poetically amplified prophecy of imminent Millennium. It is a passage that the Modest Confuter would target as a 'theatricall, big-mouthed, astounding Prayer'.[33] While Milton strove subsequently to distance himself from the stage fool, he nonetheless maintained that it is the Christian poet's role to amplify scripture in order to make it speak more fully, in part by stimulating productive investigation and discourse among an audience 'fit [. . .] though few'.[34] As Chapter 4 contends, Milton comes to the conclusion in *Paradise Lost* that Christian being is itself inexorably theatrical, and that questions of how to read, how to write, how to obey and how to interact are always questions of how to navigate between the extremes of rigid obedience to and wild improvisation upon scripture-as-script.

The Theatrical Body

The theatrical subject is a mimetic agent who acts toward a rhetorical audience complicit, or seen to be complicit, in the action; in other words, the actor's body shares a co-shaping bond with that of the spectators upon whom and for whom he acts. In Milton, this bond infuses represented action with phenomenal presence.[35]

One can inhabit theatrical subjectivity for rhetorical purposes, as Satan does several times in *Paradise Lost*. But not even Satan assumes the theatrical body independently; rather, as I demonstrate in the second half of Chapter 1, this theatrical body comes into being through the fact that it is observed. In books III and IV of *Paradise Lost*, Satan inhabits distinct modes of theatricality: in the first, he is able to deceive Uriel through disguise; in the second, his movements expose the guise when he does not know that Uriel is watching. When Uriel observes, from the sun, Satan's 'furious gestures' upon Mount Niphates, a body that is simply overcome by passions becomes analysable as a theatrical body marked by the rhetoric of *actio*. In this case, 'gestures' denotes the wild flailing of the body driven by inner torment.[36] By observing this body that does not know that it is being observed, Uriel can piece together the fact that Satan had deceived him when seeking information in the guise – a theatrical guise, straight from the tiring house of masquing culture – of a zealous cherub.

Throughout the development of Milton's theatricality, we see an increasing emphasis on spectators not only as constituting a rhetorical audience, and not only as an agential body in its own right that works upon the staged rhetor, but also as a presence that menaces authority from the periphery. Spectators and actor are not simply bound by a negotiated desire; they are also engaged in an agonistic relationship, each seeking a type of dominion over the other. The presence or imagined presence of spectators in the periphery maintains a potentially insidious influence. It becomes a menace, a power that can dismember and disintegrate. In the invocation to book VII of *Paradise Lost*, the bard laments that he is 'fall'n on evil dayes, / [. . .] and evil tongues; / In darkness, and with dangers compast round'.[37] He is not simply recalling the harrowing days of summer 1660. The idea of being 'in darkness, and with dangers compast round' also suggests his experience as a figure of public scorn and derision, as an author targeted by printed attacks, to which he was restrained from responding. His blindness would have intensified the effect.

Most immediately, however, the phrase 'in darkness, and with dangers compast round' indexes the danger that he faces as the bard of his own 'adventrous Song', his epic, his extraordinary amplification of scripture that skirts error at every line.[38] Seeking confidence to amplify the Hexameron poetically, he calls upon Urania to 'drive farr off the barbarous dissonance / Of *Bacchus* and his revellers, the Race / Of that wilde Rout that tore the *Thracian* Bard' (Orpheus). Instead, he seeks to 'fit audience find, though few'.³⁹ He is speaking from the stage, as it were, that places the author before the eyes of reader-spectators. Attempting his daunting exegetical-poetic task, he hopes to push away, at least from his creating imagination, the spectators who menace from the periphery, so that he can address his poem exclusively to those readers who are fit readers – or who would aspire to be fit readers – of the poem.⁴⁰

In both *Paradise Lost* and the *Maske* (as well as in 'Lycidas'), the Bacchantes represent the threat of mutilation or *sparagmos* – the absolute disintegrating of the body by those in Dionysian frenzy.⁴¹ If theatricality entails the negotiation of rhetorical authority between rhetor and audience, actor and spectator, the power to negotiate weakens in the periphery of sight, for in that periphery is an agency that exceeds the lens-like scope of rhetorical force. Particularly in *Paradise Lost* and *Samson Agonistes*, as detailed in Chapters 4 and 5, respectively, the seeing eyes that cannot be seen exert an influence upon theatrical bodies that they participate in moving. The periphery's effect on the theatrical body can be benign, loving, strengthening, spiritual, malicious, weakening or coercive – thus helping to pull the body into gestures of wild improvisation that can correspond with catastrophic scriptural error. Milton's mature theatricality shows interest in predominant optical theories, particularly those of Descartes and Hobbes.⁴² However, his theatricality is fundamentally at odds with Descartes' interlinked theories of optics, the passions and action, in that it underscores the constraints of vision and the control over the passions in the confrontation with a surrounding audience of spectators. And while Milton shared much of Hobbes's view of material contingency and of human sensitivity to the motive force of the passions, he actively strove to identify a quality of agency that could operate with a focused liberty within a material and social world of constraints.

Within the embodied spectacle of theatrical interaction, the rhetor, in his authority, remains menaced by the periphery, by the seeing eyes that he cannot see. Thus, the Lacanian tension between the optical focal point and the periphery corresponds with a paradox shared by rhetorical and poetic authority, on the one hand, and theatrical performance, on the other: that authority renders the author vulnerable, and that to act is, in part, to be acted upon.⁴³ For this reason, the theatrical subject runs a constant risk of being reduced to a stage fool whose body belongs more to readers and spectators than to a true self. The wayfaring Christian and the exegetical poet stray so wide of scripture-as-script that what is felt to be spiritual authority is, in fact, driven by uncontrolled passions. What is felt to be spirit is desire. What is felt as faith is self-delusion. What appears to be authority is textuality.

Notes

1. A. Marvell, 'On Mr. Milton's *Paradise Lost*', line 1.
2. See, especially, T. Burbery, *Milton the Dramatist*; J. G. Demaray, *Milton and the Masque Tradition*; Demaray, *Milton's Theatrical Epic*; and B. K. Lewalski, *Paradise Lost and the Rhetoric of Literary Forms*.
3. See T. H. Howard-Hill, 'Milton and "The Rounded Theatre's Pomp"'.
4. J. Milton, *Apology*, *CPW*, I, p. 879; see below, pp. 106, 113–14.
5. See, for instance, J. H. Hanford, 'The Dramatic Element in *Paradise Lost*'; D. Loewenstein, *Milton and the Drama of History*; and M. Nyquist, 'Reading the Fall'.
6. Plutarch, *Twelve Lives*, pp. 359–62.
7. See E. Gunderson, *Staging Masculinity*.
8. Plutarch, *Twelve Lives*, pp. 382–5.
9. Milton, *Paradise Lost*, *WJM*, II.ii, IX, lines 664–78; see below, p. 20.
10. Milton, *Of Education*, *CPW*, II, pp. 400–1; see below, pp. 18–20.
11. P. Hammond, *Milton and the People*.
12. See below, pp. 113–14.
13. For the poem's equivocality, see J. Guillory, *Poetic Authority*, pp. 18–19. For the possible role of Milton's father in the publication, see C. G. Martin, *Milton among the Puritans*, p. 70.
14. Milton, *Of Reformation*, *CPW*, I, p. 421.
15. P. Collinson, 'Ben Jonson's *Bartholomew Fair*', p. 166.
16. All biblical quotations are taken from R. Carroll and S. Prickett (eds), *The Bible: Authorized King James Version*.
17. J. Black, 'The Rhetoric of Reaction', p. 715.
18. See L. H. Carson, *Martin Marprelate, Gentleman*.
19. Milton, *Animadversions*, *CPW*, I, p. 703.
20. Anon., *Modest Confutation*, p. 32.
21. Milton, *Apology*, *CPW*, I, p. 887.
22. See below, pp. 117–20.
23. See, for instance, A. Fletcher, *The Transcendental Masque*; Guillory, *Poetic Authority*; M. Hunt, 'Managing Spenser, Managing Shakespeare in *Comus*'; and P. Stevens, *Imagination and the Presence of Shakespeare in 'Paradise Lost'*. For an essential counterpoint, see J. T. Shawcross, *John Milton and Influence*.
24. W. Shakespeare, *Hamlet*, NS, III, ii, lines 1–13, 34–40.
25. Cicero, *Orator*, p. 55. My translation.
26. The language of theatrical action is more broadly discussed in D. Bevington, *Action Is Eloquence*.
27. See below, pp. 121, 180.
28. Shakespeare, *Coriolanus*, NS, III, ii, lines 73–7.
29. Milton, *Eikonoklastes*, *CPW*, III, pp. 342, 601.
30. Shakespeare, *Hamlet*, NS, III, ii, lines 16–18.
31. D. Haskin, *Milton's Burden of Interpretation*, pp. 1–117.
32. Milton, *Paradise Regained*, *WJM*, II.ii, I, lines 259–60.
33. Anon., *Modest Confutation*, p. 22.
34. Milton, *Paradise Lost*, *WJM*, II.i, VII, line 31.

35. See L. Liblein, 'Embodied Intersubjectivity and the Creation of Early Modern Character'.
36. Milton, *Paradise Lost*, *WJM*, II.i, IV, argument; see also IV, line 128.
37. Ibid., VII, lines 25–7.
38. Ibid., I, line 13.
39. Ibid., VII, lines 33–4, 31.
40. See D. Shore, *Milton and the Art of Rhetoric*, pp. 1–18.
41. See M. Lieb, *Milton and the Culture of Violence*, pp. 15–16.
42. See below, pp. 140–2.
43. J. Lacan, *Four Fundamental Concepts*, pp. 65–119.

Chapter 1

Speaking Body: The *Vacation Exercise* and *Paradise Lost*

Did the young John Milton attend a play or two, or perhaps more? Almost certainly. We would expect a young bachelor to take in a play here and there. We would expect that re-stagings of Shakespeare and original works by Ben Jonson, or, perhaps, by Milton's Cambridge peer Thomas Randolph, might allure an aspiring poet.[1] Milton implies in two early works that he had attended plays. In *Elegia sexta*, he writes to Charles Diodati about visiting and fearing to lose himself in the playhalls. Moreover, in 'L'Allegro', we learn of the poet's desire to catch a comedy by Shakespeare or a tragedy by Jonson. Later, in the *Apology*, he would locate himself within the audience of a Cambridge play, as an intensely invested, discerning spectator who joins the crowd in hissing bad actors from the stage. There is speculative evidence, too, that Milton had experienced the popular drama of the London playhalls. A John Milton – not our poet, but perhaps his father – was, for a time, a shareholder of the Blackfriars playhall.[2]

Just as there is no evidence in Milton's writings that he viewed public theatre uncritically, so, too, is there no evidence that he abjured it, that he thought it unfit for his person. The drama, as he encountered it in books, in college or in London, offered models for his own mimeses. The metaphor driving Shakespeare's dramaturgy – of the world as a stage – was one of action, of performing bodies seen by spectators. Indeed, as so much New Historical scholarship has shown, the sign of the staged actor could work as a structural principle underlying late-sixteenth- and seventeenth-century English culture more broadly.

Accordingly, theatre in Milton absorbs its conceptual power from a number of places and centres of social organisation. He read antitheatrical literature, including Lactantius, Tertullian and, perhaps, William Prynne. He might have attended sermons that decried theatre and, like many contemporaries, might have considered the theatricality of the preachers while attending their sermons. Monarchy, of course, was inherently theatrical, a fact as evident in Milton's *Eikonoklastes* as in Shakespeare's *Richard III* and *Henry IV, Part I*, half a century before.³ Processions, academic declamations, masques, executions: these displays of power shared an essential structure – one that found in theatre its point of reference. A seventeenth-century Londoner could hope to encounter spectacles showing Native Americans, northern Africans, exotic animals and deformed bodies. Anatomy theatres, mountebanks, puppet shows – the list goes on. So Lovewit of Jonson's *Alchemist* marvels, admiringly, at how his serving-man had been able to attract crowds at his home while he was away during plague-time: 'banners / Of a strange calf with five legs to be seen, / Or a huge lobster with six claws?'; 'bawdy pictures' or 'The Friar and the Nun, of the new motion [i.e., puppet show] / Of the knight's courser covering the parson's mare'?; 'The boy of six year old with the great thing [penis]'?; 'fleas that run at tilt / Upon a table, or some dog to dance?'⁴

This chapter begins by looking at the closest thing to popular drama that Milton wrote. The text in question begins with a Latin oration and prolusion, follows with an English poem and concludes with a dramatic farce, what would be termed an 'interlude' by Milton and his contemporaries, which remains to us only as an unpromising fragment. I refer to the work in its entirety as the *Vacation Exercise* and thus carry the reference to the complete work in the title of the English poem, 'At a Vacation Exercise in the Colledge, Part Latin, Part English', which first appeared in the 1673 *Poems, etc. upon Several Occasions*. The Latin orations that constitute the first two sections of the *Vacation Exercise* were first published as 'Prolusion 6' in the 1674 *Epistolarum familiarum liber*, among an assemblage of academic exercises or declamations in the *in utramque partem* tradition. The *Exercise* was the chief part of a 'salting', an annual initiation ceremony that had developed into a distinct tradition at Cambridge and Oxford.⁵ It remains uncertain as to whether this particular salting occurred in 1628 or 1631. Gordon Campbell and Thomas Corns provide circumstantial evidence supporting the later date, though this evidence is by no means conclusive, as they acknowledge.⁶ I have chosen to accept the date assumed by previous scholarship, in part because the full title of the poem, as published in 1673, identifies Milton's age as 19 at the time of composition. Discussion of the *Exercise* has overwhelmingly focused on this English poem and has treated the poem as a register of the young Milton's prescient ambition. I follow John Hale in considering the *Exercise* as a unified, though incomplete, whole. In this chapter, I follow Hale's text for both the Latin and the English, as published in *Milton's Cambridge Latin*. Hale suggests that the *Exercise* offers a glimpse of a comedic, 'foolish' Milton; it shows 'new sides of [his] emergent personality', including 'self-confidence in performance, and a capacity for clowning'.[7] Hale includes a collation, with translation, of the textual fragments.

Scholars of Milton have been quick to accept the paradigm of the hyper-authorial, individualist author assumed in the narrative of the 'Virgilian career', a narrative that Milton wanted, in 1645, to be accepted.[8] Yet the text we have of the *Exercise*, when reassembled and re-contextualised, shows a competing narrative: of an author who comes into his own by having his identity destabilised and reiteratively refashioned on stage before spectators. Nearly half a century later, each of Milton's Restoration masterpieces would have at their centre figures of authority whose identity undergoes reiterative refashioning that is connected, whether directly, as in *Paradise Lost* and *Samson Agonistes*, or indirectly, as in *Paradise Regained*, to the stage.

The textual provenance of the *Exercise* has fractured and dissolved, as though by design, the performance's rich theatricality.[9] Most of the comedic interlude that ends the *Exercise* is gone. What began as a performance becomes, instead, a two-part academic oration, a poem and a throwaway fragment of what would have been the interlude. This fragmentation works against Milton's theatricality, against a self-staging that demonstrates a compromising and negotiation of authority.

Although the fragments were published in isolation, together they bristle with the energy of performance. Here, we see dynamism in the space between orator-actor and audience-spectators: an oscillation of desire and anxiety, placation and antagonism, and femininity and masculinity at the heart of a staged performance by an aspiring poet set forth to play before the undergraduates of Christ's College, Cambridge. The performance repeatedly manifests the theatrical potential of rhetoric while repeatedly reacting against it. We see Milton as orator, poet and actor – even, as a comedian and as a comedic actor – striving to maintain control of the situation, his words and his body.

Actor: Friend or Foe?

To understand the importance of Milton's body in this text, and in order to bring forth the significance of his interrelating with present spectators, we first need to account for the relationship between oratory and theatre. As it turns out, the staged actor lurked behind the orator long before the Roman Republic.

Rhetoric has typically been seen as the art of using language to produce a desired effect in an audience. This sense suggests an essential dislocation between orator and auditor, author and reader, and privileges words, as the medium of disembodied truth, over the body, as language's situated vehicle. Aristotle's definition of rhetoric as the power of determining what is persuasive in any situation, given available resources and constraints, suggests, of course, more of a negotiation. Even Plato's Socrates, who in 'Phaedrus' champions the intellectual rarefaction of dialectic over the performed truth of rhetoric, develops the sensuous metaphor of the chariot soul precisely to win his young auditor towards truth. The dialogue frames this persuasion in terms of sexual seduction, employing carnal rhetoric to define philosophy's true goal as the mind's transcendence of the body through discourse, aesthetic contemplation, and the aggressive curbing of sense and desire. Socrates knows that, so long as he aims to persuade this young philologist, he cannot escape rhetoric: the co-constitutive, fleshy, erotically charged negotiation of a truth through embodied, socially situated language.

Aristotle, Cicero and Quintilian emphasise the significance of bodily movement in the art of persuasion. With vocal expression, gesture belonged to the category of delivery, named either *actio* or *pronuntiatio* in the Latin, one of the five principle parts of rhetoric. Yet the vast majority of rhetorical theory, from Aristotle's *Rhetoric* to the modern college textbook, places disproportionate emphasis on composition over performance, word over body.[10] We will see that several early modern rhetoricians treat voice and gesture as necessary tools for the politician or preacher. Yet the body was essentially abandoned by Petrus Ramus, the influential sixteenth-century rhetorician whose theories closely inform Milton's own rhetorical text, the 1672 *Ars logica*. Ramus begins by distinguishing dialectic from rhetoric, or logic and grammar from style. He further divides rhetoric into *elocutio*, which essentially covers figures of speech, and *pronuntiatio*. As Walter J. Ong notes, this final category, of embodied rhetoric or *actio*, essentially 'perishes of neglect'.[11] In fact, Ramus fundamentally redefines *pronuntiatio*, which in his text ambiguously straddles written and spoken rhetoric and emphasises flourishes in style, with almost no mention of vocal pronunciation or bodily gesture. Thus, the organisation of Ramus's *Ars rhetorica* establishes a clear hierarchy that privileges the mind, provides considerable place for language and somewhat less for its ornamentation, and leaves the body almost absent. For this reason, scholars of Milton's rhetoric have largely focused on the organisation of the rhetorical text and the formal operations of logic.[12] However, abundant evidence shows that, in Milton, the classical tradition of *actio* operates side-by-side with Ramism. If we maintain our faith in Milton's Ramism, we have to accept that the principles and history of *actio* also play a significant role.

Both the historian Plutarch and Roman rhetors cite the Athenian orator Demosthenes in the context of *actio*. When asked to name the most vital aspect of oratory, notes Quintilian, Demosthenes awarded first, second and third prize to delivery.[13] Quintilian and Plutarch describe how Demosthenes failed as an orator until an actor – Andronicus in Quintilian and Satyrus in Plutarch – demonstrated how to bring to life passages from Euripides (Andronicus) or Sophocles (Satyrus) with the skills of *actio*.[14] Plutarch details the similar path of Cicero, who learnt delivery from the tragedian Aesopus and the famed comedian Roscius.[15] Valerius Maximus notes a reciprocal influence, reporting that these actors attended legal proceedings to study the gesture and pronunciation of Hortensius.[16] The theatrical body was inherent to the discipline of rhetoric.

John Bulwer, a seventeenth-century theorist of the body who authored seminal work on sign language, displays these stories of Demosthenes and Cicero on the frontispiece of his 1644 *Chironomia*, the second part of a paired volume on the rhetorical uses of the hands and fingers (Fig. 1.1).[17] The engraving is by William Marshall, of note for engraving both the botched frontispiece to the 1645 *Poems of Mr. John Milton* and the notorious frontispiece to the 1649 *Eikon Basilike*. Marshall depicts Andronicus teaching Demosthenes the art of gesture with the use of a mirror; the word *actio* appears three times at the top of the frame, representing Demosthenes' proclamation that delivery is the first, second and third most important part of oratory. From the other side, Roscius teaches Cicero to gesture while facing a mirror, also. Above Demosthenes, the Athenian orator Cleon appears engraved on the foundation of a lofted arch. Above Cicero appears the Roman orator Hortensius.

In *Of Education* (1644), Milton shows keen interest in these stories of Cicero and Demosthenes that would seem to authorise the teaching of theatrical gesture in oratorical instruction. He recommends that students, having conquered Greek and Latin, as well as Italian poetic theory, be assigned

> choise Histories, *heroic poems*, and *Attic* tragedies of stateliest, and most regal argument, [as well as] all the famous Politicall orations [...] which if they were not only read; but some of them got by memory, and solemnly pronounc't with right accent, and grace, as might be taught, would endue them even with the spirit, and vigor of *Demosthenes* or *Cicero*, *Euripides*, or *Sophocles*.[18]

Here, Milton balances Greek tragedy with political oratory, the most esteemed Greek tragedians with the most esteemed classical orators. Euripides and Sophocles are the very tragedians whom, according to

Speaking Body 19

Figure 1.1 Andronicus teaching gesture to Demosthenes and Roscius teaching gesture to Cicero, on the frontispiece, engraved by W. Marshall, of J. Bulwer, *Chironomia* (1644). William Andrews Clark Memorial Library, 1816566.

Plutarch, Satyrus applied to train Demosthenes. Milton not only positions himself at the very crease where classical rhetoric and theatre uneasily meet, but also claims that memorising and declaiming these texts will infuse students 'even with the spirit, and vigor', of the authors. The passage accords with his assertion in *Areopagitica* (1644) that books 'preserve as in a violl the purest efficacie and extraction of that living intellect that bred them', only, here, the pure extraction is not intellectual but, rather, embodied and affective.[19] Such forceful feeling, though infused from pagan authors, becomes 'spirit' and a function of 'grace' in Milton's young Protestant declaimer.

In *Paradise Lost*, Satan appears several times as an actor, as an orator and as both. During the seduction sequence in book IX, Milton compares Satan, who is preparing for his rhetorical assault upon Eve, to the great classical orators:

> Now more bold
> The Tempter, but with shew of Zeale and Love
> To Man, and indignation at his wrong,
> New part puts on, and as to passion mov'd,
> Fluctuats disturbd, yet comely and in act
> Rais'd, as of som great matter to begin.
> As when of old som Orator renound
> In *Athens* or free *Rome*, where Eloquence
> Flourishd, since mute, to som great cause addrest,
> Stood in himself collected, while each part,
> Motion, each act won audience ere the tongue.[20]

However explicitly Milton represents Satan as a classical orator ('som Orator renound / In *Athens* or free Rome'; specifically, Demosthenes or Cicero), he employs the terms of theatrical disguise and action to do so. Satan 'puts on' classical authority as a costume, a 'part' to be 'act[ed]'. Milton emphasises that the 'all impassiond' tempter relies, like his classical predecessors, first on the 'motion[s]' or gestures of the body in order to 'w[i]n audience', before commencing speech.[21] Satan's 'motion[s]' are associated with the movements of the serpent's 'tongue'; just as this tongue undulates like the gesturing body, so does that body move like the speaking tongue. The comparison evokes, again, the Ciceronian commonplace, '*est enim actio quasi corporis quaedam eloquentia, cum constet e voce atque motu*'.[22]

The movements of the body are never in the orator's complete control; something of the body is always given over to the audience. Thus, delivery ever belies the illusion of the orator's power to captivate. Consider the image of the Hercules Gallicus (Englished as 'Anglicus') in the frontispiece of Marius D'Assigny's 1699 *The Art of Memory* (Fig. 1.2).[23] It depicts the expected model of rhetorical authority, which sees the rhetor as moving and shaping the audience, as from a separate ontological plane above. Chains issuing from the tongue of Hercules link to the heads of his hearers. The slackening of the chains implies a taming by a rhetorical force that compensates for the aged hero's diminished strength. His gesturing right hand appears to reach towards the spear of Minerva. Thus, the image works to transcend the embodiment of rhetorical authority by defining the connectivity of the chains as a unilateral relationship of power grounded not in physical strength but, rather, in wisdom. Another icon of rhetorical authority (Fig. 1.3), from Marshall's frontispiece for Bulwer's *Chironomia*, similarly appears to show the Roman orator Hortensius declaiming from a pedestal to a throng below. Visible lines of influence link his gesturing hands to the heads of his hearers. In part because Hortensius stands on a pedestal alone above the blurred throng, we readily assume that, like the Hercules Gallicus, he exerts unilateral authority over audience passions and behaviour. But his hearers are not tame; they are visibly roused. Once we question whether these lines of influence may also work in the other direction, we find no way to extricate the orator's authority from the roused bodies that now seem to pull on his hands. As Bulwer notes, Hortensius's expressive gesture was both a strength and a liability, earning him reputation as an effeminate populist. 'Otherwise a man excellent', he 'was taxed with this genuine or contracted affectation of the *Hand* [. . .] and called Stage-player'.[24]

Are Satan's undulations a function of his own authority as the orator who will pervert God's creation? Or do they suggest a vulnerability, a being worked upon? What about the gestures of the young Milton during the Cambridge salting?

Low Milton

At the start of the *Vacation Exercise*, Milton associates himself directly with the Attic orators Demosthenes and Aeschines and the Roman orators Hortensius and Cicero, while flattering an audience of Cambridge undergraduates:

> I think hardly any more flocked to Athens in the old days to hear the two supreme orators, Demosthenes and Aeschines, contending for the crown of oratory: no such felicity ever befell Hortensius pleading a case; nor did so large and extraordinary a throng ever honour the orating Cicero![25]

The occasion of the *Exercise* placed Milton in a position of rhetorical authority, yet it also placed him at the centre of an audience particularly

Figures 1.2 and 1.3 Left: Hercules Anglicus (i.e. Gallicus), the orator, declaiming, on the frontispiece of M. D'Assigny, *The Art of Memory* (1699). William Andrews Clark Memorial Library, 1066770. Right: Hortensius declaiming and gesturing. Detail of Marshall's engraving for the frontispiece of Bulwer, *Chironomia* (1644). William Andrews Clark Memorial Library, 1816566.

hostile to stale humour and awkward delivery. The Oxford saltings appear to have involved abundant beer, hazing and compulsory displays of extemporaneous wit by underlings. If these spoke well, they earnt a draught of beer; if their wit failed, they were made to drink salted beer.[26] The seventeenth-century Cambridge saltings were more formal, more literary and more ordered. The Cambridge salting typically involved an oration that was followed by a more comic oration ('prolusion') and concluded with a dramatic farce or interlude incorporating several of the initiates.[27] The Academic Father, who, during the performance, assumed the roles of MC, orator, actor, playwright and stage director, likely scripted most of his speech prior to performance, and might have blocked and rehearsed the more collaborative interlude with his troupe of initiates.

Reassembled, the *Exercise* exhibits a young poet experimenting with the medium of the public stage and working to harness the energies of live performance before a raucous audience. The relationship between rhetor-actor and audience in the *Exercise* is best described as agonistic and ambivalent: 'agonistic' in the sense that both parties struggle to control the plane of representation, each simultaneously mastering and being held captive by the other; 'ambivalent' in the sense that this master–captive dialectic yields at once feelings of confidence and anxiety, sympathy and antagonism. The orator-actor holds the audience captive by means of its desires. He earns their applause by delighting them through virtuosity, wit, ingratiation and flirtation that draws them into the speech and action, making them a part of it: 'Let nobody marvel if I triumph, and feel raised to the stars, because so many outstanding talents have foregathered here – almost the whole flower of the University!'[28] He seasons his flattery with modesty, lowering himself towards his hearers. Yet their desires and judgement are essential to the emotional syntax of this flattery. He knows that his audience can explode: from *ex-plaudere*, to 'explode' means to clap the actor off the stage, a practice usually complemented by hoots and hisses.[29] Such is the actor's worst nightmare.

Milton's ambivalent identity in the *Exercise*, as both an orator and an actor, first plays out in a tension between seriousness and playfulness.[30] He represents himself as the sober scholar compelled against his will to satiate his peers' appetite for frivolity and inebriated misrule. He performs a reticence, claiming to have been 'dragged away' from his studies, 'commanded to transfer all that zest which I had destined for acquiring knowledge to trifles, to the inventing of new forms of fooling'.[31] 'My task is an arduous, uphill one', he says. 'I am to praise jocularity seriously'.[32] The oration specifically develops the argument 'that on occasion sportive exercises do not jeopardise philosophical studies'.[33]

As Milton transitions into the prolusion, he compares himself to an actor delivering the epilogue of a play:

> If anything loose or licentious is said, you are to suppose it is not my mind and nature but the rules governing the time and the spirit of the place prompting it. So then: what the comic actors entreat when they end their performance, I demand as mine begins – APPLAUD, and LAUGH![34]

Here, the students appear more like playgoers, the space more like a theatre. Milton claims that the rules governing the occasion and the very energies and expectation of the place prompt his mind and guide his actions.[35] Preparing his audience for the low comedy to come, he claims to submit his authority completely to the rules governing the salting (*'temporis rationem'*) and to the spirit of the place (*'loci genium'*). Hale's 'prompting' derives from Milton's *'mihi suggessisse'*, which carries the basic sense of 'prompt', but which also puns on *suggestus*, meaning a raised platform or stage. The *loci genium* becomes increasingly integral to his speech and movement.

The prolusion shows Milton's capacity for ribald humour. Yet this humour is not freely granted. Imperatives and admonitions attend the most hilarious portions of the *Exercise*. Milton begins the prolusion – that part of a salting in which oratorical gravity is turned upside-down – by insisting, again, that his auditors laugh.

> Let the whole place re-echo laughter; let mirth make us laugh till we cry [. . .] As for me, if I catch sight of anyone laughing only half-heartedly, I shall say it's because he is trying to hide his teeth, which are rotten and scabby and covered with disgusting gunk, or sticking out in all directions; or else he is afraid to stretch his belly any further in laughing because he has stuffed it so full at the feast already that he might give us a duet from two orifices![36]

Milton first treats laughter as a shared, communal experience: laughter will be what brings the whole performance together. He is part of the 'us'. But he immediately separates himself from his audience and antagonises. He strives for unanimity in laughter by means of a threat, albeit a light-hearted one. He will expose any non-laugher as a rotten-toothed glutton whose stomach is so full that laughing would cause flatulence, producing a 'duet from two orifices', mouth and anus. The flatulent non-laugher might then

> express some gastric riddles to us, not from his Sphinx but from his sphincter; his Posterior Anal-ytics. Such riddles I leave for the medical people to interpret, not Oedipus: I don't want any groaning posteriors to obstruct the sound of merry voices here.[37]

Milton's '*nolim*' – 'I don't want' – is at once a plea and a command, an 'oh please don't!' and a 'you better not'. The ambivalence of authority between rhetor and audience manifests as an anxiety viscerally experienced by the auditors, many of whose stomachs would have been glutted by the preceding banquet. On the one hand, Milton condescends to a penchant for the type of toilet humour appropriate to the occasion, with references to the buttocks, the sphincter, farting and an enema. Yet the passage also puts on display impressive Latin full of erudite puns and a reference to Sophocles's *Oedipus Rex*. Thus, we see both toilet humour and ostentatious erudition, a type of pandering interlaced with threats, and commands strengthened by learning.

The idea of groaning posteriors struggling to remain continent soon develops into the idea of the hiss, a sign of audience disapproval, common to the theatres, which will reappear several times in Milton's prose and later poetry:

> Next, there must be absent from this assembly that dreadful, hellish sound of hissing. If it were to be heard here today, I would think that the Furies and Eumenides were hiding amongst you, letting loose their snakes and serpents into your hearts.[38]

As Milton scripted the *Exercise*, he imagined a performance scenario where, from the stage, he could hear one or two isolated hisses – where are those furies hiding? – that work their way into the hearts of the surrounding audience, spreading as by contagion until an audience of hissing snakes surrounds him. The sound of uncontrolled bowels becomes the sound of an uncontrolled audience – a 'barbarous dissonance'.[39]

Milton's concern about how the audience would receive the performance derives, it seems, from concerns about social acceptance. He was inclined to accept the role of Academic Father in part, he says, due to his peers' 'new-found friendliness' toward him.[40] This friendliness had been confirmed, several months prior, by the favourable reception that he had received after delivering an oration in an academic exercise. 'I thought', he confesses, 'that[, then,] my excogitations would get a cold reception from you, and in fact that Aeacus and Minos' – the severe judges of Hades, here, likely, the assessing instructors – 'would judge me less harshly than would any one of you'.[41] Contrary to this assumption that he would meet with a hostile response, he found that 'against my expectation, against any slight hope I had, I perceived instead – no, I felt it – that my efforts were accepted with unusual applause from everyone'.[42] He testifies to an experience of audience response that goes beyond common perception ('*accepi*') and that is experienced as feeling ('*imo* [. . .] *sensi*').

The prolusion thus visualises two scenarios facing the staged Milton. On the one hand, the audience might hiss him off the stage; on the other, they might praise his success. Similar scenarios will be represented in the polemical prose. For instance, in the *Pro populo Anglicano defensio secunda* (1654), Milton imagines himself scanning a sympathetic audience of onlooking European nations that applaud the proceedings of Parliament, the advancement of Republican ideals, and his response to Salmasius in the *Defensio pro populo Anglicano* (1651). He is a synecdoche for the nation. From on high, he surveys European nations who now look up to him, the Republic's orator:

> I imagine [. . .] that I behold from on high, tracts beyond the seas, and wide-extended regions; that I behold countenances strange and numberless, and all, in feelings of mind, my closest friends and neighbours. Here is presented to my eyes the manly strength of the Germans, disdainful of slavery; there the lively and generous impetuosity of the Franks, worthy so called; on this side, the considerate virtue of the Spaniards; on that, the sedate and composed magnanimity of the Italians. Wherever there are natures free, ingenuous, magnanimous, either they are prudently concealed or openly professed. Some favour in silence, others give their suffrages in public; some hasten to receive me with shouts of applause, others, in fine, vanquished by truth, surrender themselves captive. Encompassed by such countless multitudes [. . .] I am bringing back, bringing home to every nation, liberty, so long driven out, so long an exile [. . .][43]

Where, in the *Vacation Exercise*, Milton identifies individual faces in the crowd and riffs humorously on their names and idiosyncrasies, here he surveys the 'countenances strange and numberless' of individual nations figured as human characters.[44] His praise of England culminates in a valorisation of his own role as a liberator. He appears as the Hercules Anglicus who left the readers of his *First Defence* 'vanquished by truth'.[45] When, five years later, all hope of a Republican government would be lost, Milton would lament that English backsliding would provoke the 'common laughter' of Europe.[46]

In the *Vacation Exercise*, Milton appears to relish his role as Academic Father even as he begins to play upon his apparent Cambridge nickname: Domina, or the Lady. He turns to the undergraduates whom he is about to lead in the farce that will lampoon Aristotle's Categories. He has now stepped into the part: 'In my role as "Father" I turn to my sons, and I look at the glorious number of them; I can see the fine rascals acknowledge me as their father by a sly nod'.[47] He is adopting fatherhood as a role, as a theatrical part. The troupe of initiates might already be on the stage with him. The play is ready to begin.

But it does not. Instead, Milton treats us to a self-aggrandising English poem about the English language and the great things that he intends to do with it as a poet.

A Bard Encompassed

The English poem published in 1673 as 'At a Vacation Exercise in the Colledge' unexpectedly precedes the interlude. If Milton had anxieties about descending into ribaldry and about staging a farce, then the English poem would seem to serve the purpose of enabling him to ascend above his peers, to isolate himself from the performance context, and to hover in the heights of divine and epic poetry. The change of genre corresponds with a change of Milton's status in relation to the spectators. Most of the poem depicts a bard eager to escape the rhetorical situation. In other ways, however, the poem serves to mediate the transition into an interlude performed in English. That is, it performs an escape from the performance context while also preparing the poet to negotiate that context.[48] The poem reflects upon poetry as writing, yet the conditions of performance impress upon its language.

The students in attendance would have been most intrigued to learn the conceit that would be brought to life in the interlude. The staging of the conceit had become a standard part of the salting: 'the daintiest dishes', says Milton in the poem, 'shall be serv'd up last'.[49] Here, he is most certainly alluding to the 1626 salting led by Thomas Randolph, who had chosen to stage a variety of victuals. Milton's chosen conceit was more cerebral, even oddly so. He would be, in his role as 'Academic Father', the figure of *Ens*, or Being-in-Essence, who interacts with his 'sons', the Aristotelian Categories of Substance. Despite this paternal role, the poem first suggests a process of childbirth and maternal nurturing:

> I have some naked thoughts that rove about
> And loudly knock to have their passage out;
> And wearie of their place do only stay
> Till thou [the English language] hast deck't them in thy best aray;
> That so they may without suspect or fears
> Fly swiftly to this fair Assembly's ears.[50]

The figure of thoughts 'loudly knock[ing] to have their passage out' plays to the anticipation of the spectators, who are eager to learn the interlude's governing conceit. As Milton's language shifts from Latin to English, the poet collaborates with his 'native tongue' to prepare these thoughts to enter society. He asks the English language to help him clothe them.

The English poem has, up to this point, gestured toward, has indeed touted, the forthcoming interlude. But Milton also gestures toward his desire to turn away: 'Yet I had rather, if I were to chuse, / Thy [the English language's] service in some graver subject use.'[51] The naked thoughts seem to transform in terms of genre. They refer no longer to the interlude's *inventio* but, rather, to the graver subjects that will be handled in the bard's later poetry:

> Such where the deep transported mind may soare
> Above the wheeling poles, and at Heav'ns dore
> Look in, and see each blissful Deitie
> How he before the thunderous throne doth lie,
> Listening to what unshorn *Apollo* sings
> To th' touch of golden wires.[52]

Milton temporarily pushes the stage below, instead looking upward and forward, as it seems, to the inspired verse of 'Lycidas', where Apollo will touch the poet's trembling ears.[53] The idea of movement away – as from the performance context – is sounded repeatedly: the mind is 'transported' and 'soare[s] / Above the wheeling poles' until arriving at 'Heaven's door'. The bard looks across the decades to *Paradise Lost*, in which he will take flight across the cosmos, following Satan's path to heaven's door, and present to us what transpires within.[54] He imagines how he will 'then sing of secret things that came to pass / When beldam Nature in her cradle was'; the Creation and the Fall come immediately to mind.[55] Finally, he imagines singing 'of kings and queens and *Hero*'s old', matter that he would include in his sketches for possible dramas a decade later. He then compares himself to the 'wise Demodocus' who sings affectingly of the Trojan War in Homer's *Odyssey*, and his auditors' souls to 'Ulysses' soul' and those of 'all the rest'. Like Demodocus, as with Homer, he will hold his readers 'with his melodious harmonie / In willing chains and sweet captivitie'.[56]

We return to the figure of the Hercules Gallicus, whose slackened chains, issuing from his mouth to the minds of his hearers, represent at once rhetorical power and a willingly captive audience. It is as though the 'suspect or fears' that require the vestments of the English language to protect his 'naked thoughts' from the hiss or explosion of 'this fair Assembly' catalyse the poetic fugue. This flight allows Milton to develop an envacuumed, divinely inspired authority; it is as though the poem serves as both an escape and a defence from the spectators waiting at the poem's peripheries. The task comes calling – 'But fie my wandring Muse how thou dost stray!' – and the demands of the audience begin to take hold once more: 'Expectance calls thee now another way, / Thou know'st it must be now thy only bent / To keep in compass of thy Predicament'.[57] 'Predicament' puns on the Aristotelian 'Predicaments' or Categories of Substance, which will shortly appear in the interlude as Milton's 'sons'. At the same time, 'predicament' also indicates the task at hand, 'a difficult, unpleasant, or embarrassing situation or circumstance'.[58] Milton resigns himself to the 'purpos'd business', specifically so 'that to the next I may resign my Roome'.[59] Hale understands the 'next' as being Milton's subsequent persona in the medley, the character of *Ens* or 'Absolute Substance'.[60] However, it seems as likely that to 'resign' the 'Roome' is meant to suggest Milton's eagerness to conclude his tenure as Academic Father. In other words, 'All right, let's get this business over with'.

As Milton faces the imminence of the interlude, an implied metaphor identifies him as a falcon under control of the falconer, who limits his flight ('bent') within the circumference ('compass') of his audience's 'call'. Indeed, we see that the poem has itself performed a falcon-like descent from 'Heav'ns dore' towards its handler. Several times in Milton's works, forms of 'compass' will demarcate theatrical spaces. In each case, the individual agent will be surrounded by audiences and spectators.[61] The relationship between the centred author and the encompassing audience produces subsidiary tensions, between desired connection and feared explosion, and between vertical and horizontal authority. We have seen a friendly hostility, or an accosting collegiality, in the struggle between two bodies, as it were. The struggle is like a game of tug-of-war, with so many unseen ropes, as each side vies not for mastery but for relative control over a centre between. As in a tug-of-war, these forces collapse into phenomenal experience, like that of the tension in the rope extending through the hands, bodily core, knees and feet. The actor does not desire connection one moment and then fear it the next; rather, the fear curves around the desire, and the desire around the fear, and delineates the other as a coherent concept.

As the interlude finally begins, Milton appears more mastered than mastering. He is a falcon who 'with no middle flight intends to soar / Above th' *Aonian* Mount', but who must, for the time being, answer to those below, who keep him within his compass and who ground him on the floorboards.[62]

Invisible Genitals

The 'naked thoughts' that Milton expresses a wish to clothe early in the English poem are near the centre of these tensions. 'Nakedness', leagued with 'suspect' and 'fear', is a condition of being exposed before scrutinising spectators. As we have seen, the rhetorical scenario of Milton's performance involves a constantly oscillating negotiation of authority between desiring bodies. Whereas the audience desires entertainment – the humorous, spectacular, wonderful or titillating – the rhetor desires its approval, if not its rhetorical domination, while also striving to maintain, at once, decorum and dignity. The experience of nakedness centres upon the genitals, the site both of pleasure and of vulnerability to castration: they are the site of phallic authority and its undoing, of what William Prynne, in the noxious anti-theatrical tome *Histriomastix* (c. 1632, dated 1633), would call an 'unman[ning] and uncreat[ing]'.[63] In short, rhetorical authority is gendered masculine, whereas the theatricalising of that authority threatens to re-gender the rhetor. Rhetoric and masculinity are further affiliated with mind and *verba*, whereas theatricality and femininity are further affiliated with the body and gesture. We recall Hortensius, identified as a 'Stage-player' for his use of flamboyant gesture to appeal to the masses.

For Milton, nakedness centres upon the genitals because they are the site of reproduction and, thus, of poetic authority. In the *Vacation Exercise*, the ambiguity of the genitals marks the contestation of rhetorical authority. As authority in the *Exercise* is unstable, the gendering of that authority is fluid – in essence, dynamically transsexual.

As 'Academic Father', Milton was responsible for introducing his 'sons', disguised as Aristotle's 'Predicaments' or Categories of Substance: Quantity, Quality, Relation, Place, Time, Posture, State, Action and Passivity. The choice was novel, ironic and, perhaps, comical; only together did the categories constitute a substance – an *ens* or 'present thing'.[64] The interlude should have given us a glimpse of Milton as a comedic dramatist. 'At a Vacation Exercise in the Colledge, Part Latin, Part English', however, contains only a fragment of what appears to be its script: forty-two lines of verse spoken by Milton, a pair of stage directions, and a concluding note, 'The rest was Prose'.[65] The fragment begins with a stage direction that introduces Milton in the role of *Ens*. *Ens* then speaks thirty-two lines to Substance. At this point, a stage direction notes that 'the next Quantity and Quality, spake in Prose, then Relation was call'd by his Name', after which we have ten more lines spoken by *Ens* to Relation, and, finally, the note that indicates and dismisses the remaining prose.[66]

The interlude identifies Milton as a father who is bringing into the world (onto the stage) ten 'sons'. Though 'Faery Ladies' and a 'drowsie Nurse' were present at their birth, the sons have no mother.[67] As both father and author, Milton has created the sons autonomously; he is both their father and their mother. Near the close of the prolusion, Milton had played upon the fact that he had earnt the nickname Domina, or the Lady, from his peers. 'Milton may have acquired the nickname', suggest Campbell and Corns, 'because of the fairness of his complexion, or because his manner or appearance was youthful or effeminate, but he prized it because it was Virgil's nickname'.[68] Milton associates his femininity with purity, their masculinity with debauchery: 'Why do I seem unmanly to them? [. . .] Perhaps because I have not proved my manhood in the way these debauchees do'.[69] He needles the audience while playing into the gender game:

> But how come I am so quickly become a Father? Ye gods! What a prodigy, surpassing the ones in Pliny! Have I killed a snake and suffered the fate of Tiresias? Has some Thessalian witch smeared me with magic ointment? Or have I been violated by some god, as Caeneus was of old, and won my masculine gender as payment for the deed, to be suddenly altered from female into male?[70]

He imagines himself as a female victim of rape, his body 'violated by some god' to 'w[i]n' his 'masculine gender as payment for the deed'.

Milton's identification with Tiresias and Caeneus further plays upon the unstable associations between sexuality and authority. Both Hesiod and Ovid recount Tiresias's transformation by Hera into a woman for smiting a pair of mating snakes with a stick. Tiresias was transformed back into a man seven years later after passing by the same pair once more. (In Ovid's account, Tiresias switches sexes after he again hits the snakes with a stick.)[71] On the other hand, as Ovid relates, Caeneus was initially a woman renowned for her beauty and chastity. After being raped by Neptune, she was granted a wish to be a male warrior in order to prevent subsequent violation.[72] Milton's classmates had gendered him female, a gender reversal that correlates with the male-to-female transformation of Tiresias. The interlude re-genders or re-sexes (here indistinguishable) him as male, as 'Father', recalling the female-to-male transformation of both Caeneus and Tiresias.

We can further see Milton's habit of gendering his poetic identity as feminine in several of the early poems and in the *Maske*, works covered in the next chapter. As in the *Vacation Exercise*, in these the poet's feminisation attends association with the public stage. Why does the poet need to occupy the subject position of the female in order to assert literary authority? And why is this subject staged? In Milton, the explicit or implied form of the stage will repeatedly help to mediate questions concerning the subjective and social dynamics of literary authority, and it will always unsettle easy resolution. Rather, its capacity will be one of foregrounding irresolutions from which text and authority emerge.

By the publication of *Areopagitica* in 1644, Milton would understand Christian agency and virtue as dependent upon the entanglements of sin and the possibility, even the inevitability, of failure, of falling into sin throughout the course of earthly engagements. The capacity of the figure of the stage to focus this vulnerability would inform the recurrent re-presenting of the author – on what might, with some liberty, be called the stage of the text – in each of the Restoration masterworks. Each of the four invocations of *Paradise Lost* would suggest a different configuration of the relationships between Holy Spirit, author and public. The invocation to book VII would place Milton in a patronage relationship with Urania, a figure of the Holy Spirit, while surrounded by the 'barbarous dissonance' of an audience of 'evil tongues'. The invocation to book I shows what Milton arguably understands as the poem's most simplistic model of authorship, one that approximates the way that Satan performs power, particularly in the early episodes. Arguably, *Paradise Lost* is, at its core, the story of how the first man and first woman come to negotiate the contradiction of their relationship as 'equal' children of God born into a gendered hierarchy. The opening invocation anticipates the irresolutions of authority through which their story (as indeed Satan's) will play out.

The *Vacation Exercise* thus appears to anticipate the contradictions of authority that are so central to *Paradise Lost* and that might be deemed, in their systemic function, the engine of the epic's poetics. The invocation of book I of *Paradise Lost* brings into focus the transsexuality suggested in the *Exercise*; the instability of sex or gender helps to mystify the contradictions, the oscillations and the ambivalences that accompany the public staging of literary authority. In the invocation, Milton explicitly identifies with Tiresias as a blind prophet. He deduces a transsexual poetic authority modelled upon a hermaphroditic, self-impregnating Creator:

> And chiefly Thou O Spirit, that dost prefer
> Before all Temples th' upright heart and pure,
> Instruct me, for Thou know'st; Thou from the first
> Wast present, and with mighty wings outspread
> Dove-like satst brooding on the vast Abyss
> And mad'st it pregnant: What in me is dark
> Illumin, what is low raise and support;
> That to the highth of this great Argument
> I may assert Eternal Providence,
> And justifie the wayes of God to men.[73]

Here, a 'Dove-like' God with 'mighty wings outspread' hovers over Chaos like a mother hen incubating the eggs of her 'brood'. Yet, the

Creator also *inseminates* Chaos, completing the picture of a hermaphroditic godhead that possesses self-sufficient procreative power. This godhead models the bard's own identity, at this point in the poem, as the creator of the epic and as a mediator between God and man. Following the hinge of the caesural colon after 'pregnant', the poet occupies the maternal subject position of Chaos, asking to be, by analogy, 'impregnated' by the light of spiritual wisdom. He suggests that his receptivity to the Holy Spirit is premised on obedience and chastity, on virtues that befit the spiritual bride of Christ and virgin priestesses. He calls upon the Spirit who 'dost prefer / Before all Temples th' upright heart and pure' to 'Instruct' him, that is, to build the structures of higher knowledge and of the Christian epic itself within him. He attributes to spiritual insemination the power to generate the poem within the darkness, chaos or body of the poet, by means of which the bard now becomes an 'assert[ive]', masculine author, whose poem re-produces in the minds of receiving readers.[74] 'Rather than a lone, masculine, inseminating or self-sufficient author', notes Amy Stackhouse, 'the poet is figured as the female who is inseminated by the generative force, and who then gives birth to a poem which disseminates authority to its readers'.[75] This unfolding of authority works like a Jacob's ladder that re-sexes authority in a series of downward inversions.

In terms of gendered poetic identity and authority, the *Vacation Exercise* can offer no resolution, only an ambiguous intertwining of flesh and the forces that move it. Its irresolution does not obscure the author: rather, it provides a liberating alternative to a narrative of poetic development constructed to fit the gradations of the Virgilian career. It shows a more compelling, because more human, picture of the poet transmorphing within and repeatedly re-emerging from the matrix of present and future audiences. As I suggest throughout this book, the Miltonic corpus is systemic in its operations in the ways that it continually reshapes the poet and his audiences.

Naked Writhing Flesh

Milton was drawn to theatre's interplay of influence and counter-influence because it offered a way to explore the challenges of materially and socially situated agency and authority. Specifically, the theatre offered a social microcosm where sinews of identification – connective threads of vision and passion – would entangle and, disentangling, leave participants altered. This corporealisation of the visual field approaches what Maurice Merleau-Ponty, in *Le Visible et l'invisible* (1964), would describe as 'the coiling over [*l'enroulement*] of the visible upon the seeing body, of the tangible upon the touching body'.[76] Theatre figures with optimal economy how vision and authority emerge from *within* the field of what is visible, 'as though it were [. . .] in a pre-established harmony' with a visible context of seeing flesh.[77]

Milton repeatedly complicates Satanic authority by suggesting through the represented body a counter-influence of passion flowing in from a fleshy field of the visible.[78] For instance, as Satan first rises from the fiery lake, he is described as throwing 'round [. . .] his baleful eyes / That witness'd huge affliction and dismay / Mixt with obdurate pride and stedfast hate'.[79] 'Witness' seems to be what the eyes are *doing* – that is, ranging over the terrain of bodies below. Yet the enjambment of 57–8 ('dismay / Mixt'), which reveals 'affliction and dismay' to be 'mixt' with 'pride' and 'hate', suggests, rather, that 'witness' should be glossed as 'show'. Thus, as Satan presents a commanding form of 'obdurate pride and stedfast hate' and expresses authority through a gaze sweeping over miserable anonymous bodies, his eyes, conduits of passion and windows to what is within, betray to onlookers profound loss and faintness of heart that place him emotionally on par with his 'followers'.[80] The form of his face cannot be extricated from the eyes of the spectators for whom it was rhetorically produced. Nor can it fully dissemble Satan's own loss and fear. Whether or not it is read, this vulnerability is readable.

From the dialectic of influence and counter-influence emerges a form of authority constantly menaced by threat of exposure. Milton repeatedly sounds audience response as hissing or 'exploding' to manifest this menace that works upon the form of authority. It also suggests the modern sense of 'bursting forth upon', a phenomenon that is similar to, but more menacing than, what Merleau-Ponty calls a 'dehiscence of Being' to describe the bursting out of the sensible upon vision, the flesh of the visible upon the flesh of the seeing.[81] In the book VII invocation, a 'barbarous dissonance' explodes upon the Orphic bard in this way, threatening dismemberment. When Satan debates Abdiel, a reluctant applause reveals the fragility of his power: 'as the sound of waters deep / Hoarce murmur echo'd to his words applause / Through the infinite Host'.[82] The applauding body churns like an ocean under lunar influence, 'waters deep' coaxed from the pull of Abdiel's zeal-imped reason towards the emotive appeal of Satanic (il)logic.[83] It moves by its own inertia, gaining momentum as though by hearing itself. 'Murmur' recalls the discontented Israelites under Moses and Aaron in Exodus 14. It registers audibly a tenuous authority that, in Satan's case, must constantly shift to meet an intermediary ground of desire.

We have seen that, as early as the *Vacation Exercise*, Milton locates the menace that attends theatricality in the genitals themselves, the epicentre of the possibly exposed. As the source of reproductive power and as the anchor of gendered identity, they are, as well, a sign of poetic authority. In the negotiations of the theatricalised rhetorical situation, the genitals are a locus of shape-shifting and of potential castration. Whereas, in the *Exercise*, Milton calls upon the clothing of English to protect his 'naked thoughts', so that they can be sent into the audience 'without suspect or fears', in *Paradise Lost* and in other texts from 1641 onwards, gesture, or the always potentially rhetorical and readable motioning of the body, works to mitigate a hostile gaze felt to issue from a social body, a panoptic God, or the conscience or superego. Fallen Adam uses fig leaves 'to hide / The Parts of each [from] other, that seem most / To shame obnoxious, and unseemliest seen'.[84] Yet in attenuating this 'guiltie shame' by veiling the naked body, this second flesh works also to expose what it veils: 'hee cover'd, but his Robe / Uncover'd more'.[85] The anti-prelatical tracts assail the 'troublesome disguises' of 'Church-maskers' who 'cover and hide' the 'righteous verity' of a 'naked' Gospel 'with the polluted cloathing of [. . .] ceremonies'.[86] Anti-episcopal readers appear as spectators menacing exposed prelatical bodies: 'O what a death it is to the Prelates to be thus unvisarded, thus uncas'd, to have the Periwigs pluk't off that cover your baldnesse, your inside nakednesse thrown open to publick view'.[87]

This view of authority as menaced by what, in *Animadversions*, Milton calls 'opposite spectators', might be clarified through Jacques Lacan's concept of the gaze.[88] Whereas Merleau-Ponty posits all phenomena as bound by the connective tissue of a reflexive optics, Lacan theorises a sadism, or a desire to dominate violently, perhaps sexually, implicit in the gaze. The subject gazing upon the object is menaced from the periphery by a generalised gaze inhabiting the field of the Other. This menace bespeaks the subject's limited control over a social and material context that, encompassing the subject, belies the illusion of a stable, independent self. This sense of menace lends urgency to the objectifying gaze and intensifies its need to express a relation of dominance.[89]

Lacan helps to explain the menace that haunts within the interconnection of flesh in the theatre space. Much of the theory of the gaze is predicated on a simple geometrical tension between centre and circumference: the gaze of a centred body focusing on a point in the circumference is menaced by an answering gaze spilling in from the periphery. Milton regularly places figures of authority at the centre of environing spectators. The 'opposite spectators' menacing Joseph Hall in *Animadversions* constitute 'the inevitable net of God, that now', Milton jeers, 'begins to inviron you round'.[90] Samson tears down a Philistine temple turned 'spacious Theatre' that, 'half round', is completed as a circle by the gazing 'throng' placed behind him: 'The other side was op'n', the Messenger tells us, 'where the throng / On banks and scaffolds under Skie might stand'.[91]

Whereas Descartes' tracts on the passions and optics develop a model of an instrumental rationality by which the agent can directly encounter menaces and overcome them, the geometrical tension between centred agent and environing spectators significantly constrains the agency of the Cartesian subject. This constraint owes to the fact that Descartes' understanding of agency depends on the structure of the eye as a focusing lens. But, once we acknowledge the blurred presence of a periphery, the hard round of the lens becomes pervious. The agent becomes menaced by the periphery, since the activity of instrumental reason can only confront one stimulus of passion at a time and, thus, cannot adequately respond to the stimuli accosting from all sides. Consider how Descartes depicts the soul's response to fear in *Les Passions de l'âme* (1649). First, a phenomenon must stimulate a passion understood *as fear*. The will cannot directly quell bad passions, but can 'indirectly[,] by the representation of things which, customarily, have been joined with the passions that we will to have, and the passions that are contrary to those that we will to reject'.[92] The mind must, as it were, take a snapshot of the passion and, viewing it, determine the fittest response. Experiencing fear when to flee is deemed cowardly, the mind recalls an image of valour. This internal mimesis inspires a passion of boldness that flows from the pineal gland through channels where the inflowing passion is met and conquered. Valorous action is willed and performed.[93] In addition to producing emotions through internal mimesis, the soul can employ rational deliberation, a staging of internal debate:

> To excite boldness in oneself and displace fear [. . .] one must apply oneself to consider the reasons, objects, or precedents that convince one that the peril is not great, that there is always more security in defence than in flight, that one will have glory and joy from having vanquished, whereas one can expect only regret and shame from having fled.[94]

For either response to work, the passion must be clearly demarcated, immediately apprehendable, and single. Both require conditions simple enough for reason or imagination to rouse countering passions as quickly as the moving body can confront them. Only by assuming a sparse reality conforming to experimental conditions, and by denying the complexity, multiplicity and ambiguity of the passions, can Descartes assert so confidently that 'there is no soul so weak that it cannot be well guided to acquire an absolute power over its passions'.[95]

In *Paradise Lost*, by representing Satan's body in the field of vision, Milton succinctly dismantles Descartes' account of instrumental reason's 'easy' and 'absolute' power over the passions. Toward the close of book III, Satan demonstrates a skill of theatrical self-presentation expert enough to deceive Uriel, 'though Regent of the Sun, and held / The sharpest sighted Spirit of all in Heav'n'.[96] Satan first sees the form of Uriel 'within kenn' among 'all Sun-Shine', which 'sharp'nd his visual ray / To objects distant farr'.[97] Satan also has the advantage of approaching Uriel while the arch-angel's 'back was turn'd but not his brightness hid'.[98] Satan, thus, has time to 'change his proper shape' into a guise that he expects will best suit his purposes. He appears in what Milton's description suggests is masquing attire: 'Under a coronet'; wearing 'wings / Of many a coloured plume sprinkl'd with Gold', 'His habit fit for speed succinct'; and carrying before him a 'silver wand'.[99] Although the disguise succeeds in gaining Uriel's trust, we are nonetheless witnessing Satanic theatricality at its utmost advantage. Uriel's exceptional perspicuity, caught 'fixt in cogitation deep', reveals him at this moment blinder than the reader, who, foreknowing, can easily see the artificiality of the disguise and the fraudulence that it conceals.[100] So far, we remain within the Cartesian paradigm, wherein the eye can see, can focus, and, through instrumental reason, can rouse the appropriate response to conquer the menace – only here, Satan's motive is not to exercise courage so as to conquer fear but, rather, to disguise and to play-act so as to deceive an angel of God.

Milton quickly demonstrates the vulnerability of Satanic theatricality to shifting contexts, to oblique perspectives and to the depth and complexity of the passions when he shows Satan's body slacken while he soliloquizes upon Mount Niphates at the start of book IV. Despite possessing a 'prospect' unto Eden that expresses a relationship of command, Satan remains vulnerable from other perspectives, including that from which 'Uriel once warnd' now views a bodily form mastered by passions from within.[101] Through countenance and gesture, Satan expresses an affective excess that belies the form that had been manageable when he had confronted Uriel directly. Now the sharp-sighted archangel 'saw him disfigur'd, more then could befall / Spirit of happie sort: his gestures fierce / He markd and mad demeanour, then alone, / As he suppos'd, all unobserv'd, unseen'.[102] Here, 'gestures fierce', or sharp movements of the body, suggest affective intensity that exceeds the now neglected control of bodily form. The defining mark of such theatrical hypocrisy is the effect of 'disfigur[ement]', the disharmonious mixing of bodily signifiers caused by dynamic, multifaceted passions that express through the simpler form that had been managed rhetorically to show a specific state of being to a single spectator.

Particularly revealing is Satan's face, which, instead of resembling one of the distinct passions catalogued by Descartes, passes through a range: 'Each passion dimm'd his face / Thrice chang'd with pale, ire, envie and despair, / Which marrd his borrow'd visage, and betraid / Him counterfet, if any eye beheld'.[103] Passions of 'ire, envie and despair', easy enough to distinguish conceptually, manifest subtly as mere shades of a single colour, 'pale'.[104] This disparity, between the layered passions and the 'borrow'd visage', reveals inauthenticity or hypocrisy to beholding eyes (especially those 'unobserv'd, unseen'). Likewise, Adam easily divines the hypocrisy of Eve's first fallen speech, which Milton depicts as inept theatre. Eve fashions her countenance so as, pre-emptively, to excuse her sin: 'in her face excuse / Came Prologue, and Apologie to prompt'.[105] Thus, Milton depicts in Eve's face a veritable theatre of exculpation that begins like any number of early modern plays: the Prologue enters and works to win over the audience by excusing elements of the play that may be distasteful to some and by emphasising which other virtues are to be expected. Instantly, Adam reads the embodied contradiction of 'distemper flushing' that 'glow[s]' in the 'Cheek' of a 'Countnance blithe' as clear evidence of fallenness.[106]

As we have seen, Milton associated poor rhetorical performance with the hiss regularly sounded in early modern theatricals by hostile audiences. The hiss not only manifests a menace but also, quite literally, works upon the staged body. In a passage from the *Apology* to which we will return, Milton depicts 'young [Anglican] Divines' who 'have bin seene so oft upon the Stage writhing and unboning their Clergie limmes'.[107] In describing the divines as wild gesturers who ape fools and vice figures, Milton pursues an ethical critique based on the bending of bodies. 'Writhing', they twist and curl. 'Unboning', they remove internal structure, becoming pliant to spectator desire. They give over flesh as though sexually to the eyes, 'prostituting' their vocation '*to the eyes* of Courtiers and Court-Ladies'.[108] This *mise en scène* captures the crucial irony that the attempt to exalt oneself in the field of vision entails a forfeiture of body and of authority. The fool, icon of vulgar posturing, embodies this paradox: 'They thought themselves gallant men', writes Milton; 'I thought them fools'.[109] He responds with hostility to the bad acting – in particular, to poor pronunciation and indecorous gesture – while in the midst of the spectators and the social energies that move through them. His hiss sounds what such acting deserves: 'they were out' – exploded – 'and I hist'.[110] Where the body's prostitution 'to the eyes' bespeaks the implicit sexuality of the actor–spectator relationship, the hiss of the discerning manifests the latent violence that threatens to 'explode' upon a desire exposed. The hiss exposes the writhing and boneless snake.

Like the actors whom Hamlet accuses of 'mouth[ing]' lines, 'saw[ing] the air too much with [their] hand[s]' and 'tear[ing] a passion to tatters' 'to split the ear of the groundlings', the Cambridge divines, seeking to stand out and gain favour, expose themselves as authored.[111] This paradox, by which the authority that would stand out as separate and self-made reveals itself to be controlled by fear and desire, is an essential characteristic of Milton's Satan. During his debate with Abdiel, Satan's imperative to show himself as radically free and supremely potent, and to convince the rebel angels of their right, requires a myth of self-creation: they 'know no time when we were not as now', were not 'formd' by 'secondarie hands' but, rather, 'self-begot, self-rais'd / By our own quick'ning power'.[112]

Sprung full-formed from Satan's head, Sin herself embodies the ruse of self-generation:

> All on a sudden miserable pain
> Surpris'd thee, dim thine eyes, and dizzie swumm
> In darkness, while thy head flames thick and fast
> Threw forth, till on the left side op'ning wide,
> Likest to thee in shape and count'nance bright,
> Then shining heav'nly fair, a Goddess arm'd
> Out of thy head I sprung: amazement seis'd
> All th' Host of Heav'n.[113]

As a parody of *inventio* that emerges full-formed in Satan's likeness, Sin is a product of the 'mind' that 'is its own place', that denies its own situatedness.[114] Yet, as an involuntary birth that 'surpris[es]' Satan with 'miserable pain', leaving his eyes 'dim' and dizzily swimming 'in darkness', she seems produced less by than upon her parent, more brain tumour than authorial offspring. The syntax models the insentience of this act of spontaneous generation. The momentary loss of control is experienced by the reader in the difficulty of 'swumm', which can be read as a past participle that takes 'thee' as its subject, but which may also extend, as a past participial adjective, the appositive phrase 'dim thine eyes' to further modify 'eyes'. In other words, the eyes have been 'swumm', or temporarily submersed, in darkness. Either way, we must suspend the logic of the syntax across the enjambment until 'in darkness' completes it.

Even during this birth, dynamic corporeal form emerges from within a surrounding field of vision, 'at th' Assembly [. . .] in sight / Of all the Seraphim'.[115] Here, the spectator context emphasises that the birth is a consequence of Satan's narcissism, as though it were an involuntary and empty gesture, a movement that surprises the would-be author with the author's own textuality. After the rebellion's defeat, Sin's body becomes not only serpentine – 'end[ing] foul in many a scaly fould / Voluminous and vast, a Serpent arm'd / With mortal sting' – but, also, a ruptured form of involuntary reproduction that is subject to repeated incestuous rape that produces 'yelling Monsters that with ceasless cry / Surround me'.[116] The sudden springing forth of Sin from Satan's head elicits a response that is appropriate to the spectator's witnessing of a monstrous spectacle: 'amazement seis'd / All th' Host of Heav'n; back they recoild afraid / At first, and call'd me *Sin*'.[117] Satan's surprise of 'miserable pain' is answered by the sudden amazement of the surrounding host, an amazement that is described as a passion that seizes, rather than is expressed by, the audience.[118] The momentary unconsciousness that coincides with Sin's birth is similarly manifested in the arbitrary naming, with no cause or explanation given, of '*Sin*'. She will be the source of endless involuntary birth and the centre of a recurring echo, 'With terrors and with clamors compast round'.[119]

Unacknowledged and undisciplined, the dialectic of influence and counter-influence would, in theory, organise into insentient mechanism, pulling actor and spectators into a closed-circuit loop, a rigid reflexivity of the debased and the debased, the authored and the authored. Such theatrical recursion would yield a zero-level of authority, an entropic ethical state distributed evenly through the system; at the same time, the system's materiality would become uncontrollably dynamic, passing through stages of naked writhing flesh in response to unacknowledged and unmanaged internal oscillations. What is ultimately a divestiture of authority comes about precisely through a commitment to a model of absolute authority that denies the dynamic connectivity of passion, vision and flesh. For Satan's relationship to the rebel throng, Milton might have looked to the spectacle of Restoration monarchy and its enabling social climate of the 'misguided and abus'd multitude', of the 'inconstant, irrational, and Image-doting rabble'.[120]

Milton brings to life such a nightmarish organisation of embodied authority during the scene of Satan's return and address to the infernal throng in book X of *Paradise Lost*. Before boasting his success in seducing Man, Satan first passes through Hell 'unmarkt, / In shew Plebeian Angel militant / Of lowest order': 'invisible [he] / Ascended his high Throne'; 'Down a while / He sate, and round about him saw unseen'.[121] Prior to emerging into view, he 'unseen' enjoys a 'round about' gaze unmenaced. He then seems to materialise *ex nihilo* as a 'shape Starr bright' emerging 'from a Cloud'.[122] It is a cheap theatrical illusion, performed 'with what permissive glory since his fall / Was left him, or false glitter'.[123] The 'throng' responds like a mass of groundlings:

'All amaz'd', they 'bent thir aspect, and whom they wish'd beheld'.[124] Collapsing the desiring to see into the seeing of what is desired, 'wish'd beheld' suggests that the throng collaborates in the field of vision to co-produce the debased theatre of Satanic oratory and monarchy.[125]

After euphorically recounting the seduction, Satan stands in his hearers' grip, 'expecting' 'universal shout and high applause', like that which is earnt by Abdiel when, 'unmov'd, / Unshak'n, unseduc'd, unterrifi'd', he 'st[oo]d approv'd in sight of God, though Worlds / Judg'd [him] perverse'.[126] Satan's display of power counters real precariousness. He declares the seduction to have been an unequivocal triumph, hence his facile misreading of the Son's curse.[127] However, as he waits, hoping for unanimous applause, divine authority supervenes to transform the scene into an allegory of symbiotic ethical abdication: 'Contrary he hears / On all sides, from innumerable tongues / A dismal universal hiss, the sound / Of public scorn'.[128]

Explosion and hissing, 'the sound / Of public scorn', pour in from 'all sides'. Satan becomes the 'shape' in which 'he sin'd', the serpentine body that, 'fawning, [had] lick'd the ground' under Eve's feet.[129] He becomes the 'writhing and unboning' fool:

> His Visage drawn he felt to sharp and spare,
> His Armes clung to his Ribs, his Leggs entwining
> Each other, till supplanted down he fell
> A monstrous Serpent on his Belly prone,
> Reluctant, but in vaine, a greater power
> Now rul'd him.[130]

Though the hissing tongues encompass Satan, the syntax, rhythm and enjambments also suggest that actor and audience oppose each other as mirroring reflections: 'Hiss for hiss returnd with forked tongue / To forked tongue, for now were all transform'd / Alike'.[131] The phrase 'hiss for hiss returnd' plots the effect of an echo on the spatial-temporal poetic line; the enjambed 'forked tongue / To forked tongue' and 'all transform'd / Alike' further translate the circular depth of the theatre onto a plane where opposing forms reflect each other.[132]

Here, rhetor and audience constitute each other, not in a negotiation of truth but, rather, in a co-dependent confirmation of self-serving desires. The monarchic Satan confirms in the rebels a sense of mission and hope, a sense of purpose that matters only as such, though not for its bitterly empty end. Satan becomes the form of that desire, a writhing form of flesh that shifts and bends, that oscillates within the fluctuations of hope and fear, deluded euphoria and desperation of Milton's infernal fallen: 'Thus was th' applause they meant, / Turn'd to exploding hiss, triumph to shame'.¹³³ This abdication of embodied authority is, through its psycho-affective structure, endlessly recursive and degenerative. It infects lesser devils who wait

> Sublime with expectation [. . .] to see
> [. . .] thir glorious Chief;
> They saw, but other sight instead, a crowd
> Of ugly Serpents; horror on them fell,
> And horrid sympathie; for what they saw
> They felt themselves now changing [. . .]
> And the dire hiss renew'd, and the dire form
> Catcht by Contagion.¹³⁴

This 'renew[al]' of 'dire hiss' and 'dire form' continues to unfold in the serpents' repeated attempts to eat the deluding apples from a newly arisen 'multitude' of 'forbidden Tree[s]': 'oft they assay'd', 'oft they fell / Into that same illusion'.¹³⁵ As 'horror on them [falls]', they are seised in a 'horrid sympathie', an inexorable magnetism of the undulating – as 'horror' and 'horrid' derive from *horrere*, to shudder and to shake.¹³⁶ 'Some say', Milton tells us, that these self-abdicated forms are 'Yearly enjoyned [. . .] to undergo / This annual humbling [. . .] / To dash their pride, and joy for Man seduc't'.¹³⁷ Thus, actor and spectators, author and audience organise into a system of theatrical recursion that brings only emptiness and a 'long and ceaseless hiss': echoing the 'clamors [. . .] and terrors' of the serpentine forms endlessly encircling the involuntarily, reiteratively birthing serpentine Sin.

Theatricality in Milton is not merely a mode of hypocrisy but is, also, one of negotiated, embodied authority: not a choice but, rather, a precondition of action. What Michael Schoenfeldt aptly describes as 'the invisible lines of force that bond one human with another, for better and for worse', are lively sinews of the poem's ethics, connecting agential bodies in the field of vision.¹³⁸ During the separation colloquy, Adam's testimony to the power of Eve's eyes upon him suggests a theatrical dimension to marriage and its cultivating labour: 'I from the influence of thy looks receave / Access in every Vertue, in thy sight / More wise, more watchful, stronger'.¹³⁹ By raising the spectre of 'shame', Eve's gaze ('thou looking on') would 'utmost vigor raise', inspiring heroic action in her defence.¹⁴⁰ Virtue appears cooperative, premised not only upon sociality but, also, upon responsiveness to the feeling of the eyes of another, or of others, upon oneself.

Sometimes, encompassing eyes, and their effect upon the passions, help to catalyse virtuous action. At the start of *Areopagitica*, a simulated speech to Parliament, Milton identifies with those 'alter'd and mov'd inwardly in their mindes' at the thought of addressing 'Governours of the Commonwealth'.[141] Where it is conventional for such pious patriots to detail 'which [passion] sway'd [them] most' to speak or write, he claims simply that this thought of his audience 'hath got the power within me to a passion'.[142] He cares not to specify *which* passion moved him but, rather, emphasises that the freedom to speak to his audience inspires a more generalised passion that is the tract's animating principle.[143] The phrase 'mov'd inwardly in their mindes' directly applies the language of passion, often seen as moving the subject from within, to describe a dynamic rationality; the productive integration of passion and reason drives his argument that pre-publication censorship will stagnate the vital force that moves writers to advance the cause of Truth. Even vicious books promote learning *because* they induce passion: 'Wherefore did [God] creat passions within us, pleasures round about us, but that these rightly temper'd are the very ingredients of vertu?'[144] The note on tragedy prefacing *Samson Agonistes*, written with a far more guarded view of the relationship between passion and reason in the public sphere, suggests that drama can work medicinally to 'purge', 'temper' or 'reduce [. . .] to just measure' unhealthy 'passions' (in part by 'stirr[ing] up' 'a kind of delight').[145] Milton's view of literature's effect on the passions and their effect on rationality corresponds with his appraisal of the public sphere: when the culture is healthy, tempered passion leads to greater health; when diseased, unchecked passion hastens decline by promoting self-deluding rationalisation.[146]

The constant oscillation between binaries that we have seen in the *Vacation Exercise* helped to condition a visceral and intellectual sense of authority differing greatly from that of the vatic, Orphic or Virgilian traditions. Authority emerges not merely from a line of literary influence, or as mode of teaching downward to a captive and infantilised audience, but, rather, from an entanglement within the body public, real and imagined: from desire and menace, from constrained condescension and from a phenomenal eroticism conjuring nightmares of rejection and dismemberment. Of course, an inspired epic poet for England does not grow into his own overnight; nor does he earn the privilege of claiming Virgil's paternity without publishing. And is not publishing quintessentially theatrical, once we understand the text to be an embodiment of authorial ethos sent out with 'suspect or fears' to the general assembly who will scrutinise, cut apart, misrepresent, violate and hermeneutically bend the author who engendered it?

Notes

1. See A. B. Coiro, 'Anonymous Milton'.
2. H. Berry, 'The Miltons and the Blackfriars Playhouse'; assumed as true in Burbery, *Milton the Dramatist*, pp. 34–5; Burbery's assumption taken as evidence in Martin, *Milton among the Puritans*, p. 70.
3. See below, pp. 117–20.
4. B. Jonson, *The Alchemist*, V, i, lines 6–26.
5. See A. H. Nelson (ed.), *Records of Early English Drama*, II, pp. 996–8; and R. Richek, '"Salting"'.
6. G. Campbell and T. Corns, *John Milton*, pp. 58–60.
7. Ibid., p. 184; see also M. A. Radzinowicz, '"To Play in the Socratic Manner"'; cf. G. Campbell, 'The Satire on Aristotelian Logic in Milton's "Vacation Exercise"'.
8. See especially L. Martz, *Poet of Exile*.
9. Scholars have rarely treated the work as a whole. The danger of parcelling the poem can be seen in N. K. Sugimura, '*Matter of Glorious Trial*', p. 24, which does not seem to recognise that the final lines of the poem are, in fact, part of an interlude.
10. See G. P. Mohrmann, 'Oratorical Delivery and Other Problems in Current Scholarship on English Renaissance Rhetoric', pp. 64–7.
11. W. J. Ong, *Ramus, Method, and the Decay of Dialogue*, p. 281.
12. See especially J. Lares, *Milton and the Preaching Arts*.
13. Quintilian, *The Orator's Education*, V, XI, iii.
14. Ibid., p. 7; Plutarch, *Twelve Lives*, pp. 359–60.
15. See above, pp. 3–4.
16. V. Maximus, *Memorable Deeds and Sayings*, p. 290; see also Macrobius, *Saturnalia*, pp. 101–4.
17. J. Bulwer, *Chironomia*, frontispiece.
18. Milton, *Of Education*, CPW, II, pp. 400–1.
19. Milton, *Areopagitica*, CPW, II, p. 492.
20. Milton, *Paradise Lost*, WJM, II.ii, IX, lines 664–75.
21. Ibid., IX, line 678.
22. See above, p. 7.
23. M. D'Assigny, *The Art of Memory*, frontispiece; see also H. F. Plett, *Rhetoric and Renaissance Culture*, pp. 501–52.
24. Bulwer, *Chironomia*, pp. 118–19.
25. Milton, *Vacation Exercise*, p. 251. *Vix etenim opinor plures olim Athenas adventasse ad audiendum duos oratores summos Demosthenem et Aeschinem de principatu eloquentiae certantes nec eam unquam felicitatem contigisse peroranti Hortensio nec tot tam egregie litteratos viros condecorasse orantem Ciceronem* (p. 250).
26. Nelson, *Records of Early English Drama*, II, p. 998; Richek, '"Salting"', pp. 105–6; see also J. G. Turner, 'Milton among the Libertines', pp. 450–1.
27. See Richek, '"Salting"', pp. 105–10.
28. Milton, *Vacation Exercise*, p. 251. *Nec miretur quispiam si ego tot eruditione insignes viros totumque pene Academiae florem huc confluxisse tanquam inter astra positus triumphem* (p. 250).

29. See below, pp. 119–20.
30. See J. Hale, 'Milton Plays the Fool'.
31. Milton, *Vacation Exercise*, pp. 245–7. *Cum his me incalentem studiis repente avocavit atque abstraxit pervetusti moris fere annua celebritas, iussusque ego sum eam operam quam acquirendae sapientiae primo destinaram ad nugas transferre et novas ineptias excogitandas* (pp. 244–6).
32. Ibid., pp. 257–9. *Sane arduum videtur et minime proclive, me iocos hodie serio laudaturum* (pp. 256–8).
33. Ibid., p. 245. *Exercitationes nonnunquam Ludicras Philosophi studiis non obesse* (p. 244).
34. Ibid., p. 267. *Aut si quid solute, si quid luxurianter dictum erit, id quidem non mentem et indolem meam sed temporis rationem et loci genium mihi suggessisse putetis. Itaque quod simile solent exuentes implorare comoedi, id ego inceptans flagito: 'Plaudite, et ridete'* (p. 266).
35. Sparse information about the staging of saltings is available. Presumably, Milton's salting took place within a dining hall or in the Christ's College Hall. See Nelson, *Early Cambridge Theatres*, pp. 65–6.
36. Milton, *Vacation Exercise*, pp. 271–3. *Profusissimo risu circumsonent omnia, et solutior cachinnus hilares excutiat lacrimas, ut iis risu exhaustis ne guttulam quidem habeat Dolor qua triumphum exornet suum. Ego profecto si quem nimis parce diducto rictu ridentem conspexero, dicam eum scabros et cariosos dentes rubigine obductos aut indecoro ordine prominentes abscondere, aut inter prandendum hodie sic opplevisse abdomen ut non audeat ilia ulterius distendere ad risum, ne praecinenti ori succinat* (pp. 270–2).
37. Ibid., p. 273. *Et aenigmata quaedam nolens effutiat sua non Sphinx sed Sphincter anus, quae medicis interpretanda non Oedipo relinquo; nolim enim hilari vocis sono obstrepat in hoc coetu posticus gemitus: solvant ista medici qui alvum solvunt* (p. 272).
38. Ibid., p. 273. *At vero absit porro ab hoc coetu horrendus et tartareus ille sibili sonus, nam si hic audiatur hodie, credam ego Furias et Eumenides inter vos occulte latitare, et angues suos colubrosque pectoribus vestris immisisse, et proinde Athamantaeos Furores vobis inspiravisse* (p. 272).
39. Milton, *Maske*, WJM, I.i, line 550; and *Paradise Lost*, WJM, II.i, VII, line 33.
40. Milton, *Vacation Exercise*, p. 247. *Vestra [. . .] in me nuperrime comperta facilitas* (p. 246). Aiming to 'remedy the misapprehension of Milton's autonomy', and to revise the 'caricature of an isolated pedant', Dobranski offers a portrait of a sociable, popular and collaborative Milton in 'Milton's Social Life', pp. 1–2.
41. Milton, *Vacation Exercise*, p. 249. *Putaremque lucubrationes meas qualescunque etiam ingrates propemodum futuras, et mitiores habituras iudices Aeacum et Minoa quam e vobis fere quemlibet sane praeter opinionem meam* (p. 248).
42. Ibid., p. 249. *Praeter meam si quid erat speculae, non vulgari (sicuti ego accepi, imo ipse sensi) omnium plausu exceptae sunt* (p. 248).
43. Milton, *Pro populo Anglicano defensio secunda*, WJM, VIII, pp. 12–15. *Jam videor mihi, ingressus iter, transmarinos tractus & porrectas latè regiones, sublimis perlustrare; vultus innumeros atque ignotos, animi*

sensus mecum conjunctissimos. Hinc Germanorum virile & infestum servituti robur, indè Francorum vividi dignique nomine liberales impetus, hinc Hispanorum consulta virtus, Italorum inde sedata suíque compos magnanimitas ob oculos versatur. Quicquid uspiam liberorum pectorum, quicquid ingenui, quicquid magnanimi aut prudens latet, aut se palàm profitetur, alii tacitè favere, alii apertè suffragari, accurrere alii & plausu accipere, alii tandem vero victi, deditos se tradere. Videor jam mihi, tantis circumseptus copiis [. . .] libertatem diu pulsam atque exulem, longo intervallo domum ubique gentium reducere. See below, p. 117.
44. See M. V. Ronnick, 'Concerning the Dramatic Elements in Milton's *Defensiones*', p. 278.
45. See S. M. Fallon, 'Alexander More Reads Milton', p. 113.
46. Milton, *The Readie and Easie Way*, *CPW*, VII, p. 423.
47. Milton, *Vacation Exercise*, p. 285. *Ad filios* [. . .] *pater me converto, quorum cerno speciosum numerum, et video etiam lepidulos nebulones occulto nutu me patrem fateri* (p. 284).
48. See Coiro, 'Anonymous Milton', p. 609.
49. Milton, 'At a Vacation Exercise', line 14.
50. Ibid., lines 23–8.
51. Ibid., lines 29–30.
52. Ibid., lines 33–8.
53. Milton, 'Lycidas', *WJM*, I.i, line 77.
54. See Milton, *Paradise Lost*, *WJM*, II.i, III, lines 501–43; and *Reason*, *CPW*, I, p. 808.
55. Milton, 'At a Vacation Exercise', lines 33–4.
56. Ibid., lines 47–52.
57. Ibid., lines 53–6.
58. 'predicament, *n.* 3', *OED Online*, available at <http://dictionary.oed.com/cgi/entry/50186764?single=1&query_type=word&queryword=predicament&first=1&max_to_show=10> (last accessed 4 March 2009).
59. Milton, 'At a Vacation Exercise', lines 57–8.
60. Hale, *Milton's Cambridge Latin*, p. 290.
61. See below, pp. 146–9, 163, 185–7.
62. Milton, *Paradise Lost*, *WJM*, II.i, I, lines 14–15.
63. W. Prynne, *Histriomastix*, p. 291.
64. Because Sugimura does not acknowledge that Milton's salting ends in a staged interlude, she misreads the philosophical implications of his invocation of the Categories ('*Matter of Glorious Trial*', pp. 17–18).
65. Milton, 'At a Vacation Exercise', after line 100.
66. Ibid., after line 90.
67. Ibid., lines 60–1.
68. Campbell and Corns, *John Milton*, p. 60.
69. Milton, *Vacation Exercise*, p. 283: *Cur videor illis parum masculus?* [. . .] *Fortasse* [. . .] *quod nunquam me virum praestiti eo modo quo quicquid est feminae* (p. 282).
70. Ibid., p. 283. *At vero unde est quod ego tam subito factus sum Pater? Dii vestram fidem! Quid hoc est prodigii Pliniana exsuperantis portenta! Numnam ego percusso angue Tiresiae fatum expertus sum? Ecqua me Thessala saga magico perfudit unguento? An denique ego a deo aliquot*

vitiatus, ut olim Caeneus, virilitatem pactus sum stupri pretium, ut sic repente ἐκ θηλείας εἰς ἄρρενα ἀλλαχ θείην ἄν (p. 282).
71. Apollodorus refers to Hesiod's text, now lost, in *The Library of Apollodorus*, III, vi, 7. Ovid, *Metamorphoses*, III, 316–38.
72. Ovid, *Metamorphoses*, XII, 146–209.
73. Milton, *Paradise Lost*, *WJM*, II.i, I, lines 17–26.
74. A. Stackhouse, 'Sleeping with the Muse', p. 143; see also J. P. Rumrich, *Milton Unbound*, pp. 94–117.
75. See below, pp. 59–62.
76. M. Merleau-Ponty, *Le Visible et l'invisible*, my translation. *La chair dont nous parlons n'est pas le matière* [the flesh of which we speak is not matter]. *Elle est l'enroulement du visible sur le corps voyant, du tangible sur le corps touchant* (p. 191).
77. Ibid. *Le regard [. . .] enveloppe, palpe, épouse les choses visibles* [the look envelops, palpates, espouses the visible things]. *Comme s'il était avec elles dans un rapport d'harmonie préétablie, comme s'il les savait avant de les savoir* [as though it knew them before knowing them] (p. 175).
78. See especially M. Schoenfeldt, '"Commotion Strange"'.
79. Milton, *Paradise Lost*, *WJM*, II.i, I, lines 56–8.
80. Ibid., I, line 606.
81. Merleau-Ponty, *Le Visible et l'invisible*, p. 375.
82. Milton, *Paradise Lost*, *WJM*, II.i, V, lines 872–4.
83. See below, pp. 55–6.
84. Milton, *Paradise Lost*, *WJM*, II.ii, X, lines 1092–4.
85. Ibid., IX, lines 1058–9.
86. Milton, *Reason*, *CPW*, I, p. 828.
87. Milton, *Animadversions*, *CPW*, I, p. 668.
88. Milton here is quoting J. Hall, *An Humble Remonstrance to the High Court of Parliament* (1641), p. 37. See below, p. 97.
89. Lacan, *Four Fundamental Concepts*, pp. 65–119.
90. Milton, *Animadversions*, *CPW*, I, p. 726. See below, pp. 99–100.
91. Milton, *Samson Agonistes*, *WJM*, I, lines 1605–10. See below, pp. 185–6.
92. R. Descartes, *Passions* (1650), translations mine. *Nos passions ne peuvent pas aussi directement etre excitées ny ostées par l'action de notre volonté; mais elles peuvent l'estre indirectement par la representation des choses qui ont coustume d'etre jointes avec les passions que nous voulons avoir, & qui sont contraires à celles que nous voulons rejetter* (p. 61).
93. Cf. Cicero, *De oratore*, II, 291–2; and Quintilian, *The Orator's Education*, V, XI, iii, 61–2, 71.
94. Descartes, *Passions*. *Ainsi pour exciter en soy la hardiesse & oster la peur, il ne suffit pas d'en avoir la volonté, mais il faut s'appliquer à considerer les raisons, les objets, ou les exemples, qui persuadent que le peril n'est pas grand; qu'il y a tousjours plus de seureté en la defence qu'en la fuite; qu'on aura de la gloire & de la joye d'avoir vaincu, au lieu qu'on ne peut attendre que du regret & de la honte d'avoir fui* (pp. 61–2).
95. Ibid. *Qu'il n'y a point d'ame si foible, qu'elle ne puisse estant bien conduite acquerir un pouvoir absolu sur les Passions* (p. 71). Consider the closing phrases of article 50: *il est evident [. . .] que ceux mesmes qui ont les plus foibles ames, pourroient acquerir un empire tres-absolu sur toutes*

      leurs passions, si on employoit assez d'industrie à les dresser, & à les conduire [it is evident that those persons who have the weakest souls could acquire an absolute empire over their passions, if they would employ enough industry to tame and guide them] (p. 74).
96. Milton, *Paradise Lost*, *WJM*, II.i, III, lines 690–1.
97. Ibid., III, lines 622, 616, 620–1.
98. Ibid., III, line 624.
99. Ibid., III, lines 634, 640–4.
100. Ibid., III, line 629.
101. Ibid., IV, line 125.
102. Ibid., IV, lines 127–30.
103. Ibid., IV, lines 114–17.
104. See article 202 of *Passions*, where Descartes describes the worst 'species of Anger, in which predominates Hatred and Sadness', as 'not so apparent at first, except perhaps in making the face turn pale [. . .] And as it is the most generous souls which have the most gratitude, so it is those which have the most pride and who are the most lowly and weak who let themselves get most carried away by this species of Anger'. *L'Autre espece de Colere, en laquelle predomine la Haine & la Tristesse, n'est pas si apparente d'abord, sinon peut estre en ce qu'elle fait palir le visage [. . .] Et comme ce sont les ames les plus genereuses qui ont le plus de reconnoissance, ainsi ce sont celles qui ont le plus d'orgueil, & qui sont les plus basses & les plus infirmes, qui se laissent le plus emporter à cette espece de Colere* (pp. 258–9).
105. Milton, *Paradise Lost*, *WJM*, II.ii, IX, lines 853–5.
106. Ibid., IX, lines 886–7.
107. See pp. 51, 55, 110, 113–14, 138, 178, 199.
108. Milton, *Apology*, *CPW*, I, p. 887.
109. Ibid., p. 887.
110. Ibid., p. 887.
111. See above, p. 7.
112. Milton, *Paradise Lost*, *WJM*, II.i, V, lines 853–61.
113. Ibid., II, lines 752–9.
114. Ibid., I, line 254.
115. Ibid., II, lines 749–50.
116. Ibid., II, lines 651–3, 795–6.
117. Ibid., II, lines 758–60.
118. Cf. Milton, 'On Shakespear', *WJM*, I.i, lines 13–16.
119. Milton, *Paradise Lost*, *WJM*, II.i, II, line 862.
120. Milton, *The Readie and Easie Way*, *CPW*, VII, pp. 452, 463; and *Eikonoklastes*, *CPW*, III, p. 601.
121. Milton, *Paradise Lost*, *WJM*, II.ii, X, lines 441–8.
122. Ibid., X, lines 449–50.
123. Ibid., X, lines 451–2. See below, pp. 188–9.
124. Ibid., X, lines 452–4.
125. Cf. the opening passage of Milton, *The Tenure of Kings and Magistrats*, *CPW*, III, p. 190.
126. Milton, *Paradise Lost*, *WJM*, II.ii, X, lines 504–5; *WJM*, II.i, V, lines 898–9; *WJM*, II.i, VI, lines 21–37.

127. Ibid., *WJM*, II.ii, X, lines 494–501.
128. Ibid., X, lines 506–9.
129. Ibid., X, line 516; IX, line 526.
130. Ibid., X, lines 511–16.
131. Ibid., X, lines 518–20.
132. For narcissism premised upon *difference* as regenerative, see M. Kilgour, 'Poetic Creation', pp. 307–39. Cf. Guillory, 'Milton, Narcissism, Gender', in C. Kendrick (ed.), pp. 194–233.
133. Milton, *Paradise Lost*, *WJM*, II.ii, X, lines 545–6.
134. Ibid., X, lines 536–44.
135. Ibid., X, lines 554, 567, 570–1.
136. See below, pp. 116–17.
137. Milton, *Paradise Lost*, *WJM*, II.ii, X, lines 575–7.
138. Schoenfeldt, '"Commotion Strange"', p. 67.
139. Milton, *Paradise Lost*, *WJM*, II.ii, IX, lines 309–11. See below, pp. 180–2.
140. Ibid., IX, lines 312–14.
141. Milton, *Areopagitica*, *CPW*, II, p. 486.
142. Ibid., p. 487.
143. Fallon, *Milton's Peculiar Grace*, sees here a 'picture of wavering and competing passions' (p. 141) as 'the pressure of self-reference leads to a distortion in the [tract's] reasoning' (p. 136).
144. Milton, *Areopagitica*, *CPW*, II, p. 527.
145. Milton, 'Of That Sort of Dramatic Poem', *WJM*, I.ii, p. 331.
146. Cf. Hammond, *Milton and the People*, p. 249.

Chapter 2

Printless Feet: Early Lyrics and the *Maske*

The embodied ambivalence that we saw in Milton's *Vacation Exercise* correlates with his view of the theatre as a cultural institution. Milton's writings about the stage distinguish, often uncertainly, between theatre as it was practised – in London, at court and in the colleges – and theatre as it *could* be practised if appropriately disciplined and mediated.

Milton's Commonplace Book, likely begun in the late 1630s, offers insight into his private hopes for theatre and objections against extreme anti-theatricality.[1] Under the heading *Spectacula*, Milton works to distinguish between the wholesale repudiation of theatre, as represented by the anti-theatrical authorities Tertullian and Lactantius, and his own qualified embrace of the stage. He notes that Tertullian 'condemns' the 'vogue' of stage plays and 'excludes' Christians from them; however, he continues, the Church father's arguments 'excoriate the pagan games *only*' (italics mine).[2] For Milton, the anti-theatrical argument is tiresome: 'Cyprian, or whoever wrote the book that deals with the same subject, rolls the same stone'.[3]

He has entered into the problem, into that crevice of ambivalence, where theatricality will pull in ongoing concerns of Milton the poet. He is actively pushing to open a space for the legitimacy of a Christian theatre. 'Nevertheless', he continues, as though with a tone of relief,

> in the epilogue of the work[, Tertullian,] with all the flowers of rhetoric directs [incites] the mind of a Christian to better spectacles, namely, those of a divine and heavenly character, such as, in great number and grandeur, a Christian can anticipate in connection with the coming of Christ and the last Judgment.[4]

In his paraphrase of Tertullian, Milton seems deliberately to soften the Church father's condemnation of theatre, focusing instead on the promise of '*better* spectacles [. . .] of a divine and heavenly *character*'. In *De spectaculis*, Tertullian unmistakably points to the divine spectacles of Apocalypse, which will show poets and players not staging religious drama but, rather, being adjudged to the flames: 'lither of limb by far in the fire' ('*solutiores multo per ignem*').⁵ Milton's 'nevertheless' ('*tamen*') suggests the force of a desired difference, to the extent that it changes the implication. His '*mentem Christiani* [. . .] *incitaverit*' – 'incites the mind of the Christian' – suggests a stirring up of the mind towards better *plays*, as though it were exhorting the Christian to write 'better spectacles' rather than providing an admonishment about divine spectacles of justice that will incinerate the vicious theatres of man.⁶

Milton moves on to Lactantius, who 'puts a stigma upon the whole dramatic art' 'by arguments no whit stronger' than those of Tertullian.⁷ Lactantius

> does not even once seem to have reflected that, while the corrupting influences of theatre ought to be eliminated, it does not follow that it is necessary to abolish altogether the performance of plays. This on the contrary would be quite senseless; for what in the whole of philosophy is more impressive, purer, or more uplifting than a noble tragedy, what more helpful to a survey at a single glance of the hazards and changes of human life?⁸

Milton's basic position toward theatre could not be clearer: 'while the corrupting influences of theatre ought to be eliminated, it does not follow that it is necessary to abolish altogether the performance of plays' ('*corruptelas quidem theatricas meritò tolli debere, omnem autem idcirco rerum dramaticarum usum penitus aboleri nihil necesse esse*'). Despite theatre's potentially 'corrupting influences', wholesale condemnation would be utterly stupid ('*insulso*'), since the best tragedies can move, edify and inspire.

In *Reason of Church Government*, Milton implies that to participate beneficially in the culture, theatre must be extracted from its commercial context and mediated by the state in a fusion of ritual and entertainment that would be 'doctrinal and exemplary to a Nation'.⁹ He suggests a proposal for state-sanctioned literary performances that would take place 'not only in Pulpits, but after another persuasive method, at set and solemn Paneguries, in Theaters, porches, or what other place, or way may win most upon the people to receiv at once both recreation, & instruction'.¹⁰ Something like the Athenian theatre festivals would reconcile poetry with ritual, theatre with religion. Milton avoids invoking anything that resembles the vices of the London theatres yet, nonetheless, pushes off against defined anti-theatrical positions. Critics of the stage, such as John Greene, continually bewailed that lapsed Christians 'flock thick and three-fold to the play-houses [. . .] when the temple of God [. . .] remain[s] bare and empty'.¹¹ Milton, however, lists theatres alongside churches as potential venues: 'porches' refers to recessed church entrances, thus marking architecturally an intended synthesis of entertainment and ritual, as the stage becomes a portal into the house of God. The phrase 'and what other place' shows willingness to break down barriers between the sacred and the profane. Where anti-theatricalists bemoaned that theatres fomented sexual license and unrest, Milton argues not only that these events could prove all the more edifying through aesthetic pleasure, but also that they could help to 'allay the perturbations of the mind, and set the affections in right tune'.[12] His justification is, implicitly, grounded in Aristotle's theory of catharsis in *Poetics* VI and anticipates his claim, in the note on tragedy that prefaces *Samson Agonistes*, that tragedy can 'temper and reduce' the passions 'to just measure'.[13]

Milton shows his strongest and most focused interest in a sacralised popular theatre precisely as social upheaval was about to compel Parliament to decree the theatres closed. Only in the early 1640s do we see him seriously thinking about writing staged drama for anything like a popular audience. During the first years of the Long Parliament, however, he was also unusually open in his embrace of a general public. Within a brief span between his return from European travels (in the late summer of 1639) and as late as 1644, he would sympathise with the opposition to Laud and episcopacy, with radicals and with Presbyterian ministers, with labourers and with landed dissenters alike – all of whom were working to build a Godly nation and to further the progress towards Millennium.

Enter Milton: The Ludlow *Maske*

The Ludlow *Maske* (i.e., 'Comus') shows a significant phase in the process by which Milton's ambivalence toward theatre became a resource in his poetry. It suggests the degree to which the effectiveness of the stage, as a medium for edification by means of delight, remains constrained by the vices and desires of the audience. Milton never embraced theatre without qualification but, rather, maintained a suspicious or critical view toward much of the theatre that was available in London. Nonetheless, his *Maske* shows him at odds with anti-theatrical writers, whom he saw as stifling the potential virtues of theatre with wholesale condemnations that defined the stage as inherently and inevitably vicious. The most ardent anti-theatricalists assailed, first and foremost, the basic constitution of theatre as staged mimesis before an audience.

Before turning to a sustained analysis of the *Maske*, I first establish how Milton, in his early poetry, looks to figures of the public stage in order to reconcile his identification as a private poet of God with his deferred role as a poet for a reading public with which he longs to merge, but which he also continues to mistrust. I then locate the *Maske* within the context of anti-theatrical criticism that defines both staged drama and the public and speaking woman as inherently unchaste. The Lady's struggles in the *Maske*, I contend, point to the failings of a libidinous climate of theatre reception that inhibits the stage's power as a vehicle to 'imbreed and cherish in a great people the seeds of vertu'.[14] The chapter locates this inhibiting power in the gaze and the 'barbarous dissonance' of the theatre audience, which is seen to work to shape represented action, and to shape the Lady herself, into the monstrous forms of its desires. The chapter then shows how Milton develops this theatrical treatment of the corrupting gaze by means of Spenser's Legend of Chastity, specifically with an eye to Britomart's journey through the House of Busyrane and her experience as a detached spectator of the masque of Cupid. I conclude by arguing that Sabrina represents a chaste theatre that, as an ideal, exerts an enabling power from outside the corrupting context of theatre reception. Sabrina's rising from the Severn opens up an alternative theatre space whereby the Lady, transfixed as a spectacle during the temptation scene, becomes a spectator confronted with the pure return of her initial footsteps. While Sabrina cannot, in herself, reform an inhibiting reception climate, she nonetheless allows Milton to hold out hope for a chaste theatre that can thrive when an audience is ready to receive it.

Building upon the account of theatre's destabilisation of Milton's sense of poetic self in the *Vacation Exercise*, this chapter continues to consider theatre as a vehicle for representing, evaluating and negotiating identity formation. Here, I mean 'identity' in the sense of an evolving conception of selfhood shaped in response to socially embedded performances of selfhood respondent to cultural norms and values.[15] This analysis focuses specifically on a process by which Milton reconciles a sense of divine poetic vocation, characterised in several early lyrics in terms of privacy and chastity, with a public sense of poetic vocation characterised in terms not only of divine and national service but, also, of sexual openness and the vulnerability of the body. I demonstrate how this process is facilitated and envisioned through Milton's Lady, whose thorny path of identity and the conditional release of its public entanglements form the *Maske*'s narrative.

As a quasi-dramatic form staged only once for a coterie audience, the *Maske* works towards integrating the sacred-and-private and the public, potentially profane poetic selves into an ideal unity.[16] The *Maske* thus represents mimetically, as drama, a crisis determined by its mode of performance, as theatre. In the first section, I examine Milton's embodiment of poetic authority in the early prose to demonstrate how the scene of writing and publication can be understood as a scene of theatrical action. Surveying representations of performance spaces and gendered authority in the early poetry, I explore how connections between staged poetic authority and gender influenced Milton's portrayal of the Lady as at once empowered and imperilled.

I call attention to how anti-theatrical discourses associating the staged/public woman with unchastity set up the basic terms of the Lady's crisis. How is she to enact publicly a chastely embodied agency amidst discursive pressures working to contaminate the self-concept and to inhibit female agency in the public sphere? I join William Kerrigan and William Shullenberger, among others, in reading the would-be bard in the powerful yet menaced voice of his Lady.[17] However, where scholars regularly picture the Lady as a temporarily stopped font of prophetic power, I focus instead on how, as a staged woman, she embodies the vulnerability of the divine poet who would be public yet who also would be chaste.

The Sacred Poet and the Staged Female Body

Milton's assertion, in the *Apology*, that the true poet 'ought him selfe to bee a true Poem, that is, a composition, and patterne of the best and honourablest things' depicts the author not as a disengaged rhetorician moulding the text from beyond but, rather, as a psychological presence in poetic language.[18] In other words, the poetic text is an ethical body. Further developing this idea in *Areopagitica*, Milton asserts that books 'preserve as in a violl the purest efficacie and extraction of that living intellect that bred them', so that 'to kill a good book' were 'as good almost [as to] kill a man'.[19] This figure of the book-as-vial implies that the author's quintessence or spirit is a vital liquid, the text a reservoir containing a distillation of a 'living' or embodied authoring mind. The metaphor suggests the potential diffuseness and contaminability of this spiritual liquid even as the vial, though (presumably) translucent, protects it from the potential contamination of the otherwise direct public encounter.

Whereas a single book holds a contained essence understood to work productively upon and within the reader, in performance, the staged body, situated within a dialectical exchange between actor and public, is much more immediately vulnerable.[20] Milton regularly locates rhetorical authority within manifest or implied theatre spaces in order to emphasise this vulnerability of the ethopoetic body. For instance, in *Animadversions*, he figures the public of 'discreet and judicious Reader[s]' as spectators capable of penetrating the varnished surface of prelatical rhetoric and, implicitly, of the actual bodies of Joseph Hall and the prelates.[21] When, in the *Apology*, he depicts young Anglicans as stage-players 'writhing and unboning their Clergie limmes', such vulnerability shapes the body as it conforms to perceived spectator desires.[22]

The threat of 'opposite spectators' in *Animadversions* makes it clear that the vial that protects the published book in *Areopagitica* no longer holds during the back-and-forth of polemical exchange. After all, Milton is in the process, here, of dissecting Hall's prose and turning it against him, just as his portrayal of the 'writhing and unboning' divines also responds to polemical attack.[23] Milton returns to theatre for its capacity to represent and explore a private–public dialectic. We might say that, as applied to print and to publication, the immediacy of performance foreshortens, into one moment, iterations of a dialectical exchange extending back in time and into the future. A poetic identity would, thus, materialise out of the experience of past iterations available in memory and future iterations anticipated in the imagination, together influencing the action of a present moment on a single stage or page. The scene of writing for print thus becomes infused with the vivid social reality of the London theatre experience, as detailed by historians of the stage such as Andrew Gurr.

Milton's path of theatrical poetic identity helps to explain the elaborate 'self-dramatization' and 'multiplication of selves' that Stephen Fallon traces in *Reason*, the first published work to which Milton attached his full name.[24] The 'interplay of the intimate and the public' observed by Fallon in Milton's justification for the second book's autobiographical digression may be taken as the driving engine of the volume's 'ethical self-representations' as well as the root cause of the very need for 'ethical proof'.[25] In the digression, Milton presents himself as a would-be divine poet called to serve 'Gods glory by the honour and instruction of my country' as an 'interpreter & relater of the best and sagest things'.[26] He considers the challenge of mediating the divine Logos to a public responsive to poetic and theatrical mediation. Seeing 'that God even to a strictnesse requires the improvement of these his entrusted gifts', the poet's most necessary acquisition is knowledge of 'how and in what manner he shall dispose and employ those summes of knowledge and illumination, which God hath sent him into this world to trade with'.[27] This challenge of 'how and in what manner [. . .] to trade' demands a 'burden of mind' that is 'sorer [. . .] and more pressing then any supportable toil, or waight, which the body can labour under'.[28] The key term here is 'trade', for it reframes poetic mediation as a transaction of Truth between the individual and his public, between an understanding of the Word emerging from an intimate communion with God and a performance of the Word informed by communal sensibilities and values.[29]

As is evident in Milton's assertion, in *Reason*'s opening passage, that 'persuasion' by 'well-temper'd discourse' is a more 'winning' means than the imposition of law to 'incite' and 'charme the multitude into the love of that which is really good', the principle of poetic mediation is founded upon sensory and affective appeal.[30] Thus, in the digression, he elevates performed poetry and drama as able, through the senses, to 'imbreed and cherish in a great people the seeds of vertue'.[31] The embodiment of poetry in performance – the phrase 'imbreed and cherish' overtly suggests insemination and incubation – can make the 'rugged and difficult' paths of virtue 'appeare to all men both easy and pleasant'.[32] Yet this same appeal to the senses also leads to a two-fold danger of carnal corruption: both for the 'youth and gentry' who 'suck in dayly' 'corruption and bane' 'from the writings and interludes of libidinous and ignorant Poetasters' and, more implicitly, for the performers, such as prelatical 'Church-maskers' who 'turne the inward power and purity of the Gospel into the outward carnality of the law[,] evaporating and exhaling the internall worship into empty conformities, and gay shewes'.[33]

The *Maske*, written for a 1634 performance, though not published with Milton's name until 1645, dramatises the plight of an agent, at once empowered and vulnerable, who struggles to maintain and express her virtue while embedded within a hostile context of sensual corruption. As such, it presents as drama a crisis of agency determined by its mode as staged performance. The 'burden of mind' facing the ethopoetic body, as a function of a private–public dialectic and of its representative locus, the theatre, becomes dramatised in the plot of a young woman returning home through the 'unhallow'd air' of an enchanted forest.[34] Arguably, the demands of the *Maske*'s occasion and the personal constitution and history of fifteen-year-old Alice Egerton, for whom the part was written, more immediately determined this character than did Milton's concerns about publication.[35] Yet, at times, it is impossible not to hear Milton's voice in the Lady's. For instance, when, during her debate with Comus, she claims a vocal power capable of moving 'dumb things [. . .] to sympath[y]', we can hear the would-be vatic poet aligning himself with Orpheus, who in 'L'Allegro', 'Il Penseroso', 'Lycidas' and *Paradise Lost* represents either poetic-prophetic power or extreme vulnerability to bodily violation.[36] Particularly as a staged female, the Lady embodies this Orphic duality. As we have seen in the *Vacation Exercise*, Milton acknowledged a nickname of Domina or 'the Lady' that was attributed to him by at least some of his Cambridge peers.[37] The fact that Milton named Alice Egerton's character 'the Lady' could not have been entirely coincidental.

For Shullenberger, the *Maske* performs a type of 'sexual initiation' that enacts 'a young woman's passage from girlhood into womanhood'.[38] Yet we might see the Lady's passage through the trials of the enchanted forest as arriving her at a starting point of legitimation *as a staged woman*. By grasping how these trials manifest anxieties that stem from the *Maske*'s theatrical mode, we can continue to resist the teleological imperative that governs much of the scholarship, which posits the emergence of a fully developed bard, an 'Author' in the most imperious, most masculine sense, possessing (sans irony) godlike poetic and prophetic power. Shullenberger's Lady, for instance, despite her physical vulnerability and victimisation, attains 'a prophetic and sublime voice' able, even, to 'transform and redeem the very nature of the public sphere'.[39] Yet the *Maske* remains acutely aware of the limitations imposed on the poet by a public sphere too menacing and powerful to be transformed so radically and suddenly.

Milton's staging of a fifteen-year-old female with substantial speaking, singing and dancing parts challenges the pronounced anti-feminism running through the anti-theatrical tracts – most directly, William Prynne's *Histriomastix* (1633/4), which met the staged, vocal female body with unequivocal hostility.[40] Less than five months before the Michaelmas staging of the *Maske*, Prynne, sentenced to life in prison and a crushing fine, was publicly pilloried, his ears cropped, for impugning Caroline masque culture. Prynne had suggested that Queen Henrietta Maria, who had participated in several court masques, was, by definition, a 'whore': 'for such are all those females [. . .] who dare dance publicly on a theatre'.[41] An index entry for 'Women-Actors', moreover, referred the reader to 'notorious whores'.[42] Where Prynne obsessively ties the stage to a feminised sexual looseness, the *Maske* heralds the chastity of a young woman whose struggles begin the moment she steps onto the stage.

Anti-theatricalists assailed theatres as 'the very markets of bawdry', glutted with content that fanned the flames of lust, provoking fornication, whoring, even rape.[43] The amphitheatres' proximity to the brothels underscored an analogy between acting and prostitution. Prynne cites:

> those venomous unchaste, incestuous kisses [. . .] those wanton dalliances; those meretricious embracements, compliments; those enchanting, powerful,

overcoming solicitations unto lewdness; those immodest gestures, speeches, attires, which inseparably accompany the acting of our stage-plays; especially where the bawd's, the pander's, the lover's, the wooer's, the adulterer's, the woman's, or love-sick person's parts are lively represented.[44]

His placement of 'the woman' upon the stage as a stock figure among bawds, panderers, seducers and adulterers underscores the vehement anti-feminism running through his tome. Stephen Gosson complains that plays besiege chastity with 'strange consorts of melody, to tickle the ear; costly apparel, to flatter the sight; effeminate gesture, to ravish the sense; and wanton speech, to whet desire to inordinate lust'.[45] Public and catering to spectator desires, theatre was a locus of be-whored femininity.

Anti-theatricalists described women playgoers as spectacles in their own right, inevitable targets of lust provoked by the stage's lewd content. As discussed by Jean Howard, the public woman was caught up in the dialectic of desire between the stage (its actors, playwrights and companies) and its paying spectators.[46] For John Northbrooke, the desiring gaze of spectators could itself corrupt a woman's chastity: 'What safeguard of chastity can there be, where the woman is desired with so many eyes?'[47] The infecting gaze enflames reciprocating desire: 'What mind can be pure and whole among such a rabblement, and not spotted with any lust?'[48] Gosson warns London's women that 'they which show themselves, openly desire to be seen': 'You can forbid no man that vieweth you to note you, and that noteth you, to judge you for entering to places of suspicion'.[49] It is but a small step to his most chilling admonition: 'If you do but listen to the voice of the fouler, or join looks with an amorous gazer, you have already made yourselves assaultable, and yielded your cities to be sacked'.[50]

By foregrounding a paragon of chastity who walks, dances, talks and sings on stage, the *Maske* counters not only the anti-feminist bent of anti-theatrical criticism but, also, the abuses of the stage that imperil the idea of chaste drama while encouraging undiscriminating anti-theatrical censure.[51] In agreeing to pen the *Maske*, Milton was turning to a notoriously 'libidinous' genre. Edward Peyton, for instance, claims in 1652 that

> the masques and playes at Whitehall were used onely for incentives of lust: therefore the courtiers invited the citizens wives to those shews, on purpose to defile them in such sort. There is not a lobby nor chamber (if it could speak) but would verify this.[52]

In *Paradise Lost*, Milton would contrast the chaste love of the marriage bed with 'Court Amours, / Mixt Dance, or wanton Mask'.[53]

'Wanton Mask' defines the medium – which often dramatised 'Court Amours' and which featured 'Mixt Dance' – according to sexual vice. As we have seen, Milton likewise depicts base comedies as 'libidinous' works proffering 'corruption and bane'. However, he voices this criticism while explaining a proposal for state-sponsored literary events that would include edifying dramas. In writing the *Maske*, he was inviting associations of wantonness in order to work his way through them.[54]

The *Maske* culminates a trajectory, traceable through the early poetry, by which Milton looks to theatre spaces and gendered embodiments of the poetic self in order to engage with the challenge of reconciling the sacred-private and the public aspects of his vocation. Several of the early poems depict the poet as a type of *vates* closed off from the world, his communion with God contingent upon privacy and sexual purity. In *Elegia sexta* (1629), he contrasts his friend Charles Diodati's poetry, which he characterises as inspired by women and wine, with the more glorified verse of the poet 'sacred to the gods': the divine poet 'is priest of the gods'.[55] Shunning wine and sex, he should 'live a simple, frugal life', eating 'herbs' and drinking 'only sober draughts from a pure spring'.[56] For the poetic imagination to soar heavenward, the divine poet must have a youth 'free of crime, pure, and chaste', a 'character unyielding' and a 'name without taint'.[57] Governed by chastity and embracing identification with the Bride of the bridegroom Christ, he serves God as a type of vestal virgin.[58] Yet he maintains his chastity specifically so that God's spirit can inhabit his body: 'The secret deeps of his soul, and his very lips alike breathe forth Jove'.[59] Poetry emerges through this spiritual inhabitation.

In *Elegia prima* (1626), an earlier verse epistle to Diodati, we see a form of the *vates* as a cloistered scholar, confined indoors yet transported through the imaginative landscape of his books. We see the poet longing to break from the enclosure and to connect with the social world. Theatre offers a means. When tired of his studies, he is welcomed by the 'splendor of the rounded theatre' ('*sinuosi pompa theatri*'), summoned to 'sound its plaudits'.[60] He seems to be describing real performances, perhaps at the Blackfriars playhall. Yet a closer look reveals stock figures of Roman comedy and a portrayal of 'furiosa Tragoedia' from Ovid, all gleaned from *books*, which 'sweep me off with them, mastering me utterly'.[61] His self-representation as urbane playgoer, applauding from within the audience, locates him more firmly within the cloister. The books open a window to an imagined future public. Milton also writes of adventures out of doors, where, from a shady grove, he revels as an erotic voyeur, gazing desirously upon passing virgins: 'There o'er and o'er one may see troops of maidens pass, stars, these, that breathe forth alluring fires. Ah, how oft have I gazed, spellbound'.[62] The public space outside of the cloister is now imagined as a space of sexual conquest. The poet directs his desire toward public spectacle but hides within the grove's umbrage, unseen and private. A sense of vulnerability accompanies the implied mastery of his shrouded outward gaze. The young women are not just objects of voyeurism, but also stars that breathe forth tempting fire.[63] 'Spellbound' and tempted, the poet feels the space of scopic pleasure as threatening to a budding selfhood. He must 'leave, with all suddenness, these walls' and with the 'aid of *moly*, plant divine', 'evade [. . .] the ill-famed halls of deceptive Circe'.[64]

From the sense of *sinuosi* ('*sinuosi pompa theatri*') as, beyond mere roundedness, a fluid and dynamic sinuosity, emerges the nightmare of ethopoetic metamorphosis within Circe's 'ill-famed halls'. This idea of theatre as a locus of beastly metamorphosis will be realised in the man-beasts of the *Maske*, which features both the son of Circe (Comus) and a variant of Homer's moly ('*Haemony*'). Theatre's scopic plenitude contrasts the hermetic privacy of the sacred ideal. Its dangers highlight the enclosure's security. The private–public divide manifests formally in the companion poems 'L'Allegro' and 'Il Penseroso' (1631), where, once again, theatre plays a role in sorting out the poetic self. Like the voyeur of *Elegia prima*, L'Allegro walks about surveying his surroundings, his eye catching a fluid procession of 'new pleasures', though now he walks 'not unseen'.[65] In lines pointing ahead to Thyrsis 'meditating' his 'rural minstrelsie' on the Severn's bank in the *Maske*, L'Allegro imagines 'feast', 'revelry', 'mask' and 'Pageantry' that offer 'such sights as youthful Poets dream / On Summer eeves by haunted stream'.[66] He drifts farther, from the exclusive audience of the court masque to the 'well-trod stage', to see a play by 'learned' Jonson or by 'sweetest *Shakespear* fancies childe'.[67] He wants to be covered in 'soft Lydian Aires' that are both 'married to immortal verse' and convivial enough to 'pierce' and entangle the 'meeting soul'.[68]

Where L'Allegro desires contact with 'meeting soul[s]', Il Penseroso resembles both the abstemious virgin priest of *Elegia sexta* and the cloistered, bookish poet of *Elegia prima*. He imagines himself walking through a forest at twilight, ending up 'in close covert by some Brook'.[69] Though near neither court nor theatre, he desires a reverie akin to what the 'youthful poets' of 'L'Allegro' 'dream [. . .] by haunted stream':

> And let som strange mysterious dream,
> Wave at his Wings in Airy stream,
> Of lively portrature display'd,
> Softly on my eye-lids laid.

> And as I wake, sweet musick breath
> Above, about, or underneath,
> Sent by som spirit to mortals good,
> Or th' unseen Genius of the Wood.[70]

We recognise, in the 'mysterious dream' that is 'laid', like Puck's fairy liquor, 'softly on [the] eye-lids', the 'sweetest *Shakespear* fancies childe' of *A Midsummer Night's Dream*. The passage evokes both the laying of drops upon the eyes and the enchantment of Bottom (L'Allegro's charismatically theatrical simpleton cousin), who wakes from enchantment believing himself to have experienced a vivid dream. Upon waking, Bottom bungles but, nonetheless, touches the essence of Paul's praise of the Spirit (1 Corinthians 2:9), which reveals divine mysteries that no eye can see, nor ear can hear.[71] Il Penseroso extracts the spirit of Bottom's dream from the context of the staged comedy and re-imagines it within an intimate wooded 'covert'.

L'Allegro and Il Penseroso can thus be seen as coming together through Bottom's dream and, more essentially, through the power of poetry and spectacle to inspire the imagination. Still, a distance separates the unseen, unheard rapture of Il Penseroso from the publicly immersed pleasure of L'Allegro.[72] Where L'Allegro fears not to be seen in court or theatre, Il Penseroso seeks inspiration 'where no prophaner eye may look', hidden 'from Day's garish eie'.[73] The poems show two aspects of the poet at a stream – L'Allegro's 'haunted stream' within the imagined court masque and Il Penseroso's 'Airy stream' of fancy 'in close covert by some Brook' – on the banks of a convergence. Yet they stand as on opposite sides, unable to unite. Their near-contact is transient, imperfect: L'Allegro turns back to his public, while Il Penseroso retreats into the 'studious Cloysters pale'. Emergence from the study, 'grove', 'cloyster' or 'covert' will require a miraculous binding of the public audience, as though contact with 'meeting soul[s]' demands the tacit violence of L'Allegro's 'notes' that 'pierce' and 'chains' of 'lincked sweetness'.[74] Scholars have argued that Milton saw Shakespearean fancy as threatening the chaste poetic mind with its overwhelming potency. Yet the image in 'On Shakespear' (1632) of an audience turned to 'marble with too much conceiving', placed with these early poems, indicates also the identification of an unproven poet desiring to perform a similar mastery.[75]

Four years after the *Maske*, Milton would find a fit embodiment of the sacred ideal in the Italian singer Leonora Baroni.[76] In the epigrams *Ad Leonoram Romae canentem* and two *Ad eandem*, he locates himself in a coterie audience as he attends to and admires Leonora. Where, in *Elegia sexta*, the poet's soul and lips 'breathe forth Jove', here, Leonora's voice 'itself sounds forth a god, a very present god', or 'the Third Intelligence of emptied heaven' (i.e., the Spirit), which 'makes its way unseen through [her] throat'.[77] Again, a divine presence inhabits the body, passing through the vocal tract (the '*ora*' of *Elegia sexta* is now '*guttura*') and emerging as song. On stage, Leonora is a focal point of desiring eyes, fully immersed in the visual field of the performance space. Yet God speaks 'in [her] alone' and makes mute the audience ('*caetera mutus habet*').[78] Her passive inhabitation by the Spirit, which empowers her voice, completely overwhelms the voice of her opposing audience. Likewise, in the third poem, though 'graced by the favouring enthusiasm of the sons of Romulus, she holds fast, by her singing, mortal men, aye, and gods, alike'.[79] What Milton had ambivalently defined as Shakespeare's preternatural power in 'Of Shakespear' now appears an unambiguous virtue in Leonora, who can 'hold fast' both men and gods. Her divine song exceeds Shakespeare's profane 'easie numbers'.[80] The poet-priest's temple is now a coterie theatre where inspired song renders the audience completely silent and immobile.

Leonora's voice again suggests Orphic power, yet this power is poised against a counter-influence that also associates the material presence of a staged singer with the Thracian bard's vulnerable body. Her voice counteracts the male desire that, according to music historian Andrew Dell'Antonio, defined an elite Roman culture of listening, which worked through oral and written discourse to overwrite the authority of staged, singing women. Dell'Antonio explains that Roman coterie audiences would aspire to *recte sentire*, a 'true way of thinking/feeling' that transformed listening from a 'passive and dangerously sensual' activity to an 'active and ideally transcendent' experience.[81] He sees Milton, in the Leonora poems, to be aspiring to a sophisticated listening that worked to wrest Baroni's 'sonic power [...] from her sinful female body' and to absorb it 'into the spiritual high-mindedness [...] of the male community of listeners'.[82] However, Milton's depiction of Leonora's song, as muting and holding fast the male audience, seems to acknowledge the erotically charged climate of reception while, at the same time, working against its gendered dynamics of power. Though the phrase 'learned sons of Romulus' likely pays tribute to the Accademia degli Umoristi, the literary club through which Milton had attended the concert, the poem attributes to Leonora far greater power. She chains and silences her auditors in order to reform them, teaching ('*docet*') mortal hearts to grow accustomed to immortal sound ('*sensim immortali assuescere*') – a unified embodiment of the multiple poetic selves that Milton, according to Fallon, would present in *Reason*.[83]

Ontology, Discursive Economy and the Disappearing Woman

The enchanter Comus's most insidious power is his ability to regulate body and agency by obscuring and distorting self-conception. The *Maske* explores the shaping power of the theatre space by dramatising how an alienation of value from the gendered body, facilitated by means of idealising (Petrarchan, dualist) and inhibiting (anti-theatrical, anti-feminist) discourses, gives rise to monstrous reflections and echoes that menace the emergent self. Milton employs a rhetoric of coinage and monetary circulation to represent this alienation of value as, at once, an economic and a theatrical problem concerning transactions between the self and the public. As I contend in the final section, Sabrina liberates the Lady by extracting her from the centre of the theatre's visual and sonic field and by resituating her as spectator. Thus, Milton complicates the spectacle–spectator dynamics that he confronted as a reader of the 'maske of Cupid' episode of book III of Edmund Spenser's *Faerie Queene*.[84] As a spectacle of inviolable chastity grounded in a terrestrial body, Sabrina represents the promise and inevitable contradictions of what the Lady calls 'uncontrouled worth': inherent value that precedes economic determination but that, nonetheless, must work within a culture of circulation in order to reform it.[85]

The drama of the Lady's public emergence requires that Milton reimagine the dualist ontology that informs the structure of antimasque and masque spectacle in numerous Stuart masques. The challenge of publicly staging a chaste female body entails the dignification of the body itself amidst discourses that work to inhibit female agency within the public sphere. As N. K. Sugimura suggests, the *Maske* 'expresses concerns about the complications arising from a purely Platonic philosophy, in which (true) Form is dangerously devoid of material association'.[86] The Attendant Spirit's opening monologue carefully sets up the problem of ontology that will inform, and in part be shaped by, Milton's representation of a spiritually agential woman who is both public and embodied. The Spirit establishes a stark distinction between the realm of immortal spirit and the corrupting material world. He hails from 'where those immortal shapes / Of bright aereal Spirits live inspher'd, / In regions milde of calm and serene Air'.[87] By contrast, the 'Earth' to which he '*descends*' (or has descended) is a 'dim spot', a 'pin-fold' where men of 'low-thoughted care' are 'confined, and pestered'.[88] The deictic 'this dim spot' and 'this pin-fold here' seem to implicate not only the earth but, more specifically, the space of performance: an earlier draft in the Trinity Manuscript reads 'this narrow spot', possibly alluding to the relatively cramped confines of Ludlow's Great Hall.[89] Milton seems to be employing the Shakespearean topos of the stage/theatre as a 'world' or 'globe' in order to make the haunted woods and the Ludlow stage co-referential. Though the opening lines posit an ontological separation of the luminous spheres from the world of flesh and shadow, the Spirit's contrast between 'calm and serene air' and 'smoke and stir' implies a material continuity more accordant with Milton's later monism. In the *Maske*'s close, the Attendant Spirit does not ascend to where 'bright aereal Spirits live insper'd' but, rather, claims that he 'can fly' or 'run / [. . .] to the green earth's end, / Where the bow'd welkin' – the horizon or sky – 'slow doth bend'.[90] The vertical distinction of the spheres above from 'this pin-fold here' below gives way to a three-dimensional perspective of a spherical earth with a distant horizon continuously curving to its vertex in the sky. Although the Spirit notes that he 'from thence can soar as soon / To the corners of the moon', he is clearly conceiving of travel between real planetary bodies rather than between ontological orders.[91]

The *Maske*'s movement toward a monist ontology is vital to restoring the Lady's sense of inherent worth and self-determination. Where dualism would insist on separating the Lady's value as a self from the body that locates that self *in this world*, a fully developed monism would insist on the full incorporation of that value. Milton would criticise in *Areopagitica* those 'who imagin to remove sin by removing the matter of sin':

> Banish all objects of lust, shut up all youth into the severest discipline that can be exercis'd in any hermitage, ye cannot make them chaste, that came not thither so: such great care and wisdom is requir'd to the right managing of this point.[92]

In the *Maske*, the Lady's embodied agency is constantly threatened by discursive appraisals of femininity that locate its value outside of the body, the theatre and public life. Specifically, corrupting male desire thrives upon the misrecognition of embodied femininity through conventions of anti-feminism, which degrades the public woman as being licentiously, even monstrously, sexual, and of Petrarchism, which excludes her as a sacred ideal from a carnal public and, even, from a material earth. The anti-feminist's rhetoric of monstrous sexuality, contributing to a climate of inhibiting hostility, sends the withering spectacle of the staged woman into the embrace of the idealist's hermetic enclosure.

In this way, the enchanter, Comus, exploits the idealisation of chaste femininity voiced by the *Maske*'s well-meaning but naïve Elder Brother.

Hoping to quell the Second Brother's concern that 'som ill greeting touch' will 'attempt the person / Of our unowned sister', Elder Brother assures him that chastity alone will make her 'secure without all doubt': 'She that has that, is clad in compleat steel'.[93] Her body is an 'unpolluted temple of the mind', that, through 'oft convers with heav'nly habitants', transforms 'by degrees to the souls essence, / Till all be made immortal'.[94] To illustrate chastity's miraculous power, he presents three images of woman sealed off from the visual field that places her in 'this dimspot', 'this pin-fold here': an armour-enclosed body, a mind enshrined as a temple, and an immortal soul.

At key moments, Milton uses economic language to theorise the transformation of embodied femininity into a cultural sign that circulates according to the demands of desire. This language first appears in the Attendant Spirit's account of how Comus's potion 'quite transforms' the 'visage [. . .] of him that drinks'.[95] The potion 'fixes' upon the partaker 'the inglorious likenes of a beast', 'unmoulding reasons mintage / Character'd in the face'.[96] 'Character'd' describes the face as a coin bearing the imprint of divine *ratio*. The metamorphosis of the manbeasts entails a process of effacing the original imprint and imposing a new 'character' that corresponds with a new value. From 'mould', meaning earthly soil or clay, 'unmoulding' suggests that this change involves a process of de-materialisation, of becoming symbolic.[97] This process does not lead to a transcending of the body; rather, it concludes in a re-materialisation of the body in the image of the symbolic. In this case, the symbolic is informed by conventional depictions of dehumanising appetite: victims of sorcerers like Homer's Circe, Spenser's Acrasia and Ariosto's Alcina, or antimasque figures like the bottles and tuns of Jonson's *Pleasure Reconciled to Virtue*. (The costumes for the *Maske*'s man-beasts might have been created, originally, for the Circean antimasque of Aurelian Townshend's 1632 *Tempe Restored*.[98]) This reminting is doubly insidious since the altered value is no longer subject to fluctuation but, now, permanently 'fixes' upon the face. Humans bearing the 'mintage' of right reason have become permanently re-cast as vices.

The economic structure of metamorphosis in the Ludlow woods is directly related to the social structure of theatrical spectacle, whereby the staged woman is subjected to values that answer the demands of spectatorial desire. 'Lust', explains Elder Brother, leads to 'defilement' not only through 'the leud and lavish act of sin', but, also, through 'unchaste looks, loose gestures, and foul talk'.[99] These centrally locate the body in a field of sound and vision. It is through the perception of such 'looks', 'gestures' and 'talk' that the soul 'imbodies, and imbrutes'.[100]

He describes a conceptual transformation that agrees with the economic structure of beastly metamorphosis: the inherent value of the gazed female body 'unmould[s]'; the gap between sign and signified is filled in by conventional associations of woman-as-spectacle with monstrosity and unchastity; the soul re-materialises in a form of anti-feminist convention (it 'imbodies, and imbrutes'). The female body, staged before spectators, is taken as the sign of a corrupted soul. Idealising dualistic discourses also respond to the body by making it disappear 'where no prophaner eye may look'.[101]

New Historical scholarship has theorised an early modern selfhood that adapts fluidly to the constraints and coercions of institutional and social contexts.[102] Such 'theatrical' identity was informed not only by the performed identities of theatre, church and state, but also by an anxious awareness of how market forces could radically destabilise value. In the *Maske*, which Blair Hoxby reads as 'Milton's first encounter with the claims of the new economic reasoning' of the early seventeenth century, economic rhetoric is used to theorise precisely the relation between a selfhood putatively essential, original and originating and a destabilising theatrical space that marks the threshold to a public capable of re-inscribing at once value and identity.[103] This language of coinage and circulation reveals Comus's most insidious power of imposing alien value to distort the self-concept, to obfuscate and to stifle self-determination, and thereby to control the body itself. 'Beauty is natures coyn', he declares to the seated Lady, and 'must not be hoorded, / But must be currant'.[104] The 'good' in beauty does not inhere but, rather, 'consists in mutual and partak'n bliss', being 'unsavoury in th' injoyment of it self'.[105] Comus is attempting to substitute the inherent value of the Lady's embodied selfhood with a 'currant' value, based on external beauty, determined by circulation. He implies that her refusal to partake reveals a miserly desire to increase her beauty's value by withholding it, by decreasing supply. He employs a metaphor of the masque-as-spectacle to persuade her that circulation determines value: 'Beauty is natures brag, and must be shown / In courts, at feasts, and high solemnities / Where most may wonder at the workmanship'.[106] The staged woman is thus a type of commodity form, an object produced by 'workmanship' and effaced by an aura of value that responds to and depends on spectator desire.[107]

Comus does not merely theorise this usurpation of value; rather, he proceeds to demonstrate it by overwriting the Lady's interiority with Petrarchan conventions that pervert her efforts of resistance by turning them into signs of love and desire: 'What need a vermeil-tinctur'd lip for' staying at home, 'Love-darting eyes, or tresses like the morn?'[108] The implication that she has applied cosmetic 'tincture' to her lips, like the reference to Aurora (noted for reddening the sky with her blush while returning from the beds of her many lovers), blurs distinctions between the Lady's body as an expression of her interiority and its culturally determined value as a sign. The phrase 'love-darting eyes' completes this usurpation of subjectivity by overwriting through the eyes, those portals to the soul, the Lady's revulsion into 'love'. At the height of her resistance, she is declared complicit in her own seduction. Her interiority, by way of the body, has become a mirror reflecting the image of the enchanter's lust. Comus has demonstrated how the woman, staged as a spectacle, becomes a circulated 'coyn' that is valued according to inherited conventions established and reiterated in order to maintain the sexual ownership of women.

Comus's man-beasts represent sonically the dissonance of the private–public transaction that works to reshape the individual woman according to publicly circulating symbols and values. Where the man-beasts embody conventions of monstrosity in their appearance, they resound such values sonically as monstrous echoes. The Lady first perceives them as a cacophonous rhythm as she prepares to emerge into view. Comus, having ordered his followers to 'knit hands, and beat the ground, / In a light fantastick round', interrupts *the Measure* upon first hearing her footsteps: 'Break off, break off, I feel the different pace, / Of som chast footing near about this ground'.[109] A recognisable similarity emphasises a striking disparity, between the 'light fantastick round' and the 'different pace' of the Lady's 'chast footing'. The 'round' dissolves at the perception of her 'chast footing', which is, in turn, stayed by fear of this 'sound / Of Riot, and ill-manag'd Merriment'.[110] Thus is the dialectic revealed: a chaste agency becomes distorted in the public space; the ensuing monstrous echo informs, in fact halts (if only for a moment), the body itself. The Lady's first response – 'this way the noise was' – makes clear that she had been out of view when she first heard the sound.[111] The 'sound / Of Riot' appears to echo in distorted form the sound of the chaste foot entering upon the stage.[112]

The Lady's 'chast footing' finds a counterpart in the 'artful strains' of Thyrsis, the Attendant Spirit's pastoral avatar.[113] In this guise, the Spirit tells the brothers of a 'barbarous dissonance' that had interrupted his solitary piping. His adoption of the pastoral persona points not only to Henry Lawes (composer of the *Maske*'s music and the Egerton children's music teacher) as the artist responsible for the 'strains' that were, at that moment, delighting the Ludlow audience but, also, to the poet behind the verse, who plays with masks as he imagines his own movement-into-public.[114] As we have seen, Milton would use the phrase 'barbarous dissonance' in his epic to describe the maenadic throng imagined to surround the bard while attempting to sing for a 'fit audience [. . .] though few'. There, the phrase will carry senses of disappointment, of wavering hope and of mistrust and resentment toward the English people, in general. In the *Maske*, 'barbarous dissonance' resounds as though from the very threshold to a poetic career.

The Spirit (as Thyrsis) narrates how, after sitting down 'to watch upon a bank', he became 'wrapt in a pleasing fit of melancholy / To meditate [his] rural minstrelsie'.[115] 'Meditate my rural minstrelsie' is a Virgilian phrase that, in 'Lycidas', refers to the practising or the contemplating of poetry, which is figured as pastoral piping.[116] The Spirit's fictive account does little to advance his plan to free the Lady, yet it connects the Lady's crisis to the poet's by embedding yet another *mise en scène* through which the poet can imagine from a distance his contact with a future public. Here, Thyrsis occupies at once the positions of actor and audience. Like the 'banks and scaffolds' set behind the 'spacious Theatre' in *Samson Agonistes*, the 'bank' functions as a type of theatre seating that allows him to listen and 'to watch'.[117] ('Bank' could also imply a raised platform or improvised stage, as in Milton's 'pulpit-mountbanck'.[118]) Just as the Lady's first steps on the Ludlow stage take her to the imperilling threshold, Thyrsis appears to trip a wire in the midst of his song. At the precise moment when 'fancy had her fill, but ere a close', 'the wonted roar was up amidst the Woods, / And fill'd the Air with barbarous dissonance'.[119] As the pastoral piper-poet sends his notes into the 'unhallow'd air', the 'sound of Riot' echoes back as a jarring explosion that permeates the 'spungy' atmosphere.[120] As we have seen, such sound manifests Milton's fear of rejection in the 1628 Cambridge 'salting' and comes vividly to life in the form of hissing snakes in *Paradise Lost*.[121] In the *Maske*, 'dissonance' indicates not only a general disharmony but, more specifically, the riotous rhythm of the rout's '*Measure*'. Is this not the sound of hostile applause and hissing, amplified and distorted?

The *Maske*'s central crisis foregrounds, in the form of the Lady's paralysed body, an arrested emergence. During the seduction scene, Comus binds the Lady to '*an inchanted Chair*' that is 'smear'd with gumms of glutenous heat'.[122] The Lady's paralysis marks her failure to imagine an active public agency due to a collapse of critical distance between the self and the cultural matrix in which that self is embedded.[123] Frozen throughout and silent for much of this central scene, the Lady is caught in the 'lime-twigs' of the theatrical space.[124] 'Lime-twigs', branches covered with a sticky paste that were used to catch small birds, figures the insidious power of Comus's rhetoric in his efforts to deprive the

Lady of an enabling sense of inherent value: the more that the 'insnared' victim engages and struggles to escape, the more that she participates in limiting her movement, in advancing the endgame of paralysis.[125] Typically, scholars either have accepted Comus's suggestion that he effects the paralysis through magic – 'if I but wave this wand / Your nerves are all chain'd up in Alabaster, / And you a statue' – or have read the Lady's stasis as signifying wilful disengagement that confirms the transcendence of her chastity over a context of carnality.[126] I propose that the conflicted sense of what causes the paralysis is symptomatic of the cause itself – namely, a conceptual slippage that obfuscates the Lady's sense of her own worth and agency.

As tempter, Comus poses the Lady no genuine threat. At no time does she come near to acceding to his evident desires. Instead, like Spenser's Archimago, he endangers as a 'Jugler' or illusionist who can manipulate behaviour by altering perception and by raising spectres in the imagination.[127] He hurls 'dazzling Spells into the spungy ayr' that have the 'power to cheat the eye with blear illusion / And give it false presentments'; he succeeds by convincing the Lady that she sees other than she does.[128] Being 'spungy', the air soaks up his spells, which imbue it with a hallucinogenic potentiality at once ethereal and corporeal. This power of illusion, linking words to perception and perception to materiality, is doubled in the power of his discourse. Late into the seduction scene, the Lady intuits that her words are working further to entrap her: 'I had not thought to have unlockt my lips / In this unhallow'd air, but that this Jugler / Would think to charm my judgement, as mine eyes / Obtruding false rules pranckt in reasons garb'.[129]

By opening her lips, she invites the rhetorical trickery of the enchanter, who works to coerce her judgement through a type of discursive magic. As the Lady's use of the conventional figure of rhetorical adornment as clothing makes clear, Comus's words translate vividly into mental perception. The man-beasts that surround her throughout the seduction scene, embodiments of reason re-minted as monstrosity, also work to strengthen the insidious rhetorical workings of 'this Jugler'.

Comus presides over a conceptual shift by which the Lady unwittingly assists in binding herself through the force of her resistance.[130] The chastity that she first describes as 'a well-govern'd and wise appetite' becomes, in his rhetoric, a 'lean and sallow Abstinence', as though to eat with discrimination were to starve oneself.[131] Juggling, he substitutes 'Chastity' with the narrower 'Virginity' in order to alter the very axis of debate: 'List Lady be not coy, and be not cosen'd / With that same vaunted name Virginity'.[132] Yet she *is* cozened with the *name* of 'Virginity', which further defines chastity as a principle of renunciation.

In a passage added to the 1637 and 1645 editions, the Lady follows her defence of the 'holy dictate of spare Temperance' with lines that further illustrate the conceptual elision underway:

> Shall I go on?
> Or have I said anow? To him that dares
> Arm his profane tongue with contemptuous words
> Against the Sun-clad power of Chastity;
> Fain would I somthing say, yet to what end?
> Thou hast nor Ear, nor Soul to apprehend
> The sublime notion, and high mystery
> That must be utter'd to unfold the sage
> And serious doctrine of Virginity.[133]

'Shall I go on?' emphasises the futility of further engagement with a juggling rhetorician. It registers at once superiority and helplessness. 'Sun-clad', the 'power of Chastity' should be shamelessly naked, yet this ideal is soon eclipsed by a 'sage / And serious doctrine' of abstemious 'Virginity'. What was an embodied virtue, of free and shameless agency and 'power', moves toward a rigid 'doctrine' of disengagement. Coaxed into embracing a Platonic dualism while embedded in degenerate carnality, the Lady seems to face two choices: to allow the context to define her by drinking from the chalice, thus giving over the body to carnal license and becoming *in essence* a monstrous form; or to allow the context to define her by rejecting the body itself, locating virtue and spiritual agency beyond earth and, thus, by ceasing to *be* there.

Earlier, the Lady had summoned Chastity as an 'unblemish't form', as an allegory accompanying 'pure-ey'd Faith' and 'white-handed Hope'.[134] She strongly identifies with this mental image of chastity: 'I see ye visibly'.[135] The allegorical trio is clearly based on Paul's 'faith, hope, and charity' (1 Corinthians 13:13), yet the Lady has substituted 'charity' – exalted by Paul as the 'greatest' and 'soul' of these virtues – with 'Chastity' as an 'unblemish't' allegorical 'form'. This 'sublime notion, and high mystery' substitutes for a virtue that 'beareth all things, believeth all things, hopeth all things, [and] endureth all things'. The rigid form eclipses a principle of confident openness that is fundamental to the fullest sense of 'charity' or 'love' as an active, public virtue.[136] The problem is not so much that the Lady invokes an idealisation but, rather, that this idealisation appears solid, monumental and self-referential. As Victoria Kahn observes, static allegory works 'to commodify truth and thus to obstruct the kind of rational exercise of the will which is the precondition of right reading and of virtue [. . .] The allegory is [. . .] one of force, of forced signification'.[137] The Lady's tendency toward Platonic conceptions of virtue and self prepare her to become a materialisation of an intellectual form that, in its hardened immobility, embodies precisely the opposite of what it was thought to represent.

Spenser's 'Maske of Cupid', Sabrina and Transformations of Perspective

When Comus asserts that 'Beauty is natures brag, and must be shown / In courts, at feasts, and high solemnities / Where most may wonder at the workmanship', the masque seems strangely divided against itself. After all, the Lady (Alice Egerton) is at this moment being 'shown' in a 'high solemnit[y]', the focal point of many wondering eyes. She sits as though fixed in place by lines of perspective emitted from each seated spectator. She is in the very grip of 'curran[cy]'. Comus has demonstrated how readily the Lady's efforts to enact her chastity will be re-encoded as evidence of unchastity. Faced with this seemingly inevitable loss of inner virtue to the 'unhallow'd air', she seems to take the way of the Platonist, withdrawing into the 'unpolluted temple of the mind'. As John Rogers suggests, the fact that she remains seated *as a body* may also imply a shoring up of 'apocalyptic energy' anticipated by her 'prophetic' claim to a voice that could 'shake the brute earth'.[138] However, even were we to grant this argument, in Ludlow's Great Hall, the here and now has been surrendered. Arguments celebrating the Lady's silent paralysis as empowered and triumphal depend on a radical extrication of her chastity, valued as transcendentally spiritual or philosophical, from the staged and imperilled body, devalued as carnal.[139] This gambit, anticipating Satan's valorisation of the 'mind' as 'its own place' is dangerous and, perhaps, even irresponsible.[140] Such praise of the Lady's stasis implicitly degrades embodied femininity, socially embedded and imperilled, in favour of an idealisation, answerable to the demands of male desire, which renders the body's coercion inconsequential and which exalts femininity only as enclosed and invisible. In this spirit, Gosson advises the women of London 'to keep home, and shun all occasion of ill speech. The virgins of Vesta were shut up fast in stone walls to the same end'.[141]

If value is determined by 'curran[cy]', then the culture of Northbrooke's lust-besotting 'rabblement' and Gosson's 'amorous gazer[s]' will ensure that Milton's 'ignorant and libidinous poetasters' and Prynne's 'immodest gestures, speeches, [and] attires', bawds, panders and adulterers will hold the stage. The seeming certainty of this impasse was to antitheatricalists a powerful inducement for banning theatre wholesale. Staged performance must withdraw into the confines of the printed book, into the closet drama, into the 'close covert' of illegal stagings. Milton does not ultimately embrace such fatalism, though resolution of the Lady's crisis does require the miracle of a magical form that is capable of acting upon and within the economy without first being determined by it. Shortly before falling silent, the Lady claims the authority to effect such a miracle, though in terms that reconstitute the opposition between the private, inspired virgin and the contaminating cultural matrix. Were she to try, she tells Comus, 'the uncontrouled worth / Of this pure cause [of chastity]' would rouse her to such 'flame[s] of sacred vehemence' that she would move 'dumb things [. . .] to sympath[y] and 'shake' the 'brute Earth', 'till all thy magick structures rear'd so high, / Were shatter'd into heaps o'er thy false head'.[142] It is the fantasy of Orpheus quelling the maenads through inspired song. (They tore his body to pieces and sent his severed head 'down the swift *Hebrus*'.[143]) The phrase 'uncontrouled worth' posits an inherent, fixed value preceding and unchanged by circulation. It would be able to shatter the 'magick structures' of discourse that blur the boundary between the real and the imaginary, that make the Lady feel that her own words are working to entangle her. Comus apprehends the threat posed by chastity as 'uncontrouled worth' – 'She fables not, I feel that I do fear / Her words set off by som superior power' – yet, having influenced her to conceive of chastity as renunciation, he has pre-empted such power from being activated decisively here and now.[144] Thus, in the very proclamation of vocal power, the Lady gestures toward her own silence: 'Fain would I something say, yet to what end?'[145] Though temporarily stilled by 'a cold shuddring dew', Comus – like Milton's Satan, anticipating, perhaps, a final sublime doom while free in the meanwhile to inflict rapine and death – nonetheless proceeds, moving towards her vulnerable body to force the chalice to her lips as the brothers rush in and she falls silent.[146]

Milton would resolve the Lady's dilemma through resources of perspective afforded by theatrical spectacle, even as the phenomenon, intrinsic to performance, of being 'compast round' by spectators most immediately captures the crisis of value that leaves her a conspicuous form of invisibility. Although the opposition between sexual license and chastity in the *Maske* has often been framed in terms of the competing influences of Shakespeare, representing the drama that Milton would (it is told) renounce, and Spenser, representing the divine poetry to which he would turn, what here helps to save the *idea* of theatre for Milton is a representation of theatrical perspective confronted in book III of Spenser's epic romance. A volume of *Milton Quarterly* has detailed *The Faerie Queene*'s influence on what, in a separate book, Annabel Patterson refers to as Milton's 'most Spenserian production'.[147]

Shullenberger has demonstrated links with book III at some length.[148] Yet the significance of Britomart's representation as a theatrical spectator viewing the 'maske of Cupid' in cantos xi–xii of the 'Legend of Chastity' has been overlooked.

Spenser's cross-dressing virgin, Britomart, concludes her maturation into a fitting representative of chastity through a process of seeing 'monstrous formes' of love as products of art and discourse. Before seeking her fated lover Arthegall, she must advance through the House where Busyrane holds the damsel Amoret chained to a pillar. Led in the 'maske of Cupid' by 'two grysie [grisly] villeins', '*Despight*' and '*Cruelty*', the 'cruelly pend' Amoret figures the scornful maid of the Petrarchan paradigm that sustains her separation from her lover Scudamore and, by extension, keeps Britomart from Arthegall.[149] ('Pend' equates literary convention with subjugation.) For Thomas P. Roche, Jr., Busyrane is 'the image of love distorted in the mind [. . .] by lascivious anticipation or horrified withdrawal'.[150] James W. Broaddus sees the House of Busyrane, its rooms ornamented with erotic art, as representing 'the attempt of an evil magician to impose a social evil upon a virtuous maiden'.[151] Both conjurer of images and author, Busyrane presides over cultural forms of male domination: he is a prototype of Milton's Comus.

Britomart first surveys a room hung with tapestries that depict the sexual conquests of predatory pagan gods. A second room displays embossed gold 'wrought with wilde Antickes, which their follies playd, / In the rich metall, as [if] they living were'.[152] These 'Antickes' or grotesque overlays, like Milton's man-beasts (his antimasque 'anticks'), offer images of sexual love that intensify and appear to vivify the horrid sexuality already unnerving in the first room: 'A thousand monstrous formes therein were made, / Such as false love doth oft upon him weare, / For love in thousand monstrous formes doth oft appeare'.[153] Britomart's ability to move past these forms depends upon her conviction that they merely 'appeare', that their power resides in the mind of the beholder. Though Spenser does not elaborate the specific content of these gold embossments, he makes clear that they emerge from thwarted male desire. The room is a 'wastefull emptinesse' of 'warlike spoiles' that give place to broken 'swerds & speres', 'rent' armour and, implicating the poet's pen, 'proud girlonds of tryumphant bayes / Troden in dust'.[154] Inscriptions on the doors tell Britomart to '*Be bold*'.[155] A final door cautions, '*Be not too bold.*'[156]

When, at the start of canto xii, Britomart enters a third room, the monstrous forms culminate in a masque presented as theatre. Demonstrating at once boldness and patience, she twice views this 'maske of Cupid' before sallying forth to rescue Amoret. As with the tapestries and embossments, the 'maske', a procession of allegorical figures that represent negative and conventionally Petrarchan responses to love (such as Doubt, Danger and Feare), places her in the position of spectator. The depiction of 'Ease' confirms that we are to see her as, specifically, a theatre spectator: 'Fit for tragicke Stage', Ease enters 'as on the ready flore / Of some Theatre' and introduces the 'Mask', after 'beckning with his hand, / In signe of silence, as to heare a play'.[157] The 'formes' represent responses to sexual love that, externalised as theatre, afford Britomart a critical perspective onto aesthetic and discursive representations of female emotion. Describing these 'maladies' to be as 'many [...] as there be phantasies / In wavering wemens wit', Spenser suggests that the fears conventionally ascribed to female objects of male desire work to *produce* the inhibitory 'phantasies' that they depict.[158] Britomart's progress through the House, thus, conditions a denaturalisation of inhibiting emotions by emphasising their artificiality and by suggesting how they may infiltrate, inhibit and constrain. 'Neither of idle shewes, nor of false charmes aghast', Britomart has, in essence, already defeated Busyrane by the time that she confronts him in the final chamber.[159]

Unlike Britomart, whose boldness is increasingly conditioned and affirmed through a critically detached perspective on love's 'monstrous formes', Milton's Lady experiences a gradually more constricting entanglement that concludes in paralysis. Beginning like Britomart 'clad in compleat steel', she becomes bound like Amoret. Yet what binds her is not fear so much as a failure to define her value and agency independently of economic determination. That is, facing the spectators from her chair on the stage, she is seeing herself through the eyes of those who sit seeing her. Milton anticipates this collapse of the self-as-spectator into the self-as-staged-spectacle when, in the Lady's first reaction to the dissonant 'Measure', her words evoke at once Spenser's 'thousand monstrous formes' and 'phantasies / In wavering womens wit': 'A *thousand fantasies* / Begin to throng into my memory / Of calling shapes, and *beckning* shadows dire, / And airy tongues, that syllable mens names'.[160] Whereas Spenser's 'phantasies' literally march 'as on the [...] flore / Of some Theatre' 'disguized [...] in masking wise', in Milton's performance, the man-beasts, perhaps donning 'masking wise' recycled from *Tempe Restored*, are re-materialisations of the self as pre-empted by circulating appraisals of embodied femininity.[161] The Lady recognises the menacing shapes, shadows and sounds of the benighted forest to be subjective 'fantasies' linked to objective phenomena. Yet the 'thousand fantasies' gather force in her memory specifically because Comus's magic so effectively blurs the real and the imaginary. Whereas in Spenser it is a prologue 'fit for tragicke Stage' who 'beck[ons] with his hand' to cue Britomart's silence and 'Ease', thus admitting a clear-minded view of psychological effects rightly recognised as productions of art, here the 'beckning' of shadows points specifically to the Lady's *lack* of critical detachment as her imagination and physical context begin to interpenetrate. This 'beckning' unnerves rather than eases. Enmeshed within that memory of shapes, shadows and tongues is the imagined theatre audience, the 'throng', emergent in her as she emerges into *its* sight.[162]

It is understandable, then, why the 'insnared' Lady cannot be freed by her well-meaning, Platonically minded brothers. She needs not only a woman's touch but, also, a new perspective on womanhood. The Spirit's plan for liberating her involves the brothers' infiltration of Comus's palace by means of the magical herb '*Haemony*'.[163] This herb will make them invisible, so that they can enter 'the very lime-twigs of his spells, / And yet c[o]me off'.[164] They must break Comus's chalice and, as the Spirit emphasises, 'sease his wand', for 'though he and his curst crew / Feirce signe of battail make, and menace high', 'Yet will they soon retire, if he but shrink'.[165] The brothers meet Comus's rod with '*swords drawn*', impotently, as the enchanter slips through their fingers like smoke.[166] As in Spenser's *Faerie Queene*, the *Maske*'s monstrous forms are linked to masculine power, to the obviously phallic 'rod'. Threaten that and they make 'feirce signe of battail' and 'menace high'; make it 'shrink' and they're gone. Yet, as we have seen, the brothers, especially the Elder, already proffer a vision of femininity informed by a complementary structure. The Elder Brother's idealisations had already anticipated his sister's status as a presence of erasure. The failure to seize the rod leaves him and his brother helpless: now, in addition to 'backward mutters of dissevering power', Comus's rod will need to be 'revers't'.[167] Both rod and 'backward mutters' once more recall the House of Busyrane, where Britomart releases the 'cruelly pend' Amoret by making the enchanter to 'his charmes backe [. . .] reverse' – that is, to recite backwards from his 'balefull booke'.[168] The reversal of the phallic rod/pen implies nothing less than an un-writing of centuries of discourse driven by the demands of male desire. Faced with this impossibility, the Spirit invokes Sabrina, the *Maske*'s other spectacle of femininity.

As a resolving *dea ex machina*, Sabrina occupies the place of the grand Stuart masque spectacles, though she implies a fundamentally different ontology than does their often manifest Neoplatonism. Whereas the ingenious devices of Inigo Jones had often represented the imposition of an ideal from above – as in the '*eight spheres seated on a cloud*' that appear just after the retreat of Circe and the man-beasts in *Tempe Restored* – Milton's Sabrina rises from the waters.[169] Not subject to the degrading transformations of 'unhallow'd air', she is, in fact, a healer of natural maladies, associated through folklore with dark magic.[170] She heals not by supernatural magic but, rather, by application of 'pretious viold liquors'. Where, in *Areopagitica*, Milton would represent books as vials holding a distilled spirit/intellect that participates in the reception culture's refinement, here Sabrina performs a purification of the Lady's self-concept, which has been contaminated by that culture's 'currant' discourses. Representing at once an inherent value that precedes the economy of desire and the *telos* of that economy's reformation, whereby sign and signified are reunited in the embodiment of an ideal, she can inspire a faith in 'uncontrouled worth' by localising it in an earthly body. She makes evident, through her staged presence and song, that the Lady is not a 'coyn' that attains value through circulation but, rather, someone who bears an inherent value that precedes public emergence. Sabrina shows, as Milton would write of Lawes in sonnet XIII (1646), that the Lady's 'worth and skill exempts [her] from the throng'.[171]

As the 'maske of Cupid' does Britomart, so does Sabrina enable the Lady by resituating her as a spectator: 'Brightest Lady look on me', she beckons, inviting identification.[172] The 'look' itself confirms the Lady's brightness, for here, whether literally or figuratively, she turns her back on the viewing audience and focuses her eyes and ears upon Sabrina. No longer is the Lady pinned as by so many lines of spectator perspective; rather, she is engaged in a transaction of sound and vision with a sympathetic woman who can 'help insnared chastity', for 'such [. . .] was her self / In hard besetting need'.[173] Sabrina offers a relation of sameness-with-difference that is capable of reinvigorating terrestrial agency by restoring an inherent value that had been warped to unrecognisability through the 'blear illusion' of 'magick structures'. Though sunk to the Severn's floor, her body was taken in by Nereus and revived with 'Ambrosial Oils' dropped 'through the porch and inlet of each sense'.[174] Nereus cured her by pouring these liquids into the 'inlets' of perception, just as she revitalises the Lady through *her* inlets: through touch, as when she sprinkles 'drops' of 'pretious cure' upon the Lady's lips and fingertip, and, especially, through sight and sound, the eyes and ears being those 'inlet[s] of [. . .] sense' through which Comus's spells have worked their magic.[175]

Sabrina's song answers the Lady's earlier incantation to an unresponsive Echo. Its prepositional indexes of place, which locate the nymph's *'sliding Chariot'* *'by the rushy-fringed bank, / Where grows the Willow and the Osier dank'*, immediately recall those by which the Lady locates Echo *'by slow Meander's margent green / And in the violet imbroider'd vale / Where the lovelorn Nightingale / [. . .] mourneth'*.[176] In calling upon Echo as a nymph *'that liv'st unseen / Within [an] airy shell'*, the

Lady had voiced an idealising relation to femininity that locates the value of chastity not in this world but beyond it, not in the moving and speaking body but in the 'soul's essence', emptied of body and 'insphear'd'.[177] The unresponsiveness of Echo, whom the Lady dubs 'Daughter of the Sphear', had anticipated the impotence of the Elder Brother's naïve Platonism.[178]

Yet while Sabrina can attend locally to the corruptions of the 'unhallow'd air', she lacks the power to reform decisively the climate itself. Comus still haunts the woods. The freed Lady must return immediately to Ludlow Castle under the escort of her brothers and the Spirit: 'Com Lady while Heaven lends us grace, / Let us fly this cursèd place, / Lest the Sorcerer us entice / With som other new device'.[179] As Shakespeare's Isabella ends *Measure for Measure*, so too Milton's Lady ends the *Maske* in silence, two hundred lines after breaking off her dialogue with Comus. Silent and rushed home under male escort, she is not quite the 'articulate [. . .] sexually mature and responsible, socially conscientious and engaged, freedom-loving Christian woman' celebrated by Shullenberger.[180] Something has changed, but what? Like a synthetic element that coheres in the laboratory for a millisecond but is incapable of manifesting naturally and sustainably on earth, staged chastity has proven itself only to vanish into the realm of possibility. Was it really here at all? Can it be replicated? Under what conditions? These questions naturally fit the decorum of the masque as an ephemeral spectacle performed but once for a coterie audience.

The *Maske* forestalls easy resolution because the Lady's future safety also requires the purification of other spectators: most immediately, the elite audience in Ludlow's Great Hall; more broadly, the reception culture at large. That the Lady can return home to what is essentially a benign representation of the *Maske* and its occasion –

> Not many furlongs thence
> Is your Fathers residence,
> Where this night are met in state
> Many a friend to gratulate
> His wish't presence, and beside
> All the Swains that there abide,
> With Jiggs, and rural dance resort,
> We shall catch them at their sport,
> And our sudden coming there
> Will double all their mirth and chere.[181]

– owes, in the *Maske*'s logic, to the benefit that the coterie spectators have received from Sabrina, an embodied ideal chastity, and from the Lady in her efforts to approach that ideal despite the extraordinary constraints awaiting her from the outset. Through this experience, it is implied, Ludlow Castle and its denizens have been proven worthy of both.

Sabrina's capacity to represent an epicentre of reform for a broader reception culture inheres in her structure as 'uncontrouled worth', as at once within and without, presently active in and antecedent to the economy of desire: the undead signified that walks with 'printless feet'.[182] Her 'printless feet', echoing (with difference) the Lady's earlier 'chast footing', point to something more substantial than the 'Airy shell' of Echo, yet they also suggest the weightless ephemerality of a ghostly body, in a state of suspended emergence, that befits the qualified presence of the resurrected drowned virgin. For Milton the would-be divine poet, she is a test case for a chaste public poetry. Both walking and leaving no mark, her 'printless feet' suggest his own reticence to print the feet of his verse, as evident in the *Maske*'s 1637 publication ushered out by Lawes. Milton not only chose to leave his authorship anonymous, but also included as his epigraph the phrase '*Eheu quid volui misero mihi! floribus austrum / Perditus*' ('Alas, what harm did I mean to my wretched self when I let the south wind blow upon my flowers?').[183] Extracted from Virgil's second *Eclogue*, the epigraph suggests again a vulnerability to the 'unhallow'd air' of reception: as Ann Baynes Coiro notes, 'The anonymous publication of *A Maske*, escorted out by a chaperon, is about as ambivalent a public appearance as one could imagine'.[184]

The paradox that Sabrina embodies as 'uncontrouled worth' reverberates forward through Milton's career; he would repeatedly experiment with dramatic form and the idea of the public theatre but would never again complete a work intended for a physically present audience. The program for public poetry and theatre implied in *Reason* would be 'solemn' and 'set', controlled, it would seem, by Parliament: 'let them in autority consult'.[185] We are, here, a long way from the popular stage. The plans for religious dramas sketched into the Trinity Manuscript would never be realised as stage plays. Like the *Maske*'s quasi-public status as a courtly masque staged once for a coterie audience, Miltonic theatre would remain somewhere in between: a threshold to an imagined, ever-changing future public, a stage for critically examining the interpenetration of the evolving author and his readers.

Notes

1. Campbell and Corns, *John Milton*, p. 89.
2. J. Milton, Commonplace Book, *WJM*, XVIII, p. 207. *Tertullianus* [...] *inscripsit damnat eorum usum et Christianis occludit*. [Tertullian's arguments] *solos ethnicos ludos convellunt* (p. 206).

3. Ibid., p. 207. *Eundem prorus lapidem volvit Cyprianus seu quis alius libro eâdem de re composito* (p. 206).
4. Ibid., p. 207. *Illud tamen optimè facit in epilogo libri ut mentem Christiani ad meliora h. e. divina et celestia spectacula quae tot, et tanta homo Christianus animo praecipere potest de adventu Christi de futuro judicio densis coloribus contortis incitaverit* (p. 206).
5. Tertullian, *Apology: De spectaculis, and Minucius Felix. Tunc histriones cognoscendi, solutiores multo per ignem* (p. 298).
6. Cf. below, pp. 121–2.
7. Milton, Commonplace Book, *WJM*, XVIII, p. 207. *Et Lactantius* [. . .] *argumentis nihilo firmioribus rem scenicam universam in vitio point* (p. 206).
8. Ibid., p. 207. *Nec semel quidem cogitasse videtur, corruptelas quidem theatricas meritò tolli debere, omnem autem idcirco rerum dramaticarum usum penitus aboleri nihil necesse esse, immo potius nimis insulum esset quid enim in totâ philosophiâ aut gravius aut sanctius aut sublimius tragoedia recte constitutâ quid utilius ad humanae vitae casus et conversiones uno intuitu spectandos?* (p. 206).
9. Milton, *Reason*, *CPW*, I, p. 815.
10. Ibid., pp. 819–20.
11. J. Greene, *A Refutation of the Apology for Actors* (1615), p. 267.
12. Milton, *Reason*, *CPW*, I, pp. 816–17.
13. See above, pp. 42–3; and below, pp. 203–8.
14. Milton, *Reason*, *CPW*, I, p. 816.
15. See J. Butler, 'Performative Acts and Gender Constitution', pp. 270–1; and J. Butler, *Bodies That Matter*, pp. 1–55. Of further theoretical influence on this chapter are Lacan, *Four Fundamental Concepts*, pp. 65–119; Lacan, 'The Mirror Stage'; L. Mulvey, 'Visual Pleasure and Narrative Cinema'; J. Rose, *Sexuality in the Field of Vision*, pp. 167–98; and K. Silverman, *The Subject of Semiotics*, pp. 149–93.
16. Scholars have tended to see the *Maske*'s genre diversely, though it is now assumed, more or less, that the masque for which Milton wrote was a provincial masque, much smaller and less elaborate than contemporary Caroline masques, with a particular focus on the Earl of Bridgewater's family. Consideration of genre has often attended questions of politics. See C. C. Brown, *John Milton's Aristocratic Entertainments*; M. Butler, 'A Provincial Masque of *Comus*, 1636'; Demaray, *Milton and the Masque Tradition*; Demaray, 'Temple of the Mind'; H. Dubrow, 'The Masquing of Genre in *Comus*'; L. Marcus, *The Politics of Mirth*, pp. 169–212; M. C. McGuire, *Milton's Puritan Masque*; D. Norbrook, 'The Reformation of the Masque'; S. Orgel, 'The Case for *Comus*'; M. Steggle, '"The Tragical Part"'; and M. A. Treip, '*Comus* as "Progress"'.
17. See W. Kerrigan, *Sacred Complex*, pp. 42–7; and W. Shullenberger, *The Lady in the Labyrinth*, pp. 203–25. See also A. Greenstadt, *Rape and the Rise of the Author*, pp. 83–139; and D. Urban, 'The Lady of Christ's College Himself a "Lady Wise and Pure"'.
18. Milton, *Apology*, *CPW*, I, p. 890.
19. Milton, *Areopagitica*, *CPW*, II, p. 492.
20. See A. Gurr, *Playgoing in Shakespeare's London*, pp. 51–7; and A. Leggatt, *Jacobean Public Theatre*, pp. 77–105. See above, pp. 20–3.

21. See below, pp. 94–100.
22. See above, p. 38; and below, pp. 113–14.
23. See below, pp. 113–17.
24. Fallon, *Milton's Peculiar Grace*, p. 93.
25. Ibid., p. 91, 89.
26. Milton, *Reason*, CPW, I, pp. 810–11.
27. Ibid., p. 801.
28. Ibid., p. 801.
29. See Haskin, *Milton's Burden of Interpretation*, pp. 29–53.
30. Milton, *Reason*, CPW, I, p. 746.
31. See above, pp. 16–17.
32. Milton, *Reason*, CPW, I, p. 818.
33. Ibid., pp. 818, 828.
34. Milton, *Maske*, WJM, I.i, line 756.
35. For familial determinants of the *Maske*, see C. C. Brown, 'Presidential Travels and Instructive Augury in Milton's Ludlow Masque'; B. Greteman, '"Perplex't Paths"'; and Orgel, 'The Case for *Comus*'.
36. Milton, *Maske*, WJM, I.i, line 796; 'L'Allegro', WJM, I.i, lines 145–52; 'Il Penseroso', WJM, I.i, lines 105–8; above, p. 11; and 'Lycidas', WJM, I.i, lines 58–63.
37. See above, pp. 30–1.
38. Shullenberger, *The Lady in the Labyrinth*, p. 15.
39. Ibid., p. 224.
40. Alice Egerton had performed a non-speaking role in Aurelian Townshend's 1632 masque, *Tempe Restored*. Townshend's masque was one of the earliest English performances to feature a woman with a speaking role, that of Circe, likely performed by a French gentlewoman of the queen's court. See K. Britland, *Drama at the Courts of Queen Henrietta Maria*, pp. 91–2; S. Tomlinson, *Women on Stage in Stuart Drama*, pp. 51–4; and J. Creaser, '"The Present Aid of this Occasion"'.
41. Prynne, *Histriomastix*, p. 292.
42. Ibid., p. 296.
43. S. Gosson, *Plays Confuted in Five Actions*, p. 109.
44. Prynne, *Histriomastix*, p. 290.
45. Gosson, *School of Abuse*, p. 25. See K. E. Maus, '"Playhouse Flesh and Blood", especially p. 603.
46. J. Howard, *The Stage and Social Struggle in Early Modern England*, pp. 73–92.
47. J. Northbrooke, *A Treatise Against Dicing, Dancing, Plays, and Interludes*, p. 5.
48. Ibid., p. 5.
49. Gosson, *School of Abuse*, p. 29.
50. Ibid., p. 30.
51. See Martin, *Milton among the Puritans*, pp. 145–73.
52. Sir E. Peyton, *Divine Catastrophe of the Kingly Family of the Stuarts*, p. 369.
53. Milton, *Paradise Lost*, WJM, II.i, IV, lines 767–8.
54. Such associations were intimately close to the Bridgewaters. In 1621, Mervyn Touchet, Earl of Castlehaven, was convicted and beheaded for

committing sodomy with his page and assisting in the rape of his wife, the earl of Bridgewater's sister. Scholars have weighed the relevance of the Castlehaven scandal to Milton's representation of chastity in the *Maske*. If anything, the scandal would have raised the stakes of Milton's staging of Alice Egerton. See Campbell and Corns, *John Milton*, pp. 69–73; and B. Breasted, '*Comus* and the Castlehaven Scandal'; cf. Creaser, 'Milton's *Comus*'. Marcus sees additional relevance in the earl's role in pursuing justice for Margery Evans, a fourteen-year-old servant who had been raped by a Welsh gentleman in 1631, in 'The Earl of Bridgewater's Legal Life'.

55. Milton, *Elegia sexta*, *WJM*, I.i, line 77. *Diis etenim sacer est vates, divûmque sacerdos.*
56. Ibid., lines 55–62. *At qui bella refert, & adulto sub Jove coelum, / Heroasque pios, semideosque duces, / Et nunc sancta canit superum consulta deorum, / Nunc latrata fero regna profunda cane, / Ille quidem parcè Samii pro more magistri / Vivat, & innocuos praebeat herba cibos; / Stet prope fagineo pellucida lympha catillo, / Sobriaque è puro pocula fonte bibat.*
57. Ibid., lines 63–6: *Additur huic scelerisque vacans, & casta juventus, / Et rigidi mores, & sine labe manus. / Qualis veste nitens sacrâ, & lustralibus undis / Surgis ad infensos augur iture Deos.*
58. For Christ-as-bridegroom, see Ephesians 5:24–7; 2 Corinthians 11:2; Revelations 19:7–9 and 21:1–2. For the role of biblical Christ-as-bridegroom metaphors in complicating the gendering of spiritual experience, see S. H. Moore, 'Sexing the Soul'; and T. Webster, '"Kiss Me with the Kisses of His Mouth"'.
59. Milton, *Elegia sexta*, *WJM*, I.i, line 78. *Spirat & occultum pectus, & ora Jovem.*
60. Milton, *Elegia prima*, *WJM*, I.i, lines 27–8. *Excipit hinc fessum sinuosi pompa theatri, / Et vocat ad plausus garrula scena suos.*
61. Ibid., lines 25–6. *Tempora nam licet hîc placidis dare libera Musis, / Et totum rapiunt me mea vita libri*; cf. Ovid, *Amores*, III, i, lines 11–14.
62. Milton, *Elegia prima*, *WJM*, I.i, lines 49–53. *Nos quoque lucus habet vicinâ consitus ulmo / Atque suburbani nobilis umbra loci. / Saepius hic blandas spirantia sydera flammas / Virgineos videas praeteriisse choros. / Ah quoties dignae stupui miracula formae.*
63. See below, p. 158.
64. Milton, *Elegia prima*, *WJM*, I.i, lines 85–8. *Ast ego, dum pueri sinit indulgentia caeci, / Moenia quàm subitò linguere fausta paro; / Et vitare procul malefidae infamia Circes / Atria, divini Molyos usus ope.*
65. Milton, 'L'Allegro', *WJM*, I.i, lines 69, 57.
66. Milton, *Maske*, *WJM*, I.i, line 546; 'L'Allegro', *WJM*, I.i, lines 127–30.
67. Milton, 'L'Allegro', *WJM*, I.i, lines 131–3.
68. Ibid., lines 136–8.
69. Milton, 'Il Penseroso', *WJM*, I.i, line 139.
70. Ibid., lines 147–54.
71. 'But as it is written, Eye hath not seen, nor ear heard, neither have entered into the heart of man, the things which God hath prepared for them that love him' (1 Corinthians 2:9); see Shakespeare, *A Midsummer Night's Dream*, IV, i, lines 199–207.

72. See E. C. Brown, '"The Melting Voice Through Mazes Running"'; and C. Finch and P. Bowen, 'The Solitary Companionship of *L'Allegro* and *Il Penseroso*'.
73. Milton, 'Il Penseroso', *WJM*, I.i, lines 140–1.
74. Milton, 'L'Allegro', *WJM*, I.i, lines 143, 140.
75. Milton, 'On Shakespear', *WJM*, I.i, line 14. See above, pp. 5, 7.
76. See Campbell and Corns, *John Milton*, pp. 111–23.
77. Milton, *Ad Leonoram*, *WJM*, I.i, lines 3–6. *Quid mirum? Leonora tibi si gloria major, / Nam tua praesentem vox sonat ipsa Deum. / Aut Deus, aut vacui certè mens teria coeli / Per tua secretò guttura serpit agens.*
78. Ibid., line 10.
79. Milton, *Ad eandem* (II), *WJM*, I.i, lines 7–8. *Illic Romulidûm studiis ornata secundis, / Atque homines cantu detinet atque Deos.*
80. Milton, 'On Shakespear', *WJM*, I.i, line 10.
81. A. Dell'Antonio, *Listening as Spiritual Practice in Early Modern Italy*, pp. 66–7.
82. Ibid., p. 87.
83. Milton, *Ad Leonoram*, *WJM*, I.i, lines 7–8.
84. E. Spenser, *The Faerie Queene*, III, xi, proem 1.
85. Milton, *Maske*, *WJM*, I.i, line 792.
86. Sugimura, '*Matter of Glorious Trial*', p. 81.
87. Milton, *Maske*, *WJM*, I.i, lines 2–4.
88. Ibid., opening stage direction, lines 5–7.
89. Milton, *A Maske: The Earlier Versions*, p. 46. Demaray sees the Great Hall as 'large enough to accommodate a stage area not very much smaller than the forty- by twenty-eight-foot area that served as the average size of court masque stages' (*Masque Tradition*, p. 100). However, the space, measuring 30 by 58 foot, was, in truth, about one-quarter the size of the Whitehall Banqueting House, which measures 110 by 55 foot; see C. C. Brown, *John Milton's Aristocratic Entertainments*, p. 36.
90. Milton, *Maske*, *WJM*, I.i, lines 1013–15.
91. Ibid., lines 1015–16.
92. Milton, *Areopagitica*, *CPW*, II, p. 527.
93. Milton, *Maske*, *WJM*, I.i, lines 405–6, 408, 420.
94. Ibid., lines 460–2. Cf. F. Bacon, *The Advancement of Learning*, p. 346: 'It is not good to stay too long in the theatre. Let us now pass on to the judicial place or palace of the mind.'
95. Milton, *Maske*, *WJM*, I.i, line 527.
96. Ibid., lines 527–9.
97. Cf. ibid., lines 17, 243.
98. Demaray, *Milton and the Masque Tradition*, pp. 101–2.
99. Milton, *Maske*, *WJM*, I.i, lines 462–4.
100. Ibid., line 467.
101. See J. Gibson, 'The Logic of Chastity'. 'A socioethical doctrine which held that women's primary virtue was chastity – followed closely by its mutually reinforcing virtues of silence and obedience – left women who were in any way "public" or autonomous open to charges of unchastity' (p. 2).
102. See, but for a few instances, S. Greenblatt, *Renaissance Self-Fashioning*;

Greenblatt, *Shakespearean Negotiations*; and S. Mullaney, *The Place of the Stage*.
103. B. Hoxby, *Mammon's Music*, p. 24.
104. Milton, *Maske*, *WJM*, I.i, lines 738–9.
105. Ibid., lines 739–41.
106. Ibid., lines 744–6.
107. See S. X. Mead, '"Thou Art Chang'd"': 'To be coined [. . .] is to be a publicly declared value that may or may not correspond to substance. It is a move away from individual identity and toward a quantifiable function of circulation' (p. 239).
108. Milton, *Maske*, *WJM*, I.i, lines 751–2.
109. Ibid., lines 143–6.
110. Ibid., lines 170–1.
111. Ibid., line 169.
112. For tensions and interplay between aristocratic and rustic music in the masque, see D. Lindley, 'The Politics of Music in the Masque'.
113. Milton, *Maske*, *WJM*, I.i, line 493.
114. Ibid., line 549. See above, p. 43; and below, p. 93.
115. Ibid., lines 542–6.
116. See Milton, 'Lycidas', *WJM*, I.i, line 66; and Virgil, *Eclogues*, I, line 2, and IV, line 6.
117. Milton, *Samson Agonistes*, *WJM*, I, line 1610.
118. Milton, *Brief Notes upon a Late Sermon*, *CPW*, VII, p. 470, where Milton uses the term to describe former royal chaplain Matthew Griffith as part priest, part quack physician and part actor; cf. *Reason*, *CPW*, I, p. 856. 'Mountebank' refers to a charlatan who vends his faux-cures from a raised platform erected in the street (etymologically, 'climb-upon-bench/platform'), as in Ben Jonson's *Volpone*, II, ii–iii.
119. Milton, *Maske*, *WJM*, I.i, lines 457–9.
120. Ibid., line 154.
121. See above, pp. 5, 25–6, 35, 41–2; and below, pp. 96–7, 110, 113.
122. Milton, *Maske*, *WJM*, I.i, stage direction after line 657; line 916.
123. See M. Gillum, 'Yet Once More, "Gumms of Glutenous Heat"'; and D. Shuger, '"Gums of Glutinous Heat" and the Stream of Consciousness'.
124. Milton, *Maske*, *WJM*, I.i, line 645.
125. Ibid., line 908. I am currently completing an article of hiding bird-liming scenes, particularly in Shakespeare's *Twelfth Night* and Marvell's 'Upon Appleton House'. Part of this article, which details the processes and strategies of bird-liming, as explained in seventeenth-century fowling manuals, was delivered recently: B. Prawdzik, 'Similitude, Deception, and the Reader of "Upon Appleton House"'.
126. Milton, *Maske*, *WJM*, I.i, lines 658–60.
127. Ibid., line 756.
128. Ibid., lines 154–6.
129. Ibid., lines 755–8.
130. See Kerrigan, *Sacred Complex*, pp. 27–9.
131. Milton, *Maske*, *WJM*, I.i, lines 704, 708.
132. Ibid., lines 736–7.
133. Ibid., lines 766, 778–86.

134. Ibid., lines 214, 212.
135. Ibid., line 216.
136. We are far here from Spenser's Charissa, who though 'chast in worke and will' and hating '*Cupids* wanton snare', appears naked with 'breasts ever open bare' (Spenser, *The Faerie Queene*, I, x, 30, lines 5–8).
137. V. Kahn, 'Allegory and Sublime in *Paradise Lost*', p. 191.
138. J. Rogers, 'The Enclosure of Virginity', p. 232.
139. See Demaray, 'Temple of the Mind'; and S. Fish, *How Milton Works*, pp. 161–84.
140. Milton, *Paradise Lost*, WJM, II.i, I, pp. 254–5.
141. Gosson, *School of Abuse*, p. 31.
142. Milton, *Maske*, WJM, I.i, lines 792–8.
143. Milton, 'Lycidas', WJM, I.i, line 63.
144. Milton, *Maske*, WJM, I.i, lines 799–800.
145. Ibid., line 783.
146. Ibid., line 801.
147. A. Patterson, *Reading Between the Lines*, p. 43; B. Quintslund and A. Escobedo (eds), *Milton Quarterly*, 37 (2003).
148. Shullenberger, *The Lady in the Labyrinth*; see also M. Quilligan, *Milton's Spenser*, pp. 209–12.
149. Spenser, *The Faerie Queene*, III, xii, 19, lines 2–3; III, xi, 11, line 1.
150. T. P. Roche, Jr, *The Kindly Flame*, p. 83.
151. J. W. Broaddus, *Spenser's Allegory of Love*, p. 96.
152. Spenser, *The Faerie Queene*, III, xi, 51, lines 5–6.
153. Ibid., III, xi, 51, 7–9. In both the Trinity and Bridgewater Manuscripts, '*The Measure*' of the man-beasts is described as a 'wild[,] rude[,] & wanton *Antick*' (Milton, *A Maske: The Earlier Versions*, pp. 64–5).
154. Spenser, *The Faerie Queene*, III, xi, 53, line 6; III, xi, 52, lines 2, 6–8.
155. Ibid., III, xi, 50, line 4; III, xi, 54, line 3.
156. Ibid., III, xi, 54, line 8.
157. Ibid., III, xii, 4, line 9, and 3, lines 5–9. As if to emphasise the 'Ease' of this detached spectatorship, Spenser has Britomart spend a day 'wandering / And gazing on that Chambers ornament' before, after a 'second watch' of the same masque, she can proceed to the next chamber (III, xii, 29, lines 1–2, 6).
158. Ibid., III, xii, 26, lines 1, 3–4.
159. Ibid., III, xii, 29, line 9.
160. Milton, *Maske*, WJM, I.i, lines 204–7, italics mine.
161. Spenser, *The Faerie Queene*, III, xii, 26, line 6.
162. Whether used as a noun or as a verb, Milton's 'throng' generally indicates a group of people (or angels or devils), usually a rabble or wild rout. See above, pp. 39–40; and below, pp. 185–6, 188.
163. Milton, *Maske*, WJM, I.i, line 637.
164. Ibid., lines 645–6.
165. Ibid., lines 652–5.
166. Ibid., stage direction after line 812.
167. Ibid., lines 815–16
168. Spenser, *The Faerie Queene*, III, xii, 36, lines 2–3; see Quilligan, *Milton's Spenser*, p. 211.

169. A. Townshend, *Tempe Restored*, p. 481.
170. See Milton, *Maske*, *WJM*, I.i, lines 841–6.
171. Milton, 'To Mr. *H. Lawes*, on his Aires', *WJM*, I.i, p. 5.
172. Milton, *Maske*, *WJM*, I.i, line 909.
173. Ibid., lines 908, 856–7.
174. Ibid., lines 838–9.
175. Ibid., lines 911–12.
176. Ibid., lines 890–1, 231–4.
177. See Sugimura, *'Matter of Glorious Trial'*, pp. 106–9.
178. Milton, *Maske*, *WJM*, I.i, line 241.
179. Ibid., lines 937–40.
180. Shullenberger, *The Lady in the Labyrinth*, p. 15.
181. Milton, *Maske*, *WJM*, I.i, lines 945–54.
182. Ibid., line 896.
183. Milton, *A Maske Presented at Ludlow Castle* [1637 version], p. 174.
184. Coiro, 'Anonymous Milton', p. 612.
185. Milton, *Reason*, *CPW*, I, 820. See above, pp. 51–2; and below, pp. 132–3.

Chapter 3

Bending the Fool: *Animadversions* and the Early Prose

'Ha, ha, ha'.[1]

More than any other line that Milton published, this burst of mocking laughter, targeting a respected Anglican bishop, in the *Animadversions upon the Remonstrants Defence against Smectymnuus* (1641), would make any pious Miltonist wince.[2] As unwieldy as its title, *Animadversions* is not Milton's finest work. Editors have found it so insignificant and off-putting that it does not appear in any collection of the selected prose. Of course, paradigm shifts can illumine value long obscured. For instance, the brutal and jagged *Titus Andronicus* was so reviled by critics that many assumed that Shakespeare could not have had a hand in it. (It is broadly accepted that George Peele wrote at least the first act.) Not until Eugene Waith's illuminations on the play's Ovidian poetics of trauma was its status in the Shakespeare canon confirmed.[3] What had seemed blemishes were now part of a sophisticated, however uncouth, artistic vision. *Animadversions* is, as it were, Milton's *Titus*. Yet if we examine it within the contexts of Milton's theatricality and the theatricality of mid-seventeenth-century polemical culture, we will see that it is one of the most significant texts in his development as an author.

Animadversions is one of Milton's first prose tracts. Milton published *Of Reformation* in May 1641 and followed quickly with *Of Prelaticall Episcopacy* in June or July. Later in July, he published *Animadversions*, which, like his previous tracts, was printed anonymously. Likely, Milton had also written the postscript to the first publication by Smectymnuus in March. 'Smectymnuus' was a corporate pseudonym composed of the initials of five Presbyterian divines: Stephen Marshall, Edmund Calamy, Thomas Young, Matthew Newcomen and William Spurstow. These responded to Bishop Joseph Hall's *An Humble Remonstrance to the High Court of Parliament*, published in January 1641, with *An Answer to a Book, Entituled An Humble Remonstrance*, in March. In April, this tract was followed by Hall's *Defence of the Humble Remonstrance*, which, in June, was answered by the Smectymnuans in their *Vindication of the Answer*, shortly before the appearance of *Animadversions*.[4] Milton appears to have radicalised, at least to some extent, in the late 1630s, around the time that he penned 'Lycidas', and he appears to have been meeting with Smectymnuans by 1640.[5]

Animadversions stands out among Milton's tracts for its form and mode of argument. Like the Smectymnuus tracts, and like countless other polemical responses in the period, Milton's tract is, first and foremost, of the genre of the animadversion, in which the author follows a point-by-point rebuttal of a previous publication. Milton's tract differs from the typical animadversion in several ways; most notably, it brings the *anima* to the page of print in punishing rejoinders that seem to transpire in the moment. Moreover, the tract not only resembles a dramatic dialogue, but also repeatedly references its theatricality: the dialogue proceeds as though in real time in the midst of spectators hostile to prelacy.

However unusual *Animadversions* might be in the context of Milton's canon, its generic hybridity fits within the social and print culture of 1641. Thomas Kranidas, in his study of Milton's anti-prelatical tracts, has argued that polemics over Church government during the early 1640s aimed not so much to provide purely logical refutations of opponent positions, but, rather, to belie the credibility that would make these positions persuasive: 'much, if not most, of the energy' of polemists in the debate over Church government 'goes into establishing their own authority and reliability, not only in their skill and comprehensiveness in presenting evidence, but in the actual presentation of self as truthteller'.[6] The style of *Animadversions*, suggests Kranidas, befitted the polemical context and the 'heterogeneous audience' that Milton was aiming to reach.[7]

Because the tracts are so focused on 'advertising rectitude', they 'subvert[t] the rules of classical rhetoric'.[8] In other words, ethos becomes central to polemical critique and defence. Since this rhetoric unfolds with rapid-fire exchange during a period of instability, decorum itself is ever on the move. Milton locates *Animadversions* within a satirical tradition that begins with the writings of the pseudonymous Martin Marprelate in the late 1580s and that would continue through Marvell's *The Rehearsall Transpros'd* (1672) and beyond – as amply detailed by Raymond A. Anselment.[9] The key marker of this tradition is the justification of satirical mode through the principle of *decorum personae*, which is derived from Horace and which was applied liberally by Marprelate in order to justify the adoption of a persona that could answer, appropriately, the characters of his antagonists.[10] In other words, if the bishops are fools because they write endless tomes of nonsense theology, it is within the bounds of decorum that I adopt the persona of a fool in order to answer them.

Here, decorum is explicitly applied to the 'players' of print exchange. The satirical mode responds to the ethos of the prose antagonist. For Milton, the prelatical ethos would entail a hypocritical disguising of the hunger for wealth and power, and a veneer of pious decency. While the exchanges of the early 1640s certainly followed a fluid and provisional sense of decorum, the polemical adoption of foolishness was, nonetheless, well-rooted in polemical tradition and elicited often predictable responses and modes of counterattack.

Moreover, once theatricalised, polemic was constrained by conventions and principles of theatrical decorum dating from Aristotle and later articulated by Sir Philip Sidney, Shakespeare's Hamlet, Ben Jonson, John Dryden and Milton, among others. As we have seen, dramatic decorum was encoded upon the body, which could, in turn, be translated into text, so that critique of the text could follow the same logic and rhetoric as could critique of the histrionic body. Discourses of dramatic decorum and critique of acting skill remained, during the seventeenth century, wedded to the classical rhetorical discourse of *actio*, which further politicised the body and, in turn, the theatricalised text.[11] As, during the early 1640s, politics were almost inevitably linked to contested modes of worship, decorum for a text like *Animadversions* – rhetorical, political, religious and theatrical – was determined by an extraordinary network of constraints that, with the political and religious tensions of the 1640s, could produce effects alternately predictable and impossible to anticipate.

As the uncouth brutality of *Titus Andronicus* owed considerably to prevalent popular tastes of the late 1580s and early 1590s, especially for over-the-top bloodiness (*Tamburlaine, Part I* and *Part II*) and revenge (*The Spanish Tragedy*), so too did the ugliness of *Animadversions* owe, in part, to popular tastes for *ad hominem* satire, iconoclastic violence and the ludic. One reason why *Animadversions* is so important to our understanding of Milton is that it initiates a realignment of his theatricality and, in so doing, a backlash against his early populism.[12] The exchanges of print during the early 1640s would place a theatrical Milton within the straits of improvisation, a space of negotiation that would help to shape his exegetical poetics and that would set the scene in the Restoration poetry.

The Populist Milieu of 1641

The Ludlow *Maske* showed the productive ambivalence held by Milton toward the institution of theatre and the implications of this ambivalence for his sense of what it meant to be an English poet of God. The *Maske* dramatised the emergence of his authorial identity from a stage that was at once a potent medium for poetic authority and a locus of contextual pressures that could destabilise and ravage this authority. Such a dialectic yielded little room for passage; the logical result was paralysis, or suspended emergence. Only a renewed vision and faith in the possibility of a theatre capable of participating meaningfully in a culture open to reform could break the impasse. Of course, Milton would write poems throughout the later 1630s, most notably 'Lycidas' (1637). The pastoral appeared in the Cambridge volume of elegies for Edward King and was signed 'J. M.' While former classmates surely knew that Milton was the author of the volume's sole masterpiece, *Justa Eduardo King Naufrago* saw limited circulation, and so knowledge of the future bard continued to circulate largely by word of mouth and inked parchment.[13] 'Lycidas' details J. M.'s struggle through an identity crisis brought on by King's death, a struggle to find a clear religious vision and 'pastures new' where to express it as poetry.[14]

Milton soon found pasture away from England, particularly in Italy, where, as he is eager to recount in *Reason*, his youthful poetry was praised by literati.[15] Yet, whether due to Charles Diodati's death or to news of the worsening religious and political crisis in England (or to both), he returned, in August, perhaps, of 1639 and settled into London, the epicentre of turmoil and change.[16] Here, under gathering clouds of blood, he would find his greenest pasture yet. Soon the world would hear the voice of Mr. John Milton, polemicist.

By the time that Milton returned from his tour of the continent, the attempt to impose Laudian reforms and a new *Book of Common Prayer* on a recalcitrantly Presbyterian Scotland had reverberated in a series of increasingly dire consequences. Soon the Second Bishops' War would lead to a Covenanter army occupying Newcastle and receiving payment from the King to prevent further incursions. What would be known as the Long Parliament was then called to levy funds. Like the Short Parliament before it, so did it withhold supply from Charles I. Rejecting prorogation until grievances with Church and State policy had been addressed, Parliament began to exploit Charles's political weakness and to tighten the vice on episcopacy. By the time that Star Chamber was officially abolished in July 1641, the gates had already opened to a deluge of print that would transform political discourse, to the extent that ideas unthinkable in 1640 would be circulated, debated and enacted by the decade's end.[17]

Milton would have absorbed the spirit of the time with excitement. He had moved to Aldersgate Street sometime between May 1640 and April 1641.[18] While state censorship began to collapse, he lived only a brief stroll from the booksellers of St Paul's and Fleet Street. Venturing just a bit farther, he would pass the Blackfriars Playhouse, while just across the river were the remaining amphitheatres, including the second Globe. The anti-prelatical tracts, especially *Animadversions*, show that he was actively considering how the institutions of prelacy and the playhouse related. There was already ample precedent for this comparison in polemics, satires, sermons, anti-theatrical tracts, and plays.

Animadversions shows Milton re-imagining theological polemic as a type of hybrid stage performance within the implied theatre of an invigorated print culture that appealed to common citizens and labourers as much as to theologians, political thinkers and Parliament. 'Between 1640 and about 1643', writes Helen Pierce, 'the English market for printed ephemera [. . .] exploded, and with it a proliferation of predominantly hostile opinions', many 'directed squarely at the archbishop of Canterbury and the unpopular Laudian regime'.[19] In *Animadversions*, Milton directly regards the spectators who were hissing the time's great antagonists – Strafford, Laud and the prelates – as though the emergent public sphere was really a 'wooden O'.

In representing the rhetorical situation as something like a dramatic scene, Milton was drawing upon an array of traditions and contexts, not the least of which was the profusion of printed 'playlets' that began to appear on London's streets after the fall of Star Chamber.[20] These three- to eight-page pamphlets resemble quarto printings of plays, with clearly demarcated dialogue, occasional stage directions and, in at least one case, division by act.[21] The playlets depict the primary actors of the religious and political drama of the 1640s, much as political cartoons and televised comedy shorts do today. Instead of merely hearing or reading about the alleged crimes of Strafford and, especially, of Laud, readers could, at little expense, see – in what Pierce terms 'an imagined space of suspended reality' – these crimes exposed and punished.[22] The prelates invited the reader into that space as judge and delighted spectator. Although there is no direct evidence that any playlet was performed, at least one, *Canterburie His Change of Diot* (1641) – apparently by Richard Overton, although the question of authorship is not settled – advertises itself as 'a new Play' and attests facetiously to a public staging at Lambeth Palace.[23] It is likely that, as had been the case with the

Marprelate tracts, these inexpensive pamphlets – costing but one or two pence – were read in taverns to the delight of boisterous sousers.[24]

Recalling and at times directly invoking the late-Elizabethan Marprelate tracts, the playlets built upon a tradition of anti-prelatical satire that catered to the tastes of radicals and Presbyterian labourers. Thus, the playlets were part of the populist stirrings that threatened a more fundamental disruption of social order than what would be countenanced by Presbyterian authorities and opposition MPs.[25] During the late 1580s, Marprelate had enlivened debate over Church government by assimilating the techniques of the popular stage clown to print in a series of incendiary tracts. Like 'Smectymnuus', 'Martin Marprelate' was a corporate pseudonym. The name cloaked a network of divines and printers, associated with the Presbyterian opposition, who risked their lives to disseminate the increasingly notorious and divisive tracts.[26]

Marprelate exposed Elizabeth's bishops as fools (idiots) while adopting the stage fool as his own satiric persona. He was, in a sense, the 'resurrected persona' of beloved stage fool Richard Tarlton, who had died only weeks before the first Marprelate tract, the *Epistle* (1588), appeared. The 'intensely theatrical' tracts, writes Patrick Collinson, represented the bishops, 'with their own inherent theatricality, [as] actors in so many comic jigs'.[27] By styling tedious theological disputation into a mode befitting amphitheatre comedy, the tracts aimed not to articulate theological arguments so much as to assail the pedantry of Anglican print in a way that would catch the ears of commoners. Adopting the stage clown's role as a mediator between the mimesis and the audience, 'Martin' often addresses his readers directly, inviting them to participate in the derision of the pedantic in this play of print.

The early Marprelate tracts quoted episcopal opponents out of context in order to fashion comically serious yet clueless personae.[28] Martin took license to needle and to make merriment of these characters as though he was translating Tarlton's post-play banter into a mess of ludic print.[29] In the *Epistle*, he asks leave to play the fool: 'otherwise dealing with master doctors booke I cannot keep decorum personae'.[30] In other words, since Martin is dealing with fools (idiots), it is necessary and appropriate for him to adopt the persona of the stage fool, a figure optimally equipped to barb idiocy humorously and lithely. He initiates what would become a standard justification of foolishness by citing the authority of Solomon in Proverbs 26:5: 'Answer a fool according to his folly, lest he be wise in his own conceit'. In *Animadversions*, Milton would appeal to the fervour of Christ and his followers – who 'have wrought up their zealous souls into such vehemencies, as nothing else could be more killingly spoken' – as well as to 'the morall precept of Salomon to answer him thereafter that prides him in his folly'.[31] He associates his righteous anger with Christ and zealous Christians and associates himself indirectly with Marprelate.

Martin's ghost would arise half a century later in response to unpopular Laudian reforms. New editions appeared in 1640, followed soon by scores of playlets that modified the Marprelate style according to contemporary dramatic sensibilities; this style was rendered more readable through the typographical advances of the printed drama.[32] These playlets include clearly demarcated interlocutions, with utterances and rejoinders separately labelled and identified. They typically follow a coherent narrative arc and in some cases include woodcuts that flesh out the dramatic scenario. Overton, later a prominent Leveller, likely re-issued Marprelate's *Hay Any Worke for Cooper* in 1641 and was publishing satirical pamphlets under the pseudonyms Martin Mar-Priest and Martin Claw-Clergie in the early years of crisis.[33]

Canterburie His Change of Diot is the most provocative of the 1641 playlets. It invites the reader (or listener) into a revenge fantasy in which the Church's most powerful religious authority, Archbishop of Canterbury William Laud, is abused verbally and physically. It includes several woodcuts and is divided into five acts. The first act shows Laud discontented with a feast of 'rarest dainties'. Instead, he desires, among other harvests of the pillory, tippets of ears: clearly those of Henry Burton, John Bastwick and William Prynne – the last punished for libelling the Queen in *Histriomastix* – who had become heroes of the anti-episcopal cause when, after enduring public mutilation and three years of imprisonment, they were released by the Long Parliament in 1640. Seeking a place to sharpen his knife, Laud is soon encountered, bound, tortured – tied to a grindstone, his nose ground to a pulp – and imprisoned by a carpenter. The carpenter places him in a birdcage with a Jesuit confessor (thus associating Laud's Church with Rome, a common strategy). The greed and abuse of power presented in the first act are justly repaid by the vengeance of a labouring class affiliated with the carpenter-Christ. The third act begins with a woodcut that shows a stage fool who taunts the captives from outside the cage. Overton evokes the Martinist principle of *decorum personae* – here wedded to the Pauline rhetoric of the wise made foolish and the foolish made wise – in the fool's mockery of Laud. The caption of the woodcut might, even, have provided a source for the 'grim laughter' of *Animadversions*: 'Ha, ha, ha, ha, who is the foole now[?]'[34] That the laughing fool is to be understood as a stage clown representing Martinist populism becomes clear in the final act, where the fool concludes the playlet in the fashion of Elizabethan comedy by performing a jig with an ecclesiastical court official ('apparitor' or 'paritor').

Animadversions does not, like *Canterburie His Change of Diot*, overtly enact a populist fantasy in which physical violence is inflicted upon an unpopular antagonist. However, the shadows of the axe and of the throng do lurk within it. Milton's persona, the Answerer, is, in part, a vehicle of popular discontent that was already erupting in violence. An armed mob of apprentices had stormed Westminster Hall and had skirmished with Colonel Lunsford, the new Tower warden, along with dozens of royal adherents.[35] On 24 January, a mob destroyed Cheapside Cross, an act of iconoclasm that Overton would commemorate in *Articles of High Treason Exhibited against Cheap-Side Crosse* (1642). 'All over England', writes David L. Smith, 'the petitions against bishops coincided with spontaneous outbreaks of popular iconoclasm, with the smashing of altar-rails and other symbols of "idolatry and superstition"'.[36] The theatres, seen by authorities as gathering places for potentially tumultuous crowds of hundreds and even thousands of boisterous Londoners, would be closed by the ascendant Parliament within months.[37]

Both Hall and Milton's early allies, the Smectymnuans, begrudged the crude satires for disrupting what they styled grave and portentous debate. Hall complains of a 'throng' of 'Libellous' pamphlets and a 'battery of [. . .] Paper-pellets'.[38] The Smectymnuus publisher blames the delayed printing of the *Vindication* to 'the crouding in of many little Pamphlets [. . .] to the great grief of the Authors'.[39] It is here, with these 'many little Pamphlets', away from the 'solemn Scenes' of debate between Hall and Smectymnus, where the author of the *Modest Confutation of a Slanderous and Scurrilous Libell* (1642) would strive to locate the author of *Animadversions*.[40]

Milton melds the populist appeal of *Animadversions* with theological disputation and the poetic expression of holy zeal. The tract includes features of both the comedic and the tragic modes. The preface argues that the tract should be taken seriously, since its satire serves a serious 'Religious Cause': 'nor can there be a more proper object of indignation and scorne together then a false Prophet taken in the greatest and dearest and most dangerous cheat, the cheat of soules'.[41] Milton works to delineate a decorum that can fit this hybrid form. It 'cannot be taxt of levity or insolence', despite the appearance 'here and there' of 'such a grim laughter, as may appear at the same time in an austere visage'.[42] Milton wears, as it were, a double mask.

Milton's justification of foolishness by *decorum personae* suggests an intended alignment not only with Marprelate but also with the playlets and, more generally, the popular literatures circulating in 1641. Indeed, the Modest Confuter would lament that the anti-Church invective of *Animadversions* offered resources for Catholics, who, he claimed, cite Marprelate 'as a grave unquestionable Authour' because of his anti-Anglican invective.[43] The Confuter would also struggle to place Milton's tract with the crude pamphlet *News from Hell* (1642).[44] The attribution owes to the pamphlet's authorial signature of 'J. M.' J. Milton French might be justified in dismissing Milton's authorship of the 'slangy, vulgar, badly printed hodgepodge' as all but 'wholly impossible'; yet, in its stylistic appeal to a popular as well as to a more learned audience, *Animadversions* gives us a rare glimpse into the possibility that, in 1641, Milton *might* have, at the least, *deigned* to dabble in populist 'low' genres.[45]

The aim of the Marprelate conspirators was to extend Church opposition to a broader base; Milton, too, might have aimed to foment discontent in order to support the push for prelatical extirpation, as Parliamentary proceedings over the 'Root and Branch Petition' were underway at the time of its appearance. The Confuter was, it seems, not entirely wrong to label the author a 'scurrilous Mime' who aimed to bring 'the very beasts of the people within the borders of the Mount'.[46] In *The Praise of Folly*, Erasmus had personated the fool, had criticised foolishness and had urged readers to pursue not ludic folly but, rather, the wise folly of the Pauline fool of Christ, who transcends the world by taking no account of its foolish wisdom. In *Animadversions*, Milton invites readers to embrace his activist foolishness and to join a community of 'opposite Spectators' who will work towards the demise of prelacy and the rise of Christ's Millennial Kingdom.

Uncasing the Prelates

In *Animadversions*, Milton pursues what he terms the 'serious uncasing of a grand imposture' that is accompanied by 'grim laughter'.[47] 'Uncasing' suggests that Milton followed the playlets in his use of personation to make crimes that had been concealed by prelatical privilege publicly visible. To uncase, here, is to peel back the paint in order to expose rottenness.

The tract's work of uncasing thus fully realises the less sustained theatrical critique of Anglican formalism in *Of Reformation* and *Of Prelaticall Episcopacy*, and later in *Reason*. In the earlier anti-prelatical tracts, Milton had characterised high Anglican ritual and worship as rigidly formal theatre.[48] *Of Reformation* begins by describing how the

Church's spirituality had become emptied, its external forms hardening into a 'crust of Formalitie'.[49] 'Professors' began to 'bring the inward acts of the *Spirit* to the outward and customary ey-service of the body', transforming 'all the Divine intercourse, betwixt *God*, and the Soule, yea, the very shape of *God* himselfe, into an exterior, and bodily forme'.[50] 'Robes of pure innocency' were replaced by 'pure Linnen, with other deformed, and fantastick dresses in Palls, and Miters, and guegaw's fetcht from *Arons* old wardrope'.[51] Now that the spirit of Reformation had been stifled by set customs and rituals, 'then was the *Priest* set to *con his motions*, and his *Postures* his *Liturgies*, and his *Lurries*' until the soul had become heavy flesh ('over-bodying her selfe') in the 'performance of *Religious* duties'.[52] Theatrical structures lurk just beneath the surface. '*Arons* old wardrope' appears to be a tiring house of diverse costumes (ecclesiastical vestments) and props (a 'guegaw' is a child's toy, perhaps here a censer or chalice). The ritual itself is described as scripted performance through the rhetoric of *actio*. The priest learns his forms by rote; he 'cons [. . .] motions', with 'motions' referring to gestures of the body while also suggesting the mechanised actions of a puppet show.[53] The priest studies how to manipulate his body and limbs ('postures') and memorises prescribed forms of worship ('liturgies') that yield a meaningless jumble of words and sounds ('lurries'). In *Reason*, the rhetoric is more explicitly theatrical: the prelates are 'Church-maskers' who, having covered Christ's 'righteous verity with the polluted cloathing of [their] ceremonies', continue to strut 'in the false vizard of worldly autority'.[54] In each case, the costume covers a spiritual nakedness while being, at the same time, a sign of that nakedness.[55]

Milton's rhetoric of hypocritical disguise and rigidly scripted performance accords with the understanding of participants in the oppositional print culture that they were stripping away the dignities of office that had protected prelates and government officials and that, moreover, they were exposing abuses of power to an encircling public that was ever more vocal and powerful. Waves of unrestricted print reshaped norms of public communication and levelled space for a speaking public. These developments, writes David Zaret, 'superseded norms of secrecy and privilege in political communication' while altering 'the *content* as well as the *scope* of political communication', which began to appeal to 'an anonymous body of opinion, a public that was both a nominal object of discourse and a collection of writers, readers, printers, and petitioners engaged in political debates'.[56]

A motif of public exposure presided over a range of publications, including *Animadversions*. 'In many ways,' writes Sharon Achinstein, 'the English pamphlets [. . .] transformed the members of their audience into spectators[, who] were invited to participate in the fray'.[57] Through personation and fictional dialogue, the playlets brought the reader into the privy chambers of power. Some invite readers to attend secret conversations that plainly reveal the guilt of conversants.[58] Others merely depict or enumerate crimes that are swiftly answered by spectacles of punishment or presage of imminent retribution. *The Bishops Potion* (1641) – also possibly by Overton – epitomises the motifs of exposure and punishment common to the anti-prelatical playlets. It manifests Laud's guilt through excrement that is forced out of his body into open view. Readers are first treated to Laud's consultation with his doctor about a urine sample: 'Your water is a most thick, dense, solid heavy, almost ragged, putrid, stinking and rotten Urine'.[59] Laud's urine materialises the ethos of the man. After ingesting a purge, Laud disgorges paraphernalia of his power and its abuse: a tobacco patent; the *Declaration of Sports and Pastimes* (1633); the Star Chamber order against Prynne, Burton and Bastwick; and the mitre itself. The exposure of crimes is quickly followed by a promise of swift justice: 'if the Miter be come, the Divell is not far off', Laud's doctor concludes: 'Farewell good my Lord'.[60] Like the playlet's concluding line, the final clause of its subtitle – 'to preserve him from being let blood in the neck, when the signe is in *Taurus*' – suggests that Laud's life will soon end on the scaffold. It was under this sign of the zodiac that Strafford had lost his head.[61]

In *Animadversions*, Milton applies Martinist techniques to the ends pursued by the playlet writers of 1641. He is able to generate an unflattering caricature of Hall by furnishing the dialogue with selective quotations from the *Humble Remonstrance* and, in most instances, from the *Defence*. This cut-and-paste technique allows Milton to respond to Hall's language with lithe and punishing rejoinders. Like the playlets, *Animadversions* differs from the Marprelate tracts in its clearly demarcated dialogue, which is suggestive of play quartos. It also differs from the genre of its namesake, the animadversion, in that it crafts, from the exchange, distinctive characters – specifically, the Remonstrant, who represents Hall, and the Answerer, who represents the anonymous author (Milton) – within a spare but lively scenario of debate. From that debate emerges the ethos of prelacy, laid bare to reading eyes.

The 'serious uncasing of a grand imposture' leaves Hall exposed to scrutiny, as though naked. Milton assails what he sees as the hypocrisy of Anglican 'decency' by calling attention to Hall's circular argumentation, logical and grammatical errors, and awkward presumptions. For Milton, Hall's words repeatedly circle around a motivating core of venality, to which each feeble effort can be traced. The ineptitude of Hall's performance elicits the 'grim laughter' of the Answerer –

menacing derision shared by the spectator-readers of the uncasing: 'God and man', declares Milton in the preface, are now ready to 'explode and hisse' Hall and episcopacy 'out of the land'.[62]

The laughter that *Animadversions* expresses and elicits is furthermore 'grim' because Milton takes pains to associate it with the morbid 'uncasing' associated with the anatomical theatre and the scaffold. Dissections of human bodies in anatomy theatres had been practised in England since at least 1570. Jonathan Sawday describes the early modern anatomy theatre, such as those in Padua and Leiden, as a theatre-in-the-round that privileges the spectator gaze upon the spectacle corpse: 'these constructions were concentric wells, into which the audience would have peered down on to the cadaver and the anatomists working at its side'.[63] William Heckscher describes a performance structure informed by theatre convention: in some instances, tickets were sold, the cadaver was enclosed in curtains before dissection began, and music was performed.[64] Sawday suggests that anatomy and textuality maintained an analogical relationship, in that 'the body – a material object in space – was gradually made a model or pattern for any spatial organisation of knowledge'.[65] Milton would describe text as body in *Reason*, *Areopagitica* and the *Apology* and would bring the King's book to life in *Eikonoklastes*.

In his *Defence of the Humble Remonstrance*, Hall had bewailed the cruelty of 'opposite Spectators' in the boisterous print culture: 'What a death it is, to think of the sport, and advantage these watchfull enemies will be sure to make of our sins and shame?'[66] Milton turns these into spectators of the anatomy theatre: 'O what a death it is', the Answerer taunts, 'to the Prelates to be thus unvisarded, thus uncas'd, to have the Periwigs pluk't off that cover your baldnesse, your inside nakedness thrown open to publick view'.[67] In this theatre of print, the prelates' 'vizards' – masks of the masquing or *commedia dell'arte* traditions – and 'Periwigs' will be 'pluk't off'. The baldness of the unmasked countenance marks a venal ethos exposed. It also evokes the practice of removing the cadaver's hair before dissection. 'Uncas'd' refers not simply to the peeling away of disguise, but also to the removal of the cadaver's skin during dissection to reveal the viscera. As the 'Remonstrant' is very much alive in *Animadversions*, we are witnessing what is, essentially, a rhetorical vivisection. Indeed, the scene of the anatomy theatre implies, also, the scene of ultimate justice, the execution scaffold, where prominent offenders could be eviscerated – 'thrown open to public view' – while still alive, before being drawn and quartered.[68] Milton literalises Hall's 'what a death it is'. The death is one of shame, but it is also one of mortification, of a textual body transformed into an embodied ethos that undergoes a grizzly torture open to all who care to read and see.

In his preface, Milton indicates that his 'serious uncasing of a grand imposture' will produce 'the speediest way to see the truth vindicated, and Sophistry taken short at the first false bound'.[69] In other words, if ethos itself is the target of polemical rhetoric, then the falsehood, worldliness, condescension and fear that constitute this ethos will manifest in every sentence. The end of argument can be reached with a single well-placed, peeling cut. Such cuts are repeated again and again, revealing the same truth.

Milton starts his encounter with Hall by developing the Remonstrant's persona from a mere fragment of text. The Remonstrant emerges from the cut-and-pasted text of the *Defence*, breaking through the preface of *Animadversions* into its *mise en scène*: 'But now he begins', proclaims the Answerer.[70] The preface becomes, retroactively, a prologue to the action. The cue '*Remonstrant*' is followed by an exact quotation of the *Defence*'s opening line – 'My single Remonstrance is encountred with a plurall Adversary' – where Hall complains that his *Humble Remonstrance*, written by himself alone, has been attacked by the 'plurall' Smectymnuus.[71]

As soon as Milton has set the scene, the discursive uncasing can begin. In the *Defence*, Hall had proclaimed that, even if the Smectymnuans were innumerable, 'my cause, yea Gods, would bid me to meet them undismaid, and to say with holy *David, Though an hoast should incamp against me, my heart shall not feare*'.[72] Milton sees here an attempt by Hall to fashion himself into the protagonist of a David-vs-Goliath narrative; after all, he is speaking David's lines (Psalms 27:3). Milton seizes upon the appositive 'yea Gods' to expose this arrogation, which is masked by a false guise of humility, from the outset:

> *Remonst.* My cause yea Gods would bid me meet them undismai'd, &c.
> *Answ.* Ere a foot furder we must bee content to heare a preambling boast of your valour, what a St. *Dunstane*, you are to encounter *Legions*, either infernall or humane.
> *Remonst.* My cause, yea Gods.
> *Answ.* What gods? unlesse your belly or the god of this world be hee? shew us any one point of your *Remonstrance* that do's not more concern superiority, pride, ease and the belly, then the truth and glory of God, or the salvation of soules.
> *Remonst.* My cause, yea Gods would bid me meet them undismaid, and to say with holy *David, though an hoast, &c.*
> *Answ.* Doe not think to Perswade us of your undaunted courage by misapplying to your self the words of holy *David*; we know you feare, and are in an agonie at this present, lest you should lose that superfluity of riches and honour which your party usurp [. . .] How shall we think you have not carnall fear while we see you so subject to carnall desires?
> *Remonst.* I doe gladly fly to the barre.[73]

Milton neither labours through Hall's citations of patristic testimony nor strains to keep pace with his arguments. Instead, he seizes upon 'my cause, yea Gods' and makes the Remonstrant speak it three times. In repeating the fragment, the dialogue quickly produces evidence of 'grand imposture'.[74] The fragment begins to voice more clearly a self-supporting assertion, that the cause for which I write – namely, the survival of the Anglican Church and its hierarchy of bishops – is also God's cause. We see at once a rhetorical *construction* of divine justification and 'the truth vindicated, and Sophistry taken short at the first false bound'. Milton's argumentation here is neither logical nor reliant upon authority; rather, it employs dramatic representation to make Hall's ethos emerge from his own words. The Answerer emphasises that, although the Remonstrant 'misappl[ies] the words of holy *David*' to claim the fearlessness of God's protected, he nonetheless speaks from a position of imminent danger, 'lest you should lose that superfluity of riches and honour which your party usurp'. A clear dichotomy has been established between pious and 'humble' spirituality and the carnal desire and fear that motivates the performance of such.

Frequently using 'we' and 'us', rather than 'I' and 'me', Milton invites his readers to attend the verbal spectacle and to participate in the Remonstrant's uncasing. When the Answerer scoffs that 'ere a foot furder' – that is, as soon as the Remonstrant begins – 'we must bee content to heare a preambling boast of your valour', the language of walking ('foot', 'preambling') and of sound ('heare') contributes to the sense that we are watching the start of a play. As the Remonstrant enters the text's implicit mimetic plane, or stage, he is represented as vaunting to a knowing audience that must 'bee content' the while. Hall, exposed with his first words, appeals to Parliament's judgement.[75] The Answerer accepts unflinchingly, offering to have him dragged to Parliament for trial: 'To the barre with him then'.[76] Thus, Milton's theatricality flows into a new configuration: the 'opposite spectators' – the audience, the readers – will also be jurors. He operates quickly to bring them into a process of judgement and punishment that follows from their discernment and delighted identification with the Answerer.

When, near the close of *Animadversions*, a horrified Remonstrant acknowledges the theatre of print that surrounds him, bewailing the 'watchfull enemies' and 'opposite spectators' who will make 'sport and advantage [. . .] of [the prelates'] sinne and shame', the Answerer explains that this hostile audience is, ultimately, an instrument of divine judgement: 'This is but to fling and struggle under the inevitable net of God, that now begins to inviron you round'.[77] Uncased by Milton and exposed to popular ridicule, the Remonstrant flails in an ever-tightening net, encompassed by a populace doubling as the 'inevitable', constricting 'net of God'. The net tightens as the Remonstrant commends, in a desperate *non sequitur*, the 'so many eminent schollers, learned preachers, grave, holy and accomplish'd Divines' of the 'Church of *England* [...] at this day'.[78] Where the fool of *Canterbury His Change of Diot* had mocked Laud from outside of the Archbishop's cage, so Milton's Answerer mocks the Remonstrant: 'Ha, ha, ha', an outburst of 'grim laughter' that logically follows the constriction of the audience around the helpless, silver-tongued apologist of prelacy.[79]

Delivery and Decorum in Polemical Print

The theatricality of *Animadversions* emerges from a confluence not only of genres, but also of cultural dynamics, stereotypes and polemical memes. The shared rhetorical and representational strategies circulating in and mutating through print culture were informed by the spectacular aesthetics of religious ritual, as well as distinct worship styles, emotional registers and interpretive relations to scripture. These strategies were also derived from the classical tradition of *actio*, the discipline of gesture and pronunciation employed to accentuate or project authentic emotion. After 1640, the use of this rhetoric worked, generally, to delegitimise claims to spiritual authenticity by calling attention to the constructedness of spiritual affect. The body, in its representation, became a centre of contention for opposing religious and political creeds.

Polemicists characterised Anglican worship as ritual theatre, in that set forms and the actions of minister and congregation followed what appeared to be a constraining script. Little ambit was given to spiritual expression or to action that strayed from the guidelines of the *Book of Common Prayer*. On the contrary, Presbyterian and more enthusiastic worship was presented as waywardly improvisational, promoting the self while transgressing bounds of scripture and decorum. Heated reformist sermons and zealous worship were marked with the stigma of overweening populism, due in part to the association of excessive gesture with popular comedy in the *actio* tradition. These coordinates of gesture, comedy and populism would also apply to the representation of later enthusiasts, especially the early Quakers.[80]

At the core of these debates was the relationship between worship and emotion and, by extension, spirituality. Debora Shuger argues that Hellenic rhetoric influenced early modern sacred rhetoric by offering a psychological justification for artifice in preaching. Especially important to Shuger's case is *Peri ideon* or *Types of Style* (c. 400 BC) by Hermogenes, who divides rhetoric not into canons but, rather, into broad styles delineated by their effect on audience emotion. Manuals situated within this affect-oriented paradigm instructed preachers in how to move parishioners to God through the passions, which, by way of Augustinian theology, did not necessarily undermine rationality but could 'wing the mind's search for God and truth'.[81]

Before the Laudian reforms, the imperative to rouse passions in order to elevate congregates spiritually was not so exclusively assigned to Presbyterians and enthusiasts. In 'The Windows', George Herbert had posited that the preacher's body requires zeal to channel scripture, just as the high Anglican ornamentation of stained-glass windows in Salisbury Cathedral requires luminescence to vitalise it: 'Doctrine and life, colours and light, in one / When they combine and mingle, bring / A strong regard and aw: but speech alone / Doth vanish like a flaring thing, / And in the eare, not conscience ring'.[82]

In an elegy for John Donne that was re-published in Bulwer's *Chironomia* (1644), Jasper Mayne employs the language of *actio* to describe the Dean of St Paul's as a brilliant rhetor who could save souls through his gesturing body alone:

> Yet have I seen thee in the Pulpit stand,
> Where one might take notes from thy look & hand;
> And from thy speaking action beare away
> More Sermon then some Teachers use to say.
> Such was thy cariage, and thy gesture such,
> As could devide the heart, and conscience touch:
> Thy motion did confute, and one might see
> An error vanquish'd by deliverie.[83]

Mayne describes Donne's body as communicating a non-verbal sermon more effectively than most preachers could speak it. The words 'action', 'gesture', 'motion' and 'delivery' ground this praise of Donne's sacred rhetoric in the tradition of *actio*. Yet the idea that such a zealous self-presentation could touch upon the various passions of the 'heart' and stimulate 'conscience' suggests that *actio* could easily fit within the broader affect-oriented paradigm of seventeenth-century sacred rhetoric.

This paradigm enabled sacred rhetors to obviate taboos against ornamental artifice, such as the tropes, figures and rules of delivery set forth by Cicero and Quintilian. Such flourishes, verbal or embodied, could then be justly re-assimilated to sacred rhetoric, because it was instrumental to rousing and directing the passions.[84] Preachers strove to achieve a transmission of sublimating affect in a way that was, problematically, analogous to the transmission of what the anti-theatricalists saw as carnal affect, from the lascivious actor to the mindlessly imitative audience. The dangerous proximity of worship to playacting required codes of constraint and decorum in order for preachers and worshippers to maintain the credibility of a spiritual affect that could otherwise be undermined as histrionic. By far the most important style detailed by Hermogenes was *semnotes*, or 'solemnity', which he identified as the most appropriate style for sacred expression.[85] This style agreed with the decorum of solemnity or gravity that, given the intensification of interdenominational strife during the 1640s, increasingly required fortification. Breaches of solemnity were described in language that was suggestive of physical comedy. Notably, Parliament's 1642 ordinance closing the playhouses defines the decorum of London at the outset of civil war as one of 'solemnity' that required 'profitable and seasonable' humility: 'publike Stage-playes [do not agree] with the Seasons of Humiliation, this being an Exercise of sad and pious solemnity, and the other being Spectacles of pleasure, too commonly expressing lascivious Mirth and Levitie'.[86]

The 1637 *Booke of Common Prayer* and the 1645 Presbyterian *Directory for the Publike Worship of God* demonstrate underlying structures of Anglican and Presbyterian theatricality, respectively, while also employing an anti-theatrical criticism of gesture to encourage the restraint of embodied zeal. Almost every page of the *Book* reveals a compelling basis for criticisms that its rigidly formalised scripting transformed the worship of God into spirit-stifling, carnal rehearsal (Figs 3.1 and 3.2). At the start of morning prayer, the minister 'shall reade with a loud voyce some one of these Sentences of the Scriptures that follow. And then he shall say that which is written in the said Sentences'.[87] If we consider the space of Anglican preaching and ritual as a stage, then these 'Sentences' and the *Book*'s set prayers become features of a play-script that prompts the words to be spoken, the manner and volume of utterance, and the 'gestures' of worship:

> A generall Confession to be said by all that are present after or with the Deacon or Presbyter, all humbly kneeling [. . .] [The prayer.] The Absolution or Remission of sinnes to be pronounced by the Presbyter alone, he standing up and turning himself to the people, but they still remaining humbly upon their knees [. . .] The people shall answer. Amen.[88]

While the *Book*'s focus throughout remains the establishment of consistent, predictable and uniform worship, it nonetheless attempts to command an authentic humility that underlies enjoined gestures. The prompts subordinate the gesture ('kneeling') to the mode ('humbly'), even as they work to constrain and to compel from the outside in.[89]

The *Book* also promotes the conformity of bodily affect as instrumental to curtailing the spread of heresy, the wayward interpreting

Morning prayer.

¶ A generall Confession to be said by all that are present after the Presbyter, all humbly kneeling.

ALmightie and most mercifull Father, Wee haue erred and strayed from thy Wayes lost sheepe, Wee haue followed too much the deuices and desires of our owne hearts: Wee haue offended against thy holy Lawes: Wee haue left undone those things which wee ought to haue done, and wee haue done those things which wee ought not to haue done : and there is no health in us : but thou, O Lord, haue mercy upon us miserable offenders : Spare thou them, O God, which confesse their faults : Restore thou them that be penitent, according to thy promises declared unto mankinde in Christ Iesu our Lord : and grant, O most mercifull Father, for his sake, that wee may hereafter liue a godly, righteous, and sober life, to the glory of thy holy Name, and the saluation of our own soules. Amen.

¶ The Absolution or Remission of sinnes to be pronounced by the Presbyter alone, he standing up and turning himselfe to the people, but they still remaining humbly upon their knees.

ALmightie GOD, the Father of our Lord Iesus Christ, who desireth not the death of a sinner, but rather that he may turne from his wickednesse and liue, and who hath given power and commandement to the Presbyters of his Church to declare and pronounce to his people being penitent, the absolution and remission of their sins : The same Almighty GOD pardoneth and absolueth all them which truly repent, and unfainedly beleeue his holy gospel. Wherefore wee beseech him to grant us true repentance and his holy Spirit, that wee may receiue from him absolution from all our sins, that those things may please him which wee do at this present, and that the rest of our life hereafter may be pure and holy, so that at the last we may come to his eternall ioy, through Iesus Christ our Lord.

Amen. The people shall answer,

Then

Morning prayer.

Then shall the Presbyter or Minister begin the Lords prayer with a loud voyce. And in this, and all other places of the Liturgie, where the last words, for thine is the kingdome, &c. are expressed, the Presbyter shall reade them. But in all places where they are not expressed, he shall end at these words, but deliuer us from evill. Amen.

OUr Father which art in heaven, hallowed be thy Name. Thy kingdome come. Thy will be done in earth, as it is in heaven. Giue us this day our daily bread. And forgiue us our trespasses, as we forgiue them that trespasse against us. And leade us not into temptation: but deliuer us from evil, for thine is the kingdome, the power, and the glory, for ever and ever. Amen.

Then likewise he shall say,

O Lord open thou our lips,
    Answer,
And our mouth shall shew forth thy praise.
    Presbyter.
O God make speede to saue us.
    Answer.
O Lord make haste to helpe us.

¶ Then all of them standing up, the Presbyter shall say or sing,

Glory be to the Father, and to the Sonne : and to the holy Ghost.
    Answer,
As it was in the beginning, is now, and ever shall be : world without end. Amen.
    Answer.
Praise ye the Lord.
    Answer,
The Lords Name be praised.

¶ Then shall be said or sung, this Psalme following.
Come let us sing unto the Lord: let us make a ioyfull noise to the rocke of our saluation. Let us come before his presence with thanksgiuing, and make a ioyfull noise unto him with psalmes,

Venite ex- ultemus Domino. Psal. 95.

for

Figures 3.1 and 3.2 *The Booke of Common Prayer* (1637), fols. A2–A2v. William Andrews Clark Memorial Library, 1005889.

of scripture that was manifested in the improvisational gestures of enthusiasts. In the preface, Charles I, apparently quoting the Lords of Congregation under Edward VI – though the ascription is dubious – defines the *Book*'s set forms against wild forms of enthusiastic worship:

> *Religion was not then placed in rites and gestures, nor men taken with the fancie of ex-temporarie prayers.* Sure, the publike worship of God in his Church, being the most solemne action of us his poor creatures here below, ought to be performed by a Liturgie advisedly set and framed, and not according to the sudden and various fancies of men.[90]

The decorum of solemnity ('solemne action') provides the norm against which enthusiastic worshippers are marked as aberrant; enthusiastic 'gestures' mark dissenting practices as capricious ('sudden'), multiform ('various') and wildly imaginative ('fancies'). Like theatrical improvisation, the prayers themselves are 'ex-temporarie'.

The Presbyterian *Directory* of 1645 offers considerably more latitude to both preachers and worshippers. Worship is constrained not by script but by norms of style, and particularly by the decorum of solemnity. Adverbial prompts establish tone and manner but admit room for what we might call improvised ('ex-temporarie') speech and action (Fig. 3.3). Within the unstable political-religious climate of the 1640s, obedience to solemn decorum required admonitions against unseemly gesture in order to protect decorum's always ambiguous boundaries. The preacher must perform 'gravely, as becometh the Word of God, shunning all such gesture, voice and expressions, as may occasion the corruptions of men to despise him and his Ministry'.[91] Thus, the *Directory* defines unseemly gesture against the dominant style of solemnity ('gravely') in order to ensure that worship that is liberated from set forms does not transgress the boundaries that protect the reformed Church's legitimacy. Its concern that certain 'gesture, voice and expressions' may provoke some parishioners to contempt (through the 'corruptions of men') shows acute sensitivity to the vulnerability of the spiritual body to the distortions of theatricalising polemical discourse.[92]

Bulwer's volumes on the rhetorical gestures of the hand warn against gestural excess. Although Bulwer embraces trained gesture as 'that elegant Expositour of Nature', he protects the privileged category of the natural – associated with authentic emotion – by defining it against the overtly theatrical and, especially, the comedic.[93] The gesture of striking the forehead with the hand should 'bee confined to the Theatre, and the ridiculous Hands of Mimicks'.[94] 'The trembling *Hand* is scenicall, and belongs more to the theatre, then the forum'.[95] Nature, writes Bulwer, recalling Quintilian, 'unlesse illustrated by Art, and

Of Assembling the Congregation.

The Congregation being assembled, the Minister, after solemne calling on them to the worshipping of the great name of God, is to begin with Prayer.

In all Reverence and Humility acknowledging the incomprehensible Greatnesse and Majesty of the Lord, (*in whose presence they do then in a speciall manner appear*) *and their own vilenesse and unworthinesse to approach so neer him; with their utter inability of themselves to so great a Work: And humbly beseeching him for Pardon, Asistance, and Acceptance in the whole Service then to be performed; and for a Blessing on that particular portion of his Word then to be read: And all, in the Name and Mediation of the Lord Jesus Christ.*

The Publike Worship being begun, the people are wholly to attend upon it, forbearing to Reade any thing, except what the Minister is then reading or citing: and abstaining much more from all private whisperings, conferences, salutations, or doing reverence to any persons present, or comming in; as also from all gazing, sleeping,

Of Publike Reading holy Scriptures.

sleeping, and other undecent behaviour, which may disturbe the Minister or people, or hinder themselves or others in the service of God.

If any, through necessity be hindred from being present at the beginning, they ought not, when they come into the Congregation, to betake themselves to their private Devotions, but reverently to compose themselves to joyne with the Assembly, in that Ordinance of God which is then in hand.

Of Publike Reading of the holy Scriptures.

Reading of the Word in the Congregation, being part of the publike Worship of God, (wherein wee acknowledge our dependence upon him, and subjection to him) and one Means sanctified by him for the edifying of his People, is to bee performed by the Pastors and Teachers.

Howbeit, such as intend the Ministery, may occasionally both read the Word, and exercise their gift in Preaching in the Congregation, if allowed by the Presbyterie thereunto.

All the Canonicall Books of the Old and New Testament, (but none of those which are commonly called Apocrypha) shall be publickly read in the vulgar Tongue, out of the best allowed Translation, distinctly, that all may hear and understand.

How large a portion shall be read at once, is left to the wisdom of the Minister: But it is convenient that ordinarily one Chapter of each Testament be read at every meeting; and sometimes more, where the Chapters be short, or the coherence of matter requireth it.

confirmed by exercitation, is [. . .] but as a field untill'd, which runs wild with disorder'd productions'.[96] The art of delivery also works to moderate, or to cultivate, the expression of authentic feeling; moreover, it not only facilitates the outward appearance of genuine feeling but also curbs inward passions that threaten to make the rhetorical body unrestrained and thus discreditable.[97]

A decorum of solemnity, which demands constrained modulation of voice and movement of body, is also apparent in instruction for preachers. The solemn preacher, inspired by zeal and a caring love for his parishioners, is seen to act naturally, without the restraints or embellishments of art. Nonetheless, even such a degree of bodily freedom is rare in gestural instruction for preachers, which tends heavily toward the proscriptive. For instance, Richard Bernard, in handling delivery at the close of the oft-reprinted *Faithfull Shepheard* (1607), teaches that the preacher's countenance must not be 'lumpish, not frowning or irefull, not light, smiling as too full of laughter: but sober, grave and modest, framed after the godly disposition of the heart'.[98] 'A reverend gesture' of the body 'is to be observed. The bodie stable and right up, as nature hath framed it. The head not wagging, the eies moveable, and thy right hand onely as occasion shall be offered, but not always moving'.[99] The preacher's body must essentially be a column, 'stable' and erect, signifying virile authority. The description of the eyes and 'right hand onely' as 'moveable' suggests just how delicate, measured and sparing the preacher's gesture must be: the eyes and a single hand can move, yet only when appropriate, 'as occasion shall be offered'. For Bernard, unseemly gesture can arise from 'rash boldnesse, or an inconsiderate zeale [. . .] and by heat of affection, which have moved [preachers] to violent motions'; 'by too great feare and bashfulnesse', which yields aberrations such as coughing or nervous fidgeting; or 'els by acting upon a stage, [for preachers] cannot but shew their vaine and phantasticall motions ridiculously in a Pulpit, which they have used in prophane pastimes'.[100] The ridiculously theatrical or 'thrasonicall' style may be amended by 'serious consideration of the difference of the actions' – that is, by thinking upon the difference between 'prophane' comedic acting and solemn preaching that is motivated by authentic zeal and brought into form through the subtle art of restrained delivery.[101] In *The Schismatick Stigmatized* (1641), Richard Carter laments the histrionic style of enthusiastic preachers who 'affect an odd kind of gesture in their Poopits [Pulpits], vapouring and throwing heads, hands, and shoulders this way, and that way, puffing and blowing, grinning, and gerning ['yawning' or 'snarling'], shewing their teeth, and snuffling thorow their noses'.[102]

By the early 1640s, polemicists could draw from a rich vocabulary of theatrical rhetoric, marking rigid formalism or gestural excess, which was both rooted in the rhetorical tradition of *actio*, as it had been enriched during the golden age of London theatre, and which was, with an eye to Marprelate, infused, with increasing colour and variety, into print culture. No author made more of this vocabulary than Milton, whose political, religious and poetical development becomes clearer as we continue to trace his rhetoric of *actio* through the rapid-fire polemical exchanges of the early 1640s. Association with the stage fool threatened the legitimacy of a Presbyterian style that embraced an extemporaneousness regulated by mode or decorum.

Beating the Fool

Milton's first attacker in print styled him an indecorous buffoon. The anti-theatrical lunges of the *Modest Confutation* (early 1642), published in the midst of Parliamentary debate over the Root and Branch Petition by an anonymous author – perhaps Hall or his son – might appear from our vantage comically off-target.[103] Yet if we consider how the *Modest Confutation* altered the trajectory of Milton's theatricality, and thus how it helped to shape prominent concerns of his literary identity and poetics, we can see that it struck home woundingly.

In *Animadversions*, Milton had channelled an oppositional mode of theatricality based on improvising wit that peeled back a false modesty. Though his preface nods to the principle, from Proverbs 26:5, that it was justifiable to 'answer the fool according to his folly', Milton was by no means answering Hall in kind. Hall's rhetoric is polished and punctual. *Animadversions* is, like Milton's early prose in general, poetically effusive and metaphorical, though here that eloquence is besmirched with the scatological and vitriolic. In a polemical climate that translated literary or discursive styles into modes of bodily transgression, *Animadversions* left Milton wide open to counterattack. The *Modest Confutation* proved instructive the proverb that immediately precedes Solomon's justification of foolishness: 'Answer *not* a fool according to his folly lest thou be also like unto him' (Proverbs 26:4, italics mine). It is a verse that Milton neglects to acknowledge in *Animadversions*, yet it offered a lesson that he would not forget.

The Confuter's title suggests his strategy: since *Animadversions* was 'slanderous', he would answer it, first and foremost, by 'modestly' illustrating its immodesty (although, in truth, much of the *Modest Confutation* is comparably unrestrained and *ad hominem*[104]). The

Confuter would bring to the fore the 'scurrilous' nature of Milton's tract. The Latin *scurra* denotes both the idle, fashionable fop and the buffoon or clown of Roman comedy.[105] While 'scurrility' is proper only to the fool, it furthermore carries a sense of nasty invective. The Confuter would locate this scurrility within a context that demanded solemnity and thus would expose the author's embarrassing indecorum to ridicule.

In his preface, the Confuter suggests that the author of *Animadversions* had been 'vomited out' of the 'University [. . .] into a Suburbe sinke about London'.[106] 'Where his morning haunts are I wist not; but he that would finde him after dinner [i.e., in the afternoon], must search the Play-Houses, or the Bordelli, for there I have traced him'.[107] Of course, the Confuter has only 'traced' Milton to the 'Suburbe sinke' of Southwark through language in *Animadversions* that is associated with it: 'old Cloaks, false Beards, Tyres, Cases, Periwigs, Modona Vizzards, nightwalking Cudgellers, and Salt Lotion'.[108] (Milton would, in the *Apology*, rehearse this 'tracing' in turn, arguing that, upon the same faulty logic, the Confuter, too, must then be a dissolute playgoer.)[109] Nonetheless, the Confuter does appear to write from intelligence of Milton's time at Cambridge and what might have been Milton's habits in London shortly before the wars. The Confuter grapples with a new adversary; he *might* have known Milton's name, but he struggles to wrap his mind around this divided identity, this author who seemed at once erudite and populist, tragic and comedic. Milton did not reside far from the 'Suburbe sinke', which had been home to amphitheatres such as the Swan, the Rose and the Globe. In 1641, he would have easily been able to catch a play at the second Globe – rebuilt in 1614 – and might have seen, if he so chose, fencing, fighting or animal baiting. His nephew, Edward Philips, reported in 1675 that 'once in three Weeks or a Month', his uncle

> would drop into the Society of some young Sparks of his Acquaintance, the chief whereof were [. . .] two Gentlemen of *Gray's*-Inn, the *Beau's* of those Times [. . .] With these Gentlemen he would so far make bold with his Body, as now and then to keep a Gawdy-day.[110]

Philips might be trying to soften the Restoration caricature of Milton as a dour Puritan, yet the information is nonetheless specific enough to be more than plausible. As Campbell and Corns note, 'make bold with his Body' 'remains a puzzling phrase', yet its association with 'Gawdy-day' seems to suggest that, during these alleged forays with 'young Sparks', Milton took license to wear more fashionable and colourful attire that his modesty might otherwise have kept locked away.[111] We can imagine something of the licentious rake depicted by the Modest Confuter:

dawdling in the suburbs, frequenting playhouses and taverns, and even womanising. As we have seen, the younger Milton had, in the *Elegia sexta*, suggested that the playhouses – 'the infamous halls of faithless Circe' – had a potentially contorting pull upon him: 'I must flee'.[112]

The Confuter's implication that the author bends below his social rank to enjoy the allurements of the suburbs serves a strategy of characterising him as a 'Ringleader' of 'the very beasts of the people'.[113] The author, suggests the Confuter, descends, in his profane diction, to 'canting', a dialect of suburban rogues fetishised by gallants in Jacobean city comedies and closely associated with the suburban amphitheatres: 'Such language you should scarce hear from the mouths of canting beggars', let alone 'in a treatise of controversall Theologie, as yours might have been thought, had you not thus prevented it'.[114] Milton's tract violates decorum because it descends to a level of discourse that belongs in the sewer of Southwark.

The Confuter begins the prefatory epistle by noting that the reader is likely 'acquainted with the late and hot bickerings between the Prelates and Smectymnuans'.[115] He then cleaves Milton from his Smectymnuan allies by characterising him as an awkward disrupter of serious theological dispute:

> To make up the breaches of whose solemn Scenes, (it were too ominous to say Tragicall) there is thrust forth upon the Stage, as also to take the eare of the lesse intelligent, a scurrilous Mime, a personated, and (as himself thinks) a grim, lowring, bitter fool.[116]

Here, the Confuter moves to identify the author with Marprelate, whose first tracts were intended to serve as a type of interlude, between weightier polemics, that would work to 'take the eare of the lesse intelligent' – that is, of the mass of common labourers who leaned toward reformist Protestant principles. By translating the 'late and hot bickerings' into 'solemn Scenes', the Confuter is able to represent Milton as an indecorous interluder who enters 'in[to] the breaches' of these scenes only to disrupt them. 'Scurrilous' identifies Milton with the buffoon or stage clown, while 'Mime' identifies him, specifically, with the gesturing pantomime. The prose of *Animadversions* is rendered into body. Its offences to the dignity of religion are translated into gestures that exceed propriety, given the solemn scenario.

Even as the Confuter characterises *Animadversions* as a theatrical gaffe, he nudges himself outside of the theatre of print by suggesting that, while tragic decorum is here more appropriate than comedic indecorum, 'tragedy' is too extreme a label for the struggle over Church government: 'it were too ominous to say Tragicall'.[117] A moderate, non-violent solution can be achieved more congenially. The phrase also works to distance the debates from the dynamic pacing of dramatic interaction and the economy of dramatic time. Tragedy, it suggests, presents events too ominously and is not a fit framework for cultural debate, which requires time, patience, moderation and, above all, solemnity.[118]

In the *Apology*, a response to the *Modest Confutation*, Milton carefully engages with, transforms and redirects the terms of the anti-theatrical attack levelled against him. He responds to the Confuter's strategy in a way that distances his person from theatricality without entailing a disavowal of theatricality and that remakes the gesturing, self-pandering fool into a characteristically Anglican figure. Responding to the accusation that 'plays had been seen' – the passive voice suggesting a bemused belittling of the charge – Milton concedes that, yes, he did attend plays, at least as their attendance was compelled when he was a student at Cambridge.[119] He writes of one Cambridge performance – quite possibly the disastrous staging of Peter Hausted's *Rival Friends* during a royal visit in 1632 – in which would-be Anglican divines had been hissed off the stage because of their exaggerated declamation and gesture.[120] As we have seen, he portrays them as 'writhing and unboning their Clergie limmes to the antick and dishonest gestures of Trinculos, buffons and bawds; prostituting the shame of [the ministers' vocation] to the eyes of Courtiers and Court-Ladies, with their Groomes and *Madamoisellaes*'.[121] Kranidas, addressing scholarly speculation about the reference to 'Trinculos', observes that Milton, here, might be drawing upon the recent pamphlet, *The Plot Discovered and Counterplotted* (1641), in its similar attack on the Anglicans:

> *Tom Trinkilo* was never more acted to the life, than by many of these, who go under the name of the Angells of the Church of *England*, and by their mimicall, apish, and ridiculous cariages seek to please the humours of the grave sparks and gallants of our times.[122]

Before beginning to break this passage down further, I would like to take us a bit deeper into anti-theatrical culture by further pursuing this figure of Trinculo. Of course, there is the Trinculo of Shakespeare's *The Tempest*, a foolish figure who would not be out of place on such a stage. Milton certainly knew the play, as evident in a stage direction, as it were, that appears in *Paradise Regained*.[123] Both Milton and the author of *The Plot Discovered and Counterplotted* refer to a 'Trinculo' in a casual reference that would seem to suggest that readers could readily recall the figure. 'Trinculo' is a player in the discourses of theatrical culture. As it turns out, there is a far more reliable source text for Milton's reference, yet I present it with the caveat that, even here, the reference remains casual enough to suggest a general and broad familiarity with the figure of Trinculo.

Both the '*Tom Trinkilo*' of *The Plot Discovered and Counterplotted* and Milton's 'Trinculo' derive from satirical moralist Richard Brathwaite's poem 'An Age for Apes'. The work exists only in a 1658 publication titled *An Excellent Piece of Conceipted Poesy; Divided into Two Subjects: A Voice from the Vault; and An Age for Apes*. The ability to identify 'An Age for Apes' as a source rests upon a footnote, added to page 249, which indicates that the 'Novels' or news mentioned just above 'relate to the time wherein they were first writ, being according to the Original. An. 32'.[124] The note clarifies that 'An Age for Apes' appeared first, in some form, in 1632. Brathwaite's strategy – to satirise various groupings of English society by representing them as so many 'apes' (hence 'apish' in *The Plot Discovered*) – agrees with the vogue of estates satire that Martin Butler locates in late-Caroline city comedies – and that informed characterisation in the playlets during the early 1640s.[125]

Although Brathwaite would identify as a royalist during the civil wars, Milton would have looked sympathetically to his critiques of general debauchery and of legal, mercantile, property, clerical and court corruption. Milton also would have taken interest in Brathwaite's abundant use of theatrical rhetoric, which Brathwaite repeatedly deployed to detail the vain posturings of the unprincipled within a society of spectators. Brathwaite was also a Caroline dramatist, though his plays do not survive. He appears to have collaborated with Thomas Randolph and is best known for the riotous *Barnabae itinerarium* (1636) and *Mercurius Britanicus, or The English Intelligencer* (1641).[126] The latter is a closet play that targets the judges of the 1637 ship-money trial of John Hampden; it announces itself as '*a tragic-comedy at Paris: acted with great applause*'.[127]

'An Age for Apes' is so saturated with themes and diction that appear in Milton's account of the playacting divines that an inventory would be excessive. We see courtiers posturing to catch the eyes of spectators. We see the corrupt advancement of university graduates taking orders. 'Courtiers', 'Court-Ladies', 'grooms', Madamoiselles, 'Fooles' and buffoons appear aplenty, as do bawds and prostituted women. The Ape of Vaine-glory notes his

> affection [. . .] to bestow
> My bounty on some publique Antick show,
> So I may have my name endors'd at large,
> That it was reared at my proper charge,
> Then building of a *Church*, or any use

Which simple people terme religious:
These works I hate.[128]

Through the theme of 'aping', the poem surveys forms of imitation, colouring them with the language of theatre and of *actio*. The passage that most directly informs Milton's depiction of the young Anglicans in the *Apology* occurs in the speech of the Chymicall Ape, an alchemist-turned-con-turned-incompetent-doctor. After foreswearing alchemy, the Chymicall Ape recruits

> a companie
> Of wittie *Rake-hells*, roaringly profest,
> And in all forlorne courses bravely flesh't.
> Flankt were my troups with *bolts, bauds, punks,* and *panders,*
> *Pimps, nips* and *hints*[?], *Prinado's, highway-standers*;
> All which were my *familiars*, and would doe
> With quick dispatch whats'ere I put them to.
>   [. . .]
> For to relate those nimble *tricks* we plaid,
> Though on the publick Stage they be displaid,
> As th' subtile-headed *Alchimist* can show;
> Or th' *Alchimists* own Ape, *Tom. Trinculo*,
> One hold I fitting to be here exprest
> By which you may judge better of the rest.[129]

Tom Trinculo then speaks, explaining how some in this gang of scoundrels – of bawds, panders, pimps and prostitutes, of pickpockets, cons and robbers – played elaborate cheats at a card game at court. The 'nimble *tricks*' are 'on the publick Stage [. . .] displaid' because Trinculo is attesting to them in a printed book. Brathwaite is riffing from Jonson's *The Alchemist*, which features a smaller gang of cons, including the prostitute Doll Tearsheet and Subtle, who plays the alchemist ('subtile-headed *Alchimist*'). Tom Trinculo may be understood as a version of *The Alchemist*'s Jason or 'Face', whose role in the scheme is, in part, to organise the cons of the 'venture tripartite' while finding gulls in the city and preparing them to be cozened.[130] The Trinculo of Milton's *Apology*, thus, is not so much a foolish figure as a deft con, a comedic criminal whose roots pass through literary culture as deep as Jonson. So much for 'Trinculo'.

The passage from the *Apology* reconstitutes several anti-theatrical barbs from the *Modest Confutation*. If he had attended a play, Anglicans were the actors. If he had embodied the gesturing fool for the sake of satirical effect, the Anglicans are gesturing fools through and through. If he was at once a 'scurrilous Mime' and a brothel patron, the Anglicans go further by taking prompts from the 'buffons and bawds' with whom they share the stage: *they* are the prostitutes of their ministry and of their own spiritual bodies. If Milton had breached decorum, these 'overacted', thus undermining the coherence of the dramatic situation.¹³¹ If he had 'sought to catch the eare of the less intelligent', these sycophantically employ 'antick and dishonest gestures' to catch the eyes of aristocrats and their adherents. The scenario suggests that antic gesture is the logical corollary of Anglican formalism. What resolves the paradox is that, here, wild gesture marks a failure to restrain the external manifestation of an ethos that has been forfeited to spectator desire. While obedience to set forms contrarily creates a 'crust of formalitie', the process of the spiritual body's transformation is essentially the same: the Anglicans 'bring the inward acts of the *Spirit* to the outward and customary ey-service of the body'. Such change of 'the very shape of *God* himselfe, into an exterior, and bodily forme' signals the same forfeiture of the spiritual body.

Just as 'God and man [were] now ready to explode and hisse' prelacy 'out of the land', so do Milton and his fellow spectators hiss these unskilled actors from the stage:

> There, whilst they acted and overacted, among other young scholars, I was a spectator: they thought themselves gallant men, and I thought them fools; they made sport, and I laughed; they mispronounc'd, and I mislik'd; and, to make up the *atticism*, they were out, and I hist.¹³²

Milton no longer appears on stage as the overacting comedian who is unable to discern that his breaching of 'solemn Scenes' would be wildly inappropriate; rather, he is an engaged and discerning spectator of theatre and a critic of Anglican theatricality. If in *Animadversions* he had placed his authorial persona upon an implied stage and had rallied a broad audience to participate as discerning spectators of a textual uncasing, here he changes subject position: now a spectator, he can no longer be associated with the fools on stage but is, rather, their antagonist. The radical pliancy of the Anglican spiritual body violates a more essential spiritual decorum; that body belongs fully to the world and not to God. 'Writhing and unboning', the divines become, as it were, uncontrolled oscillations of flesh; while forfeiting the ethical and spiritual infrastructure that allows one to stand approved in the sight of God, they have given themselves over to the forces of wealth and worldliness, allowing these to misshape their spiritual being.

Milton performs a similar move when handling the Confuter's 'likening of those grave controversies' over Church government 'to a piece of Stagery'.¹³³ He names Hall, 'whether in Buskin or Sock', the 'chiefe Player' of the prose drama, 'be it a boasting *Thraso*, or *Davus that troubles all things*, or one who can shift into any shape'.¹³⁴ Hall is thus associated with the braggart soldier and the servile *scurra* of Plautine and Terentian comedy. Like the staged Anglican divines, he is a shapeshifter without a stable ethical or spiritual centre.¹³⁵ His body corresponds with a discourse that feigns modesty and paternal care to conceal carnal motivations – wealth, power and fear. Milton is thus able to switch between theatrical critiques of rigid formality and of comedic excess, since each demonstrates a venality that manifests bodily in a way that belies an appropriate spiritual relation to scripture. At times, he mixes modes within the same phrase, as when, later in the tract, he refers to the 'finicall goosery' of the Anglican 'neat Sermon-actor'.¹³⁶ Here, the fastidiousness of the minister accords with the 'neat' manner by which he performs his stunted sermon, following script without feeling the scripture. And yet, his affected fastidiousness makes him come off ridiculously, as a pulpit goose.

Milton's phrase, 'to make up', or to complete, 'the *atticism*' is rooted in the politics of classical *actio*. It indexes the relationship between polemical culture and theatrical representation. It demonstrates Milton's self-consciousness of the dangers of rendering his authorial identity theatrical and suggests sensitivity to the abuses of theatricalising rhetoric and representation. He acknowledges himself to have been playing, in his critique of actor-Anglicans, the role of one who conforms to the refined and stilted predilections that Cicero associates with the stoic Brutus, a chief oratorical rival. In *Orator*, Cicero imagines the harsh reception that an Asiatic orator, singing 'in a whining voice with violent modulations', might have received at the hands of a strict Athenian audience: 'who would have put up with him [. . .] who would not have cried "Put him out?"'¹³⁷ Yet, Cicero does not aim to criticise Asiatic oratory but, rather, to emphasise the narrowness of a stoic taste that militates against the body and its expressiveness as a rhetorical medium. Seemingly diverging from Cicero, but in fact sharing Cicero's reservations, Milton creates a scene through which he can turn the critique of enthusiastic gesture back upon the Confuter and the prelates. At the same time, by drawing upon Cicero's critique of stoic restraint, Milton indexes how the aspersing rhetoric of 'antick and dishonest gestures' is manufactured within polemical exchange. The Confuter's 'make up the breaches' becomes 'make up the *atticism*' in Milton, who thus explodes the Anglicans by placing them within the dramatic scenario that they have created.

If we consider Milton's efforts to distance himself from the foolish persona that he had fashioned in *Animadversions*, it is surprising that he adopted Proverbs 26:5 as the epigraph for the 1645 *Colasterion*, which was appended to *Tetrachordon*, the last of Milton's divorce tracts. Where Milton had struggled, in the anti-prelatical tracts, to establish a credible voice for liberty, both the *Doctrine and Discipline of Divorce* (1643) and *Areopagitica* (1644) made that struggle all the more difficult, as they quickly earnt him notoriety, to some as a divorcer and a libertine. 'The criticism which his views attracted', writes Hammond, 'routinely associated him and them with the lower-class radicals who in the mid-1640s were promoting a range of heretical ideas, and his doctrine was often seen as an invitation to libertinism and a rejection of divine and human law'.[138]

It might seem odd that Milton would have devoted an entire tract to defending himself against the anonymous *An Answer to a Book Intituled, The Doctrine and Discipline of Divorce* (1644), for he was, admittedly, facing no formidable adversary. Indeed, Milton seems entirely concerned with lashing an ignorant and presuming inferior – the title of the tract means 'place of punishment' – so as to consolidate his own worthiness and dignity as an author. In response to this purpose, foolishness returns wholly transformed. Rather than once again locating himself on a figurative stage of print, in *Colasterion*, Milton answers the fool according to his folly while going out of his way to distance himself yet further from that contorted, populist body. To answer a fool according to his folly does not, in *Colasterion*, equate to adopting a foolish vehicle for satire but, rather, to punishing the fool in a manner appropriate to the crime – in this case, a presumptive ignorance. In answering, Milton targets his opponent's lower social status. He counters the populism that inflects the fool's utterance and body with a brisk, unapologetic elitism. And he counters the generic affiliation of this populism with comedy by renouncing the comedic as a polemical and poetic mode. Once more, he does not renounce theatricality per se; rather, he affiliates himself with tragic dignity.[139]

Those seeking a populist Milton in the later 1640s and 50s might be surprised to see that *Colasterion* is both intellectually and socially elitist, and self-consciously so. Milton's nameless opponent is an 'illiterate' and 'arrogant presumer', guilty of 'peasantry rudeness'.[140] He wears a 'Livery cloak' and speaks 'pretended Languages with such a low and home-spun expression of his Mother *English* along'.[141] His 'stile [is] flat and rude, and the matter [...] shallow and [...] unwary'.[142] Milton claims that the vocation of his assailant had, by occasion, been revealed to him: 'ratifi'd to bee no other, if any can hold laughter, [...] then an actual Serving-man', a 'creature' who had 'turn'd Solliciter' 'to the improvement of his wages'.[143] Where the Modest Confuter had 'traced' Milton to the playhouses and brothels of London's suburbs, so Milton claims intelligence of the anonymous author's demeaning social status. By the end of his preface, Milton has not only defamed the author but has, moreover, insulted the poor and labouring generally: illiterates, peasants, servants, domestic thread-spinners ('home-spun') and inconsequential men of law.

The anti-populist rhetoric of *Colasterion* returns Milton twice to the figure of the stage fool. Yet where, in *Animadversions*, Milton had identified directly with the fool and its associations with popular opposition and satire, here the fool is brought upon the stage of print to be disavowed formally. The Confuter had represented the author of *Animadversions* as awkwardly performing an indecorous interlude, yet, here, Milton's target is the interluder. Milton justifies the treatment of the 'trivial' opponent by suggesting that, 'though hee bee the lowest person of an interlude, hee may [yet] deserv a canvasing'.[144] As 'canvassing' primarily refers to a punishment that involved tossing the offender in a canvas sheet, it would seem that Milton, here, associates the 'lowest person of an interlude' with the shaming rituals of the rural poor. Indeed, the tract may be understood as a punitive tossing of the clownish presumer in sheets of print, the tract itself the 'place of punishment' (the meaning of the Greek, *colasterion*).

As Milton concludes, he bids the fool farewell:

> I have now don that, which for many causes I might have thought, could not likely have bin my fortune, to bee put to this under-work of scowring and unrubbishing the low and sordid ignorance of such a presumptuous lozel. Yet *Hercules* had the labour once impos'd upon him to carry dung out of the *Augean* stable. At any hand I would bee ridd of him: for I had rather, since the life of man is likn'd to a Scene, that all my entrances and *exits* might mix with such persons only, whose worth erects them and their actions to a grave and *tragic* deportment, and not to have to doe with *Clowns and Vices*.[145]

Milton's scorn for labour here is unusually sharp. It is his 'fortune' to be compelled to perform the 'under-work' of house servants. He compares the compelled labour of answering his opponent to polishing kitchenware and to house-cleaning: 'scowring and unrubbishing'. He has performed the fifth labour of Hercules; yet this labour is no heroic task but, rather, the drudgery of clearing dung from the stables of Augeas. Milton is eager to move on: 'I would bee ridd of [this author]'. His distinction of Hercules from the basest labourer immediately translates into distinctions between 'gravity' and levity, tragedy and comedy, the noble and the foolish, and the heroic and the vicious. He seeks exclusive company: 'that all my entrances and *exits* might mix with such persons only, whose worth erects them and their actions to a grave and *tragic* deportment'. 'Worth' implies wealth as readily as it does virtue. Genre, class and style converge: on one side, this 'clown', at once a country dolt and a stage fool; on the other, our noble poet – still, implicitly, theatrical, but no fool.

Milton would continue to tangle with opponents by animadverting their prose, repeatedly returning to the Modest Confuter's *ad hominem* strategy of digging up or of fabricating narratives about his opponent. He employed this strategy with particular relentlessness to Alexander More, whom Milton knew to have played a role in the publishing of *Regii sanguinis clamor* (1652), a response to Milton's *Pro populo Anglicano defensio* (1651, '*First Defence*'). While Milton's *Pro populo Anglicano defensio secunda* (1654, '*Second Defence*') and *Pro se defensio* (1655, '*Defence of Himself*') indulge in the gleeful scurrility so abundant in *Animadversions*, Milton has stopped playing games with foolish personae and with the language of theatrical foolery. 'Milton's personal onslaught', note Campbell and Corns, 'really functions as the spice to reward his readers for their effort, rather than as part of the serious argument of his response. He needed a victim'.[146] From another perspective, Milton's *ad hominem* attacks are merely signs of a heavier, duller pen.

More's surname gave Milton every opportunity to drag him to the place of punishment *as a fool*. Indeed, Milton uses the name to generate several puns. Since *morus* names the mulberry tree in Latin, and since Milton finds More clouded in sexual scandal, his opponent doubles as a sculpture of Priapus that is made of mulberry wood.[147] Transliterated from the Greek, *morus* also means a fool or simpleton, whence 'moron'. But we are no longer dealing with stage fools here, only, as it were, a sexually out-of-control stupid person. As we have seen in Chapter 1, Milton does stage himself in the *Second Defence*, though here he is a triumphant orator, befitting a decorum of solemnity, who observes the admiring spectators of European nations:

> I behold countenances strange and numberless, and all, in feelings of mind, my closest friends and neighbours [...] Some hasten to receive me with shouts of applause, others, in fine, vanquished by truth, surrender themselves captive. Encompassed by such countless multitudes [...] I am bringing back [...] liberty [...] so long an exile.[148]

Rather than dealing with '*Clowns* and *Vices*', he faces the world with 'a grave and *tragic*', however exultant, 'deportment'.

We see Milton deploying a more flexible anti-theatrical rhetoric in *Eikonoklastes*. As Daniel Shore argues, the tract aims to extract, from the admirers of the *Eikon Basilike*, those readers who should be worthy enough to see through the King's self-martyrising and into its self-serving motivations.¹⁴⁹ The anti-theatrical rhetoric serves three strategies. Rather than representing the King himself as a fool, Milton represents those taken in by the *Eikon Basilike* as the type of base audience that, in earlier tracts, sought the stage fool as fodder. Merely the name of a 'King' as the author, he claims,

> needs no more among the blockish vulgar, to make [the book] wise, and excellent, and admir'd, nay to set it next the Bible, though otherwise containing little els but the common grounds of tyranny and popery, drest up, the better to deceiv, in a new Protestant guise, and trimly garnish'd over.¹⁵⁰

If Charles I is to be taken, as Milton proposes, as though 'in his Book alive', then the book presents a Charles who playacts to catch the eyes and sympathies of the throng.¹⁵¹ To do so, the book has to 'dress' over Charles's 'tyranny and popery [...] the better to deceiv'. Charles appears sympathetic, in part, because the book shows him 'in a new Protestant guise'.

The disguising of the tyrant as a person of the people leads Milton to Shakespeare. Milton compares the King's 'overlate Apologies and Meditations' to the 'the last will of *Caesar* being read to the people', a set-piece of Shakespeare's *Julius Caesar*.¹⁵² The scene of Antony's eulogy illustrates that 'what bounteous Legacies' Caesar 'had bequeath'd' the Romans 'wrought more in that Vulgar audience to the avenging of his death, then all the art he could ever use, to win thir favor in his life-time'.¹⁵³ So with *Eikon Basilike* and the English people. Milton refers to the prayers of Charles in *Eikon Basilike* as 'these Soliloquies' – whether or not truly those of 'the late King, as is vulgarly beleev'd, or any secret *Coadjutor*' (i.e., John Gauden).¹⁵⁴ Identifying Shakespeare as 'one whom wee well know was the Closest Companion of these his [the King's] solitudes', Milton compares Charles to Shakespeare's Richard III. He compares one of Charles's professions of good will to four lines of Richard's dialogue, where the tyrant speaks 'in as high a strain of pietie, and mortification, as is utterd in any passage of this Book'.¹⁵⁵

Imagery and language associated with the Caroline court masques extend the argument that the King's book is a theatrical performance of Charles 'in his Book alive'. The attack on the masquing Charles is, to some extent, opportunistic, in that it recalls the fact that the execution scaffold was erected along Whitehall Palace, the venue of several of the most lavish Caroline masques. Milton seizes upon William Marshall's notorious frontispiece: the King at prayer is 'drawn out to the full measure of a Masking Scene, and sett there to catch fools and silly gazers'.¹⁵⁶ The 'quaint Emblems and devices', as well as the Latin motto, that adorn the portrait are 'begg'd from the old Pageantry of some Twelfth-night's entertainment at *Whitehall*'.¹⁵⁷ The 'silly gazers', who never had access to the masques, now have a masquing King Charles I in their pockets.

Moreover, the rhetoric of *Eikonoklastes* works to diminish Charles as a frivolous enthusiast of profane theatricals. To begin with, the King indulged in 'the superstitious rigor of his Sundays Chappel'.¹⁵⁸ Like high Anglican worship, the King's secretly Catholic devotions are ritual theatre. Next, Milton faults 'the licentious remissness of his Sundays Theater', evoking the common reformist complaint against the attendance of plays on the Sabbath.¹⁵⁹ Milton sees opportunity to impugn the 1637 *Book of Sports and Pastimes* – 'that reverend Statute for *Dominical Jiggs* and May-poles, publish'd in his own Name, and deriv'd from the example of his Father *James*'.¹⁶⁰ Milton culminates his argument that the King's devotions are inherently theatrical – both false and intended to win the passions of the vulgar – by observing that one of Charles's prayers, supposedly expressed on the eve of the execution, was pilfered almost verbatim from Pamela's prayer in 'the vain amatorious Poem of Sir *Philip Sidney's Arcadia*; a Book in that kind [prose romance] full of worth and witt, but among religious thoughts, and duties not worthy to be nam'd'.¹⁶¹ Milton pivots on the genre of prose romance to strip the King's scaffolded body of tragic dignity.

> Yet hardly it can be thought upon (though how sad a thing) without som kind of laughter at the manner, and solemn transaction of so gross a cousenage: that he who had trampl'd over us so stately and so tragically should leave the world at last so ridiculously in his exit, as to bequeath among his Deifying friends that stood about him such a pretious peece of mockery to be publisht by them, as must needs cover both his and their heads with shame [. . .] if they have any left.¹⁶²

Milton's claim of plagiarism turns focus on the tragedy of the King's beheading to the tragedy of the manner by which he left the world: 'how sad a thing'. However, no matter how sad, the pilfering of Pamela's prayer cannot be answered 'without som kind of laughter'. The act defines Charles as a risible comedic figure. The King, 'who had trampl'd over us so stately and so tragically', is now seen to have departed 'so ridiculously in his exit'. The phrase recalls Milton's expressed wish, in *Colasterion*, 'that all my entrances and *exits* might mixe' with only those of 'a grave and *tragic* deportment'.

In *Eikonoklastes*, the various depictions of Charles I as a theatrical deceiver, cheap masquer and comedic figure aim specifically to alter the way that the admirers of *Eikon Basilike* conceptualise themselves.

They are, in each case, implicated in the King's theatricality. The reader is discouraged from identifying with the King's 'Deifying friends that stood about him', that now 'must needs cover both his and their heads with shame'. It is tempting to shake one's head at *Eikonoklastes* as a failed rhetorical document. After all, it passed through just two editions while *Eikon Basilike* was passing through scores. Yet it is mistaken to assume that Milton's goal in writing *Eikonoklastes* ever was to win over the people at large. Rather, he had his eye, at once, on powerful supporters of Charles and on those hostile to the Rump Parliament, including the Scottish Presbyterians, who would drive the next and final stage of the conflict in an effort to restore the monarchy. Milton was not merely encouraging them to see through the King's disguise and to discern its poor quality as a performance; he was also encouraging them to distinguish themselves from the throng that idolised him 'in his Book alive', a book intended to 'catch the worthles approbation of an inconstant, irrational, and Image-doting rabble': 'The rest, whom perhaps ignorance without malice, or some error, less than fatal, hath for the time misledd [...] may find the grace and good guidance to bethink themselves, and recover'.[163] The rabble was not the rhetorical audience but, rather, a foil for that audience.

Although Milton would leave the stage fool behind after *Colasterion*, the exchanges of print during the early 1640s would help to condition the flexibility of anti-theatrical rhetoric that we see in *Eikonoklastes* and would anticipate the more complex theatricality of the Restoration masterworks. The stage fool is formally disavowed in *Colasterion* yet would be absorbed into Milton's poetics and his identity as an exegetical poet – until it would be set loose again in *Samson Agonistes*.

Exegetical Poetics and the Straits of Improvisation

Stanley Fish has argued that the claims of scriptural self-sufficiency in *Of Prelaticall Episcopacy* render Milton's first anti-prelatical tract aimless, with nothing to do but to deny its own supplementarity: it performs an exegesis that 'is superfluous, and because it is superfluous, it is also, potentially at least, impious'.[164] For Fish, the all-sufficient scripture encourages the reader's interpretive stasis, associating 'danger and impiety [...] with movement'.[165] Movement is precisely what *Animadversions* brings to Milton's exegesis and to his poetic relation to scripture.

While Milton does, at moments in each of the anti-prelatical tracts, continue to employ the rhetoric of the plain or naked scripture, the theatrical tactics of *Animadversions* lead him beyond himself to a poetic-prophetic fugue that anticipates the exegetical advances to come. From the alternately stichomythic and more discursive exchanges of *Animadversions* comes a sustained flight that carries the tract's style from comedic satire to the heights of a prophetic song that celebrates victory over prelacy and the imminence of a New Jerusalem.[166] The passage anticipates what Milton would describe, in *Reason*, citing the theologian Don Paraeus, as the 'majestick image of a high and stately Tragedy, shutting up and intermingling her solemn Scenes and Acts with a sevenfold *Chorus* of halleluja's and harping symphonies'.[167]

The Modest Confuter would absorb the millenarian passage into his anti-theatrical strategy. He defines it as a 'long, tedious, Theatricall, big-mouthed, astounding Prayer'.[168] 'Big-mouthed' and 'astounding' imply indecorous *actio*, recalling once more Hamlet's admonishment against stage-foolery to those who 'out-Hero[d] Herod' in order 'to split the ears of the groundlings'.[169] 'Theatricall', the fugue is a mere performance of holy zeal – not the real thing.

In the *Apology*, Milton would defend the passage as not 'a prayer so much as a hymne in prose frequent both in the Prophets, and in humane authors'.[170] The 'stile' was therefore 'greater then for an ordinary prayer'.[171] The 'hymne in prose', he continues, 'consisted most of Scripture language' and 'had no *Rubricke* to be sung in an antick Coape upon the Stage of a High Altar'.[172] Not relying on a rubric, it is authentic, driven by holy zeal. It produces, then, inspired prophecy that reworks the matter of scripture into new form; in essence, it improvises upon scripture-as-script within the theatre of print. Milton maintains the anti-theatrical assault on high Anglican formalism while projecting the characteristic rhetoric of wayward zeal – 'antick and dishonest gestures' – onto the overwrought costume to be worn on the stage of Anglican ritual.

The 'hymne in prose' of *Animadversions* brims with the energy of renewal and re-creation that is enabled by the new dispensation of Christ and that is to fulfil Old Testament prophecy. Consisting 'most of scripture language', it responds to a call for creative outpouring that accompanies the 'renovating and reingendring Spirit of God', which, in the 'present age', has 'manifestly come downe among us, to doe some remarkable good to our Church or state'.[173] It exalts and harnesses the Spirit that mediates the dispensation, that makes new ('renovates') and re-creates ('re-ingendr[s]'). Milton compares the English people, at the dusk of episcopacy, to the Israelites in Exodus wandering the desert after the destruction of their enemies in the Red Sea. He invokes the ordinances of Leviticus, comparing episcopacy to the bread of the 'old levin'.[174] Thus, the Mosaic Law is associated with Leviticus, particularly with the injunction against the leavening of bread; Milton's 'hymne', on the other hand, moves toward Revelation, as though rising with yeast. Revising the account of the Israelites' construction of the tented temple in Leviticus, he cites 'the brightnesse of thy descending cloud that now covers thy Tabernacle' and claims to see God walking through the sanctuary, 'amidst those golden *candlesticks*, which have long suffer'd a dimnesse amongst us through the violence of those that had seiz'd them, and were more taken with the mention of their gold then of their starry light'.[175] The language of Leviticus – of the old law, of the old forms and indeed of the old Church, of the old episcopacy, of the old carnal superficiality – is giving way to the pure light of Revelation: 'Come therefore O thou that hast the seven starres in thy right hand, appoint thy chosen *Priests*'.[176]

In the 'renovating and reingendring Spirit of God', Milton locates an invocating of zealous, inspired song. God has 'sent out the spirit of prayer upon thy servants over all the Land', and has 'stirr'd up their vowes as the sound of many waters about thy Throne'.[177] He calls upon God to 'perfect, and accomplish thy glorious acts'.[178] These come with acts of the faithful, who in their gratitude 'may [. . .] perhaps take up a Harp, and sing thee an elaborate' – produced through artful labour – 'Song to Generations'.[179] The theatre of print resounds not only with heckling, hissing and explosion but also, at a much higher register, with a hymn sung by the poet amidst a chorus of the faithful. A theatrical structure has been maintained: the 'opposite spectators' have become praying and singing 'servants'; the spectacle of satirical punishment has become the spectacle of apocalypse: 'thy Kingdome is now at hand [. . .] Now the voice of thy Bride calls thee, and all creatures sigh to bee renew'd'. The improvising wit and gesturing body of the 'grim fool' has become the voice of Christ's true Church.[180]

The phrase 'most of scripture language' looks forward to the straits of improvising exegesis that Milton would explore, and would attempt to navigate, in his Restoration poetry. He would do this, in part, by repeatedly staging his body as the poet-exegete and, in part, by foregrounding each protagonist's efforts to navigate those straits. The seeds of a scripture that will raise trying questions – How can the Fall be justified? What caused it? To what degree does equality extend to women before and after the Fall? Is Samson a hero or an anti-hero? What motivates him? When and how did Jesus defeat Satan and regain Paradise, or the promise of Paradise? – burst open here. The dramatic sketches in the Trinity Manuscript aimed above all to *show* scripture for the sake of moral edification. But in *Paradise Lost*, *Paradise Regained* and *Samson*

Agonistes, Milton would actively seek out scriptural problems as sources of poetic creation.

In 1641, Milton had stepped into the persona of the satirical stage fool while bolstered by the justification of Proverbs 26:5. By the time that Laud was beheaded in 1645, Milton's relation to foolishness had become significantly constrained. Proverbs 26:4, 'Answer not a fool according to his folly, lest thou also be like unto him', would have seemed intimately wise. The fool was disavowed, but it was not wholly relinquished. Rather, it was beaten, flipped, transformed and submerged, and would attain new energy and purpose in differing genres and modes. For the remainder of his life, Milton would continue to associate theatricality with the problems of discerning spiritual authenticity and of properly managing the scriptural mandate to reveal and to fulfil its truths in a spirited re-engendering through creative exegesis. But what were the boundaries between which zealous verbal and physical expression could be legitimately spiritual and scripturally obedient? If obedience to God and to the Spirit requires poetic acts of renewal and re-creation, at what point does such improvisation become erroneous or transgressive? If there are boundaries, do these shift or change when the social or cultural context of exegesis and utterance also shifts or changes? From all that we have seen of Milton's theatricality, surely they do. But at what point does spirited performance become antic and dishonest gesturing?

It is not surprising that the invocations of *Paradise Lost*, in each of which Milton again stages himself, explore the questions that theatricality poses for him as an exegetical poet writing to an audience. How can I, he searches, reconcile my intimate communion with God with my vocation as a teacher and as a prophet for an audience 'fit [. . .] though few'? To what extent does the public essence of printed poetry threaten to distort the ethos of the poet under God, to bend the spiritual body into transgression, into irrevocable error? How can I fulfil the scriptural mandate to renovate and re-engender without breaching the bounds of divine decorum, let alone solemn decorum, and without ruining sacred truths? How can I move poetically in the Spirit without overreaching, to the explosion of God?

> Least from this flying Steed unrein'd, (as once
> *Bellerophon*, though from a lower Clime)
> Dismounted, on th' *Aleian* Field I fall
> Erroneous there to wander and forlorne.[181]
>   [. . .]
>   Higher Argument
> Remaines, sufficient of it self to raise

> That name [of Tragedy], unless an age too late, or cold
> Climat, or Years damp my intended wing
> Deprest, and much they may, if all be mine,
> Not Hers who brings it nightly to my Ear.[182]

Notes

1. Milton, *Animadversions*, *CPW*, I, p. 747.
2. See R. Kirk and W. P. Baker, Preface to *Animadversions*, *CPW*, I, especially pp. 653–6.
3. E. M. Waith, 'The Metamorphosis of Violence in *Titus Andronicus*'; for the authorship controversy, see J. D. Carroll, '*Gorboduc* and *Titus Andronicus*'.
4. For discussion of these publications and their dating, see D. M. Wolfe, Introduction, *CPW*.
5. Campbell and Corns, *John Milton*, p. 137; see J. A. Miller, 'Milton and the Conformable Puritanism of Richard Stock and Thomas Young', pp. 89–92.
6. T. Kranidas, *Milton and the Rhetoric of Zeal*, p. 89.
7. Ibid., p. 102.
8. Ibid., p. 93.
9. R. A. Anselment, '*Betwixt Jest and Earnest*'. See also J. Egan, 'Milton and the Marprelate Tradition'.
10. Horace, *The Art of Poetry*, line 316: *reddere personae scit convenientia cuique* (the poet 'knows how to assign each character that which is appropriate to that character'; translation mine).
11. See above, pp. 6–10, 17–18; and below pp. 177–8, 194–6.
12. See Hammond, *Milton and the People*, pp. 43–9.
13. See Coiro, 'Anonymous Milton', p. 612.
14. Milton, 'Lycidas', *WJM*, I.i, line 193.
15. See Milton, *Reason*, *CPW*, I, pp. 809–10; also Campbell and Corns, *John Milton*, pp. 109–23.
16. Campbell and Corns, *John Milton*, p. 131.
17. G. E. Aylmer, *Rebellion or Revolution?*, pp. 8–34; C. Hill, *Century of Revolution*, pp. 9–107; L. Stone, *Causes of the English Revolution, 1529–1642*, pp. 117–33.
18. E. Jones, 'The Loyalty and Subsidy Returns of 1641 and 1642', p. 237. See also Campbell and Corns, *John Milton*, p. 133, n. 9.
19. H. Pierce, 'Anti-Episcopacy and Graphic Satire in England, 1640–1645', p. 813. See also S. Achinstein, 'The Politics of Babel in the English Revolution'; and D. Cressy, *England on Edge*, pp. 281–376.
20. See M. Butler, *Theatre and Crisis*, pp. 181–249; and S. Wiseman, *Drama and Politics in the English Civil War*, pp. 19–39.
21. See below, pp. 92–3.
22. Pierce, 'Anti-Episcopacy and Graphic Satire', p. 826.
23. R. Overton [?], *A New Play Called Canterburie His Change of Diot*, title page; see M. Heinemann, *Puritanism and Theatre*, pp. 237–57.
24. Cressy, *England on Edge*, p. 300.

25. Hill, *Century of Revolution*, pp. 104–5.
26. See above, pp. 5–6.
27. Collinson, 'Ben Jonson's *Bartholomew Fair*', p. 166; for possible staging of playlets, see Wiseman, *Drama and Politics in the English Civil War*, pp. 81–7; and M. Butler, *Theatre and Crisis*, pp. 238–48: 'It seems quite possible that these playlets represent a further development of the jig or afterpiece, that satirical dialogue or song-and-dance by the clowns so popular in the Elizabethan theatre' (p. 238).
28. See Egan, 'Milton and the Marprelate Tradition', p. 104.
29. For Tarlton, see Gurr, *Playgoing in Shakespeare's London*, pp. 150–8.
30. M. Marprelate [pseud.], *Oh Read over D. John Bridges [The Epistle]* (1588), p. 1.
31. Milton, *Animadversions*, *CPW*, I, pp. 662–3; see Milton's justification of this passage in the *Apology*, *CPW*, I, p. 904.
32. Black, 'The Rhetoric of Reaction', pp. 724–5.
33. Egan, 'Milton and the Marprelate Tradition', p. 107; see D. R. Como, 'Secret Printing, the Crisis of 1640, and the Origins of Civil War Radicalism'; N. Smith, 'Richard Overton's Marpriest Tracts'; and Hill, 'Radical Prose in 17th Century England'.
34. Overton [?], *A New Play Called Canterburie His Change of Diot*, p. 4.
35. Wolfe, Introduction, *CPW*, I, p. 178.
36. D. L. Smith, 'From Petition to Remonstrance', p. 209.
37. One playlet that addresses the imminence of the shut-down is the anonymously written *Stage-Players Complaint*.
38. J. Hall, *An Humble Remonstrance to the High Court of Parliament* (1641), p. 1.
39. Smectymnuus, *A Vindication of the Answer to the Humble Remonstrance* (1641), p. 220.
40. Anon., *Modest Confutation*, fol. A3.
41. Milton, *Animadversions*, *CPW*, I, p. 664.
42. Ibid., pp. 663–4.
43. Anon., *Modest Confutation*, p. 32.
44. Ibid., p. 32; Anon., *News from Hell, Rome and the Innes of Court*.
45. J. M. French (ed.), *The Life Records of John Milton*, II, p. 43.
46. Anon., *Modest Confutation*, p. 23.
47. Milton, *Animadversions*, *CPW*, I, p. 663.
48. See L. Potter, *Secret Rites and Secret Writing*, pp. 168–9.
49. Milton, *Of Reformation*, *CPW*, I, p. 522.
50. Ibid., p. 520.
51. Ibid., p. 521.
52. Ibid., pp. 521–2.
53. Cf. Milton, *Areopagitica*, *CPW*, II, p. 527.
54. Milton, *Reason*, *CPW*, I, pp. 828, 833.
55. See above, pp. 34–5.
56. D. Zaret, 'Petitions and the "Invention" of Public Opinion in the English Revolution', p. 1498.
57. S. Achinstein, *Milton and the Revolutionary Reader*, p. 103.
58. See, for instance, Anon., *The Discontented Conference Betwixt the Two Great Associates* (1641), which stages Laud and Strafford as they survey

their wrongs, exchange blame and resign themselves to imminent justice; also L. Price, *A New Disputation betweene the Two Lordly Bishops* (1642), which shows Laud and Archbishop of York John Williams bickering as neighbours in the Tower.
59. Overton [?], *The Bishops Potion*, p. 2.
60. Ibid., p. 4.
61. Ibid., p. 4; see M. Butler, *Theatre and Crisis*, pp. 242–5. Consider the more figurative regurgitation in Anon., *Canterbury's Will* (1641), which shows Laud recording his crimes and fears in his last will and testament.
62. Milton, *Animadversions*, *CPW*, I, p. 662. See above, pp. 23, 40–2.
63. J. Sawday, *The Body Emblazoned*, p. 67.
64. W. Heckscher, *Rembrandt's Anatomy of Dr. Nicolaas Tulp*, pp. 32, 98; as cited in P. Mitchell, *The Purple Island and Anatomy in Early Seventeenth-Century Literature, Philosophy, and Theology*, p. 414.
65. Sawday, *The Body Emblazoned*, p. 135.
66. Hall, *Defence* (1641), pp. 23–4.
67. Milton, *Animadversions*, *CPW*, I, p. 668.
68. The connection between the anatomy theatre and the scaffold is strengthened by the fact that the bodies of the executed were often used in the anatomy theatre; Sawday, *The Body Emblazoned*, pp. 3–4.
69. Milton, *Animadversions*, *CPW*, I, p. 664; cf. Lieb, 'Milton's *Of Reformation* and the Dynamics of Controversy', pp. 68–9.
70. Milton, *Animadversions*, *CPW*, I, p. 664.
71. Ibid., p. 664.
72. Hall, *Defence*, p. 1. See M. Grossman, 'The Dissemination of the King', pp. 250–81.
73. Milton, *Animadversions*, *CPW*, I, pp. 665–6.
74. See H. S. Limouze, 'Joseph Hall and the Prose Style of John Milton'.
75. Cf. Hall, *Defence*, pp. 1–2: 'The truth of God, which I maintaine, shall beare me up against the discouragements of my confessed weaknesse; In which just confidence I doe gladly fly to the Bar of this high and honourable Court, craving no favour but justice'.
76. Milton, *Animadversions*, *CPW*, I, p. 666.
77. Ibid., p. 726.
78. Ibid., p. 726.
79. See above, pp. 40–2.
80. See below, pp. 177–8, 194–6.
81. Shuger, *Sacred Rhetoric*, p. 47.
82. G. Herbert, 'The Windows', lines 11–15.
83. J. Mayne [1633], 'On Dr. Donne's Death', p. 20.
84. Shuger, *Sacred Rhetoric*, p. 193.
85. Hermogenes, *'On Types of Style'*, pp. 19–26.
86. An Ordinance of Both Houses, for the Suppressing of Stage-Playes, no page number.
87. Church of England, *The Booke of Common Prayer*, fol. A2.
88. Ibid., fol. A2.
89. Cf. Milton, *Animadversions*, *CPW*, I, p. 682.
90. Church of England, *The Booke of Common Prayer*, fol. A3v.

91. General Assembly of the Kirk of Scotland, *A Directory for the Publike Worship of God*, p. 29.
92. Cf. M. Le Faucheur, *An Essay upon the Action of an Orator* (1680). '*All Affectation* is *odious* [. . .] The *Orator* must manage his *Gesture* so nicely, that there may be nothing, if possible, in all the *Dispositions* and *Motions* of his *Body*, which may offend the *Eyes* of the *Spectators*' (p. 174); for instance, 'you must never *clap* your *Hands*, nor *thump* the *Pulpit*, nor *beat* your *Breast*; for that smells of the *Juggler* and the Mountebank' (p. 196).
93. Bulwer, *Chirologia*, p. 28.
94. Bulwer, *Chironomia*, p. 50.
95. Ibid., p. 104.
96. Ibid., pp. 20–1.
97. Cf. Anon., *Advice to a Parson* (1691); and R. Rapin, *Reflections upon the Eloquence of these Times* (1672), pp. 111–12.
98. R. Bernard, *The Faithfull Shepheard* (1607), pp. 88–9; reprinted 1609 and 1621.
99. Ibid., pp. 88–9.
100. Ibid., pp. 88–9.
101. Ibid., p. 90.
102. R. Carter, *The Schismatick Stigmatized*, p. 7.
103. For discussion of authorship and date, see Campbell and Corns, *John Milton*, pp. 145–6.
104. See, for instance, Anon., *Modest Confutation*, fol. A4: 'Horrid Blasphemy! You that love Christ, and know this miscreant wretch, stone him to death, lest your selves smart for his impunity'.
105. See Milton, *Areopagitica*, *CPW*, II, p. 510: 'scurril *Plautus*'.
106. Anon., *Modest Confutation*, fol. A3v.
107. Ibid., fol. A3v.
108. Ibid., fols. A3, A3v.
109. Milton, *Apology*, *CPW*, I, pp. 885–6.
110. Quoted in Campbell and Corns, *John Milton*, p. 134.
111. Ibid., p. 134.
112. See above, pp. 59–60.
113. Anon., *Modest Confutation*, p. 23.
114. Ibid., p. 2; cf. T. Dekker and T. Middleton, *The Roaring Girl* (1611), V, i.
115. Anon., *Modest Confutation*, fol. A3.
116. Ibid., fol. A3.
117. Ibid., fol. A3.
118. Soon after the opposition playlets began to appear, a range of moderationist playlets also appeared that aimed to sway public discourse and parliamentary action away from root-and-branch extirpation of episcopacy and towards more moderate reforms. See, especially, Anon., *A Dialogue Betwixt Three Travellers* (1641); and H. Peacham, *Square-caps Turned into Roundheads* (1642). See also Potter, *Secret Rites and Secret Writing*, pp. 33–4.
119. Milton, *Apology*, *CPW*, I, p. 887.
120. See Coiro, 'Anonymous Milton', p. 616.
121. Milton, *Apology*, *CPW*, I, pp. 887–8.
122. As quoted in Kranidas, 'Milton's Trinculo'; also Campbell and Corns, *John Milton*, p. 46.

123. See below, p. 189.
124. R. Brathwaite, *An Excellent Piece of Conceipted Poesy*, p. 249.
125. M. Butler, *Theatre and Crisis*, pp. 141–80.
126. See J. Sanders, 'Brathwaite, Richard (1587/8–1673), poet and writer', in H. C. G. Matthew and B. Harrison (eds), *Oxford Dictionary of National Biography* (Oxford: Oxford University Press, 2004), available at <http://www.oxforddnb.com.ezaccess.libraries.psu.edu/view/article/3290> (last accessed 4 August 2016).
127. Brathwaite, *Mercurius Britanicus*, title page.
128. Brathwaite, *An Excellent Piece of Conceipted Poesy*, pp. 143–4.
129. Ibid., p. 231.
130. Jonson, *The Alchemist*, I, i, line 170.
131. Milton, *Apology*, *CPW*, I, p. 887; see above, pp. 8–9.
132. Ibid., p. 887.
133. Ibid., p. 879.
134. Ibid., p. 879.
135. Brathwaite, *An Excellent Piece of Conceipted Poesy*, p. 124: 'Now this *Politicall* time-studied *Ape* / Could soone transform himself to any shape; / For if with *holy-men* hee had to deal, / He could pretend a counterfeited zeale'.
136. Milton, *Apology*, *CPW*, I, p. 935.
137. Cicero, *Orator*, p. 325: *Quonam igitur modo audiretur Mysus aut Phryx Athenis, cum etiam Demosthenes exagitetur ut putidus? Cum vero inclinata ululantique voce more Asiatico canere coepisset, quis eum ferret aut potius quis non iuberet? Ad Atticorum igitur auris teretes et religiosas qui se accommodant, ei sunt existimandi Attice dicere* (p. 324).
138. Hammond, *Milton and the People*, pp. 70–1.
139. See Egan, 'Rhetoric, Polemic, Mimetic'.
140. Milton, *Colasterion*, *CPW*, II, p. 724.
141. Ibid., p. 725.
142. Ibid., p. 725.
143. Ibid., pp. 726–7.
144. Ibid., p. 726.
145. Ibid., pp. 756–7.
146. Campbell and Corns, *John Milton*, p. 260.
147. See Milton, *Pro populo Anglicano defensio secunda*, *CPW*, IV, p. 566; and *Pro se defensio*, *CPW*, IV, p. 722.
148. See above, p. 26.
149. Shore, *Milton and the Art of Rhetoric*, pp. 30–5.
150. Milton, *Eikonoklastes*, *CPW*, III, p. 339.
151. Ibid., p. 341.
152. Ibid., p. 342.
153. Ibid., p. 342; see the discussion of '*Andronicus Comnenus* the *Byzantine* Emperor', who learnt by 'imitation' the style of 'Saint *Pauls* Epistles', and who was torn to pieces by the people 'notwithstanding his Saints vizzard' (p. 361).
154. Ibid., p. 346.
155. Ibid., p. 361.
156. Ibid., p. 342.

157. Ibid., p. 343.
158. Ibid., p. 358.
159. Ibid., p. 358.
160. Ibid., pp. 358–9.
161. Ibid., p. 363.
162. Ibid., p. 364.
163. Ibid., p. 601.
164. Fish, 'Wanting a Supplement', p. 44.
165. Ibid., p. 44.
166. Cf. Milton, *Areopagitica*, *CPW*, II, p. 554: 'What wants there to such a towardly and pregnant soile, but wise and faithfull labourers, to make a knowing people, a Nation of Prophets, of Sages, and Worthies. We reck'n more then five months yet to harvest; there need not be five weeks, had we but eyes to lift up, the fields are white already'.
167. Milton, *Reason*, *CPW*, I, p. 815.
168. Anon., *Modest Confutation*, p. 22.
169. Shakespeare, *Hamlet*, *NS*, III, ii, lines 12, 9.
170. Milton, *Apology*, *CPW*, I, p. 930.
171. Ibid., p. 930.
172. Ibid., p. 930.
173. Milton, *Animadversions*, *CPW*, I, p. 703.
174. Ibid., p. 705.
175. Ibid., pp. 705–6.
176. Ibid., p. 706.
177. Ibid., p. 706. Cf. above, p. 34.
178. Ibid., p. 706.
179. Ibid., p. 706.
180. Ibid., p. 707.
181. Milton, *Paradise Lost*, *WJM*, II.i, VII, lines 17–20.
182. Ibid., *WJM*, II.ii, IX, lines 42–7. The compelling but rarely voiced argument that Milton's invocations dramatise different versions of the poet, and that, in fact, tell the story of the poet, is explored in R. McMahon, *The Two Poets of Paradise Lost*.

Chapter 4

Theatre of Vegetable Love: *Paradise Lost*

During the early 1640s, the theatre of print, as Milton imagined it, showed him encompassed by an allied audience, performing a type of exegetical poetics that, despite being impelled by zeal, was nonetheless constrained by cultural discourses and interpretive manoeuvres that he was beginning to understand but that he could not fully control. At the same time, he was theorising a type of drama that appears, for the most part, devoid of the struggles and complexities of character that defined his own experience in print culture and that would be so integral to the greatness of *Paradise Lost*. His consideration of the public staging of dramas in a newly reformed London manifested in scores of sketches, in the Trinity Manuscript, for dramas based on stories from scripture and British history. Together, these evince his desire for England to achieve the moral and spiritual edification that would be required of a nation aspiring to be a vanguard of the coming Millennium.

However, by the time that Milton began to write *Paradise Lost* in the mid-1650s, his faith in a general populace would be all but gone. The final passage of the second edition of the *Readie and Easie Way to Establish a Free Commonwealth* (1660) implored, on the eve of the Restoration, a remaining

> abundance of sensible and ingenuous men [...] to bethink themselves a little and consider whether they are rushing; to exhort this torrent also of the people, not to be so impetuos, but to keep thir due channel [...;] to stay these ruinous proceedings; justly and timely fearing to what a precipice of destruction the deluge of this epidemic madness would hurrie us through the general defection of a misguided and abus'd multitude.[1]

Paradise Lost (1667) opens with a view to the innumerable fallen angels, who are 'rowling in the fiery Gulfe', the 'fiery Deluge', after having been 'Hurld headlong flaming [...] / With hideous ruine and combustion down / To bottomless perdition'.[2] The final passage from the *Readie and*

Easie Way and the opening scene of *Paradise Lost* form a continuity of various implication. (It is perfectly plausible that they were composed at or near the same time.) Hammond understands the scene in Hell, a political scene dramatising the co-dependencies of a tyrant and a 'misguided and abus'd multitude', as one of three microcosms or 'proto-communit[ies]' by which Milton explores the troubled relationship between liberty and democracy in the epic.[3] In the first chapter, we saw the relationship between the bodily form of the tyrant and the bodily form of the infernal throng as theatrical and as recursive; a community and a leader maintained a balance of power based on a sympathy of loss, vulnerability, fear and desire. We have seen variations of this theme played out repeatedly in Milton's works. But, just as the epic follows a shift between forms of epic heroism, a shift from the Virgilian Satan towards 'the better fortitude / Of Patience and Heroic Martyrdom', so too does Milton's theatrical poetics, in *Paradise Lost*, retract from politics to focus on the relationship between individuals as a site of potential regeneration.[4]

Leaving Hell and mid-century political culture behind, we enter, now, into a realm of flowers and holy light. It is the scene of Hammond's second 'proto-community', where we find two spouses struggling to strengthen each other in obedience to God, despite the threat of an impinging and insinuating Satan. With an eye to the theatrical operations of the Garden, we will continue to deal with Milton's antitheatrical concern that the spectators who encompass the subject loosen embodied spirituality and fortitude. Yet we will also see Milton turning inward to consider how smaller social configurations can regenerate and thrive under God, within an inexorably theatrical world. First, however, we need to consider why a 'Milton the dramatist' could not have written *Paradise Lost*.

Aristotle, Dramatic Time and the Problem of Eve

Efforts to redefine Milton as a dramatist have often leaned on the fact that the Trinity Manuscript contains two *dramatis personae* lists and two substantial sketches for a drama about the Fall. Thus, the story goes, *Paradise Lost* was a product of Milton the dramatist in addition to being the work of Milton the epic poet. There might be some truth in this assertion, if only because these sketches factored in his turn *away* from performed drama as a literary genre and toward theatricality, a mode of representation that could account more adequately for the psychological and affective transformations of characters beyond the bounds of dramatic time. Milton absorbed theatricality into the fabric of epic. This absorption proved critical in resolving perhaps the most difficult question that faced the poet who would strive to justify the ways of God to humankind. How could the Fall have happened if humankind was born 'sufficient to have stood, though free to fall'?[5]

Far from 'the writings and interludes of libidinous and ignorant Poetasters', the dramas suggested in the Trinity Manuscript sketches would have served, in Milton's mind at that time (1640–2), a restructured, Presbyterian state as 'doctrinal and exemplary to a Nation'.[6] To some extent, they are, in aim and in much of their subject matter, heirs of the Corpus Christi (or 'mystery') plays that were performed as late as the middle of the sixteenth century. Besides providing entertainment, the Corpus Christi plays brought to life the stories of scripture, to which lay audiences had no direct access in the written scripture. Like the Corpus Christi plays, most of Milton's sketches suggest little complexity of character. Rather, they appear conceived to teach religion and to inspire English nationalism.

Timothy Burbery, in his attempt to find in Milton the popular playwright, suggests that Milton's proposal for 'set and solemn Paneguries' was, in earnest, a 'plea' and 'request to the authorities to keep the theaters open', in part 'based on his (partial) ownership of one of those theaters'.[7] The idea is pure make-believe and completely bereft of supporting evidence. Rather, in the idea of 'set and solemn Paneguries', Milton was suggesting a proposal that would contribute to his efforts of civic reform. Several of Milton's early prose tracts were proposals. *Reason* laid out what he believed, at the time, was the most rational and scripturally supported structure for a state church. *Areopagitica* did not merely criticise Parliament for re-enacting papal censorship; it also suggested how 'bad books' could be digested into virtue by a readership nourished by a liberated book trade.[8] *Of Education*, a proposal directed to Samuel Hartlib, sketched forth a less scholastic and more holistic educational program that could help to advance the 'repair[ing] of the ruins of our first parents'.[9] The *Doctrine and Discipline of Divorce* called directly for a new way of thinking about and of legislating divorce.

The sketches in the Trinity Manuscript – as we understand them through the lens of the proposals for 'set and solemn Paneguries' in *Reason* – appear intended to be some part of a government program. As Milton understood it, the design would redirect the public's appetite for drama to a tradition 'set' by government and 'solemn' in decorum; it would help to shape England into a Godly nation.[10] The plays that he imagined would work at once affectively, helping to temper cultural angst, and didactically, offering models of vice and virtue while teaching the Bible and British history. To meet these aims, the dramas would closely follow principles of Aristotelian dramaturgy, including *peripeteia* (reversal), *anagnorisis* (recognition) and *catharsis* (the purging of emotion through identification). Milton would have first encountered the *Poetics* in Daniel Heinsius's *De tragica constitutione* (1611), which presented the emended Greek beside the Latin.

Scholars have laboured to locate traces of the sketched dramas in the epic. Merritt Y. Hughes calls *Paradise Lost* an 'epic built out of dramas' – but here 'drama' can mean little more than self-contained episodes of dialogue or, simply, represented scenes. As easily can the scene, in Spenser's *Faerie Queene*, of Redcrosse Knight's dissolute bathing with Duessa, or of his grinding down by Despair, etc., be considered 'dramas' built into his epic.[11] Barbara Lewalski sees a type of pastoral drama in book IV; a 'brief moral interlude', a georgic dialogue and comedic resolution in book V; a 'dialogue of love' in book VIII; 'Aristotelian tragedy' in book IX; and 'Christian tragedy' in book X.[12] The helpfulness of these labels is limited, in that they presuppose a determining link between genre and purpose, in that they impose questionable generic labels, and in that they unravel a polychrome poetics into a neat sequence of monochrome threads.[13]

John G. Demaray has been more successful in linking the Trinity Manuscript sketches to the epic. In particular, he shows that the masque of allegorical maladies that appears in the most developed sketch on the Fall – 'Adam Unparadiz'd' – makes its way into the prophecies delivered by Michael in books XI and XII.[14] Although Milton first began to imagine *Paradise Lost* as a drama during the time when he was writing the anti-prelatical tracts, he would, in the supervening decades, develop a keen sense of the limitations of dramatic mimesis. In particular, a drama on the Fall would never be able to justify the ways of God to humankind because it could never do justice to Eve. Milton would address this problem not in a drama but, rather, in the theatrical poetics of an epic.

When Milton flipped through the pages of scripture to locate stories that might serve the purpose of state theatre, such as implied by the 'set and solemn Paneguries' mentioned in *Reason*, he readily fell back on the principles described by Aristotle in the *Poetics*. For examples of the dominance of Aristotelian dramaturgy in the sketches, we can look to 'Abram from Morea, or Isack redeemd' and 'Cupids Funeral Pile. Sodom Burning', two of only a handful of sketches that Milton developed beyond the sparsest of notes. 'Abram from Morea' focuses exclusively on interactions and turbulence that take place within Abraham's home during a brief span on 'the fift or sixt day after Abrahams departure'.[15] Milton omits from his sketch the crisis of faith by which the story is best known: Abraham's test of obedience to God, despite his paternal love, to sacrifice his only son, Isaac. Instead, Milton focuses on what unfolds at Abraham's home as he prepares to return. Tension builds during the speeches of Abraham's steward and of a chorus, which relates the 'sorrow', '*per*plexity' and 'frigh[t]full dreams' of Sarah.[16]

The drama would hinge on two *peripeteia* that correspond with the revelations of messengers. First, 'some shepheard or companie of merchants', who had been 'passing through the mount in the time that Abram was in the mid work', reveal the horror of infanticide to Sarah.[17] 'Lamentations, fears, [and] wonders' ensue that are, for the audience, invitations to pathos.[18] Abraham remains absent in the drama, until a second reversal brings about a joyful conclusion. Having not sacrificed Isaac, 'last he himselfe comes in with a great Train of Melchizedec whose shepheards being secret eye witnesses of all passages had related to thir master, and he conducted his friend Abraham home with joy'.[19] Milton follows Aristotle closely in exploiting turning points and discoveries, which Aristotle identifies as the most powerful strategies for inducing catharsis.[20] The drama appears to be a consummate Aristotelian tragedy until the second reversal makes it a tragedy of happy closure.[21] Most of the Biblical and British sketches follow the Sidneyan moral-aesthetic logic that the good should be made imitable examples through their fortune, whereas the bad should be made examples, through their downfall, of what not to imitate.

In the vast majority of the sketches, Milton follows Aristotle's prioritisation of plot over character. Abraham might come off as an imitable example of obedience, yet the sketch suggests no intent to develop his character, to provide any sense of the depth of his struggle and of the quality of his obedience. We have no access to his thoughts and passions, to the twists and turnings of his inner drama; rather, we are shown simply that he has obeyed God and that he has returned home with joy. Indeed, the reversals and recognitions focus exclusively on Sarah and her household. However, Sarah is not represented as a moral agent; thus, her character would not appear to develop. This focus may suggest Milton's attempt to distinguish the drama from Theodore Beza's *Abraham sacrifant* (1552, translated into English by Arthur Golding in 1577) – just as the brief description for a drama on Macbeth deviates markedly from Shakespeare's *Macbeth*.[22] Regardless, the choice to exclude Abraham's spiritual, psychological and emotional crisis sidesteps a unique challenge for the dramatist and his intended audience. Given its turn toward happy closure, the drama might have also been intended as helping to 'allay the perturbations' of minds during a time of great uncertainty for the nation.

Several of the Trinity Manuscript sketches follow Aristotle in employing spectacle as an additional instrument to induce cathartic pity and fear. If staged, plays such as 'The Golden Calfe', 'The Quails', 'The Murmurers' and 'The Deluge' likely would have foregrounded spectacles of divine punishment.[23] In 'Cupids Funeral Pile. Sodom Burning', the catastrophe occurs during the Sodomite 'Solemnity', which recalls the banquet scene of the *Maske* in resembling a debased court masque.[24] The catastrophe would proceed with an avenging angel of the Lord that descends from above as a *deus ex machina* 'all girt with flames'.[25] The angel's delivery of God's vengeance would define the 'Solemnity' as an antimasque that is annihilated by the spectacle of divine judgement.[26] Sodom's king and Lot's son-in-law 'fall down with terror' at the sight of the flames.[27] As the play would end with the Angel's 'short warning to all other nations to take heed', the 'terror' would elicit emotional response that would be based on identification further inflected or intensified by moments of reversal and recognition.[28] We hear the implicit call for vigilance over England's moral and spiritual fortitude. Lot, spared this punishment, becomes an imitable example of the obedient one just man. 'Cupids Funeral Pile' was a sketch for a drama intended to serve the purpose of nurturing virtue in the English people by showing the spectacular punishment of the wicked, thus teaching spectators to 'deplore the general relapses of Kingdoms and States from justice and Gods true worship'.[29]

In *Reason*, Milton not only endorses drama's capacity for teaching through exempla of vice and virtue, but also suggests that it could – like epic poetry – invite the audience to navigate the 'wily suttleties and refluxes of mans thoughts from within'.[30] Wiliness and subtlety are traits associated with the crafty slaves and knaves of Roman comedy. They are also associated with insidiousness or intellect that moves behind the surface of the outward person. Shakespeare's Iago and Hamlet come immediately to mind. The phrase 'refluxes of mans thoughts from within' represents dynamic interiority in terms of churning water. It suggests traces of humoral theory and anticipates Milton's interest in the passions as a conflux.[31] Milton is just beginning to feel out how he might further revise Aristotelian dramaturgy for his purposes. Of course, he would never fulfil these purposes in staged drama; however, he would in the epic. While considering the genre of epic in *Reason*, he wonders whether 'the rules of *Aristotle* herein are strictly to be kept, or nature to be follow'd, which in them that know art, and use judgment is no transgression, but an inriching of art'.[32] The reality of 'nature' – of human nature, in particular – is beginning to drift from what is capable when 'strictly' following 'the rules of *Aristotle*'. The deeper interest and understanding of this 'nature' would further the 'inriching of' Milton's 'art' – even if this enriched aesthetics would further limit his audience.

The drafts for a drama about the Fall include a pair of relatively spare *dramatis personae* lists, a sketch, titled 'Paradise Lost', which contains some details of plot and division into acts, and a more developed sketch under the title 'Adam Unparadiz'd'.[33] Where 'Abram from Morea' occludes the critical scene of a thwarted infanticide, so, too, does 'Adam Unparadiz'd' omit what would be the epic's centrepiece: the temptation and Fall of humankind. In the sketch, the narrative of temptation and fall is related through Gabriel, a chorus and Lucifer. Adam and Eve enter as beings already fallen: 'having by this time bin seduc't by the serpent [. . .] confusedly cover'd with leaves'.[34] We see conflict only as Adam and Eve 'accuse one another' – 'especially Adam', who 'layes the blame to his wife' and 'is stubborn in his offence'.[35] The sketch's capacity for catharsis that backs moral example hinges on the moment when, after viewing 'a mask of all the evils of this life & world', Adam 'is humbl'd[,] relents, [and] dispaires', as he will in book XI, lines 495–511 of *Paradise Lost*.[36] The spectacles of suffering and Adam's response are intended to induce pity and fear, just as the spectacle of the Lord's avenging angel induces the lamentations of Sodom's king and Lot's son-in-law in 'Cupids Funeral Pile'. In the epic, the turn from despair to regeneration will play out, largely, in the dialogic agon between Adam and Eve in book X; yet, in the sketch, Milton employs allegories that externalise and foreshorten the process of emotional transformation.[37] Adam – it is unclear what Eve is doing at this time – is further instructed by 'faith, hope, & charity', before he 'repents[,] gives god the glory[, and] submits to his penalty'.[38] Whereas *Paradise Lost* will seek out the audience 'fit [. . .] though few' – one that will need to be adept to its complexities of character development – 'Adam Unparadiz'd' focuses on material and techniques that would have been more effective in reaching a broader audience that included the uneducated.

The sketches were as a much a product of Milton the religious and civic reformer as they were of Milton the poet. The Hellenistic 'Paneguries', which he imagined could contribute to the consolidation of a Godly state, were never held, of course.[39] The theatrical entertainments of the mid-1650s – such as William Davenant's *The Siege of Rhodes* and its sequel – served an entirely different purpose; like the Stuart masques, they addressed elite audiences. The sketches, in allowing Milton to dwell on the essence and workings of catharsis, and to explore the relationship between dramatic time and his increasing sense of original sin's theological complexity, nonetheless had a formative impact on the theatricality that would be seen in *Paradise Lost*, *Samson Agonistes* and *Paradise Regained*.

The Fall raised daunting challenges at the intersection of character and theology. The question of how the unfallen Eve could have come to commit original sin had caused the exegetes no end of difficulty.[40] Was she created imperfect, already fallen? Did she fall suddenly, or did a fall *in occulto*, a secret and shadowed lapse into evil desire, precede the transgression? This crux, hinging upon a mysterious causality, unfolded into a problem of narrative. What kind of narrative could lead to the Fall of humankind without slipping into readily available clichés about Eve? For the exegetes, these questions easily became questions of, indeed accusations about, Eve's character. Should Eve be shown as inherently flawed, even as wicked, as predestined to fall? As a generally good character who falls through a sudden error in judgement? Or as a psychologically complex character who develops tragic depth throughout a process of action? If the Fall demands a *lapsus in occulto* in order to avoid the failures of previous exegeses, then what kind of timeline would such representation demand? If the theology of original sin *requires* the idea of a secret Fall, then could a drama represent this process to spectators?

Had Milton been familiar with other Fall dramas published in the seventeenth century, he would have noted the regularity by which the problem of causality found a theologically unsatisfying resolution in the defamation of Eve's character. Dramatic depictions of Eve failed to represent the Fall plausibly within dramatic time without avoiding a lapse into the circularity of anti-feminist exegesis, whereby the wickedness of woman is established by the Fall, while the Fall, in turn, depends upon Eve's *a priori* wickedness. *L'Adamo* (1613), by Giambattista Andreini, depicts Eve as seduced by a snake with a female human head, torso and arms. The figure of Vain Glory remains hidden and watching and emerges once Eve plucks and eats. *Adamo caduto* (1647), by Serafino della Salandra, likewise employs the woman-serpent to make Eve her own tempter.[41]

Milton was likely familiar with the *Adamus exul* (1601) of the Dutch jurist Hugo Grotius, whom he had met in 1638, while in Paris.[42] Milton's replacement of the title of 'Adam in Exile', which he crosses out, with 'Adam Unparadiz'd', might suggest that he demurred from Anglicising Grotius's title.[43] *Adamus exul* shows a more sympathetic Eve who resists the serpent, yet even she confesses that the serpent 'deceived with cunning [her] simplicity', since she was 'made by [her] very sex susceptible to wiles'.[44] The tradition of the self-tempted Eve was well rooted in Renaissance culture. Milton, when visiting St Peter's Basilica in 1638, could not have missed Michelangelo's Eve on the ceiling of the Sistine Chapel.[45] There, Eve reaches with her left hand toward the apple in the left hand of the serpent that is twined around the Tree of Knowledge – the serpent's body merging into the hips, torso, breasts, shoulders and head of a woman.[46]

While Milton scholars have shown keen interest in the idea of a dramatic, and particularly a Shakespearean, influence on *Paradise Lost*, the problem of causation and characterisation, which requires the substructure of a *lapsus in occulto*, depends on a different type of influence.[47] We have seen this type of influence in the ways that spectators worked upon the staged actor. This is the influence that, in the *Apology*, makes the bodies of the staged divines 'writh[e]' and 'unbon[e]' their limbs while 'prostituting' their vocation 'to the eyes' of the elite.[48] We have seen, in abundance, that the way that Milton evaluates theatre depends on how he understands the desire that links actor to audience and audience to actor.[49] Epic was, for Milton, a genre that could productively render a range of literary genres into a single fabric. The challenges of psychological, affective and bodily liquidity posed by staged performance could function flexibly within the epic, as means to profound characterisation.

The Nature of Milton's Optics

Milton's response to the problem of causation and character would require the further 'inriching' of his poetry through his exploration of 'nature' – not merely human nature, but, also, the workings of an ecology that he understood to be imbued with divine spirit. In this nature resides the 'influence' of eyes upon the theatrical body.

In the last two decades, scholars have variously pursued how Milton's writings engage with discoveries of the New Science. Angelica Duran and Angus Fletcher have explored Milton's response to a rapidly evolving mathematics, physics and cosmology.[50] Recently, some have turned to Newton.[51] Scholarship has also focused on the post-Baconian empirical science that informed the experiments and publications of the Royal Society. Karen Edwards surveys the presence of 'natural history' in the poem, exploring Paradise's plants and animals for their symbolic and heuristic significance as part of the 'Book of Nature'.[52] Her approach is, itself, discernibly empirical: she collects the flora and fauna of Milton's Garden and analyses their semiotic functions within the narrative. Joanna Picciotto reads *Paradise Lost* as extending post-Baconian experimentalism, which provided methods and instruments abetting empirical discovery as a means to corporate knowledge integration.[53]

As with Edwards, Picciotto offers an empiricist – or 'experimentalist' – who appears bound to the subject–object structure of empiricism itself. Picciotto turns both reader and author into experimenters, the poem itself into an 'instrument', whereas Edwards gives us the delight of the collector.[54]

The remainder of this chapter considers how the cosmology, horticulture and materiality of Milton's Eden enabled him to represent the spousal drama of Adam and Eve and to dramatise the transformation of the subject-in-motion. His representation of these aspects of Edenic nature helped him to absorb theatricality into a much more limited and focused social scenario. Particularly through the insights of optical theory, Milton was able to represent unfallen beings who are capable of emotional fluctuations, their touch, communication and acts of looking played off against the force of encompassing spectators lurking unseen. Of course, *Paradise Lost*, in which a single piece of fruit plays an epic role, does depict elements of the natural world as objects – collectible, nameable, describable, semiotic. Yet these are connected entities of a Garden-in-motion and of a horticulture that is intimately linked with a marriage under negotiation. Indeed, the nature of Eden plays a vital role in the epic's human drama; it allows Milton to represent the *lapsus in occulto* that is necessary to reconcile the theological challenge posed by the Fall.

Now-classic studies by Fallon and by Rogers have shown, beyond doubt, that Milton's poetics evolved alongside idiosyncratic theories of animist materialism, or vitalism.[55] But these studies, too, incline toward a misleadingly individualistic paradigm, in this case through an unqualified sense of Miltonic 'liberty' and 'freedom' as radical and absolute, rather than as 'strenuous', as 'contiguous' and as inextricable from the material universe.[56] Fallon asserts that Milton's materialism frees him from a 'mechanism threatening to his conception of freedom of the will', and that he 'moved toward the position that all corporeal substance is animate, self-active and free'.[57] Rogers connects vitalism to antinomianism by grounding 'the dangerously anti-authoritative logic of the Vitalist Moment' in the interests of radical religious politics: 'The figure of autonomous material agency peculiar to animist materialism' spoke to 'politically minded radicals seeking a liberatory conception of individual political agency'.[58] The insights of these studies shine more brightly once we allow the Miltonic subject to break from the glowing armour of the self-moving individual into the dialectics of material, biological, social and spiritual being.

The poem's theatricality is intimately linked with its rhetoric and representations of optics and botany. We will see that Milton's plants *move*. We will see how the Garden's vegetables *behave* like humans, and how humans, in turn, behave like vegetables. Most importantly, we will see how these plants encode a loosening of a spousal bond that is at once psychological, affective and physical, a loosening that invites a coherent causal narrative of the Fall. Milton's theatrical framing of the Garden helps to show how the optical field connecting husband to wife, man to angel, woman to flowers, and prelapsarian subject to God and the environing world conditions Eve's occult or secret Fall towards a position where Satan's words can 'into her heart' win 'too easie entrance'.[59]

One of the ways that Milton's materialism frees him from 'mechanism threatening to his conception of freedom of the will' is in his engagement with longstanding concerns of optics. As Stuart Clark details in his exhaustive intellectual history of optical theory during the early modern period, philosophers of optics worked through a crisis of the 'derationalization of vision' to achieve a modern basis, informed by scepticism, for the scientific study of the natural world.[60] The remainder of this section differs from Clark in two fundamental ways. First, I do not intend to account for a cohesive intellectual history but, rather, wish to illustrate what I see as Milton's unique contribution to the theory of optics, particularly in its distinction from the theories of Descartes and Hobbes. As such, I do not account for predecessors of these key figures, such as Johannes Kepler (1570–1630), or contemporaries, such as Marin Mersenne (1588–1648). Secondly, I am far less interested in examining the act of seeing than I am in exploring the mechanics and psychology of *being seen*, which entails a preconscious affective experience that seeps into consciousness.

In the middle decades of the seventeenth century, Hobbes and Descartes advanced theories that linked the mechanics of vision to the agency of the subject. For each, a unique theory of optics became the foundation for theories of metaphysics, ontology, the passions, rationality and agency. Hobbes and Descartes present what might be termed 'intromissive' accounts of vision, in that perception and sight are effected, first, by phenomena that pass into the retina and through the optic nerve.[61] Thus, their accounts do not seem, at first, much different from the Aristotelian theory of *species*, which, as Clark explains, 'supposed that objects in the world gave off resemblances and replicas of themselves (*species*) which then travelled to the eyes and, via the eyes and the optic nerves, into the various ventricles of the brain to be evaluated and processed'.[62] Problems associated with dreaming, deception and anamorphosis influenced the gradual abandonment of this view and rendered exigent a scientific basis for a more reliable account of vision and its vagaries. Descartes and Hobbes developed early modernity's most cogent answers to longstanding questions about the essence of vision during the late 1640s. Vision became understood to be a function of perspectival derivations or material motions that enabled the brain to 'see'.

Descartes, explains Clark, developed a 'mechanistic and corpuscularian account of perceptual cognition in which the essence of matter became extension and its only properties the geometrically derived ones of shape, size, position, and motion'.[63] In this account, sense perception occurs when refractions pass through the retina into the optic nerve. This information traces itself upon the pineal gland; then, 'in a state that is mind–body interactive, effects are produced in the mind which again correspond exactly to these motions'.[64] 'In both these stages, assuming normal conditions, certainty is guaranteed by the regularities and correspondences of mechanical physiological sequences'.[65] Vision is completed through the soul's divinely ordained ability to judge – that is, to arrive at an exact rational account of the object, despite whatever distortions occur naturally or artificially. Thus, 'it is the soul that sees, and not the eye'.[66] The entire process is instantaneous, entailing a mechanism that operates much like a camera, a copy-machine or, perhaps most accurately, the digitisation of images and video. And, of course, the eye functions instrumentally as a lens.

Descartes' optics would have attracted Milton due to its conservation of rational, and thus of ethical, agency. Yet its minimising of the passions as an agent in perception – we recall Descartes' confidence that any rational mind can attain 'easy' and 'absolute' control over the passions – would have seemed reductive, as it failed to account for the entanglements of the visual field that challenge the materially situated subject.[67] Hobbes's optics seems at first identical to its near precursor. But Hobbes's emphasis on the operations of the passions/heart over and above the mind leads to radically different implications – indeed, ultimately, the vast implications of his epistemological relativism. In Hobbes, no soul dwells within the pineal gland. Reason is far more mastered than mastering; it rationalises so as to protect self and body. Light's pulsations – rapid oscillations of material light moving through material air – place upon the eye pressure that passes through the eyeball, through the optic nerve, to the brain, and into the heart. The heart, seat of the passions, rebounds this pressure through the brain, where it is projected onto the world not as idea or as exact resemblance but as an 'appearance', as a 'representation' or a 'seeming'.[68] Such 'appearances' occupy the imagination and the memory, where they continue to work upon the passions whence they emerged.

Nonetheless, Hobbes inherited from Descartes the model of the retina as functioning like a lens that brings the propulsions of light from all sides of its curvature to a point. As a result, there is no evident concern for peripheral vision, for that liminal space in which objects emerge into or fade from vision. We might note the difference between a photograph of Half Dome, a famous rock structure of Yosemite National Park, and our view of Half Dome through the eyes. Viewing the photograph, we can peek or zoom into its corners and see, to a greater or lesser extent, what is there. But let us imagine that, as we stood upon an outcropping at Glacier Point, we took this photograph just as a bear was emerging from the left to push us off the cliff into the valley thousands of feet below. The photograph would never record this event. Yet what did we experience as we took a step back from the tripod and snapped the shot? We heard a sound and intuited a presence in the preconscious mind as the bear passed into the periphery of sight. Whereas the photograph shows sublimity, we were seized by terror – even if we never came to know its source.

Early modern optical theories did not account for peripheral vision, which proves central to the psychology of the Fall. Descartes' theory leaves no room for the periphery, since sight functions according to a subject–object model that privileges the eye as a lens that can focus on the object and can, thus, direct a response to what is perceived.[69] It is more surprising that Hobbes would neglect the periphery of sight, since, in his materialism, we are bombarded sensorily from all sides at all times. An illustration of the eye included in the English manuscript, *A Minute or First Draught of the Optiques* (1646), suggests that, by adhering less to a model of the instrumental lens, by rendering the eye-as-lens paradigm more flexible, Hobbes might have accounted for causes and effects of peripheral vision.[70] His illustration of the optical mechanism shows all parts of the eyeball to be connected to the brain by the layered wires feeding into the optic nerve (Fig. 4.1). Thus, it is easy to speculate that propulsions could pass through a perceptual limen that touches the optic nerve indirectly. Yet, in Hobbes as in Descartes, the optic nerve pulls sense information into a unity; sense does not glance the nerve but, rather, is pulled into the nerve. An extension of Hobbesian optics to peripheral vision would suggest the further power of the visible, as well as of what we might call the visible imaginary, to disturb the passions while avoiding the focus of the lens and averting conscious apprehension.

The counterpoint to 'intramission' is 'extramission', whereby the eyes are understood as projecting a power, operating like beams of light that illumine what is seen.[71] Despite being broadly discredited before the

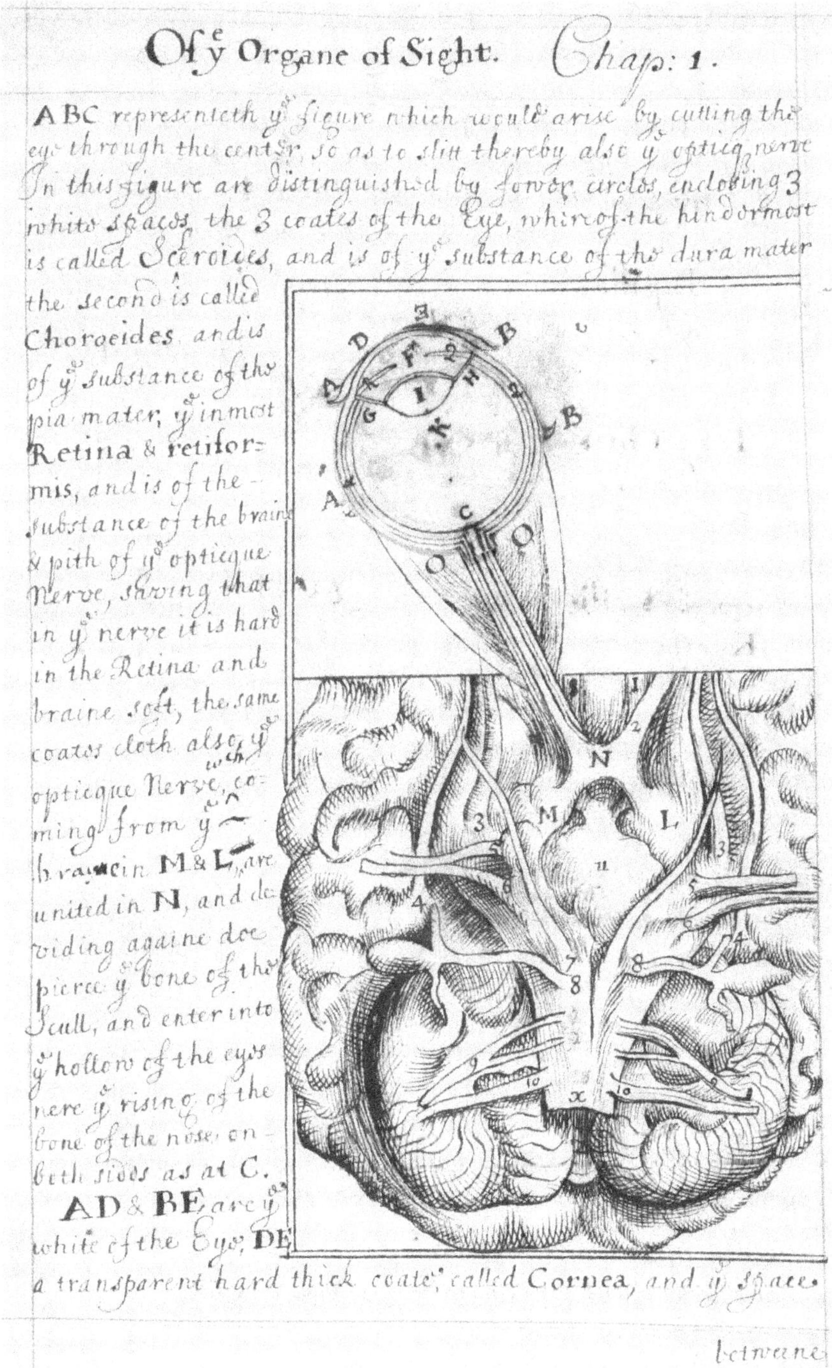

Of y̆ᵉ Organe of Sight. Chap: 1.

ABC representeth y̆ᵉ figure which would arise by cutting the eye through the center, so as to slitt thereby also y̆ᵉ optiq̆ nerve. In this figure are distinguished by fower circles, enclosing 3 white spaces, the 3 coates of the Eye, wherof the hindermost is called Sc̆eroides, and is of y̆ᵉ substance of the dura mater. the second is called Choroeides and is of y̆ᵉ substance of the pia mater, y̆ᵉ inmost Retina & retiformis, and is of the substance of the brain & pith of y̆ᵉ optique Nerve, shewing that in y̆ᵉ nerve it is hard in the Retina and braine soft, the same coates doth also y̆ᵉ optique Nerve, coming from y̆ᵉ braine in M & L are united in N, and deviding againe doe pierce y̆ᵉ bone of the Scull, and enter into y̆ᵉ hollow of the eyes nere y̆ᵉ rising of the bone of the nose, on both sides as at C. AD & BE are y̆ᵉ white of the Eye; DE a transparent hard thick coate, called Cornea, and y̆ᵉ space betwene

Figure 4.1 From T. Hobbes, *A Minute or First Draught of the Optiques* (1646), British Library, Harley MS 3360.

seventeenth century, extramissive theory still offered early modern poets a compelling metaphorical tool. Consider sonnet XX of Philip Sidney's *Astrophel and Stella*, in which the speaker describes his fatal first glimpse of Stella's eyes, the glance of which is figured in Cupid's heart-slaying arrow. As the poet enters a clearing, he notes a 'dark bush', 'that sweet black which veils the heav'nly eye' – an eyebrow, an eyelash or the iris itself – which conceals his killer.[72] As the speaker lingers to admire 'the sweet prospect of the place' – Stella's face – 'straight I saw motions of lightning grace, / And then descried the glist'ring of his dart: / But ere I could fly thence, it pierced my heart'.[73] The emitted power of vision pierces the heart, leaving the speaker mortally wounded in his amorousness. Milton also makes poetic use of extramission theory. For instance, during the separation colloquy of *Paradise Lost*, Adam implores Eve's presence so as to preserve her gaze's inducement to virtue: 'I from the influence of thy looks receave / Access in every Vertue, in thy sight / More wise, more watchful, stronger'.[74] Similarly, the speaker of Milton's 'L'Allegro' delights in imagining contests 'Of wit, or Arms', 'With store of Ladies, whose bright eies / Rain influence'.[75] It is the knowledge of being watched, the seeing that one is being seen, that allows these eyes to 'rain influence', to rouse the passions and to impel martial chivalry. While, in each of these instances, women are seen to emit a power that flows from their eyes, that power arguably transmits in cooperation with the male eyes that perceive the gaze that looks upon them. In the theatrical poetics of *Paradise Lost*, phenomena of more scientifically grounded intromission work symbiotically with phenomena of extramission.

'Influence', a flowing into the eye and spirits of an animating gaze, extends to perception the longstanding theory of stellar influence, whereby planetary bodies, particularly the sun, moon and stars, were understood to determine or to inform human actions and earthly events. Milton refers to this sense of astrological influence several times in his works. For instance, the Elder Brother of the *Maske* calls upon 'ye faint Stars, and thou fair Moone' to send down 'your influence' upon the dark woods obscuring their lost sister.[76] Such sense of 'influence' appears frequently in *Paradise Lost* to describe both the spiritually luminescent interrelations of heaven and the effect of these bodies on the experience of Adam and Eve. Raphael pictures the constellation of the Pleiades as dancing before the sun, 'shedding sweet influence'.[77] He describes the 'Suns Orb' as 'made porous to receive / And drink the liquid Light', which in turn is drawn into the 'gold'n Urns' of lesser stars.[78] The 'holy Light' that is hailed by the bard in the book III invocation is, thus, described as 'bright effluence of bright essence increate'; light is what flows from God, who is understood as a brilliant essence in His uncreated or unextended state.[79] References to 'sacred', 'selectest' and 'kindly heate / Of various influence' accompany others to 'bad influence' and 'influence malignant'.[80] Whereas God can claim that 'if I foreknew, / Foreknowledge had no influence on their fault', Satan's influence, a power of insinuation leagued with the stars, will help to condition the lapse towards transgression.[81] Granted that the theory of stellar influence has little scientific basis, early moderns, nonetheless, would have felt changes in light much as we feel such today, the sunlight working, often, to elevate mood and, for many, to bring a sense of serenity and to imply a pervasive divinity in nature.

I suggest that, in depicting the Eve of *Paradise Lost*, Milton was interested precisely in this experience of preconscious apprehension, though one that initiated more complex psychological and affective operations because the unseen objects in question were eyes looking upon her. In developing his treatment of Eve, Milton placed the predominant optical theories of the middle seventeenth century and Restoration into conversation with the more mythical, more poetic, yet scientifically ungrounded extramissive theory of stellar influence. This conversation allowed him to ask the following questions: What does it mean to see that eyes are seeing you? How do eyes seen as seeing back continue to work in the imagination and upon the passions? How does the consequent unsettling of the passions inform the spiritual and social ethics of the seeing subject? How does this process participate in impelling bodily movement? And to what end?

Satan's opening gambit in the seduction sequence of book IX shows Milton's interest in peripheral vision and its role as a potential gateway to pernicious influence. The serpent 'Curld many a wanton wreath in sight of *Eve*, / To lure her Eye; shee busied heard the sound / Of rusling Leaves, but minded not'.[82] The serpent resides 'in sight' but is not 'minded', Eve's 'Eye' not 'lured' to apprehend the presence that she intuits aurally. ('Minded' here means both 'seen' and 'processed by the mind'.) Despite not at first being 'minded', Satan soon hooks the glance that sees that which is seeing back: 'Hee boulder now, uncall'd before her stood; / But as in gaze admiring'; 'His gentle dumb expression turnd at length / The Eye of *Eve* to mark his play'.[83] Satan stands directly before Eve, yet remains unseen, hovering still in the periphery of sight. His 'gaze admiring' and 'gentle dumb expression' are what finally 'turn' her eye. 'Turnd' suggests that Satan's presence has been dimly perceived but has not been encountered visually until 'mark[ed]' and that, moreover, this perception, however dim, can compel body and eyes to move in order to achieve full apprehension of the object.

Thus, Satan begins the final stage of seduction by entering Eve's 'mind' through the periphery. Such a mode of insinuation is central to Satan's strategy throughout. He stirs Eve's passions not only by manipulating, through the ear, the 'Organs of her Fancie' while she sleeps, but also, and more sustainedly, by populating the periphery of her visible imaginary with gazing eyes.[84]

The Theatre of Vegetable Love

We first encounter the Garden through the lens of Satan's vision. He is a spectator who views an unfolding scene, a type of drama similar in content to, but essentially different from – in its abandonment of dramatic time, its treatment of causation, and its dynamic characterisation – the Fall dramas of Grotius, Andreini and della Salandra. Here, the distance from the Trinity Manuscript sketches becomes immediately apparent. As we have seen, 'Adam Unparadiz'd' does not represent prelapsarian life at all. In the preceding sketch, 'Paradise Lost', Milton employs Moses as a prologue to tell the imagined audience that, because of original sin, and because of 'the purity of [th]e pl[ace]', 'certaine pure winds, dues, and clouds', they cannot, or are forbidden to, 'se[e] Adam [and Eve] in the state of innocence'.[85] In the epic, Milton handles the problem of accommodation by revealing the Garden to us through what appears to be the filter of Satan's eyes. When we first encounter Eve, we are looking with Satan, whether through him or alongside him. If we are seeing a drama, then we are seeing a drama that, from the start, is conscious that it is being seen.[86]

As Satan enters the Garden, Milton explicitly describes the wall of Paradise as a theatre gallery constituted by trees. Less clear is whether this gallery is part of the Garden's interior or its exterior. It seems equally to frame Satan in his approach and to frame the unfallen, as yet unseen, Adam and Eve in their innocence. As Satan nears the Garden's wall, we learn that 'over head up grew / Insuperable highth of loftiest shade, / Cedar, and Pine, and Firr, and branching Palm, / A Silvan Scene, and as the ranks ascend / Shade above shade, a Woodie Theatre / Of stateliest view'.[87]

Among others, Lewalski and James Turner have assumed that the galleries frame the approaching Satan, as 'Scene', interchangeable with 'scaena', suggests that Satan stands before a *frons scaenae* while surrounded by galleries of trees.[88] Lines above, we had learnt that Satan's 'gestures fierce' and 'mad demeanour', 'as he suppos'd all unobserv'd, unseen', had been 'markd' by 'Uriel once warnd'.[89] The 'insuperable highth' and 'ascend[ing]' formation seem, furthermore, to indicate that the approaching Satan is solely foregrounded. This reading finds further support in its echo of *silvis scaena* in Virgil's *Aeneid*.

Tum silvis scaena coruscis
desuper horrentique atrum nemus imminet umbra;
fronte sub adversa scopulis pendentibus antrum,
intus aquae dulces vivoque sedilia saxo,
nympharum domus.
[Next, a glittering sylvan scene
hangs over a dark, shady grotto,
a cave, under the brow of pendant rocks,
within which are luscious waters and seats of stone –
the home of the nymphs (i.e., the Nereiads).][90]

There, the *scaena* is clearly intended to evoke a *frons scaenae*, the ornately adorned wall backing the stage of a Roman theatre. The structure of such a theatre is further suggested, in Virgil, by the stone seats beneath.

However, others have assumed that this 'Woodie Theatre' surrounds not Satan but, rather, Adam and Eve. For instance, John Dixon Hunt locates a source for this structure in the fashions of continental gardens.[91] Thomas Luxon, editor of the Dartmouth online edition, glosses 'Scene' and 'Theatre' as 'suggest[ing]' the Garden to be 'a stage upon which the tragic drama of the Fall will take place'.[92] Milton could not have been unaware of the glorious frontispiece – featuring Adam and Eve in a lush, apparently transatlantic Garden – of John Parkinson's monumental herbal, the 1629 *Paradisi in sole* ('Paradise in the Sun') (Fig. 4.2). Milton would also have known that *Theatrum botanicum*, or 'Plant Theatre', was the title of Parkinson's subsequent herbal, published in 1640 (Fig. 4.3). In the lines describing the 'Woodie Theatre / Of stateliest view', we encounter an odd and seemingly superfluous allusion to 'our general Sire', as he looks over the Garden's wall. The 'Sire' is usually glossed as Adam, for whom the 'verdurous wall of paradise' 'gave prospect large / Into his neather Empire neighbouring round'.[93] Yet we cannot exclude Satan as the referent, since his progeny, Sin and Death, will infect and devour all bodies of *his* postlapsarian empire 'neighbouring round'. This description of the world outside the Garden as 'neighbouring round' implies that the galleries curve around behind the referent's either side. If the *silvis scaena* of Virgil is clearly meant to resemble a *frons scaenae*, then we must also note that, in *Paradise Regained*, the 'woody Scene' that is prepared by Satan to deceive Jesus is, unmistakably, a scene of theatrical action.[94] As we are, in *Paradise Lost*, brought up to and over the wall of the Garden, the phrase 'general Sire' seems to curve both

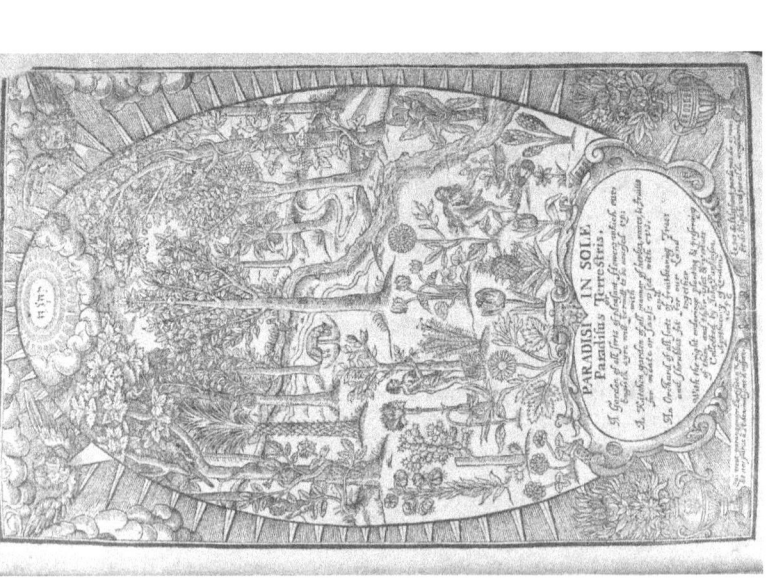

Figures 4.2 and 4.3 Left: frontispiece of J. Parkinson, *Paradisi in sole* (1629). William Andrews Clark Memorial Library, 2580743. Right: frontispiece of Parkinson, *Theatrum botanicum* (1640). The Folger Shakespeare Library, HH159/20.

ways, thus making it more difficult for us to visualise the aspect of these arboreal galleries.

The passage that describes the 'sylvan scene' is, in its ambivalence, typically Miltonic. The disparate senses that readers take from these lines do not derive from the unintended opacity of an inferior artist. As with so many moments in the Miltonic corpus, we face the challenge not only of seeing the ambiguity from both sides, but also of working out how such ambivalence or ambiguity signifies. Either way, we face a geometrical quandary. If surrounding Satan, the galleries would bend outward from the Garden. If surrounding Paradise, they would bend around the Garden to permit the 'general Sire' a prospect unto an Eden 'neighbouring round'. The ambivalence of the passage is best illustrated by Demaray, who, like Lewalski and Turner, assumes that the 'sylvan scene' 'unfolds before [Satan's] gaze' 'as [he] approaches'.[95] Yet, Demaray cannot resist a reference to the 'woody theatre of Eden' when developing his reading of the Garden as a masquing scene.[96]

Indeed, Milton's 'Woodie Theatre' makes the most sense if we read the galleries as, figuratively, bending at once both ways from the hinge of the Garden's wall. Although this is a physical impossibility, it is, yet, a poetically productive paradox. Milton activates this ambivalence at the moment of crossing over in order to suggest that the Garden is, as it were, *infected* by theatricality, heretofore a Satanic mode, at the tempter's entrance, which immediately places him in the subject position of spectator of the spousal drama of unwitting actors. With Satan switching from seen theatrical spectacle to unseen theatrical spectator, the line of sight that first issues from Uriel in the sun continues through the Satanic lens, translocates through various Edenic beasts, and constricts towards the blissful couple, until Satan is perched as a gazing cormorant atop the Tree of Life: 'O Hell! what doe mine eyes with grief behold?'[97] Thus, he watches from what would appear a lower arboreal gallery. What do such unseen seeing eyes *do*?

Vegetable Gesture

Just as early moderns represented the movement of plants and flowers as these responded to the light of the sun, that great eyeball in the sky, human bodies in Milton, as we have seen, also respond to onlooking eyes. *Paradise Lost* represents the human as a type of responsive vegetable; moreover, he represents the vegetable world as responsive to the human. As such, the visual field becomes a place of extraordinary relations of embodied movement. To represent the human body as vegetable, as responsive to direct or refracted luminescence, is to capture the essence of peripheral influence, since the vegetable does not see by optic lens but, rather, moves in accordance with both the light of the sun and the refracted light flowing into the vegetable body from all sides. In this sense, the vegetable is all eyes.

Milton employs specific language to capture the spirited movement of the plants and humans of the Garden. Behind the arboreal theatre galleries, narrates Milton, 'the verdurous wall of paradise up sprung'.[98] The phrase 'up sprung' refers to vertical plant growth towards the sun. Milton uses 'sprung' seventeen times with this sense in his poetry, fourteen of which appear in *Paradise Lost*. 'Spring' appears thirteen times in the epic with the same sense, again a preponderance of instances. Relatedly, 'droop', which suggests an evacuation of spirit and a downward bending of plant or body, appears five times in the poem. Both the springing and the drooping of plants correspond with embodied spirit or passions, whether of vital instinct, of hope, of longing or of deflating sadness.

The direct upward growth implied by 'sprung' or 'spring' corresponds – except for one important exception – with a directly vertical inclining toward God and 'holy Light'. We see such a relationship between vegetable subject and solar God in George Herbert's 'The Flower'. Here, Herbert's speaker seasonally reinvigorates, shooting upwards in response to the sun's congenial beams, which represent God's love: 'Many a spring I shoot up fair / Offering at heaven, growing and groaning thither'.[99] Here, too, Herbert plays upon the meaning of 'spring' as to shoot upwards. 'Shoot[s]' also suggests the young sprouts of early spring. Adam relates to Raphael that, upon waking to consciousness, 'By quick instinctive motion up I sprung'.[100] He comes to life as an automatically obedient being, from whom will soon branch rational and ethical capacities. But he responds first as a vegetable that springs toward the holy light 'instinctive[ly]'.[101] Although we are seeing an embodied spirituality, the behaviour is, at first, distinctly mechanistic, free of the ethical challenges that will confront Adam and Eve as early as their first meeting.

In tension with the perfectly vertical, obedient springing in Adam's account is the appearance of Eve as a drooping daffodil in hers. The bloom of the top-heavy daffodil, often flourishing in shade, bends downwards like Ovid's Narcissus, who lends the daffodil its Latin name (Fig. 4.4).[102] Eve finds herself 'under a shade of flours' before approaching her reflection in the pool: 'As I bent down to look, just opposite, / A Shape within the watry gleam appeerd / Bending to look on me'.[103] Where Adam had sprung instinctively towards the sun, Eve bends towards eyes seen seeing back in 'the cleer / Smooth Lake, that to me seemd another Skie'.[104] We would be hasty to assume that these movements up and down the vertical axis correspond with contradicting character and capacity. Both incline or decline towards a seeing sky, or what appears as such; both share the language of Ovid's Narcissus; and both are associated, during their first meeting, with the shade.[105]

The appearance of Adam 'under a Platan' suggests strong verticality. Eve first describes him as 'tall', despite being 'less winning soft, less amiablie milde / Then that smooth watry image'.[106] The platan's thick trunk might suggest a phallic authority that accounts for what seems to be Eve's timorousness or hesitancy. It has been suggested that Milton chose the name of 'platan' over 'plane tree' in order to associate the episode with Platonic philosophy and, in particular, with Socrates's habit of teaching under a platan, as in *Phaedrus*, to distinguish between truth (associated with Adam) and illusion (associated with Eve).[107] Admittedly, I am eager to reject arguments that read into Milton's theodicy only a modified version of the already-imperfect, vainly narcissistic Eve of the hackneyed exegetical, aesthetic and dramatic traditions that he inherited, and that he is so busy examining and unsettling in the poem. Milton makes it clear that Adam and Eve are both imperfect – incomplete – as, within God's paradigm, they need each other to complete themselves in a union of flesh with flesh, so as 'to manifest / His single imperfection, and beget / Like of his like, his Image multipli'd, / In unitie defective, which requires / Collateral love, and deerest amitie'.[108] As such, through the fortitude to resist temptation, obedience gains strength from a horizontal alignment between two, and ultimately between many, in bonds of '*collateral* love'. Where Adam's exactly vertical response to the sun is both pure and instinctive, 'collateral' points to the difficult rational, affective and physical negotiations, facilitated by love, between human agents along a horizontal or lateral axis. The fact that these negotiations *require* collateral love indicates that horizontal identifications are necessary in man's obedience to God.[109]

Considering that spousal interrelations work collaterally in order to strengthen a vertically conceptualised obedience, the 'platan' where Eve first sees Adam suggests other implications. Milton has in mind here the Oriental plane (*platanus orientalis*) or, perhaps, its close variant, the London plane (*platanus acerifolia*), both of which appeared as arboreal ornaments in seventeenth-century parks and gardens, in England as in Europe.[110] While the plane tree is tall, its most striking characteristic is the girth of its branches, which spread outwards from the trunk like reaching arms. They reach parallel with the ground, striving for access to the sun, as each level provides a dense canopy of leaves – Adam here is well-shaded – resembling those of the maple. John Evelyn extols 'the incomparable and shady *Platanus*': '*Pliny* tells us there is no *Tree* whatsoever which so well defends us from the *heat* of the *Sun* in *Summer*, nor that admits it more kindly in *Winter*'.[111] Where the vine and elm more readily figure the happy union of two 'Imparadis't in one anothers arms', these massive reaching branches may be seen to figure the heavy-handedness of Adam's efforts to win Eve, for she first demurs: 'I espi'd thee, fair indeed and tall, / Under a Platan, yet methought less faire, / Less winning soft, less amiablie milde, / Then that smooth watry image; back I turnd [. . .]'[112] The tree is an appropriate metonymy for the man who will chase Eve grasping with 'gentle hand / Seis[ing]'.[113] The action of seizing might ultimately work toward disorienting Eve's sense of place in the Garden as an agential rational equal, but, if it leaps over an appropriate process of courtship, it nonetheless shows the couple for the first time establishing a collateral physical bond that will evolve into a stronger 'collateral love'.

Adam and Eve are bestowed the labour of gardening in order to strengthen and maintain collateral love, which will, in turn, help them to grow in firmer obedience to God. The interplay between the two axes of connection is emblematised in the horticultural practice of binding plants together in order to sustain a cooperative growth. Milton describes Adam and Eve's hair in botanical terms: Adam's 'Locks' are 'Hyacinthin', like the hyacinth, a flower closely related to the narcissus.[114] As with the daffodil, the hyacinth appears early in spring and features blooms that, like the platan's branches, shoot horizontally in stacked layers (Fig. 4.5).[115] Eve's 'unadorned golden tresses [. . .] / Dissheveld' and 'wanton ringlets' are 'as the Vine curl[ing] her tendrils'.[116] They figure the spousal bond described in book V as they garden

> where any row
> Of Fruit-trees overwoodie reachd too farr
> Thir pamperd boughes, and needed hands to check
> Fruitless imbraces: or they led the Vine
> To wed her Elm; she spous'd about him twines
> Her marriageable arms, and with her brings
> Her dowr th' adopted Clusters, to adorn
> His barren leaves.[117]

The metaphor of the vine and the elm tightly twines gardening with spousal discourse and touch; it concludes with an implication of progenitive sexual intercourse. It posits the marriage bond as one of collateral love that complements the vertical growth and horizontal sprawl of the trees, plants and flowers that the spouses groom. Just as the 'boughes [. . .] needed hands to check / Fruitless imbraces', so is it necessary for

Figures 4.4 and 4.5 Daffodils (left) and hyacinths (right), in Parkinson, *Paradisi in sole* (1629), pp. 71 and 121. Williams Andrews Clark Memorial Library, 2580743.

Adam and Eve's labours of collateral love to 'check' potentially vain attachments.

Raphael's comparison of the obedient subject to a flowering plant underscores the difficulty of perfectly vertical growth. Just as the flower begins in earth, becomes more refined, and 'spirits odorous breathes', so 'Your bodies may at last turn all to Spirit, / Improv'd by tract of time, and wingd ascend / Ethereal [. . .] / If ye be found obedient, and retain / Unalterably firm his love entire'.[118] While, by all appearances, the sociable archangel discourses with Adam and Eve with the best of intentions and does not fail to fulfil his mission, as he understands it, the implications of his metaphors can fall wide of the mark. The metaphor of the flower suggests the spiritual growth of a single individual, though Raphael's speculation that 'Your bodies may at last turn all to Spirit' makes clear that the flower is meant to be a model for both Adam and Eve. As we have noted, this obedience and 'unalterably firm' retention of God's love requires the continuing collateral support of spousal love. We do not see here a 'vitalist process of material self-organization' but, rather, a more cooperative model of growth, one that binds God and humankind, on one hand, and husband and wife, on the other.[119] Raphael's concept of long-term spiritual growth and sublimation is translated into the image of floral growth and suspiration, phenomena that Adam and Eve would see occurring – as it seems, with increasing rapidity – every morning. Eve's dream in book V implants a fantasy of proleptic vertical ascendancy. Adam, awed, sees Raphael as the embodiment of such sublimation before him. If not read correctly, the compelling metaphor of the spiritual flower invites danger. It projects an improvement by 'tract of time' onto an image of ephemerality, with 'tract' connoting, also, the historically emergent sense of a digestive canal – another figure of comparably rapid change.[120] The image of the flower, of an individual being, would also seem to dissociate obedience from the 'collateral love' that such growth 'requires'. One might imagine the consequences of prolonged 'autonomous [. . .] agency' in marriage.[121]

Adam's identification with this image of spiritual ascendancy, an identification that is reinforced by the presence of the glorious being before him, does not seem to strengthen the dialectical buttressing of spouses. After Eve's transgression, and at the moment when Adam's 'vehemence of love' will compel his own, Milton offers a contrasting floral symbol.[122] Upon perceiving Eve's fallen state – 'in her face excuse / Came Prologue, and Apologie to prompt' – he releases the garland, the gift of flowers with which he had intended to crown her: 'From his slack hand the Garland wreath'd for *Eve* / Down drop'd, and all the faded Roses shed'.[123] The clipping, falling and shedding of wreathed roses is emblematic of a spousal sundering that is followed soon by fall and demise. The crown is itself a 'fruitless embrace'. The fact that these roses are already 'faded' may suggest the immediate effect of Eve's fall on groaning nature, but it also emphasises that these roses have been sundered from their life-supporting stems, that a botanical clipping had preceded a fatal falling – that a temporary sundering of the ties binding spouses had preceded a fall that was, in part, its consequence.

The possibility of re-connection, and thus of regeneration, is restored with the unfolding of the Son's 'Curse' after the Fall.[124] Book X ends with the 'penitent' couple 'prostrate', falling under God, 'with tears / Watering the ground' and 'with thir sighs the Air / Frequenting'.[125] Thus, Raphael's flower image returns as an act of spousal cooperation in humility and prayer. Instead of regenerating in upward ascension, Adam and Eve first fall to earth. They re-establish the process of vegetable growth by 'watering the ground' 'with tears'. The suspiration of Raphael's flower becomes the 'sighs' of spontaneous, formless prayer. The prayer is received by the 'Son' (sun) and is presented as 'spirits odorous' (incense) to the Father. Adam and Eve's motions are catalysed by a revised understanding of the solar godhead as merciful and as enabling their regenerative growth in the light of a restored righteousness. Adam recalls that, even at God's angriest, 'favor, grace, and mercie [had] shon' in his 'look serene'.[126] Adam moves the pair closer to hope and prayer by imagining a godhead who will 'relent and turn / From his displeasure'.[127] Just beneath the surface is a structure of divine spectatorship of an obedient performance – unscripted humble weeping and prayer that compels the affective response ('relent') and movement ('turn') of the spectator-God.[128]

Book XI begins with the 'prostrate' couple now 'in lowliest plight repentant st[anding]', like a reinvigorated plant, enabled by 'Prevenient Grace descending' from the 'Mercie-seat' of God 'above', which 'remove[s] / The stonie from thir hearts' and makes 'new flesh / Regenerate grow instead'.[129] The Son, beckoning ('See Father'), presents the prayers as though he were a Prologue gesturing toward a spectacle of the *theatrum mundi*.[130] He describes the prayer as 'first fruits on Earth [. . .] sprung / From thy implanted Grace in Man', 'Fruits of more pleasing savour from thy seed / Sow'n with thy contrition in his heart, then those / Which his own hand manuring all the Trees / Of Paradise could have produc't, ere fall'n'.[131] We know that Adam and Eve have regenerated because their actions have borne fruit, indeed, fruit more 'pleasing' to God than anything that their gardening had accomplished before. God is not simply pleased to see the fallen couple humbled and realigned in tenuous obedience; rather, the 'pleasing savour' of this postlapsarian fruit owes to the fact that a primary cause of the Fall – a loosening of affective connection playing out through the field of vision – has been worked into control. Affective negotiations have culminated in a 'repairing' and rising. As Kevis Goodman argues, book X dramatises a process of humiliation and of a re-negotiation of feeling that rejoins the estranged couple through a labour of sympathy: Eve 'in *Adam* wraught / Commiseration'.[132] The repeated 'repairing' connotes three interrelated meanings: the fixing of a temporarily broken marriage; the coming together of two as one in collateral bond; and the re-alignment with God's will for the sake of continued growth in obedience.

Yes, the theology of a *felix culpa* rests, ultimately, upon the crucifixion, the resurrection and the return of Christ. However, at a more mundane level, we are seeing a marriage that is grown stronger because each spouse has not only felt loneliness but has, moreover, found expression of powerful, but heretofore unarticulated and unknowable, emotions.

Stellar Eyes and the Secret Fall

Eve's unsettling dream, in book V, is part of Satan's long game, a second key stage in a process by which Eve will gradually move toward the decision to act upon her need to understand her place in the Garden and in Adam's affection. Her transgression must be understood as, in part, a violation of the first law that will require atonement and a new dispensation through Christ. But it is not only a 'sin against the Word', a Satanic corruption of unfallen language, as argued by John Reichert.[133] Eve also struggles to find a vocabulary to express affective disturbance and contradictory senses of her place in Paradise.[134] Two temporalities – synchronic and diachronic – must be operative in order to deliver Eve from the facile prejudices of exegetical tradition and, thus, to justify God. Milton also encodes a *lapsus in occulto*, or secret Fall, whereby Eve's violation of the prohibition is first gradually conditioned by Satan.[135] The tempter deftly works upon Eve's imagination and passions by gradually shaping her early curiosity about the stars into a sense of both being watched and being invisible within the Paradisal theatre.

Adam and Eve's garden becomes increasingly difficult to manage at the same time that signs related to vision, the body and the spirited vegetable infer a loosening of the spousal bond and a mismanagement of largely ineffable passions. Doubt is revealed in book V, after Eve's dream, which takes form through Satan's manipulation of her fancy and his vocal insinuation through her sleeping ears. After the dream, Adam kisses Eve's tears 'as the gracious signs of sweet remorse / And pious awe, that feard to have offended'.[136] The tears *may* express 'sweet remorse', as Adam interprets them, but they also seem to express a troubling incoherence. 'As' and 'signs' indicate an authorial intention to destabilise assumptions about prelapsarian emotion.

We need not doubt that both Adam and Eve are 'sufficient to have stood'. However, according to the horticultural logic of obedience in *Paradise Lost*, their standing requires firm collateral love, the loosening of which leaves them vulnerable. We see a loosening of this bond dramatised in the silent departure of Eve early in book VIII. The sudden appearance that is revealed by her rising to leave tends to catch first-time readers off guard. After thousands of lines recounting Lucifer's apostasy, the War in Heaven, the Hexameron and more, discourses that seem shared exclusively between aspiring husband and a male-gendered archangel, we learn that the men, as it were, have been under observation: Adam 'by his count'nance seemd / Entring on studious thoughts abstruse, which *Eve* / Perceaving where she sat retir'd in sight', 'Rose, and went forth'.[137] A constellation of optical signifiers forms a telling picture. First, the 'seem[ing]' of Adam's countenance suggests that his facial expressions might purposefully be fashioned to confirm to Raphael his fitness as an intellectual partner. While Adam fixes on Raphael, Eve is intensely 'perceaving' – both seeing and reading – their interaction and, more specifically, Adam's facial expression.

'Retir'd in sight' calls attention to Eve's own status in the group as there-but-not-there, or as the invisible visible – within glance of teacher and husband but, nonetheless, peripheral to the conversation and to the eyes and minds of the conversants. Though Eve is 'not with such discourse / [Un]delighted', the text suggests that she departs with a muted longing for the conversation of tangibly loving spouses:

> Her Husband the Relater she preferr'd
> Before the Angel, and of him to ask
> Chose rather; hee, she knew would intermix
> Grateful digressions, and solve high dispute
> With conjugal Caresses, from his Lip
> Not Words alone pleas'd her.[138]

Beneath the playful eroticism of these lines is the suggestion of a genuine longing, not only for conjugal discourse, 'she sole Auditress', but also for caressing touch.[139] 'Relater' collapses communication into 'relationship'; the root, *latus*, 'carried or conveyed', further evokes the imperative of 'collateral love'. Moreover, 'caress', with 'care' at its root, suggests a touch that works to soothe, to heal and to guide. Eve will read the Forbidden Fruit as the 'Cure of all' before her fatal bite.[140] 'Cure', rooted in *cura* – which denotes not only soothing attention but also a horticultural rearing – links the need for caress with the cure for that need.

Visual signifiers continue to glimmer through the text. Eve embodies 'Grace that won who saw to wish her stay'.[141] Of course, none has urged her to stay because none has been seeing or minding – until her rising – that grace of presence. Meanwhile, 'from about her shot Darts of desire / Into all Eyes to wish her still in sight'.[142] This strange description of her body as shooting arrows into 'all Eyes' – and here we might recall the piercing 'arrow' of Sidney's sonnet XX – is not merely a commentary on her beauty and its effect on gazers. It makes as much sense to read the 'desire' of these darts as her own. These 'Darts of desire' seem intended to make neglecting eyes 'wish her still in sight'. 'Still', moreover, suggests not merely 'remaining' but also 'always'. It recalls Satan's claim, during the dream sequence, that Eve is 'Nature's desire, / In whose sight all things joy, with ravishment / Attracted by thy beauty still to gaze'.[143]

Meanwhile, 'shot', the past tense of the botanically resonant 'shoot', offers to align these optical signifiers with sprouting vegetation, as though Eve's body, in its departure, is extending, through her need, an invitation to vegetable reconnection. If Adam neglects spousal care, Eve knows where to find a substitute. She walks immediately to the 'Fruits and Flours', 'bud and bloom' of 'her Nurserie', 'to visit how they prosper'd': 'they at her coming sprung / And toucht by her fair tendance gladlier grew'.[144] Just as Adam and Eve often behave as, and are at times described as, spirited vegetables, so too do these flowers exhibit human feeling that corresponds with motion. Milton might have had in mind the 'sensitive plant' or *mimosa pudica*, a favourite of early modern herbalists (Fig. 4.6). The sensitive plant is given special attention in the herbals because its leaves niftily retract when touched. This seeming gesture of sensitive withdrawal – the opposite of what Eve's flowers are doing here – earnt the plant the namesake of an emotional vegetable.[145] To Eve's flowers Milton attributes 'gladness', a characteristic both of their physical appearance and of their emotional lives; affect materialises physically along the horizontal axis upon Eve's approach. Her rising toward the nursery is expressed in the past tense of 'rise' – 'Rose'. If we can imagine, here, a floral pun, then we can see a rose-like human moving towards human-like blooms that spring towards her.[146] This reciprocity between the gestures of man and flower can also be seen in the *Self-Portrait with a Sunflower* (1633) by Anthony van Dyck, a favourite painter of Charles

I's court. Here, van Dyck's hair reflects the densely layered petals of the large, face-sized sunflower blossom. A smaller bloom, to the right of the flower, complements the right hand of Van Dyck as it gestures toward the bloom (Fig. 4.7).[147]

Eve is not alone in her vulnerability. Her departure precedes Adam's surprising revelation to Raphael of his diminished self-esteem, his sense of vulnerability that intensifies when he is overwhelmed with sensual desire.[148] Adam relates that he longs to feel closer to Eve's inner being. He feels that he can only 'approach / Her loveliness' as though he were nearing an impenetrable 'awe / About her, as a guard Angelic plac't'.[149] The image of emotional distance places him outside of the Garden, as though he were already banished thence. Eve appears a walled Garden that he can only hope to 'approach'.

Adam and Eve's mutual sense of emotional separation leads to a physical separation after the dispute that begins the day in book IX. Raphael's almost shockingly anti-feminist admonition to Adam, toward the close of book VIII, may well be disastrous in the result. In that speech, Raphael encourages Adam to maintain his superior rationality and to make it show: for Eve 'sees when thou art seen least wise'.[150] At this point, we are fully unaware that she might be watching at this very moment. We soon learn that, after leaving to tend her flowers, Eve had once more become the seeing invisible. During the separation colloquy, in response to Adam's admonition about the lurking Satan, she alerts him that she had already learnt this lesson. 'That such an Enemie we have, who seeks / Our ruin, both by thee informed [. . .] / And from the parting Angel over-heard / As in a shadie nook I stood behind, / Just then returnd at shut of Evening Flours'.[151] What feelings are moved, what thoughts provoked, when one overhears an archangel telling your husband that you are an assemblage of 'show[s]: / Made so adorn to delight [him] more', an 'outside' that must 'yield' to his 'realities'?[152] It is difficult not to conclude that Adam and Eve would have been better prepared to resist the tempter had they spent that afternoon together alone.

Milton's theodicy of original sin requires of the Fall a double cause. The first cause is easy to apprehend. Here, Satan catches Eve at the wrong time and tricks her into biting the fruit: 'The Serpent me beguil'd and I did eate'.[153] But there are two problems, here. First, this conclusion defines the transgression as a consequence of rational failure, which renders moot the emotional and psychological drama of Edenic marriage and which leaves God unjustified. Second, it adheres to the hackneyed exegetical tradition that Milton inherited and that he wrote an epic poem, in part, to challenge and to re-theorise. Rational error would seem to require, first, a strong affective disturbance, so that faulty reason

160 *Theatrical Milton*

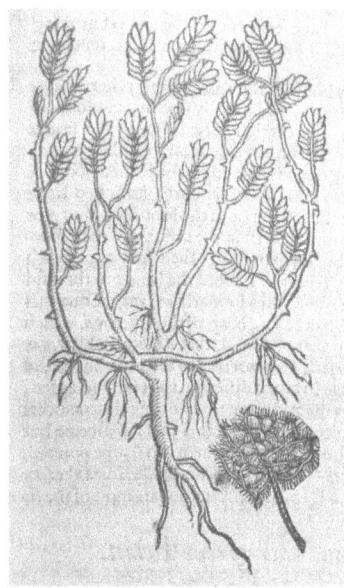

Figures 4.6 and 4.7   Left: the *mimosa pudica* or 'sensitive plant', in J. Gerarde, *The Herball*, (1636) (first published 1597), p. 1599. William Andrews Clark Memorial Library, 1508681. Below: A. van Dyck, *Self Portrait with Sunflower* (c. 1633). Private collection.

would be, in actuality, rationalisation. We see a relationship between passions and reason that is distinct from that detailed by Milton in *Areopagitica*. For instance, the intense passion that Adam feels for Eve derails his intellect: 'here passion first I felt, / Commotion strange'; 'Wisdom in discourse with her / [. . .] like folly shewes'.[154] The proximity of emotional disturbance and rational error allows Satan's words to enter into Eve's heart 'too easi[ly]'. Milton renders the transgression plausible as an emotional and psychological phenomenon, yet he is still able to maintain the legalistic sense of the Fall as the transgressing of a divinely imposed prohibition.

Eve's slide into original sin depends on the transposition of imagined eyes onto stars. The sun's influence on spirit and body, substituted by the stars in its nightly absence, infiltrates the imagination to generate a subconsciously operative theatrical structure that continues to work from the periphery. In book IV, Eve had followed her assertion to Adam that 'God is thy Law, thou mine: to know no more / Is womans happiest knowledge and her praise' not only with a loving lyric poem but also – and we should not miss the irony – with a question about the stars: 'But wherfore all night long shine these, for whom / This glorious sight, when sleep hath shut all eyes?'[155] An enjambment momentarily isolates the phrase, 'wherefore all night long shine these, for whom[?]'. It briefly suspends the sense that Eve is curious about the stars' operation as spectators of a 'whom'. After the line break, a sense of curiosity appropriate to Paradise is secured with 'this glorious sight'. Now Eve is but a pious spectator of God's works.

If, as early as book IV, Eve is seeking to understand her place in the Garden as at once equal and inferior, then Adam's response to her curiosity would seem merely to exacerbate the disturbance that impells it. Having already observed that the two have 'nothing merited, nor can performe / Aught whereof [God] hath need', Adam suggests that he and Eve are only two among 'millions of spiritual Creatures' who behold God's works with 'ceasless praise'.[156] This redirection is analogous to the shift from a Ptolemaic to a Copernican and Galilean cosmos, a shift that, during Milton's lifetime, continued to alter humankind's sense of place within an ever more boundless universe.[157] Are Adam and Eve peripheral, even unnecessary spectators – 'nor think, though men were none, / That heav'n would want [i.e., lack] spectators, God want praise' – or are they centred spectacles?[158] Is Eve merely an onlooker, or does she 'performe / Aught whereof' God, or whereof Adam, 'hath need', given her secondary status as meet help?

When Satan later reworks this material into the dream of book V, the subconscious desire for a centred sense of self is seized by Satan as an opportunity to exacerbate internal disturbance, for which Eve yet lacks a paradigm to understand and a vocabulary to express: 'Heav'n wakes with all his eyes, / Whom to behold but thee, Natures desire, / In whose sight all things joy, with ravishment / Attracted by thy beauty still to gaze'.[159] In the dream's playing out of the Fall, Eve is unquestionably the spectacle, the sole object of admiration upon whom all things fixedly gaze and thrill, the very centre of the viewing universe. The Ptolemaic cosmos is restored, and Eve marks the very centre of its centre. During the temptation, Satan will further develop upon this strategy. He will repeatedly assert Eve's status as centred, admired spectacle, not so much to arouse vanity but, rather, to exacerbate her sense of invisibility and disorientation. In the dream, Satan provides the answer that Eve seems all too eager to hear: 'Wherfore all night long shine these, for whom?': 'whom to behold but thee'. Of the stars, Adam had noted that 'these soft fires / Not only enlighten, but with kindly heate / Of various influence foment and warme, / Temper or nourish, or in part shed down / Thir stellar vertue on all kinds that grow'.[160] So, too, will the eyes that 'behold' Eve's beauty and that fix upon her, these eyes sown in the sky of the imagination, continue to work upon her passions as does light on plants and as do spectators' eyes upon on the actor's body.

The gaze plays a critical role in the seduction sequence of book IX, where the visual field constricts around Eve as it will around the Fruit. Satan's rhetoric cooperates with the 'gaze', a word repeated six times during the temptation. Forms of 'to admire' – that is, 'to look towards' – appear five times with significance. Satan's gaze and the constricting gaze of the imagination intensify the horizontal challenge to the spousal bond, which has loosened to the degree that Adam and Eve have separated, for the morning. As in the dream, here Satan repeatedly declares that Eve is the admired spectacle whom 'all things living gaze on', 'there best beheld / Where universally admir'd'.[161]

Substitutions and inversions continue, working to narrow the conceptual space between subject (Eve) and object (forbidden fruit). Since the spousal bond is loosened through an exacerbated sense of *not* being seen, Satan's words rub the very wound that they caress. Thus, Eve projects a subconscious, ineffable and thus undefinable sense of lack – 'to add what wants / In Femal Sex, the more to draw his Love, / And render me more equal', perhaps 'a thing not undesireable' – onto the Fruit. As such, she inverts her position from object to subject of the gaze: 'Fixt on the fruit she gaz'd'.[162] The word 'fixt', which suggests a locking of desiring eyes upon the object of temptation, echoes Satan's 'still' in the dream sequence, heaven's 'eyes' being 'attracted by [Eve's] beauty still to gaze'. This intense admiration of the object betrays a deflating self-consciousness: in this psychodrama, to gaze upon the apple is, in the end, to see oneself as invisible, to know that flattering delusions have no basis in reality, and, ultimately, to see the 'cure' for one's need for 'care'. To incorporate the apple is to absorb its visibility and its pre-eminence of place, as well as to absorb the 'caress[ing]' affection for which it has become a substitute.

The spiritual body has been theatricalised, roused and pulled into motion, through the influence of surrounding eyes in the imagination. The effect of environing pressures is the motion of plucking an apple, a gesture that fuses the theatrical with the horticultural. The reaching hand of Eve meets at the apple the straining branch of the Tree of Knowledge. From the visual field comes forth something like an 'antick and dishonest gestur[e]', a fatal 'unboning' of the spiritual body divided from its propping co-partner as it moves laterally toward the tree reaching.

The horizontal axis of vision will be strongly aligned with obedience in Michael's teaching, after the Fall, that 'God attributes to place / No sanctitie', but that His 'presence' will in the world be readable, 'still following thee, still compassing thee round', 'his Face / Express' in 'many a signe'.[163] The signs of God's presence recall the 'neighbouring round' seen from atop the Garden's sylvan galleries, as well as many other circular fields of vision that we have explored already.[164] With the idea of God displaced from the vertical axis that is definitive of perfect vertical growth and projected onto the environing Book of Nature, the visual field will pose in itself incessant ethical and spiritual challenges. There, we will be called to negotiate strenuous obedience with a faithful social ethics amidst environing pernicious influences: 'Wherefore did he creat passions within us, pleasures round about us, but that these rightly temper'd are the very ingredients of vertu?'[165]

> What wisdome can there be to choose, what continence to forbeare without the knowledge of evill? He that can apprehend and consider vice with all her baits and seeming pleasures, and yet abstain, and yet distinguish, and yet prefer that which is truly better, he is the true wa[y]faring Christian.[166]

Pernicious influences work alongside surrounding forces of grace, faith, caress, social support and spiritual guidance. Michael's view of God as compassing and following the wayward Christian through the world and its challenges logically follows upon the forces that undermined humankind's initial obedience to the sole prohibition.

Where discourses of the New Science privilege the subject–object workings of the individualist experimenter, *Paradise Lost* shows Milton harnessing and modifying its insights so as to focus on the complementary workings of social and spiritual bonds. Perhaps the greatest benefit of a theatrical paradigm is that it inevitably belies the all-too-credited fable of the individualistic Milton who seeks radical freedom and who, with god-like power and prescience, lights the way to Enlightenment.[167] It is possible that an author so admirable as to be fetishised from early Romanticism to the present was capable of recognising the dangers of 'autonomous' spiritual 'agency' pervasive in the antinomian discourses of the 1650s. It is possible that he could use these insights to zero in on the challenge to social bonds that, as bonds of cooperation enabled and strengthened in strenuous liberty, could forestall or prevent the emergence of the modern subject – even as empiricism and industrial mechanism were fostering this emergence.

The theatricality diversely inscribed in *Paradise Lost* and throughout Milton's corpus has, at the same time, been all but eclipsed by genre scholarship, which has tended to confine the drama to a purely literary/aesthetic, didactic, rhetorical or indoctrinating mode. While the book VII invocation suggests that Milton is isolated, encompassed and menaced, it also shows him reaching for a 'fit audience [. . .] though few' that can meet the terms of cooperation. In other words, theatricality, which precedes, informs and follows the Fall, extends radially outward through civilisation and its history, in its dogged ambivalence. It persists in Hammond's third 'proto-community', that of the Israelites, and it persists far beyond Milton's time and ours.

Milton may well have understood drama as one of many rhetorical modes during the early 1640s, when he considered how a drama on the Fall might have benefitted a broad English audience. Yet decades of political and religious turmoil helped to sprout a theatrical poetics that was unbound to genre and that allowed the poet to capture and to explore the complex rational, spiritual and passionate events of human interaction.[168]

Notes

1. Milton, *The Readie and Easie Way*, CPW, VII, p. 463. See Hammond, *Milton and the People*, pp. 205–9; cf. Shore, *Milton and the Art of Rhetoric*, pp. 5–6.
2. Milton, *Paradise Lost*, WJM, II.i, I, lines 52, 68, 46–7.
3. Hammond, *Milton and the People*, p. 218.
4. Milton, *Paradise Lost*, WJM, II.ii, IX, lines 31–2.
5. Ibid., WJM, II.i, III, line 99.
6. See above, pp. 51–2.
7. Burbery, *Milton the Dramatist*, pp. 34, 35.

8. Milton, *Areopagitica*, CPW, II, p. 512.
9. Milton, *Of Education*, CPW, II, pp. 366–7.
10. See above, pp. 51–2.
11. M. Y. Hughes, Introduction to *Paradise Lost*, in *John Milton: Complete Poems and Major Prose*, p. 173.
12. Lewalski, *Paradise Lost and the Rhetoric of Literary Forms*, pp. 199, 214, 222.
13. See above, pp. 1–3.
14. Demaray, *Milton's Theatrical Epic*, pp. 102–14.
15. Milton, 'Abram from Morea', CPW, VIII, p. 557.
16. Ibid., p. 557. See Hanford, 'Appendix B: Notes on Milton's *Paradise Lost* and Other Biblical Scenarios', CPW, VIII, pp. 591–2: 'Milton has created an interesting person in Sarah [. . .] Nowhere else does he portray a good but distracted woman torn by anxiety about her husband'.
17. Milton, 'Abram from Morea', CPW, VIII, p. 557.
18. Ibid., p. 557.
19. Ibid., p. 558.
20. Aristotle, *Poetics*, VI, xiii–xiv.
21. See Aristotle, *Poetics*, XIV.
22. Cf. T. Beza, *Abraham sacrifant*, published as *A Tragedie of Abraham's Sacrifice*.
23. Milton, 'Appendix A: Milton's Outlines for Tragedies', CPW, VIII, p. 555.
24. Milton, 'Cupids Funeral Pile', CPW, VIII, p. 559.
25. Ibid., p. 559.
26. See Demaray, *Milton's Theatrical Epic*, pp. 41–4.
27. Milton, 'Cupids Funeral Pile', CPW, VIII, p. 559.
28. Ibid., p. 559.
29. Milton, *Reason*, CPW, I, pp. 816–17.
30. Ibid., p. 817.
31. See Schoenfeldt, *Bodies and Selves in Early Modern England*, especially pp. 1–39.
32. Milton, *Reason*, CPW, I, p. 813.
33. For the *dramatis personae* lists, see Milton, 'Appendix A: Milton's Outlines for Tragedies', CPW, VIII, p. 554; for 'Paradise Lost', see pp. 554–5; and for 'Adam Unparadiz'd', see pp. 559–60.
34. Ibid., VIII, p. 560.
35. Ibid., VIII, p. 560; cf. Milton, *Paradise Lost*, WJM, II.ii, X, lines 124–62.
36. Milton, 'Adam Unparadiz'd', CPW, VIII, p. 560.
37. Ibid., VIII, p. 560.
38. Ibid., VIII, p. 560.
39. Cf. Milton, *Samson Agonistes*, WJM, I, lines 1596–604.
40. See W. Poole, *Milton and the Idea of the Fall*, pp. 21–39; and Turner, *One Flesh*, pp. 96–123.
41. English translations of these dramas are provided in W. Kirkconnell (ed.), *Paradise Lost in World Literature*.
42. Campbell and Corns, *John Milton*, p. 106.
43. See Steadman (ed.), 'Appendix A: Milton's Outlines for Tragedies', CPW, VIII, p. 567, n. 120.

44. H. Grotius, *Adamus Exul*, V, line 1873, in Kirkconnell, *Paradise Lost in World Literature*.
45. Campbell and Corns, *John Milton*, p. 116.
46. Milton might have had some familiarity with the Dutch poet Joost van den Vondel's *Lucifer* (1654) and *Adam in Ballingschap* (1664), though, almost certainly, the latter came too late to have attracted Milton's notice, let alone to have had any impress on the epic.
47. See above, pp. 33–4.
48. Milton makes it clear that theatre can serve as an effective vehicle for elevating an audience towards God, yet theatre's didactic efficacy inevitably depends on its ability to entertain. The delightfulness of drama can make the 'rugged and difficult' paths of virtue 'appear to all men both easy and pleasant'; yet this delightfulness also makes theatre an alluring vehicle for 'vitious principles', as though vice were placed within 'sweet pils to be swallow'd down', making 'the tast of vertuous documents harsh and sowr'. See above, p. 56.
49. Milton, *Reason*, *CPW*, I, p. 818.
50. A. Duran, *The Age of Milton in the Scientific Revolution*; and Fletcher, *Time, Space, and Motion in the Age of Shakespeare*.
51. The eleventh annual International Milton Symposium, Exeter, 2015, included a roundtable session – featuring S. Fallon, S. Hutton, L. L. Knoppers, J. Rogers and N. Smith – that explored the topic of whether Newton was anywhere within Milton's orbit. Fallon also presented the paper 'Living Matter in John Milton and Isaac Newton'. In 2013, Rogers presented the paper 'Milton: Heresies of Creation in the *Principia* and *Paradise Lost*' for a plenary address at the Conference on John Milton in Murfreesboro, TN.
52. K. L. Edwards, *Milton and the Natural World*, p. 5.
53. J. Picciotto, *Labors of Innocence*, especially pp. 405–19.
54. See Picciotto, *Labors of Innocence*, pp. 476–93; Edwards, *Milton and the Natural World*, pp. 40–63.
55. Fallon, *Milton among the Philosophers*; Rogers, *The Matter of Revolution*.
56. Milton, *Samson Agonistes*, *WJM*, I, line 271; *Areopagitica*, *CPW*, II, p. 555.
57. Fallon, *Milton among the Philosophers*, pp. 107, 81.
58. Rogers, *The Matter of Revolution*, pp. 27, 9.
59. Milton, *Paradise Lost*, *WJM*, II.ii, IX, line 734.
60. S. Clark, *Vanities of the Eye*.
61. This discussion of optics owes considerably to the clarifications offered in J. Prins, 'Hobbes on Light and Vision', pp. 129–56.
62. Clark, *Vanities of the Eye*, p. 2.
63. Ibid., p. 338.
64. Ibid., p. 340.
65. Ibid., p. 340.
66. Descartes, 'Optics', p. 172.
67. See above, p. 36.
68. T. Hobbes, *Leviathan* (1651), p. 3.
69. See above, p. 37.
70. Hobbes, *A Minute or First Draught of the Optiques* (1646), p. 1.
71. See B. Eastwood, *Astronomy and Optics from Pliny to Descartes*.

72. P. Sidney, *Astrophel and Stella*, sonnet XX, lines 3, 7.
73. Ibid., lines 10, 12–4.
74. Milton, *Paradise Lost*, *WJM*, II.ii, IX, lines 309–11.
75. Milton, 'L'Allegro', *WJM*, I.i, lines 121–3.
76. Milton, *Maske*, *WJM*, I.i, lines 330, 335.
77. Milton, *Paradise Lost*, *WJM*, II.i, VII, line 375.
78. Ibid., VII, lines 361–5.
79. Ibid., III, lines 1, 6.
80. Ibid., II, line 1034; *WJM*, II.ii, IX, line 107; *WJM*, II.i, VII, line 513; *WJM*, II.i, IV, lines 668–9; *WJM*, II.i, V, line 695; *WJM*, II.ii, X, line 662.
81. Ibid., *WJM*, II.i, III, lines 117–18.
82. Ibid., *WJM*, II.ii, IX, lines 517–19.
83. Ibid., *WJM*, II.ii, IX, lines 522–3, 527–8.
84. Ibid., *WJM*, II.i, IV, line 802.
85. Milton, 'Paradise Lost', *CPW*, VIII, p. 554; Milton's note to self to 'compare this ["Adam Unparadiz'd"] with the former draught ["Paradise Lost"]' (p. 560) makes it clear that he considered both sketches, indeed all four, to be stages in a process toward a single work.
86. See Lieb, '"Two of Far Nobler Shape"'.
87. Milton, *Paradise Lost*, *WJM*, II.i, IV, lines 137–42.
88. Lewalski, *Paradise Lost and the Rhetoric of Literary Forms*, p. 79; Turner, *The Politics of Landscape*, pp. 28–9.
89. Milton, *Paradise Lost*, *WJM*, II.i, IV, lines 128–30, 129, 125.
90. Virgil, *Aeneid*, lines 164–8.
91. J. D. Hunt, 'Milton and the Making of the English Landscape Garden', pp. 93–5.
92. T. Luxon (ed.), *Paradise Lost*, IV, on *The John Milton Reading Room*, note to the word 'Theatre', line 141, available at <https://www.dartmouth.edu/~milton/reading_room/pl/book_4/text.shtml/> (last accessed 6 September 2016).
93. Milton, *Paradise Lost*, *WJM*, II.i, IV, lines 143–5.
94. Milton, *Paradise Regained*, *WJM*, II.ii, II, line 294. See below, pp. 188–9.
95. Demaray, 'Love's Epic Revel in *Paradise Lost*', p. 11.
96. Ibid., p. 15.
97. Milton, *Paradise Lost*, *WJM*, II.i, IV, line 358. See Grossman, *Authors to Themselves*, p. 87. Cf. E. Bradburn, 'Theatrical Wonder, Amazement, and the Construction of Spiritual Agency in *Paradise Lost*'; and Fish, *Surprised by Sin*, pp. 100–7.
98. Milton, *Paradise Lost*, *WJM*, II.i, IV, line 143.
99. Herbert, 'The Flower', lines 24–5.
100. Milton, *Paradise Lost*, *WJM*, II.i, VIII, line 259.
101. Cf. Ibid., III, lines 51–3.
102. See J. Parkinson, *Paradisi in sole* (1629), pp. 67–108.
103. Milton, *Paradise Lost*, *WJM*, II.i, IV, lines 451, 460–2.
104. Ibid., IV, lines 458–9.
105. See C. M. Champagne, 'Adam and His "Other Self" in *Paradise Lost*'; and Kilgour, '"Thy Perfect Image Viewing"'.
106. Milton, *Paradise Lost*, *WJM*, II.i, IV, lines 478–80.
107. M. H. Arnold, 'The Platan Tree in *Paradise Lost*'.

108. Milton, *Paradise Lost*, *WJM*, II.i, VIII, lines 422–6.
109. See K. A. Pruitt, *Gender and the Power of Relationship*, especially pp. 45–59.
110. See W. Aiton, *Hortus Kewensis* (1789), p. 364.
111. J. Evelyn, *Sylva* (1664), pp. 57–8; Aiton, *Hortus Kewensis*, describes the leaves of the London plane as *transversis* – as moving or lying across, as at a right angle from the trunk (p. 364).
112. Milton, *Paradise Lost*, *WJM*, II.i, IV, lines 477–80.
113. Ibid., IV, lines 488–9; see below, pp. 221–2.
114. Ibid., IV, line 301.
115. See Parkinson, *Paradisi in sole*, pp. 111–32.
116. Milton, *Paradise Lost*, *WJM*, II.i, IV, lines 305–7.
117. Ibid., V, lines 212–19.
118. Ibid., V, lines 482, 497–502.
119. Rogers, *The Matter of Revolution*, p. 114; cf. p. 111.
120. 'tract, n.3.3.b', *OED Online*, available at <http://www.oed.com.ezaccess.libraries.psu.edu/view/Entry/204234?rskey=XiUjcS&result=3&isAdvanced=false> (last accessed 6 August 2016).
121. See above, p. 139.
122. Milton, *Paradise Lost*, *WJM*, II.ii, IX, argument.
123. Ibid., IX, lines 853–4; see above, p. 38; IX, lines 892–3; see below, pp. 157–9.
124. Ibid., X, line 640.
125. Ibid., X, lines 1097, 1099, 1101–3.
126. Ibid., X, lines 1096, 1094.
127. Ibid., X, lines 1093–4.
128. See Aristotle, *Poetics* VI, especially κρίμα and πάθος, or 'pity' and 'pathos', in the discussion of catharsis. See below, p. 185.
129. Milton, *Paradise Lost*, *WJM*, II.ii, XI, lines 1, 3, 2, 3–5.
130. Ibid., XI, line 22.
131. Ibid., X, lines 22–3, 26–9.
132. K. Goodman, '"Wasted Labor"?', especially pp. 431–5.
133. J. Reichert, *Milton's Wisdom*, p. 143; cf. Nyquist, 'Reading the Fall'.
134. See M. Kietzman, 'The Fall into Conversation with Eve'; and E. Liebert, 'Rendering "More Equal"'.
135. Augustine, *City of God*, XIV, xii.
136. Milton, *Paradise Lost*, *WJM*, II.i, IV, lines 134–5. See K. R. Lehnhof, '"Impregn'd with Reason"'.
137. Milton, *Paradise Lost*, *WJM*, II.i, VIII, lines 39–41, 44.
138. Ibid., VIII, lines 52–7.
139. Ibid., VIII, line 51.
140. Ibid., *WJM*, II.ii, IX, line 776.
141. Ibid., *WJM*, II.i, VIII, line 43.
142. Ibid., VIII, lines 62–3.
143. Ibid., V, lines 45–7.
144. Ibid., VIII, lines 44–7.
145. See, for instance, J. Gerarde, *The Herball*, p. 1599; Parkinson, *Theatrum botanicum*, pp. 1617–18; and S. Blake, *The Compleat Gardeners Practice*, p. 73.

146. Cf. above, p. 41.
147. A. van Dyck, *Self-Portrait with a Sunflower* (1633), oil on canvas, collection of the Duke of Westminster.
148. See Guillory, 'Milton, Narcissism, Gender'.
149. Milton, *Paradise Lost*, WJM, II.i, VIII, lines 546–7, 558–9.
150. Ibid., VIII, line 579.
151. Ibid., WJM, II.ii, IX, lines 274–8.
152. Ibid., WJM, II.i, VIII, lines 575–6, 568, 575.
153. Ibid., II, line 555.
154. Ibid., VIII, lines 530–1, 552–3.
155. Ibid., IV, lines 637–8, 657–8.
156. Ibid., IV, lines 418–19, 677, 679.
157. See M. Brady, 'Space and the Persistence of Place in *Paradise Lost*'; cf. P. Borel, *A New Treatise Proving a Multiplicity of Worlds* (1658).
158. Milton, *Paradise Lost*, WJM, II.i, IV, lines 675–6.
159. Ibid., V, lines 44–7.
160. Ibid., IV, lines 667–71.
161. Ibid., WJM, II.ii, IX, lines 539, 541–2.
162. Ibid., IX, lines 821–4, 735.
163. Ibid., XI, lines 836–7, 352–4, 351.
164. See above, pp. 35–6, 99–100, 146–7, 149.
165. Milton, *Areopagitica*, CPW, II, p. 527.
166. Ibid., pp. 514–15.
167. See Martin, *Milton among the Puritans*, pp. 4–14.
168. See above, pp. 34–5.

Chapter 5

Passion's Looking-Glass: *Samson Agonistes*

Samson Agonistes would seem to lend itself easily to a book on Milton's theatricality. After all, it is Milton's one true drama – albeit, one 'never [. . .] intended' to be staged – and at its heart is a protagonist who performs on stage in a 'spacious Theatre'.[1] By now, the general case is closed: theatre meant a great deal to Milton the poet; it provided a range of representational resources from which he drew often; it helped to transform his poetic response to scripture; it helped him to represent the Fall and a postlapsarian ethics based in the passions; and it continually worked to reshape his understanding of interiority and of his own role as a poet. Yet the presence of Samson on stage at the point of the drama's catastrophe – when he actually tears down a theatre – poses extraordinary challenges. For the most part, we have considered the signification of the theatrical body; while such signification is often complexly systemic and, to a greater or lesser extent unstable, *Samson Agonistes* works to create an aesthetic *experience* of polysemic theatricality. In an important contribution to scholarly discussion, Fish observed that the *failure* of Samson's body to signify – a failure that is, in the event, ultimately indistinguishable from polysemy – is central to the reading experiences dramatised within the text and the experience of the reader without. The broadest purpose of this chapter is to explore how the ambiguities that have generated so many disparate views do signify, and were intended to signify, in Milton's theatrical poetics.[2]

Scholars have shown extraordinary creativity in arguing how, why and to what effect Samson is prompted by God – either in his decision to go with the Philistine Officer to perform in the Dagonalian festival or in his final act of strength – to murder three thousand people and to kill himself in the process.[3] Samson is a deeply troubling character, a problem for which solutions have been many and diverse: *Samson Agonistes* dramatises a refinement of carnal passions into spiritual intellect.[4] The drama is a Christian tragedy that shows a 'modern' Samson 'becom[ing] his own man'.[5] God recuperates him by sending him 'secret refreshings' that help to refine his heart and mind, and thus to realign him with God's purposes.[6] Samson acts like the Pauline 'fool of Christ' and affirms his status as a hero of faith.[7] His violence answers the Old Testament God's vehemence toward idolatry.[8] He represents Charles I, and his heroism suggests Milton's royalism.[9] The responses of Manoa and the Chorus, who immediately and without questioning embrace Samson's act as heroic, anticipate his most confident defenders.

It would be wise to remind ourselves of the extent to which Milton's thought changed during the civil wars, the Protectorate and the first decade of the Restoration. The prose tracts and later poetry record changes in his views of Parliament, the Kirk, women, Cromwell, scriptural exegesis and the polis. Often undergirding readings of the drama is an adherence to the image of Milton the Revolutionary, who justified the beheading of a king and who tempted horrid death by publishing and republishing a lamentation for the Good Old Cause. This Milton is a strongman, a hero of liberty, a man of unflinching principles, the imperious bard whose shadow would haunt generations of quaking Romanticists. And, of course, Samson the Hero is the author's avatar. To some extent, this Milton is haled from the 1640s and 50s. To some extent, he never existed. The question as to why Miltonists have so often embraced Samson as a hero returns us to one of this book's refrains – namely, that the scholarship has regularly fetishised Milton's authority and has often, without question, accepted his narratives about himself. As we have seen, the idea of a theatrical Milton immediately calls this narrative into question, as it points to Milton's own interest in unsettling the author he creates.

Given these scholarly tendencies, it is not surprising that Christopher Hill and David Loewenstein, among others, have placed the drama in the context of radical Protestant enthusiasm, which saw its height in the 1650s.[10] Their readings draw analogies between the 'rouzing motions' that impel Samson to the theatre and the unmediated Spirit of enthusiasts, most notably the early Quakers.[11] Hill went so far as to claim that 'Samson was as entirely dependent on the motions of the spirit as Quakers, Ranters and other extreme radicals', and that the drama was Milton's 'call of hope to the defeated'.[12] The Quaker context is particularly informative, since the questions of spiritual authenticity recurrent in debate over the 'rouzing motions' were central to the literatures of enthusiasm that proliferated after 1650. Indeed, for contemporaries, the Chorus's claim that Samson pulls down the theatre 'with inward eyes illuminated' would readily have brought the Quakers to mind.

However, the span 1656–71 was a time when the Quaker movement divided against itself over the problem of spiritual discernment and the persistent threat that carnality could infiltrate and undermine the Spirit. In particular, the James Naylor crisis of 1656 marked the beginning of the end for the movement's confrontational enthusiasm, as it rendered the Quakers exceptionally vulnerable to polemical attack and to political repression. Moreover, the movement turned toward quietism on the axis of anti-feminism, as the threat that carnality posed to spiritual authority became interchangeable with the threat of female seduction. As such, it is all the easier to place Samson the revolutionary hero in the Quaker context *prior* to 1656. Yet the Samson we confront in Milton's closet drama is as much or more informed by the Quaker context *thereafter*.

Laura Knoppers, in her General Introduction to the drama in the recent Oxford edition of Milton's works, sees piercingly through the accumulated distortions of scholarly will in considering 'the 1671 poems as products of the Restoration period in which they were published'.[13] She works to reconstruct for the drama a context that accounts for continuing strife over Church and State, repression of sectarians, discourses of toleration and discourses of opposition to conformity. At the same time, this work of contextualisation assumes what much previous scholarship has assumed about Milton's view to political and religious opposition in the 1671 poems. Despite Knoppers' caution, a gravitation toward the revolutionary Milton remains palpable. One of the goals of this chapter is to consider how *Samson Agonistes* relates to other discourses of the late 1650s and the Restoration period. Specifically, it considers how the drama speaks to Milton's intensified suspicions about the driving forces of religious enthusiasm.

Milton's closet drama evinces both tolerationist sympathy and scepticism toward Quaker claims to immediate spiritual revelation. Consistent with his equivocal discussion of the Holy Spirit in *De doctrina Christiana*, Milton remains unwilling to exclude the possibility of direct revelation while he is, at the same time, committed to scrutinising the ambiguous melding of Spirit and body in the passions. The ambiguity of *Samson Agonistes* is consistent with its generic identity as closet drama, as it invites the reader into a space of deliberation, rather than into a plot arc leading through conflict to resolution. Indeed, the prefatory note, 'Of That Sort of Dramatic Poem Which Is Call'd Tragedy', supports this reading by linking 'rouzing motions' to Aristotelian catharsis and, thence, to a medicinal effect of 'temper[ing] and reduc[ing] to just measure' the passions.[14] However, as we will see, Milton inverts the expected operations of catharsis in order to encourage readers to internalise an agon that is intended to play out far longer than dramatic time permits. In essence, the drama helps to condition the state of patient introspection and scriptural deliberation that is modelled in the Jesus of *Paradise Regained*.

The high tide of enthusiasm and the swelling of tolerationism during the 1650s and 60s brought a number of polemical texts that represented themselves as 'mirrors' or 'looking-glasses' enabling the Christian reader to scrutinise the passions. *Samson Agonistes* performs an analogous function in holding itself up to Milton's reader as such a mirror – instrumental to the scrutiny of the passions that give rise to a delusional zeal capable of justifying the worst violence. In this way, the antimonies of the debate over Samson's spiritual authenticity have manifested, to some extent inevitably, from Milton's intention to create a dramatic text that could, through its ambiguity and its availability for repeated readings, allay passions that had contributed to decades of violent upheaval and persecution. Milton found the fittest vehicle for this enterprise in a read-only drama that centres on the staged body of a blind man.

Samson's Body and Early Quaker Thought

The drama immediately indicates that Samson is, indeed, a body. In fact, he does not seem much more than that: 'Thou art become (O worst imprisonment!) / The Dungeon of thy self; thy Soul' 'In real darkness of the body dwells'; 'My self, my Sepulcher, a moving Grave'.[15] What exactly happens to this body? If Samson is impelled by the Spirit or if he achieves a state of enlightened reason, does he then transcend the body or does the body play some role in either trajectory? And if it does, then what problems might the body impose upon our evaluation of his character and his actions?

These questions troubled early Quaker theology. Early Quaker beliefs straddled the Spirit–flesh divide in ways that invited critique focused on the body and its motivation. Though their nascent theology was far from settled or consistent, we might posit that early Quakers broadly believed (1) that all men and women are incorporate with Christ, with whom their (spiritual) bodies participate but do not individually contain; (2) that salvation is an experience that emerges into open awareness through the embrace of 'inner light'; (3) that this inner light or Spirit infuses the believer with immediate spiritual knowledge prompting immediate actions and prophetic utterance in speech or writing; (4) that such utterance was living prophecy that could be understood to supersede, in its authority, the written scriptures; and (5) that the inner light transforms the believer entirely, making her perfect in Christ. Critics of the early Quakers commonly located the source of the proclaimed Spirit in the body. For Quakers, illumination by the Spirit bypassed the problems of the flesh. Since the inner light was immediate, the body could not corrupt it. The inner light transformed the sense of the body, revealing the believer's incorporation with Christ. It followed that the illumined flesh was unimpeachable.[16]

Milton regarded Friends and other enthusiasts with sympathy, committed to the belief that they, as other Protestants, should be free from persecution for practising their consciences.[17] His later prose – particularly *A Treatise of Civil Power* (1659) and *Of True Religion* (1673) – shows sustained commitment to toleration. We know that Milton was congenial with Quaker contemporaries, most notably Thomas Ellwood, the man who claimed to have first suggested to him that he should write *Paradise Regained*.[18] Yet, in themselves, these facts do nothing to indicate that Milton was an antinomian spiritualist or that he was personally invested in the type of antinomianism that Quakers epitomised.[19]

In her analysis of George Fox's *Journal*, Hilary Hinds delineates a model of early Quaker subject formation in which the subject forms in reaction to the structure of Calvinist double-predestination. Fox's tone of anxiety, during his account of early spiritual struggle, transforms into one of God-like confidence that is expressed in rhetoric indicative of Old Testament heroes moved by sudden gusts of God's power. While double-predestination 'combine[s] an acute sense of spiritual responsibility with a crippling absence of spiritual agency, the [Quaker] doctrine of the indwelling Christ presupposes a human, but divinely endowed agency – the power to turn to the inward light'.[20] The Calvinist subject is formed at the border of conflict between an internalised alien (the Devil) and an omnipotent external authority (God), whereas Quaker subject formation

> effectively reverses the encounter, such that the external authority is to a significant degree internalized, understood to inhere within and be transformative of the human subject, while the alien – the forces of ungodliness at work in the fallen world – is fully externalized.[21]

Both Calvinist and Quaker subject formation depend upon the antithesis between the elect/illuminated and the reprobate/unilluminated. Thus, while Quakers proclaimed that the ability to access the inner light is universal, their status as a persecuted minority encouraged a sense of special status as children of light standing against encompassing forces of darkness. The Quaker's belief in his incorporation with Christ fortifies confidence, steeling him against persecution and the stigma of reprobation; this confidence is maintained through the othering of those who reject the light; the assertion of divine presence and perfection alienates those who do not accept the light and unsettles power structures dependent upon the anxious uncertainty of Calvinist double-predestination; respondent anxiety then fuels persecution of Quakers in the courts, the streets and the press; such attacks inspire potent typological associations that point to the chosen, persecuted few; this sense of being the persecuted righteous facilitates polarisation.

Defenders of Samson have tended to attribute to Milton an antinomian spiritualism largely on the basis of a single passage from *De doctrina Christiana*. Milton's assertion that 'the Spirit itself' is the 'utmost and supreme of all' authority has been misapplied since it has not been understood in the context of Protestant community that Milton addresses in *De doctrina* and elsewhere.[22] His elevating of the Spirit to a status 'utmost and supreme' is part of his position that 'under the Gospel we possess [. . .] a double Scripture; one external, of the written word, the other internal, of the Holy Spirit, inscribed [. . .] upon the hearts of believers'.[23] Scholars have not paused often enough to consider how the two scriptures relate. Loewenstein infers from 'pre-eminent and supreme authority' that Milton believed that the 'spiritually illuminated inner scripture superseded all human laws and should therefore be followed by faithful saints'.[24] However, Milton makes clear that the external or written scripture is of fundamental importance in matters of disagreement among believers: 'Scripture alone is the judge of controversies; or rather, each is to decide for himself from scripture through [the guidance of] the Spirit of God'.[25] This belief that the Spirit does not overwrite scripture but rather helps to guide the Christian's understanding of it was rather commonplace.[26] The Baptist preacher Thomas Collier expresses a similar view in his anti-Quaker tract, *A Looking-Glasse for the Quakers* (1657):

> I know the letter of the Scripture is the rule of Saints, and the Spirit the guide to that rule: I know that the Gospel is the ministration of the Spirit; yet not without the letter but in and according to it.[27]

The myriad scriptural annotations that Milton uses as support for the theological positions of *De doctrina* further demonstrate that he understood the external and internal scriptures as intended to guide each other in the faithful's labour of understanding God's will and ways. Milton does not exalt the solitary antinomian but, rather, locates the believer within a discursive community that collectively negotiates essential Christian truths: 'To protestants [. . .] whose common rule and touchstone is scripture', he writes in *Treatise of Civil Power*, 'nothing can with more conscience, more equitie, nothing more protestantly can be permitted then a free and lawfull debate at all times by writing, conference or disputation of what opinion soever, *disputable by scripture*'.²⁸ The scriptures are the only 'divine rule or autoritie'; yet

> these being not possible to be understood without this divine illumination, *which no man can know at all times to be in himself, much less to be at any time for certain in any other*, it follows cleerly, that no man or body of men in these times can be the infallible judges or determiners in matters of religion to any other mens consciences but thir own.²⁹

It is in *Treatise of Civil Power* that Milton would make his strongest case for toleration, with the persecuted Quakers in mind; however, his arguments for toleration cut the other way, too. While, doubtlessly, he would have defended the Quakers against the arm of civil power, he also would have viewed antinomian spiritualism sceptically and even critically. For Milton, imperfection – inevitable and indefinite – defines the state of humanity after Christ, as before. This imperfection mandates the 'touchtone' of the written Word, which forms the basis of religious truth even as its intertextuality enables a spirited creativity to augment and, thus, to reveal divine truth.³⁰ While direct revelation is not only possible but is also more authoritative in matters of conscience, the further that this truth is extended into civic life, the more that it is likely to encounter conflict and the more that scripture and rational debate become necessary.

The Jesus of *Paradise Regained* epitomises this principle of spirited renovation based on a rigorously intertextual exegesis, a 'revolving' that enables him to understand and embody his messianic identity and role.³¹ His triumph on the pinnacle involves the creative reconstitution of a single verse from Deuteronomy into a proclamation of messianic selfhood.³² Indeed, Jesus's speech act exemplifies the perfectly obedient improvisation of scripture-as-script. It repurposes a prohibition from the Mosaic code, from Deuteronomy 6:16 – 'Ye shall not tempt the Lord thy God' – into a confirmation of who Jesus is and of what it means to be the Messiah. Attending this scriptural improvisation is a corresponding motion of the body: 'also it is written, / Tempt not the Lord thy God; he said and stood'.³³ Essentially, Jesus re-enacts Adam's instinctive upward springing to God, but he performs it as a deliberative action within a dialogue and within the ethical and spiritual entanglements of postlapsarian existence.

Greatly expanded space and time are essential to this achievement. Jesus is first confronted by Satan after wandering forty days in complete solitude. Samson, on the other hand, is confined within dramatic time and achieves no distance from the noise and gaze of spectators. He begins the drama 'retiring from the popular noise'.[34] That noise immediately returns to him with the arrival of the Danites. Within a space of hours he will place himself amidst the extraordinary 'popular noise' of thousands of theatre spectators. Where Jesus performs the rigorous exegetical labour implied by Milton's view of the 'double-scripture', Samson remains characteristically impetuous, seemingly moved by gusts of spirit that are difficult to distinguish from bodily impulses.[35] Samson acts from down in the centre of a theatre, while Jesus stands high above Jerusalem on the pinnacle, where none sees but Satan and God. The accounts of Samson's life in Judges and in the closet drama follow spiritual rhythms similar to those of Quaker testimonies, such as Fox's *Journal* and Barbara Blaugdone's *Account*.[36]

The legitimacy of early Quaker worship hinged upon a spiritual interiority that could be asserted ardently but could neither be verified nor disproved empirically. What if the spiritual agent confuses God's will with a rationality deluded by the senses of the flesh? Aiming to falsify the supposed purity of Quaker interiority, polemicists repeatedly subjected the Quaker body to critical analysis. The preface to *The Perfect Pharise* (1654), authored by five Presbyterian ministers from Newcastle, points to the 'so many monstrous shapes, and varieties of appearances into which [Satan] transformeth himself' to more successfully 'intangle' deluded souls, 'according to the diversities of the temper of hearts'.[37] Yet, by the mercy of God, 'even when Satan would appear most like an Angel of light [...] something ever doth break forth in his closest contrivances, that makes the design of the Serpent very visible'.[38] We readily think of Satan's 'furious gestures', observed unknown by Uriel.[39] For critics, the easiest way to read Satan's presence in the Quaker was through the trembling of the body. This trembling, for the Quakers a sign of the Spirit, signified to critics either counterfeit spirituality or unnatural and unbridled passions.

Polemicists and satirists frequently deployed the rhetoric of *actio* that had evolved in political discourses during the preceding decades. The Quaker was repeatedly represented as ludic and theatrical. For instance, *The Perfect Pharise* cites the Quakers' 'mimical gestures' and 'hypocritical carriages in the streets'.[40] The (often satirised) satirist Samuel Austin's *Character of a Quaker in His True and Proper Colours* (1672) describes the Quaker as a 'Puppet of Religion, contrived to amuse the Rabble, that receives its motion from his Holinesses invisible hand behind the Curtain'.[41] Here, Quaker worship appears as theatre staged by the Pope to amuse a base audience. Francis Higginson, in the *Brief Relation of the Irreligion of the Northern Quakers* (1653), argues that the trembling of the Quaker body could not be theatrical and must, therefore, be caused by demonic possession. The contention rests on the peculiar ground that Quakers in northern England could not have experienced theatre: 'Surely it must needs bee some black Art that works so turbulently on mens Spirits or bodies, and conjures them into such Surprizes', for they 'never knew what belonged to Stage-playing'.[42]

Critics often rooted Quaker gesture in the inordinate and confused passions. While theatrical performance and outrageous passions appear mutually exclusive, as we have seen, they are resolved in the registers of comedy; they are precisely the coordinates of the wayward spiritual body epitomised by the stage fool, whose 'writhing and unboning' denotes a forfeiture of self, of spirit and body, to carnal inducements.[43] Donald Lupton writes in the 1655 *Quacking Mountebank* that

> their gestures in the time of their publick *tumultuous* Meetings are *various* and *strange*, sometimes *standing*, sometimes *sitting*, sometimes *tumbling*, *wallowing* from one side to another, *lying* on their *bellies*, sometimes on their *backs*: never *kneeling*, shaking their hands as though troubled with a deep *Palsey*; strangely *Casting up* and distorting their *Eyes*, and *wreathing* their Mouthes, lying as *dead* as in a trance or a *Swoune*, strangely *whining*, *squealing*, *yawling*, *groaning*, *foaming*, at mouth, as troubled with the *Falling sicknesse*.[44]

Details such as the rolling ('distorting') of the eyes and the contorting ('wreathing') of the mouth suggest a manipulation of the body that was intended to signify a spiritual presence (hence the double meaning of 'quack' in Lupton's title).[45] However, Lupton's Quakers also lack control. Their '*squealing, yawling, groaning*' and '*foaming*' suggest not imitation but, rather, violent internal disorder producing a grotesque body.

Polemicists cited the case of John Gilpin, who, in *Quakers Shaken* (1653), confessed that his own quaking fits had been caused by Satanic possession. The anonymous *Quakers Dream* (1655) features a woodcut of Gilpin's near-naked, contorted body (Fig. 5.1).[46] Gilpin writes that, when failing to perceive a spiritual presence during one Quaker meeting, 'I still expected the appearance of that light within me and earnestly desired that I might fall into quaking and trembling[,] apprehending that I should thereby attaine to the immediate discoveries of God unto me'.[47] He then claims to have been possessed by Satan at the conventicle. Thus, Gilpin attributes to possession what his own prose suggests is an epiphenomenon of group-think, where both the spectators and the actors are complicit in seeing and enacting performance as reality.[48]

Dutch painter Egbert van Heemskerck rendered a series of *Quaker Meetings*, from roughly 1675 to 1690, that feature ambiguous details open both to sympathetic and to critical interpretations.[49] These were painted decades after the high point of early Quaker enthusiasm, during

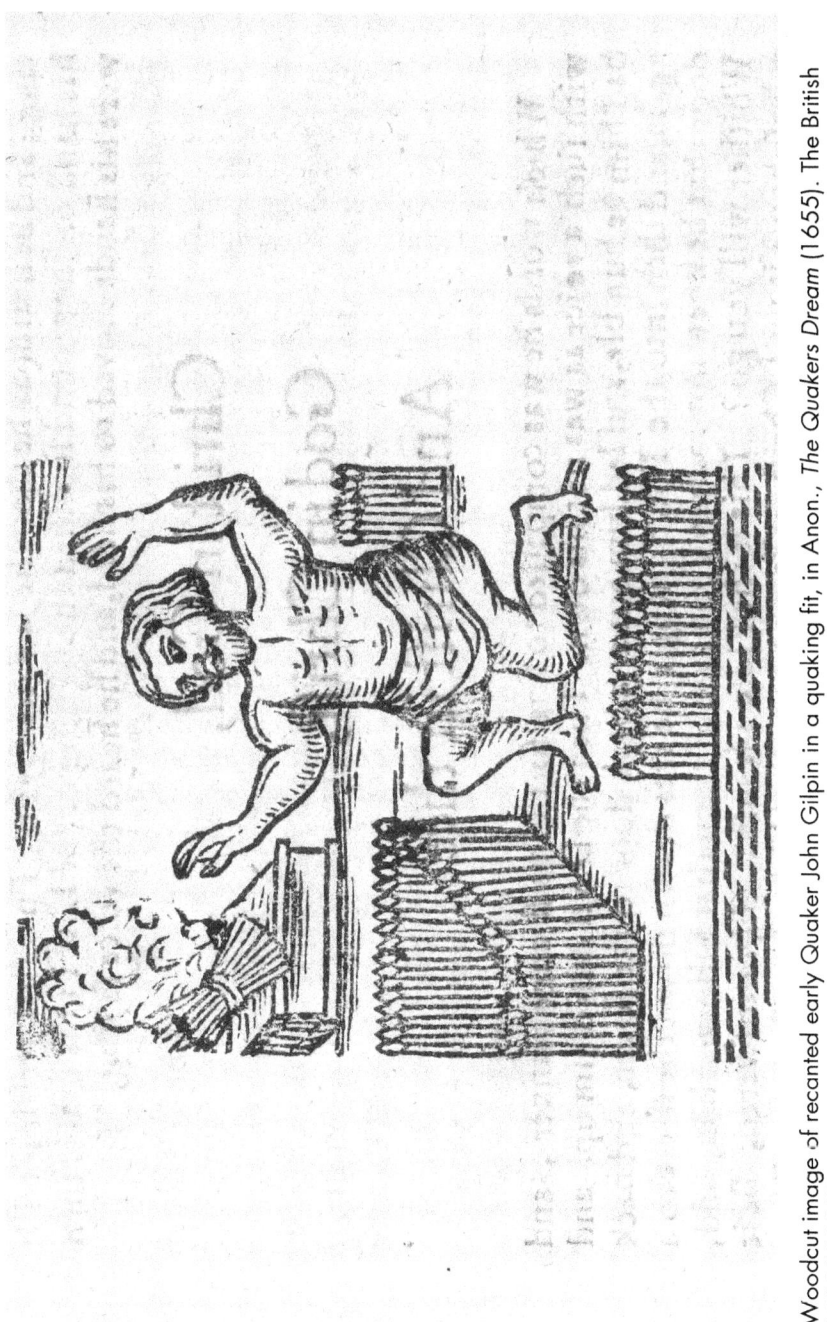

Figure 5.1 Woodcut image of recanted early Quaker John Gilpin in a quaking fit, in Anon., *The Quakers Dream* (1655). The British Library, BLL01001329933.

a time when the movement was consolidating in discipline and belief. Nonetheless, some conventions of representation persist in the painting. The *Quaker Meeting* shown here – 'lost' until 2009 – suggests verisimilitude offset by details that seem to speak to conventions of Quaker satire (Fig. 5.2).[50] The female worshipper in the foreground, mouth ajar, expresses spiritual presence through gestures. She stands, knees slightly bent, with right arm lowered and bent with closed fist and with left arm raised with hand open (Fig. 5.3). The posture resembles that shown in the woodcut of Gilpin. Another woman, anchoring the lower left corner, clenches both fists and tilts from a stool to her right. Heemskerck appears to intimate possible 'black Art' through the peculiar whites of eyes (protruding blotches of white paint) that peer disturbingly from throughout the meeting room.[51] The Friends were not intended buyers; rather, the paintings appear to answer an allure of mystery, offering a peek into the forbidden conventicle. Were these strange Englanders possessed by the Holy Spirit or by the Devil?

Loewenstein's contention that Samson embodies attributes of early Quaker enthusiasm finds support in the drama. Not only does Samson's body, as described by the Messenger, resemble the trembling body of the Quaker, but the relationship between Samson's signifying body and his obscured interiority also raises the same epistemological questions faced by polemicists and, consequently, by Friends themselves. Quaker worship involved the waiting upon the motions of the Spirit, the ecstatic experience of the Spirit moving through the body, and, finally, the expression of the Spirit through the body's trembling and prophetic speech. So, too, Samson waits during the early movements of the drama for evidence of divine presence, believes that he feels it, and, finally, acts upon it with speech and violence that involves bodily trembling. The apparent movement from self-searching contemplation to illumination seen by Samson's champions does not resolve the epistemological crisis but, rather, throws it into sharper relief.

The comparison of Samson to the early Quaker is inevitably reductive because it bypasses – at least preliminarily – the workings of Samson's reason. Nonetheless, the Messenger's description of Samson's body foregrounds distinct similarities: 'Straining all his nerves he bow'd, / As with the force of winds and waters pent, / When Mountains tremble, those two massie Pillars / With horrible convulsion to and fro / He tugg'd, he shook, till down they came'.[52] The language of the 'trembling' and 'horrible convulsion' resonates throughout the anti-Quaker literature, as in the 'trembling of all the parts of their body' and the 'horrible noyse' noted by the Newcastle ministers, or the 'tremblings, palsie-motions [. . .] and horrid screechings' noted by Higginson. 'Convulsion', signifying the

Figures 5.2 and 5.3 Left: E. van Heemskerck, *Quaker Meeting* (c. 1680). William Andrews Clark Memorial Library. Although a mezzotint copy by J. Bowles has circulated, the painting itself was 'lost' until identified by Prawdzik in 2009. (I thank Carol Sommer of the Clark for pointing me to it.) Detail from the painting is shown on the right. Photograph by Jennifer Bastian.

'violent irregular motion and agitation of a limb or of the whole body', is synonymous with 'quaking', while 'horrid' and 'horrible' take as their root *horrere*, meaning 'to shake, tremble, shiver, shudder, or quake'.[53] While it is assumed that 'with horrible Convulsion' describes the pillars as Samson tugs and pulls them, the phrase can just as easily modify 'he'. It would then describe the quaking of Samson's body as corresponding with the straining of his nerves. In which case, it would not be his body but, rather, the pillars that he 'bow[s]' or bends toward the breaking point.

As Fish demonstrates, the Messenger's description variously indexes the impenetrability of Samson's interiority.[54] Yet the comparison of Samson to a trembling mountain pent with winds and waters seems to bring us closer to this core by calling attention to the force of the passions that move him. Classical theories still current in early modernity attributed earthquakes either to 'winds' or 'waters' 'pent' within cavities of the earth, including what were presumed to be the hollows of 'Mountains'. Michel Pederson Escholt's *Geologia Norvegica*, translated to English by Daniel Collins in 1663, describes how

> when such hollow places are filled with subterraneous water [...] then is the inclosed Air, expelled, and forced thence [...] If the earth be so close, Tight, and solid, that the Air cannot so suddenly get passage to depart away, it breaks out by force; and when this conflict and breach betwixt the subterraneous Air and Water happens: then the earth [...] must certainly quake, tremble, shake, and be moved.[55]

Forensic and sensationalist accounts of earthquakes, in England and abroad, attracted readers. *A True and Exact Relation of the Late Prodigious Earthquake of Mount Aetna*, by Heneage Finch, Earl of Winchelsea, went through four editions in 1669. Finch describes a 'dreadful convulsion of the earth' that threw off 'the stones about it', which 'fell like a crust of vast bigness', a 'force' that 'caused a shaking and trembling in our buildings' that struck 'so great a Terror into the People'.[56] Other earthquake literature of the period reads quakes as omens of divine judgement. Quakers played upon the connection between tremors and their derisive namesake to suggest the earth-shaking power of the Spirit. The fifth chapter of Fox's *Journal* is titled 'One Man May Shake the Country for Ten Miles'.[57] Edmund Burrough's *A Trumpet of the Lord Sounded out of Sion* – its subtitle announcing '*a certaine sound in the eares of all nations [...] a true noyse of a fearfull earthquake at hand, which shall shake the whole fabrick of the earth, and the pillars of its standing shall fall*' – went through three editions in 1656, the year of the Naylor crisis.[58]

No event in early Quaker history prompted so great an outcry, and so public an inquiry into Quaker interiority, as the enthusiastic Quaker James Naylor's October 1656 re-enactment of Christ's Palm Sunday entrance into Jerusalem. Naylor entered a muddy Bristol on a donkey, with adherents Hannah Stranger and Martha Simmonds singing 'Holy, Holy, Holy'. The act was broadly interpreted as damnable blasphemy, and Naylor was punished accordingly after a public trial. Loewenstein recounts the event in the process of framing Samson's destruction of Dagon's theatre as an act of revolutionary enthusiasm. And yet the Naylor crisis outraged many within the movement as well as without. The scandal had far-reaching consequences, not only for the legal status of nonconformity, but also for the future of Quaker organisation and discipline. It effectively resolved a leadership struggle between Naylor and the more conservative Fox.[59] 'The fissures of the dispute between' them, writes Katie Peters, 'stretched forward into Quaker history, and splits in the later seventeenth century were still attributed to the followers of James Naylor', who 'cast a long shadow over the movement'.[60] Naylor's performance as the Palm Sunday Christ provoked a torrent of anti-Quaker literature. For critics, the event was decisive evidence of Quaker delusion, carnality, madness, outrageous indecorum, and idolatry – all terms bound up within the discourses of ludic theatricality.

Complaints that Quakers 'Idolize[d] their owne fancies' were common in the polemical literatures. 'You call it the light within, the voice of Christ, the true Word', addresses Collier to Naylor in 1657, 'when it is but your own lying fancies at the best'.[61] In *Antichrist in Man the Quakers Idol* (1655), Presbyterian Joshua Miller dubs self-justification through the inner light 'mans grand Idol, and Christs arch enemy', noting that the Devil 'is said to work mightily [. . .] with forcible and strong impulsions on the spirits of men'.[62] In *Antichrists Strongest Hold Overturned* (1665), John Wigan defines 'idol' as 'anything (besides the true God) that mans imagination feigns to it self to be a God, and to which he ascribes a Deity, whether it be exhibited to the body, or mind'.[63] 'To worship this [inner] light as the Redeemer, is to worship an imaginary and fictitious Christ, and indeed an Idol, and in effect to deny the person of the True Jesus'.[64]

For critics, this imagination indicated a 'light' that was, in truth, a sign of darkness and delusion. 'This Light', bewails Ralph Hall in the *Quakers Principles Quaking* (1656), 'so full of confusion, darkness, and disorder, is no other than the enlightening of the Prince of Darkness, darting out Scripture words without either sence or reason'.[65] '[I]t is no marvell', writes John Tombes in *True Light Exalted above Pretended New Light* (1660), that men that boast so much of light within them, shew so much darknesse of mind in their expressions, it being true of them, as Christ said of the Pharisees, *Joh.* 9.41. *Because ye say, We see, therefore your sin*, or blindnesse, *remains*.[66]

The assertion of divine vision is, for Tombes, direct evidence of spiritual blindness. For Collier, the Quakers are a 'poor blind deluded people' who 'turn from the light shining in Scriptures to follow their own inventions'.[67] In the same spirit, Edward Dodd adds to his *Innocents No Saints* (1658) the subtitle '*A Paire of Spectacles for a Dark-Sighted Quaker. Whereby; If He Be Not Wilfully Blind, He May Discern Truth from Lies*'.[68] Those hoping to understand, to prove or to disprove the phenomenon of the inner light faced an insurmountable epistemological barrier: within the border of the flesh, between that which appears from without and that which moves from within.[69]

Should we believe the Chorus's judgement that Samson acts upon the stage 'with inward eyes illuminated'?

Passions in the Round

Scholars of *Samson Agonistes* have struggled to avoid reductive accounts of how the passions relate to the drama's plot. Some have observed a gradual transformation of a womanising killer into a triumphant rational Christian humanist, or even into a type of Christ who anticipates the abrogation of Old Testament Law. For instance, Joan Bennett sees 'the development of a rational faith', Samson's violence answering a voluntary obedience to the Spirit that, founding a typological bridge, advances an ethics of Christian liberty.[70] For Mary Ann Radzinowicz, the drama 'imitat[es] the structure of thought itself'; it shows readers 'a mind being changed [...] by dialectic leading to resolution, internal drama leading to integration, conflict leading to harmony'.[71] Her language suggests the Platonic antagonism of rationality to flesh – a 'mind' refines through 'dialectic' into a state of 'harmony' – and is indicative of a tendency in the criticism towards a mental over and above a material Milton.[72] But, as we have seen, Milton repeatedly turns to the passions because their tendency toward ambiguation proves especially productive of a poetics that explores the psychological, ethical and spiritual challenges attending the integration of an animist materialism with a libertarian rational humanism. The body, with its passions, must be confronted in the drama as, at once, a foundation of Christian agency and as the greatest threat to that agency.

The narrative of the passions in *Samson Agonistes* constitutes an indispensable middle of the drama that entails the accumulating interventions of the Danites, Manoa, Dalila, Harapha and the Officer. The drama suggests what might appear to be a gradual process of regeneration if it were not undercut, at every turn, by a counterplot of exacerbated passions that concludes in the explosion, as it were, of a powder keg. Even as the drama maintains possibilities of rational-spiritual regeneration and of immediate divine intervention, it also plots, in detail, a process whereby Samson's passions are provoked in a variety of ways that answer the complexity of the passions and their tendencies to fuse in and out of each other. The cumulative effect could be the catastrophic delusion of a mind revealed to be vulnerable to the inducements and the provocations of the flesh.[73]

We have seen that the passions of the spiritual body are at the epicentre of Milton's theatricality and Christian ethics, and that the theatrical round repeatedly offers Milton a means of representing how the body is challenged in its struggle to activate, at once, freedom and obedience within a material and social existence. Vanita Neelakanta argues that Dagon's theatre represents a *theatrum mundi*, of which God remains a possible, but unrevealed, spectator. For Neelakanta, Samson's challenge is to reject the surrounding audience so as to perform only for the Hebrew God.[74] However, in each chapter of this book, we have seen how essential the social presence is to Milton's theatricality; without this presence, this theatricality flattens, while ethical challenges 'in the field of this World' immediately dissolve, since the only challenge becomes that world's rejection.[75]

A closer view of the architecture of Dagon's theatre shows an intention to re-create this round. Among Milton's most significant revisions of the Judges account is his transformation of the House of Dagon into

> a spacious Theatre,
> Half round on two main Pillars vaulted high,
> With seats where all the Lords and each degree
> Of sort, might sit in order to behold,
> The other side was op'n, where the throng
> On banks and scaffolds under Skie might stand.[76]

The half-round shape instantly suggests the Greek and, especially, the Roman amphitheatres, with their semi-circular galleries sloping downward to the stage. The structure may reflect aspects of theatres that Milton had studied in the *De architectura* of Vitruvius or had visited in Italy, such as the Coliseum or the enclosed Teatro Olimpico in Vicenza. These included columned *frons scaenae* set before the towering backdrop of the *scaena*. The columns might have modelled a suitable place from which Samson could bring down the building.

Despite the theatre's semi-circular shape, Milton nonetheless completes the round that appears so frequently in previous works: 'The other side was op'n, where the throng / On banks and scaffolds under Skie might stand'. The phrase 'the other side' indicates that the throng stands in an open space *behind* Samson while still able to view the feats performed under the roof. The platforms might be understood to be exceptionally high or to be built upon ground near-level with the top of the theatre, which may be imagined as built into a depression.

It may also be possible that Milton thought to include features of London's amphitheatres, some of which remained open until 1642. Like Milton's 'throng', amphitheatre groundlings stood under open sky, while the more well-to-do enjoyed the benefit of a thatched roof. Milton may be seen as switching centre for circumference. As in the Globe, the amphitheatres typically included two pillars resembling Greek columns that upheld a roof known as 'the heavens'.[77] The 'two main Pillars' of Dagon's theatre support a vaulted roof that extends above 'the heads of all who sate beneath'. A roof both massive and somehow supported by two columns, within the grasp of a single man, cannot be rendered plausible.[78] Although such columns were too far apart to be grasped at once, the concept offers the benefit of placing Samson on stage, in the round's centre, at the moment of catastrophe. Moreover, the idea of the 'heavens' crashing down upon Samson and the Philistine elite reproduces the central ambiguity of the drama. Does the roof's collapse suggest divine retribution or is the divine presence merely an artificial construction?

Samson's end, which occurs on stage while surrounded by thousands of frenzied spectators, appears to be the logical culmination of a reiterative and cumulative process that constitutes the drama's 'middle'.[79] Samson's susceptibility to self-contempt, lust and rage makes him particularly vulnerable to prodding from without, as does his blindness. Just as Milton had been 'in darkness, and with dangers compast round' at the dawn of the Restoration, so, too, is Samson in Gaza.[80] 'Blind among enemies', he finds himself 'dark in light expos'd'.[81] His inability to see what surrounds him intensifies his vulnerability to the gaze: 'O dark, dark, dark, amid the blaze of noon'![82] He is the 'scorn and gaze' of his enemies, 'to visitants a gaze / Or pitied object'.[83] He is 'Eyeless in *Gaza*', which carries the sense of being unable to gaze while in the midst of the gaze.[84] This social structure, of a blind man surrounded by a real and imagined gaze – a spectacle to visitors who emerge from the darkness, from, as it were, an unbroken periphery – anticipates his status as a staged spectacle surrounded by thousands during the catastrophe.[85]

The Trinity Manuscript includes titles for several possible dramas about Samson. As we know, Milton's dramaturgy had fundamentally changed: once focused on the didactic effects of plot and staged spectacle, now it was focused on the way that readers could imagine themselves into the situation of the spectacle staged.[86] In this light, *Samson Agonistes* appears to share its closest affinity with *Baptistes*, Milton's sketch for a drama about Herod's beheading of John the Baptist, which deviates markedly from George Buchanan's closet drama of the same title.[87] Milton's sketch sticks out from others in the Trinity Manuscript as an early experiment in a type of plotting focused on the passions. As such, the sketch 'follows nature' in depicting the 'refluxes of mans thoughts from within'.[88] In the sketch for *Baptistes*, Herod appears influenced by a combination of affective provocations that blurs distinctions between the passions and the rational mind. We first see him '*persuaded on his birth day*' to release John from prison.[89] This persuasion is effected either by a counsellor or by the Queen, who seeks John's release in order to 'draw him into a snare by his freedom of speech'.[90] After the Queen engineers a public spat with John, she accuses him of a 'contumacious affront' and thereby 'praepares the K[ing] to some passion'.[91] The phrase 'prepares [. . .] to some passion' suggests that the Queen establishes in Herod a general agitation that makes him vulnerable to further catalysts. This agitation appears to lead fluidly into sexual arousal as the Queen concludes her coup through Salome: 'and at last by her daughters dancing effects it'.[92] To suggest further how Salome's dance might be the final determinant of Herod's order for John's beheading, Milton notes that 'it may also be thought that Herod had well bedew'd himself with wine which made him grant the easier to his wives daughter'.[93] Thus, Herod's decision to behead John follows a multi-step process of physiological manipulation that begins with agitation based on falsehood and is succeeded by uxorious vulnerability, incestuous sexual arousal, and, perhaps, drunkenness. Herod thus embodies a rationality that has been obscured by a conflux of passions: a synthesis of psychological, affective and physiological stimulation manipulated from without.

Baptistes thus anticipates a turn from an Aristotelian dramaturgy dependent upon plot towards a more fluid theatrical structure centred in the activated passions. In *Samson Agonistes*, this process of arousal – to whatever degree spiritual – is facilitated, framed and ambiguated by means of a social round that gives way to an explicitly theatrical round. We first see Samson 'retiring from the popular noise', seeking 'some ease':

> Ease to the body some, none to the mind
> From restless thoughts, that like a deadly swarm
> Of Hornets arm'd, no sooner found alone,
> But rush upon me thronging, and present
> Times past, what once I was, and what am now.[94]

His thoughts, likened to a swarm of hornets, assail him with images of his former self. This 'thronging' 'swarm' anticipates the theatre audience that the Messenger will later identify as a 'throng': a word that, as we have seen, Milton uses in earlier works to denote an encompassing populace.[95] Milton suggests that Samson's thoughts, as 'Hornets arm'd', sting the mind as though stinging the body.

In *Paradise Regained* – also in an opening interior monologue – Milton's Jesus gives voice to a structure of thought that appears similar but is, rather, essentially different:

> O what a multitude of thoughts at once
> Awakn'd in me swarm, while I consider
> What from within I feel my self, and hear
> What from without comes often to my ears,
> Ill sorting with my present state compar'd.[96]

Milton's Samson and Jesus do not embody two modes of heroism so much as they demonstrate different relationships between mind, body, distance and time. Where Samson's thoughts sting him from without like a 'swarm' of hornets, Jesus's 'swarm' is 'awakn'd *in* me'. Where Samson feels the pain of bombarding remembrances, Jesus is intently focused on calibrating 'what *from within* I feel' with what he has heard from the mouths of others. Samson evinces a consciousness that cannot escape externalised imaginative forces that are figured as afflicting him, whereas Jesus's feelings remain absorbed into a process of patient rational deliberation. Although we first apprehend a Samson seeking to escape from the 'popular noise', he does not achieve the time or distance required to develop into an understanding of self and of that self's role in God's will. Indeed, he spends his only time alone in the opening soliloquy. Jesus notes it 'the better to converse / With solitude, til far from track of men'.[97]

In book II of *Paradise Regained*, the scene of temptation to feast while fasting helps to illustrate the disparity between Jesus's theatricality and Samson's. Satan chooses to tempt Jesus by staging a banquet scene within a desert oasis. In *Paradise Lost*, the wall of the Garden was described as affording 'our general Sire' (either Adam or Satan) 'prospect large / Into his neather Empire neighbouring round'.[98] Similarly, Jesus climbs toward a hill 'From whose high top to ken the prospect round'.[99] Thence, 'in a bottom', he sees 'a pleasant Grove', towards which he descends, 'determin'd there / To rest at noon'.[100] He enters 'soon the shade / High rooft and walks beneath, and alleys brown / That open'd in the midst a woody scene'.[101] The 'woody scene' evokes the 'Woodie Theatre / of Stateliest view' seen as Satan approaches the Garden in *Paradise Lost*.[102] Although, 'to a Superstitious eye', the scene appears to be 'the haunt / Of Wood-Gods and Wood-Nymphs', Jesus, characteristically, scrutinises it: 'he view'd it round'.[103]

The perceived artificiality of the scene helps to prepare Jesus's easy dismissal, despite his hunger, of the costumed Satan's offer of delicacies. In part, Jesus's patience and perspective work toward reversing the Fall because they alert him that Satan is trying to pull him into a scene of his own design, just as he had worked to condition Eve in the 'Woodie Theatre' of the Garden. Revealing a sumptuous banquet, Satan points out that 'no interdict / Defends the touching of these viands pure, / Thir taste no knowledge works, at least of evil'.[104] The danger of Satan's offer is that it will tempt Jesus into acting directly into Satan's script. Rather, the regaining of Paradise requires that he continue to work out and to act out his own: 'Shall I receive by gift what of my own, / When and where likes me best, I can command?'[105] In the banquet's disappearance, its conspicuous theatricality exposes Satan's failure: 'Both Table and Provision vanish'd quite / With sound of Harpies wings, and Talons heard'.[106] Milton borrows from a stage direction in Shakespeare's *The Tempest* that describes stage effects produced by Ariel when he makes disappear the illusory banquet of Act III, Scene iii: '*Thunder and lightning. Enter Ariel like a harpy, claps his wings upon the table, and with a quaint device, the banquet vanishes*'.[107]

Jesus is able to make the theatre disappear by rejecting his participation in it. Samson, of course, also makes a theatre disappear. He claims to work 'of mine own accord', and yet he is on a theatre stage as part of a festival dedicated to a pagan God. The question of what motivates Samson to pull down the theatre is also a question of the nature of the script that he is performing. If his act is one of pure improvisation, then is he following the will of God, as he thinks he is, or have the invisible stage directions become catastrophically muddled?

Although regenerationist accounts tend to see a gradual refinement of Samson's passions into a salvific self-awareness or readiness to move in harmony with the Spirit, a clearer view to the relationship between his visitors and their effects upon him does not easily suggest incremental spiritual growth. Rather, whatever rational or spiritual awakening that Samson experiences seems out of line with his disturbed emotions.

The Danites are first to re-shake the hornets' nest. Samson hears 'the tread of many feet stearing this way; / Perhaps my enemies who come to stare / At my affliction, and perhaps to insult, / Thir daily practice to afflict me more'.[108] The sound of footsteps immediately prompts Samson to think of his enemies who stare and scoff, who bring 'the sound / Of public scorn'.[109] Such blind assaults from the perimeter appear to find 'secret passage [. . .] / To th' inmost mind', where torment 'exercise[s] all his fierce accidents' and on the mind's 'purest spirits prey[s], / As on entrails, joints, and limbs'.[110]

It would be easier to embrace a logic of regeneration if this structure did not continue to recur. The sudden arrival of Manoa agitates Samson further: 'Ay me, another inward grief awak't, / With mention of that name renews th' assault'.[111] Samson's passions have not, at this point, been tempered, as once again his inner vision of a physical presence registers as 'assault'. A father both doting and chiding, Manoa compels Samson to face, with stinging shame and regret, the folly of his actions and the magnitude of his fall. Manoa foregrounds his son's vulnerability to the sensual temptations of women: 'feminine assaults', 'tongue-batteries' and 'over-potent charms'.[112] Samson, too, faults what he understands as his own 'foul effeminacy':

> At times when men seek most repose and rest,
> I yielded, and unlocked her all my heart,
> Who with a grain of manhood well resolv'd
> Might easily have shook off all her snares:
> But foul effeminacy held me yok't
> Her Bond-slave.[113]

The anti-feminist discourse that Samson employs in his own self-criticism provides further evidence of his struggle to respond to agitation, as he redirects the blame upon those – especially Dalila – who expose his weakness. We might still conclude that the dialogue evinces a clearer and humbler self-awareness if the vulnerability and failure that it foregrounds were not immediately re-apparent upon Dalila's entry.

Given news of Dalila's approach, Samson describes her as the 'chief affliction' and 'anguish of my Soul, that suffers not / Mine eie to harbour sleep, or thoughts to rest', thus again reiterating the psycho-affective structure expressed in the opening monologue.[114] Although Samson, in his discourse with Dalila, takes further responsibility for his own failures, the encounter nonetheless testifies to her continuing power over his emotions and, even, his physiology. However invigorated his rationality might be, the passions within prove a formidable challenge to a historically weak intellect. He finds loathsome the prospect of being freed, through Dalila's persuasions, only to remain in her care within the home, where, ever surrounded by the physical presence and gaze of the woman who seduced and betrayed him, he would remain helpless, emasculated and never more vulnerable. Most strikingly, he shows himself to be horrified viscerally by her body in its proximity: 'My Wife, my Traytress, let her not come near me', he implores at her arrival.[115] Her touch is the greatest threat. When she requests, with apparent tenderness, to 'Let me approach at least, and touch thy hand', he reacts with extraordinary violence, in a manner that anticipates his encounter with Harapha: 'Not for thy life, lest fierce remembrance wake / My sudden rage to tear thee joint by joint. / At distance I forgive thee, go with that'.[116] Susan Woods suggests that Samson's warning to Dalila to keep her distance – as opposed to dismembering her actually – is indicative of the drama's pedagogy of violence, whereby violent language gives way to pacifying alternatives or, as with the Danites, cautionary examples of bad reading.[117] Yet, even if Samson's restraint indicates improved decision-making, the episode nonetheless shows that his passions are as, or more, open to provocation as they were from the outset. As Dalila departs, the Chorus suggests, upon ample precedent, that Samson's fury follows not from a sense of betrayal but, rather, from residual erotic magnetism and sense of love lost: 'beauty, though injurious, hath strange power' and cannot 'be easily / Repuls't, without much inward passion felt / And secret sting of amorous remorse'.[118]

The suspicion that the inner light had its source in the carnal passions was part cause, part effect of the frequent association of the Quakers with the so-called Ranters, deviants whose muddling of spiritual and sexual ecstasy allegedly manifested in demonstrations of public nakedness and fornication, drunken orgies, seductions and the holding of wives in common.[119] The association of Quakers with Ranterism was promoted by polemics and satires such as the *Devil Turned Quaker* (1656), which describes the Friends as 'turning the grace of God into wantonness [. . .] leading captive silly Women, laden with divers lusts, going naked about the streets, in a most odious and beastlike manner'.[120] The absurdly lurid *Quaker Turn'd Jew* (1675) tells the narrative of a Friend who uses his guise of piety to seduce a young virgin. Plagued by conscience afterwards, he preaches condemningly to his penis before dolling out punishment with a knife.[121]

The role of Dalila, as both a corrupting influence and as a victim of anti-feminist aspersion, finds a corollary in the role that Martha Simmonds played in Naylor's downfall. The theme of carnal passions, a theme that threatened the legitimacy of the movement from its inception, was closely associated with that of female seduction. Letters seized from Hannah Stranger, who accompanied and sung with Simmonds during the ride into Bristol, revealed apparent adoration for Naylor coloured with the erotic language of Canticles: 'Oh thou fairest of ten thousand, thou onely begotten Son of God, how my heart panteth after thee; O stay me with flagons, and comfort me with Wine', began one letter that would figure prominently in Naylor's interrogations and trial.[122] Opponents 'were particularly eager to find evidence that Naylor had sexual relations with his female admirers', writes Leo Damrosch, 'and if possible to prove that he thought it harmless to do so, which would have identified him with the Ranter position'.[123] For critics, Naylor epitomised Quaker delusion by the flesh; he was an extreme case of a spirit misguided by passions stoked by 'over-potent charms'. A contingent of Quakers accused Simmonds of influencing Naylor's lapse into spiritual crisis and error. 'This became the standard Quaker position', writes Damrosch, 'excusing or at least explaining Naylor's errors by displacing them onto his female associates'.[124] Though Stranger reconciled with the Friends, Simmonds bore heavy blame as the movement became further consolidated and disciplined under Fox. The idea that the Bristol fiasco was caused by 'over-potent charms' encouraged further repression of women preachers in the movement and influenced the gradual relegation of authoritative women to the domestic tendance to other female Friends.[125]

The tenuously restrained violence that we see during Dalila's visit manifests more overtly during Samson's exchange with the giant Harapha. This declared rival immediately seeks to humiliate Samson by openly objectifying him as spectacle: '[I] now am come to see of whom such noise / Hath walk'd about, and each limb to survey, / If thy appearance answer loud report'.[126] This taunt immediately provokes Samson's first bid to fight: 'The way to know were not to see but taste'.[127] However crestfallen Harapha will leave the encounter, he nonetheless shows keen awareness of Samson's susceptibility to provocation: 'Dost thou already single me; I thought / Gives and the Mill had tam'd thee'.[128]

Particularly disturbing during the rhetorical duel with Harapha is Samson's readiness, in the heat of his passion, to arrogate God's will. Samson twice implies that evidence of his superior strength will prove the superiority, and even the existence, of the Hebrew God:

> [I] challenge *Dagon* to the test,
> Offering to combat thee his Champion bold,
> With th' utmost of his Godhead seconded:
> Then thou shalt see, or rather to thy sorrow
> Soon feel, whose god is strongest, thine or mine.
>   [. . .]
> All these indignities, for such they are
> From thine, these evils I deserve and more,

> Acknowledge them from God inflicted on me
> Justly, yet despair not of his final pardon
> Whose ear is ever open; and his eye
> Gracious to re-admit the suppliant;
> In confidence whereof I once again
> Defie thee to the trial of mortal fight,
> By combat to decide whose god is god
> Thine or whom I with *Israel*'s Sons adore.[129]

Samson regains confidence that God will 'readmit the suppliant' in his penitence, and scholars have reasonably seen here evidence of his renewed faith in himself and in God's mercy: 'these evils I deserve and more, / [. . .] yet despair not of his final pardon'. However, he also conflates God's strength with his own: the fight will determine 'whose god is strongest'. The phrase 'thine or mine' troubles on two counts, since 'or' gestures away from monotheism while 'mine' objectifies God as Samson's ideation. Samson's most potentially blasphemous assertion is that 'mortal fight' can 'decide whose god is god'. The claim perverts the Old Testament motif of God's capacity, if He will, to determine the outcome of 'combat'. Harapha, though himself an idolater, notes this impiety: 'Presume not on thy god, what e're he be'.[130]

Whatever process of rational clarification Samson achieves within the span of a few hours' traffic, at no point does the text demonstrate with any clarity that the 'inward passion' stung at the outset becomes moderated during the process of the drama's middle. Rather, as in the earlier sketch of *Baptistes*, we see a strongman with limited rational capacity prodded in various ways from the periphery, these assaults affecting the conflux of the passions. Moreover, we might consider the additional complication of the Danites' status as spectators during Samson's latter engagements. Does the spectator presence encourage Samson to demonstrate his masculinity and strength, to overextend his claims to divine favour into impiety, even idolatry? To what extent does this theatrical structure anticipate the dynamics of the catastrophe?

It requires an extraordinary leap to read in Samson's agon with Harapha, as does Norman T. Burns, 'the operations of faith in the life of a hero moving toward true liberation'.[131] After Samson dismisses Harapha – 'Go baffl'd coward, lest I run upon thee, / Though in these chains, bulk without spirit vast, / And with one buffet lay thy structure low' – he will welcome death and note that those who aim to destroy him might 'with mine / Draw thir own ruin'.[132] These lines imply an analogy between the impetuous rage evinced in the bout with Harapha and the obscured workings through which Samson will lay low the 'pile high-built and proud' and share in the Philistines' ruin.[133]

Ludic Samson

In the prefatory note on tragedy, Milton emphasises distaste for the comedic and, especially, for the mingling of tragic and comedic modes and characters.[134] He aims 'to vindicate Tragedy from the small esteem, or rather infamy, which in the account of many it undergoes at this day with other common Interludes'.[135] Specifically, he cites 'the Poets error of intermixing Comic stuff with Tragic sadness and gravity; or introducing trivial and vulgar persons [...] brought in without discretion, corruptly to gratifie the people'.[136]

The statement expresses, once more, Milton's aversion to the stage fool and distaste for the mingling of comedy with tragedy. And yet, despite being an Old Testament tragedy greatly in debt to the Hellenic tragedies of Sophocles and, especially, of Euripides, Milton's closet drama is suffused with the comedic.[137] Samson continually worries that his fall will leave him to posterity as a 'fool'. On his way to 'play' in the theatre of Dagon, he appears in a train of ludic figures. For Anna K. Nardo, Samson is a trickster whose foolishness becomes integral to his Christian heroism; Arnold Stein, too, sees him as 'the patient Fool of God' who has 'master[ed] [...] the final consequences of his folly'.[138] These accounts do not acknowledge the unstable place of the fool in Milton's previous writings, where the rhetoric of ludic *actio* worked to undermine political strategies and forms of authenticity; nor do they acknowledge the overwhelming tendency in contemporary polemical literature to activate negative characterisations with this rhetoric.

By the middle 1650s, the word 'gesture' readily conjured a framework of physical comedy. For instance, Boston merchant Joshua Scottow's *Johannes Becoldus redivivus: Or, The English Quaker, the German Enthusiast Revived* (1659) projects the language of antic gesture onto its source text, a century-old anti-Anabaptist tract by Guy de Brès, a disciple of Calvin and Beza. Scottow promises that, in his translation of de Brès, 'the spirit, countenance, language, garb, gestures and practices of [...] Quakers' will 'lively appear'.[139] In the preface, he encourages the reader to consider 'whether the adversary of mankind hath not in our native soil, already acted the comical part of the German enterlude [...] in the sequel; and whether he watcheth not his season to bring in the Tragical part also'.[140] Neither the theatrical framing nor the language of ludic *actio* appears in either the original tract or in Scottow's translation; rather, the language of the ludic in the preface and title page clearly appealed to contemporary fascination with the bizarre sectarians.

The language of gesture, rooted in the rhetoric of ludic *actio*, was widely used by Quaker opponents.[141] Cartographer Richard Blome's *Fanatick History* (1660), a comparative view of the Quakers and the German Anabaptists, advertises in a subtitle 'Mad mimick Pranks, and [. . .] ridiculous actions and gestures, enough to amaze any sober Christian'.[142] 'Pranks' refers to indecorous demonstrations of spiritual presence, as by one Quaker who allegedly 'got into the Pulpit' during the singing of a psalm and 'there sate on the cushion with his foot on the stool or seat, and with a needle and thread sowed a pocket, untill pulled down'.[143] 'Mimick' defines these demonstrations as imitative street theatre, yet the other modifying adjective, 'mad', points away from feigning to indicate unbridled passions. Similarly, recanted Quaker George Emmot's *Northern Blast* (1655) announces that within 'are shewed the manner of their Meetings [. . .] their Quakings, Shreekings and ridiculous Actions'.[144] Whether by design or through cultural transfusion, these tracts appear to simulate earlier quartos of tragedies and history plays that enticed buyers by alluding on their title pages to comedic material. Consider the first quarto of Shakespeare's *Henry IV, Part I*, which advertises 'the battell at Shrewsburie' in the first subtitle, just above, in the second subtitle at centre page, 'the humorous conceits of Sir Iohn Falstaffe'.[145]

Polemicists who called attention to the gestures of Quaker worship understood the gesturing body as a physical manifestation of spiritual error. In *Samson Agonistes*, the rhetoric of the ludic works similarly to mark decisions and actions that push, and push beyond, the boundaries of Hebrew law. Samson's marriage to Dalila demonstrates a troubling proximity of adherence to the Law, responsiveness to the Spirit and vulnerability to female sensuality. The Chorus absolves his marriage to the bride of Timna, accepting his defence that God had 'prompted' him 'against his vow of strictest purity, / To seek in marriage that fallacious Bride, / Unclean, unchaste', in order to help him gain advantage on the Philistines: 'what I motion'd was of God; I knew / From intimate impulse'.[146] They accept that divine dispensation 'quits her of unclean', that 'unchaste was subsequent, her stain not his'.[147] But the marriage to Dalila stands on frailer support. Samson claims that he had understood the marriage as 'lawful from my former act, / And the same end; still watching to oppress / *Israel*'s oppressours'.[148] Yet this first logical justification does not square with his claim to Manoa that he had acted upon 'Divine impulsion prompting': God pushed him from within to marry her.[149] Perhaps Samson's reasoning worked only to affirm the 'Divine impulsion': do we see here not reason but, rather, rationalisation? Did lust have something to do with his sense of 'Divine impulsion'? Does the claim to divine impulsion and the rational defence of the marriage upon this claim work, rather, to obscure a true cause in the passions of the flesh?

Samson's identity as a Nazarite introduces similar problems. Numbers 6 explains that the Nazarite renders himself 'holy' and 'separate unto the Lord'. 'Why was my breeding order'd and prescrib'd', asks Samson in his opening monologue, 'As of a person *separate to God*, / Design'd for great exploits'?[150] His final act will leave him a body 'sok'd in his enemies blood' and 'with these immixt': his blood, flesh and limbs blended together with unclean Philistine flesh.[151] Nonetheless, his failures to remain 'separate to God' – whether in his politics, violence or sex life – are not definitively transgressions of vow and Law. Where the Nazarite vow is usually voluntary, Samson is consecrated a Nazarite from birth: one of few Biblical exceptions, including Samuel, John the Baptist and Jesus, the supreme dispenser of the Law. Samson's unsupported assertion, that by going to Dagon's Theatre he will do 'nothing [...] be sure, that may dishonour / Our Law, or stain my vow of *Nazarite*', is suspicious, and yet his adherence to God's power to dispense with the Law finds ample enough support in the New Testament and leaves room for plausibility.[152] And, since the drama must hold open the possibility of immediate spiritual power – attested by Paul in Hebrews 11 – that cannot be disproven, nothing can possibly shake this plausibility.

What we might call Samson's tendency toward legal improvisation corresponds with a rhetoric of theatrical performance. The improvising Samson might bear a 'renovating and reingendring' relation to the Law – a capacity to shadow forth the new dispensation through Christ – or might bend beyond the Law both in letter and in spirit. The Messenger narrates that, within Dagon's theatre, Samson 'still *perform'd* / All with incredible, stupendious force'.[153] 'What your commands impos'd / I have *perform'd*', Samson addresses his spectators.[154] He will 'of [his] own accord' '*shew* [...] strength' that will 'with *amaze* strike all who *behold*'.[155] The word 'act' describes Samson's achievements ten times. 'This day will be remarkable / By some great *act*', he predicts before his final exit to the theatre.[156] 'Play' appears several times in the context of the catastrophe. In the argument, Milton explains that Samson will be beckoned 'to *play* or *shew* his strength in [the Philistines'] presence'.[157] Not long before changing his mind, Samson considers '*shew*[ing] them feats and *play*[ing] before thir god' to be 'the worst of all indignities': 'how vile, contemptible, ridiculous, / What act more execrably unclean, profane?'[158] Manoa notes that Samson has left 'to *play* before them at thir Feast'.[159] Both the legal and the theatrical readings involve the ambiguity of improvisation: does it creatively fulfil or does it, rather, violate scripture-as-script? The two uses of the word 'prompt' – Samson claims to have been 'prompted [...] / Against his vow of strictest purity' to marry the Timna bride, and to have been moved by 'divine impulsion prompting' to wed Dalila – carry the double sense of a movement, whether from without or from within, to push the boundaries of law in a way that threatens to break it in its bending.

Milton puts Samson's 'play' within Dagon's theatre into conversation with the story of David 'playing' before the Ark in 2 Samuel 6. As David and the Israelites transport the Ark from Judah to Jerusalem, 'David and all the house of Israel played before the Lord on all manner of instruments made of fir wood, even on harps, and on psalteries, and on timbrels, and on cornets, and on cymbals' (2 Samuel 6:5). Upon entering Jerusalem, David 'danced before the Lord with all his might', girded sparsely in a 'linen ephod' (2 Samuel 6:14). Of particular interest is the way that the story emphasises David to be a potentially unclean spectacle who justifies his dancing as, rather than shameful public idolatry, an honouring of God. Michal, the daughter of Saul, 'looked through a window, and saw king David leaping and dancing before the Lord; and she despised him in her heart' (2 Samuel 6:16). 'How glorious was the king of Israel to day', she scoffs when confronting him, 'who uncovered himself to day in the eyes of the handmaids of his servants, as one of the vain fellows shamelessly uncovereth himself!' (2 Samuel 6:20) David vindicates himself by attesting,

> It was before the Lord, which chose [...] to appoint me ruler over the people of the Lord, over Israel: therefore will I play before the Lord. And I will yet be more vile than thus, and will be base in mine own sight. (2 Samuel 6:21–2)

Again, the evidence speaks equivocally to the central interpretive crux of *Samson Agonistes*. On the one hand, David's assertion that his action was not idolatrous because he was dancing to honour Israel's God agrees with Samson's self-justification and the opinion that he is, during the catastrophe, a regenerate fool in Christ. Yet Samson does not play before the Ark but, rather, before the grand idol of his enemies; this suggests that he improvises for reasons closer to his self and body.

To play before the idol is, in essence, to worship an idol within, to worship the god of one's own making, whose supposed will is the supposer's conviction. The drama questions the degree to which Samson is not only uncontrollably self-willed but also, in the words of *Animadversions*, a 'Men-please[r]', whose concerns repeatedly turn away from God toward the public eyes he desires more.[160] Samson yields his secret to Dalila, allows Harapha to goad him into idolatrous boasting, and dispenses with Nazarite vow and Hebrew law by performing before Dagon. He remains acutely sensitive to the judgement of the general public: 'Tell me Friends', he asks just after scorning himself as 'Fool' for revealing his secret 'to a deceitful Woman', 'am I not sung and proverbd for a Fool / In every street, do they not say, how well / Are come upon him his deserts?'[161] The idea of foolishness is directly associated with the forfeiture of self to whims of others: 'still as a fool, / In power of others, never in my own'.[162] When, on the verge of the catastrophe, Samson claims that he will 'Act of my own accord', it is unclear whether we are seeing a rational or a rationalised choice. Is there not a spiritual basis for this choice? Or is that basis really in the passions? If so, are they too un-tempered to be trusted?

The phrase 'proverb for a Fool' cites the fool described in Proverbs as the antithesis of the man of wisdom. Although Samson would not be familiar with this later Old Testament text – though he might well have known the proverbs themselves – it was, for Milton, closely associated with the stage fool, as we have seen both in *Animadversions* and in *Colasterion*. Proverbs, in its fool, reveals instance after instance of character traits observable in Samson: 'fools despise wisdom and invite destruction' (Proverbs 1:7): 'what is strength without a double share / Of wisdom [. . .] / Proudly secure, yet liable to fall?'[163] 'Shame shall be the promotion of fools' (Proverbs 3:35): 'Had I sight, confus'd with shame / How could I once look up[?]'[164] 'The wise in heart will receive commandments: but a prating fool shall fall' (Proverbs 10:10); 'the mouth of the foolish is near destruction' (Proverbs 10:14); 'A fool's mouth is his destruction, and his lips are the snare of his soul' (Proverbs 18:7): '[I], Fool, have divulg'd the secret gift of God / To a deceitful Woman'.[165] 'A fool is right in his own eyes' (Proverbs 12:15): 'Yet that he might dispense with me or thee / Present in Temples at Idolatrous Rites / For some important cause, thou need'st not doubt'.[166] 'A fool's wrath is presently known' (Proverbs 12:16); 'In the mouth of the foolish is a rod of pride' (Proverbs 14:3); 'The fool rageth, and is confident' (Proverbs 14:16); 'He that is soon angry rageth foolishly' (Proverbs 14:17); 'A fool's lips enter into contention, and his mouth calleth for strokes' (Proverbs 18:6); 'It is an honour for a man to cease from strife: but every fool will be meddling' (Proverbs 20:3): 'Answer thy appellant [. . .] Who now defies thee thrice to single fight, / As a petty enterprise of small enforce'.[167] 'Every wise woman buildeth her own house: but the foolish plucketh it down with her own hands' (14:1): 'The Edifice where all were met to see him / Upon thir heads and on his own he pull'd'.[168] 'A fool despiseth his father's instruction' (Proverbs 15:5): 'I cannot praise thy Marriage choises, Son, / Rather approv'd them not'.[169] 'He that begetteth a fool doeth it to his sorrow: and the father of a fool hath no joy' (Proverbs

17:21); 'A foolish son is a grief to his father' (Proverbs 17:25); 'A foolish son is the calamity of his father' (Proverbs 19:13): 'I pray'd for Children [. . .] / Who would be now a Father in my stead? / O wherefore did God grant me my request?'[170] 'As a dog returneth to his vomit, so a fool returneth to his folly' (Proverbs 26:11): 'I thought it lawful from my former act'.[171]

Where Samson's seven references to himself as a fool earlier in the drama apply more generically to the unwise fool of Proverbs, the culminating reference is unambiguously theatrical. Samson imagines the train of physical performers and comedians who will enter the theatre before him. When the Officer first summons him 'to appear as fits before th' illustrious Lords', he disdains to join a list of performers – 'Swordplayers, and ev'ry sort / Of Gymnic Artists, Wrestlers, Riders, Runners / Juglers and Dancers, Antics, Mummers, [and] Mimics' – who, he assumes, will perform at the feast.[172] The list moves towards the physically comedic, suggesting that Samson, the last of this train, might be understood to be the culmination, the most entirely comedic in his feats of strength. While the list begins with athletes, after the enjambment it moves through roles increasingly associated with the pliant, improvising body. These include magicians ('Juglers') and 'Dancers'. 'Antics', 'Mummers' and 'Mimics' follow. As we have seen, 'Antic' and 'Mimic' held important meanings for Milton.[173] The first he used to characterise, as rigidly and as ridiculously formal, adherents of prelacy, and to denote the wild gestures of the 'writhing and unboning' spiritual body. As a noun, 'antic' essentially means 'stage clown', while in the age of the Stuart masques it also denoted the grotesque minions of the antimasque. The Modest Confuter had dubbed Milton a 'scurrilous Mime': a vitriolic buffoon or stage fool. Like a 'Mimic', a 'Mummer' too is a type of stage clown; both are actors who imitated more by gesture than by declamation, or who imitated by gesture alone. We can see these characters as forming a type of antimasque that prepares the way for Samson's masque of divine destruction; yet we can also see Samson as the leading figure of this antimasque:

> Can they think me so broken, so debas'd
> With corporal servitude, that my mind ever
> Will condescend to such absurd commands?
> Although thir drudge, to be thir fool or jester,
> And in my midst of sorrow and heart-grief
> To shew them feats and play before thir god,
> The worst of all indignities?[174]

The catastrophe could resemble the judgement brought upon the Sodomites in Milton's sketch for 'Cupids Funeral Pile. Sodom Burning' in the Trinity Manuscript. There, the masque of divine destruction follows upon the vicious antimasque of the Sodomites in their celebration of carnal love.[175] Does Samson channel God's will? Or, while claiming to act of 'mine own accord', is he not already bound up with the Philistines as a wild improviser, already 'with these immixt'?

Passion's Looking-Glass

The polysemy of 'motions' in early modern discourses helps to explain why scholars, seeking to pin down Samson's interiority during the drama's final episodes, have arrived at such disparate conclusions. The ability of 'motions' to activate senses of interiority and behaviour – often at the same time – serves the drama's function as an instrumental text enabling reflection and discernment.

Samson's apologists might have made the best case for the trouble of 'motions' in their eagerness to dismiss it. It is clear to Anthony Low that Samson 'knows immediately that this is a divine calling'.[176] 'The "motions" are divine inspiration, to be sure', affirms Bennett.[177] 'We need not adopt a position of extreme scepticism that prompts us to doubt [their] profound source', assures Loewenstein: in other words, we need not be sceptical of the 'profound source' since it is a 'profound source'.[178] The extraordinary plenitude of meanings attributed to 'motions' in the seventeenth century may suggest that 'extreme scepticism that prompts us to doubt' is, really, just common sense.

At times, Milton uses 'motions' to describe celestial movements over which God exerts control. For instance, in *Paradise Lost*, Raphael describes the 'harmonie Divine' in the 'motions' of angelic 'Mystic dance'.[179] Belial refers to the 'motions vain' of the fallen angels in Hell, which God 'sees and derides'.[180] In *Areopagitica*, Milton uses 'motions' to describe obedient action performed without rational agency, as by 'a meer artificiall *Adam*; such an *Adam* as he is in the motions', with 'motions', here, indicating puppet shows that depict scripture.[181] In *Of Reformation*, 'con his motions' describes the prelate memorising theatrical gestures by rote.[182] In *Tenure of Kings and Magistrates*, Milton compares Anglican rhetoric both to theatrical gestures and to troop movements, suggesting that 'Divines, if ye observe them, have thir postures, and thir motions no less expertly, and with no less variety, then they that practise feats in the Artillery-Ground'.[183]

Scholars of *Samson Agonistes* have long emphasised that 'motions' can indicate rational or spiritual awakening. And it can. Milton uses the word twice in this way: in *Treatise of Civil Power*, where he claims that

God impels the Christian through 'the inward perswasive motions of his spirit and by his ministers', and, accordingly, in *Paradise Lost*, where God attributes Adam and Eve's regenerative prayer to 'my motions in him'.[184] Yet 'motions' also commonly indicated 'emotion' or 'affect'. Like the passions, affect might best be understood as an ambiguous middle space between spiritual feeling and pure physiology. In the 1644 *Chirologia*, Bulwer uses 'motions' to refer not only to gestures, as in the 'Speaking Motions, or Discoursing Gestures [. . .] of the Body', but also to the physiological source of corporeal movement, as in the 'inward and secret motions of beasts'.[185] In his 1649 *Pathomyotamia, or, A Dissection of the Significative Muscles of the Affections of the Minde*, he attempts to demonstrate how the 'voluntaire or impetuous motions of the mind' lead to specific contractions in the muscles of the face and head.[186] And, of course, William Harvey had provided early moderns a familiar reference to motion in the title of his pioneering book on blood circulation: *De motu cordis*, or, *On the Motion of the Heart and Blood* (1628).

'Motions', like 'gestures', also activated satirical associations. In both its inward sense as affect and in its outward sense as gesture, 'motions' appears in satires of Quaker worship. The Devil, writes Miller, 'is said to work mightily, that is with forcible and strong impulsions on the spirits of men; therefore the Scripture must try all such strong motions, or else God knows whither such strong powers will lead'.[187] Here, 'motions' is interchangeable with 'impulsions'; unexamined, they 'will lead' to 'God knows' what. In Blome's account of Gilpin, 'motions' describes the movement of 'his body and all the members'.[188] Yet Gilpin, notes Blome, reported that 'he acted not in the least, but was altogether passive': Gilpin's body directly expresses the turbulent 'motions' within.[189] The senses of 'motions', straddling performance and interiority, internal disorder and 'divine impulsion', converge at the fault-line of scholarly controversy.

It is almost incredible that the one appearance of 'motions' in the King James Bible has been neither acknowledged nor explored by Milton's scholars. While Milton was familiar with the Vulgate and Geneva Bibles as well as with much of the Hebrew and Greek, he chose overwhelmingly to quote – often from memory – the elegantly poetic King James Version. Here, the word 'motions' appears once, in Romans 7:5: 'when we were in the flesh, the motions of sin, which were by the law, did work in our members to bring forth fruit unto death'. The verse is particularly significant for *Samson Agonistes* because it pinpoints the relationship between the Law and the new dispensation through Christ that has been a prominent focus of the scholarship. 'Motions' appears right in the middle of Paul's discourse on Christ's dispensing of the Law. It anticipates the dialectical registers of flesh and spirit that run throughout the drama.

Specifically, Romans 7:5 claims that, when the Jews were confined within Hebrew Law, embodied sexual arousal ('motions of sin') leading to penile erection and emission ('did work in our members') produced children ('bring forth fruit') born into the spiritual death of that Law ('unto death'). This sexual reproductive metaphor implies the barren carnality of Mosaic Law, which becomes obliterated by the regenerative and saving Spirit through Christ. If we can entertain the King James Version's only instance of 'motions' to be a source text for the 'motions' experienced by Samson, then his rising to go with the Officer to Dagon's theatre would suggest penile erection, and his murderous violence would suggest sexual reproduction yielding death within the Law.[190] This reading finds further support in the adjective that modifies 'motions', 'rouzing', which connotes not only impulsion from within but, also, a rising upwards – as in sexual '*arou*sal'.[191] Moreover, 'did work' translates Paul's *energeito* – 'was enacted' – which further defines 'motions' as stirred up from the outside. Of course, Milton does not make Samson into a penis, yet he does have this idea in mind while attempting to set the parameters of experience implied by 'motions'. If one pole of interpretation (such as Hill's) sees impulsion by pure Spirit, the other extreme would see a body of roused flesh that moves involuntarily into a state of erection leading, as it were, to emission.

The significance of *Samson Agonistes* inheres in the power of its ambiguities to pull readers into the evidence, to engage them individually and collectively in a reiterative negotiation. The drama's ambiguities thus render it instrumental rather than exemplary or straightforwardly didactic. We can see how the drama functions instrumentally by considering Milton's efforts to place Romans 7:5 into conversation with Aristotle's definition of catharsis in *Poetics* VI. The King James Version's 'motions' derives from the Greek *pathemata* of Paul's original. The most direct translation of *pathemata* is 'passions', the word used in both the Wycliffe and Rheims versions. Tyndale and Cranmer choose 'lustes', while Geneva is the only earlier version to translate *pathemata* as 'motions'.

In *Poetics* VI, Aristotle uses the singular form of Paul's *pathemata* – *pathematon* – to signify the 'passion' stirred up within the spectator while viewing tragedy. Milton quotes *Poetics* VI three times before the drama begins. Prominently featured below Milton's name appear only the first words of *Poetics* VI, in Greek, which indicate that a tragedy represents a serious action.[192] This is immediately followed by a somewhat enlarged Latin translation, where Milton introduces the theory of catharsis, translating *pathematon* into *affectuum*, as in 'affect' or 'emotion'.[193] His English translation, which begins the note on tragedy, returns *pathematon* to the plural 'passions' (*pathemata*), as in Paul.[194] It would seem, then, that what Milton describes as the aesthetics of dramatic experience centres upon the obscured motions operative during the *peripeteia* and, arguably, the catastrophe.[195] As such, 'motions' becomes an ambiguous sign of carnal, spiritual or hybrid passions that encourages the reader, through an experience of spectacle translated into an experience of text, to identify with Samson and his passions and, thereby, to work toward discerning and testing those passions within.

However indebted, Milton is nonetheless playing coy with Aristotle. For Aristotle, the experience of catharsis depends on a clear and compelling mimesis of an embodied emotional state, so as to strengthen identification aiding the purgation of emotion that tragic experience incites. Thus precision, and not ambiguity, is of the essence: we need to know confidently what the tragic hero is *feeling*. Yet 'motions' is the epicentre of the drama's ambiguity. The experience of stirring up and purging the passions would be blocked, since identification would fail if we did not know how to evaluate what we are presented. What saves the drama from being a failure in terms of catharsis is only its status as closet drama: the failure to see intensifies a probing for insight that inevitably turns inward, focusing a reflective process conventional to closet drama.[196] It would seem that Milton, anticipating the blockage of catharsis, aimed to turn the reading eye back upon the self and into the self, encouraging the reader to examine those passions from within. The goal was never to purge the passions but, rather, to help the reader by means of this inversion to explore and to understand them – and, thus, to ameliorate them. The drama thus creates a process of right reading that the Chorus neglects when it embraces Samson as a self-evidently signifying spectacle, one that permits the cathartic release of tribal dejection and shame and, indeed, of terror: 'O dearly-bought revenge, yet glorious!'[197]

In the note on tragedy, Milton presents his fullest – modified and extended – translation of Aristotle's definition of catharsis.[198]

> Tragedy, as it was antiently compos'd, hath been ever held the gravest, moralest, and most profitable of all other Poems: therefore said by *Aristotle* to be of power by raising pity and fear, or terror, to purge the mind of those and such like passions, that is to temper and reduce them to just measure with a kind of delight, stirr'd up by reading or seeing those passions well imitated. Nor is Nature wanting in her own effects to make good his assertion: for so in Physic things of melancholic hue and quality are us'd against melancholy, sowr against sowr, salt to remove salt humours.[199]

Milton immediately links the concept of catharsis to that of moral profitability, indicating that the representation of the passions works to some edification. He adds to Aristotle's 'pity and fear' in a way that tends toward inclusiveness: tragedy is of a power to raise 'pity and fear, or terror [. . .] and such like passions'. Kahn has argued that Milton's emphasis on 'terror' indexes the drama's intended effect of reducing the paralysing fear of subjects under tyranny so as to encourage them into a readiness for political action.[200] And yet the phrase 'pity and fear, or terror' does not foreclose potential reader responses to Samson's 'rouzing motions'; 'such like passions' is even more broadly inclusive.

Milton defines the function of tragic drama as medicinal. It operates, he suggests, according to homeopathic theory or the 'Law of Similars', whereby like provides the cure for like, as in the practice of inoculation.[201] In this case, outward seeing and identification become internalised to cure the reader-patient from within. The unstably signifying textual spectacle works upon the complexity of the passions within the reader, whose heightened critical engagement with the Samson of the drama corresponds, ideally, with sharpened perspicacity and discernment of passions and Spirit. Just as 'in Physic things of melancholic hue and quality are us'd against melancholy, sowr against sowr, salt to remove salt humours', so does tragedy – and particularly a tragedy that invites identification with an ambiguous hero with an ambiguous interiority – work to 'temper and reduce' heightened passions 'to just measure'.

Milton thus brings catharsis into productive contact with Aristotle's humoral theory, specifically as it relates to enthusiasm in the *Problemata physica*. Although the *Problemata* is the accumulation of several authors over the course of several centuries, in Milton's day, Aristotle's authorship was not in doubt; the tract ran through several editions in English from the late sixteenth century.[202] Book XXX of the *Problemata* – incidentally, the section believed most likely to be authentically Aristotelian – explains that both melancholy and mania derive from excesses of black bile, or the humour of 'melancholic hue and quality'. The melancholic's bile is cold, whereas the manic's is overheated:

> Those [. . .] in whom the bile is considerable and cold become sluggish and stupid, while those with whom it is excessive and hot become mad, clever or amorous and easily moved to passion and desire, and some become more talkative. But many, because this heat is near to the seat of the mind, are affected by the diseases of madness or frenzy.[203]

'Sowr' likely refers to a peevishness, also associated with melancholy, that might be associated with an acidic stomach. In Shakespeare's

Richard II, Henry Percy declares that 'the Abbot of Westminster, / With clog of conscience and sour melancholy, / Hath yielded up [Richard's] body to the grave'.[204] In *Comedy of Errors*, Adriana laments to Luciana that 'This week [Antipholus] hath been heavy, sour, sad, / And much different from the man he was; / But till this afternoon his passion / Ne'er brake into extremity of rage'.[205] Thus, 'sowr' suggests a moody aspect to melancholy that is capable of breaking forth into rage. On the other hand, 'salt humours', recalling the reference to 'salt lotion' in *Animadversions*, is to be understood as a cure for intemperate lust. John Marston, in *The Scourge of Villeiny*, refers to 'salt humour' as 'letchers dropsie'.[206] As such, the 'Physic' described by Milton is definitively psycho-physiological and focuses, largely, on excesses of the passions that are, at least to some extent, exhibited by Samson and that are prominent in anti-enthusiastic discourse.

The drama's concluding lines, in which the Chorus asserts that God has provided his servants with 'new acquist / Of true experience' as well as with 'calm of mind', 'all passion' having been 'spent', makes sense in two ways.[207] If we read as do the Danites, then we are acquiring a true experience that is, in truth, deluding. 'Calm of mind', then, would follow upon the purging of those disturbances that come with the ambiguation of tragic experience. The effect would be an exhilaration attending repression; the spectator becomes locked into Aristotelian catharsis and thus locked into reductive interpretation that palliates the emotion. Moreover, the catastrophe of *Samson Agonistes* occurs off-stage and at an 'obscure' distance from even the one Danite who can claim, at this point, to have viewed it. Yet, if we read the closet drama as closet dramas tend to encourage, then we have made a virtue of this distance, which facilitates the 'true experience' of inwardness and patient reflection. The time, distance and reiterability that distinguish closet drama from staged performance work towards the 'calm of mind' characteristic of Jesus in *Paradise Regained*: a peace achieved through a lengthy period of solitude, during which Jesus was 'revolving' scriptural matter and, accordingly, calibrating self-awareness. The right reader would reject the 'calm of mind' that 'dismis[ses]' and, instead, will work towards the 'calm of mind' conditioned through prolonged introspection.

As Marta Straznicky has shown, the closet drama, by translating the public experience of theatre performance into the intimate experience of reading, is also especially fit for enacting the interface between the private and the public and for closely examining the relationships between them.[208] Throughout this book, the flesh, that perforated boundary that masks and reveals, that is always both within and without, has been this interface. The drama, in its consideration of the dangers of deluded enthusiasm, participates in mediating between the internal scripture to which Milton attributes 'supreme authority' in *De doctrina Christiana* and the submission of this 'divine illumination' – 'which no man can know at all times to be in himself' – 'to free and lawfull debate [...] by writing, conference or disputation of what opinion soever, disputable by scripture'. Where the drama's difficult and dangerous conflux of passions promotes a turn inwards, so does discernment work outward from the individual into broader discursive communities.

From pervasive scepticism about the authenticity of the unmediated Spirit emerged a new variation of the century's old genre of 'looking-glass' literature. Before the 1650s, texts proposing to serve as 'mirrors' provided not means to introspection but, rather, representations of ideal virtue and cautionary exempla of vice. Most notably, volumes of Tudor poetry titled *A Mirror for Magistrates* – as compiled and published, between 1559 and 1584, by William Baldwin, Thomas Blenerhasset, John Higgins, Anthony Munday, Richard Niccols and George Whetstone – offered 'examples passed in this realme, with howe gree[v]ous plagues, vyces are punished in great princes & magistrats, and how frayle and unstable worldly prosperity is founde, where fortune seemeth most highly to fauour'.[209] This literature on the 'Fall of Princes' was joined by scores of volumes offering 'mirrors' of ideal behaviour for knights, merchants, sailors, women, Catholics, drunkards, regicides and citizens generally. Thomas Lodge's late-Elizabethan play, *A Looking Glass for London*, modifies the tale of Job in Nineveh in order to promote the penitence and reform of contemporary playgoers. In each of these examples, the word 'mirror' implied either a reflected ideal intended to shape the reader in its image or a reflected cautionary example intended to instruct the reader what to avoid.[210]

Samson Agonistes repeatedly calls attention to Samson's status as an example: 'Of such examples adde mee to the roul', he tells the Chorus, citing other Israelite heroes betrayed by their people.[211] Milton's inclusion of as many as five sketches for possible Samson plays in the Trinity Manuscript suggests as many ways of perceiving the strongman as an example, whether of heroism or of vice. Yet as the complexity of Samson's character deepens during the drama's movement toward the *peripeteia* and catastrophe, his exemplarity necessarily changes. He no longer becomes readable in relation to specific Old Testament referents but, rather, develops an allure that promotes increasing questions with increasingly elusive answers.

The looking-glass literature took a corresponding turn with the surge of antinomian sects at mid-century. Where earlier such publications had taught exclusively through their renderings of exempla, after 1650 they developed a different instrumentality. New 'mirror' texts promoted themselves as instruments whereby polemical targets could discern the workings of their inner being so as either to discern the falsehood of their 'inner light' or to discern between spiritual impulses and worldly, carnal influences. The inward turn is clear from such titles as Samuel Morris's 1655 *A Looking-Glasse for the Quakers or Shakers, Wherein They May Behold Their Errours, Acknowledge Their False Doctrines, and Be Converted*; and Lodowicke Muggleton's 1668 *A Looking-Glass for George Fox the Quaker, and Other Quakers; Wherein They May See Themselves to Be Right Devils*.

Muggleton's looking-glass for Fox is replete with the prophet's characteristic vitriol and argument by assertion, just as Morris's looking-glass for Quakers does not so much aim to 'convert' them as it does to enumerate their errors and condemn their ways for the benefit of the common reader. However, with the increasing volume and credibility of tolerationist discourses, looking-glass tracts were, after 1656, often more tolerant and often promoted introspection and discernment. Although Collier's *A Looking-Glasse for the Quakers* mostly details Quaker errors and delusions, Collier turns to address the Friend directly, beseeching him to discern and to reform:

> Oh all you Quakers [. . .] do you not witness it to the World, that you hearken not to the voice of Christ in Scripture, nor obey him on the account of faith? but to the voice of Satan, or at best your own deceitfull hearts; though contrary to all rules of Scripture. You call it the light within, the voice of Christ, the true Word, &c. when it is but your own lying fancies at the best [. . .] Oh you Quakers, be ashamed and tremble to exalt your selves, and [to] condemn the Saints that live in the sight and sense of their corruptions, warring against sin [. . .] If the Saints deceased are not yet perfect [. . .] tremble at the pride and hypocrisie that exalts you in your own imaginations.[212]

The looking-glass text that most closely approaches the instrumentality of *Samson Agonistes* is the moralist and evangelist Richard Younge's *An Experimental Index of the Heart: Or Self-Knowledge*, by which both civil and profane sinners can see 'As in a Looking-Glasse [. . .] what need they have of a Redeemer'.[213] Younge's text – published in four editions between 1658 and 1660 – follows a dialogue between a libertine and a convert. The text does not participate in the denominational aspersions so common to the genre. Younge speaks in the voice of a man who was once confident in his own goodness but who learnt the subtlety by which sin makes its way into the heart of those who, though not truly evil, are convinced of their purity. He writes in a spirit of concern that characterises the more tolerant literature critical of

Quaker belief and practice, such as John Batchiler's *Christian Queries for Quaking-Christians* (1663).[214]

We cannot know how many contemporary readers would have benefited from the instrumentality of *Samson Agonistes* as a textual looking-glass prompting and aiding the discernment and testing of the spirits. By 1671, Milton had long abandoned writing to a popular audience in which he hoped to 'imbreed and cherish the seeds of vertu'.[215] Rather, he was writing to the 'fit audience [. . .] though few'. The Danites immediately respond to knowledge of the catastrophe by affirming that Samson 'heroicly hath finish'd / A life Heroic, on his Enemies / Fully reveng'd' – 'Come, come, no time for lamentation now'.[216] The Danites are wrong both in the manner of their interpreting and in their conclusion. Even if Samson 'hath left' the Philistines 'with years of mourning', it is *Israel* that will 'still serv[e] with all his Sons'.[217] In a drama that foregrounds blindness – Samson's, the Danites', the reader's – and yet works towards the cultivation of insight, the final judgement of Judges is implied: 'In those days there was no king in Israel: every man did that which was right in his own eyes' (Judges 21:25; also 17:6).

Yet however 'few' its 'fit' readers might have been, Milton's 1671 volume continues to eye future audiences. The drama's function speaks equally well to the two possible historical trajectories apparent in books XI and XII of *Paradise Lost*: just as the text could be a vehicle toward and for that 'fit' readership, for a regenerative culture, so could the failure of reading modelled by the Danites point to the failure of progress and to the likelihood of a punishing, rather than a progressive, apocalypse. The closure promised by an imminent Millennium had slipped from imminence into vast deferral. *Samson Agonistes* does not seek revolution or a revival of the Good Old Cause; rather, it speaks to the unforeseeably long meanwhile. 'Tempering' suggests 'temporality' and, accordingly, requires due time. *Samson Agonistes* also served an autodidactic purpose, as it provided yet another means – the most focused, the most explicitly theatrical – for the poet to re-stage his own spiritual body and thus to discipline the conditions by which scriptural exegesis would most harmoniously respond to the scriptural letter and to the Spirit. In so doing, it allows him opportunity to look back over a career in which there were undoubtedly errors and regrets. For Milton was a human being, a spirited body with a brilliant intellect that evolved and self-corrected through stages of idealism and optimism, to turbulence and conflict, to a resignation that was as hopeful as it was sceptical.

We have come full circle to Marshall's engraving of Demosthenes and Cicero practising gestures before a mirror under the tutelage of actors.[218] We might understand this image as figuring the productive tensions and paradoxes of Milton's theatrical poetics as it culminates in *Samson Agonistes*. After all, Milton was a rhetor who developed and practised skills that could help him to shape the audience that was, inevitably, helping to shape him. He was poignantly aware of how the *imitatio Dei* in his poetics could, and inevitably sometimes would, pull the spiritual body out of line; and so his late works participate in his most significant and daring feats of poetically improvising exegesis while also incorporating mechanisms by which the theatrical body's gestures, its improvisations, could be checked, restrained or redirected.[219]

At the core of *Samson Agonistes* is a doubleness that seems characteristic of Milton's living literary corpus: physical and immaterial, visible and invisible, concrete and elusive, a torsional texture of semiotic sinews. The drama seems characteristic of the Miltonic text as a theatrical body that, in exerting authority through the negotiations of a contingent relationship, ensures its own transformation while struggling to manage and delimit the re-sedimenting work of reception. The corpus reiteratively exfoliates the very skin of this crossing over that is a given of rhetorical, and thus of poetic, production. The most remarkable characteristic of this corpus is the degree to which it actively encourages textual renegotiations, not merely on the surface but also, much more deeply, in the poetic and exegetical traditions in which this flesh takes root. We are not dealing with radical indeterminacy but, rather, systems of signification that return us to polarities through which we may continue to work out – both in Milton's texts and beyond – key questions answered only with difficulty and with time. The systemic nature of this process defends Milton's poetics from disintegrating into the forces of cultural desire and offers it as a means to the repairing of ruins and the reintegration of Truth.[220]

The author relinquishes control with his death in 1674. The vial of the book, once thought to 'preserve [. . .] the purest efficacie and extraction of that living intellect that bred [it]', falls and breaks, while this quintessence spreads into the spirits of the living.[221] In the fading of consciousness, the author can see the divide between himself and his audience dissolving into a blur of flesh. And yet, the actor remains, training and correcting just above the shoulder.

Notes

1. Milton, 'Of That Sort of Dramatic Poem', *WJM*, I.ii, p. 331; *Samson Agonistes*, *WJM*, I, line 1605.

2. Influential treatments of the drama's ambiguity (or indeterminacy) include Achinstein, '*Samson Agonistes* and the Drama of Dissent'; Fish, 'Spectacle and Evidence in *Samson Agonistes*'; G. Teskey, *Delerious Milton*; and J. A. Wittreich, *Shifting Contexts*.
3. The earliest challenges to the paradigm of the heroic Samson include I. Samuel, '*Samson Agonistes* as Tragedy'; and Wittreich, *Interpreting 'Samson Agonistes'*.
4. Radzinowicz, *Toward 'Samson Agonistes'*.
5. M. Freedman, 'Waiting for Samson', p. 44.
6. R. Leo, 'Milton's Aristotelian Experiments'.
7. A. K. Nardo, '"Sung and Proverb'd for a Fool"'; D. M. Rosenberg, '*Samson Agonistes*: "Proverb'd for a Fool"'; and A. Stein, *Heroic Knowledge*, pp. 200–1.
8. Lieb, *Theological Milton*, pp. 184–209; and R. Schwartz, 'Revelation and Idolatry'.
9. D. Clay, 'Royal Samson'.
10. Hill, *Milton and the English Revolution*; Loewenstein, 'Revenge of the Saint'; Loewenstein, *Representing Revolution in Milton and His Contemporaries*.
11. Milton, *Samson Agonistes*, *WJM*, I, line 1382.
12. Hill, *Milton and the English Revolution*, pp. 447, 441.
13. L. L. Knoppers, General Introduction, in *The Complete Works of John Milton*, II, p. xcv.
14. Milton, 'Of That Sort of Dramatic Poem', *WJM*, I.ii, p. 331.
15. Milton, *Samson Agonistes*, *WJM*, I, lines 155–6, 159, 102.
16. See N. Smith, *Perfection Proclaimed*, especially chapter 1.
17. Campbell and Corns, *John Milton*, p. 329.
18. See Knoppers, General Introduction, in *The Complete Works of John Milton*, II, pp. lxxxviii–xc.
19. See A. Balla, 'Wars of Evidence and Religious Toleration in Milton's *Samson Agonistes*'.
20. H. Hinds, '"And the Lord's Power Was over All"'.
21. Ibid., p. 863.
22. Milton, *De doctrina*, *WJM*, XVI, p. 274, translations mine: *Interna vero cuique, summa atque suprema, est ipse spiritus.*
23. Ibid., p. 272: *Duplicem enim habemus sub evangelio* [. . .] *scripturam; externam verbi scripti, et internam sancti spiritus, quam is* [. . .] *in cordibus credentium* [. . .] *exaravit.*
24. Loewenstein, 'Revenge of the Saint', p. 162.
25. Milton, *De doctrina*, *WJM*, XVI, pp. 266–8: *Scriptura* [. . .] *controversiarum etiam iudex nisi ea, nemo; aut saltem ex ea sibimet quisque cum spiritu Dei.*
26. 'The Bible [. . .] says nothing about what the Holy Spirit is like, how it exists, or where it comes from – a warning to us not to be too hasty in our conclusion' (*De doctrina*, *CPW*, VI, p. 281).
27. T. Collier, *A Looking-Glasse*, p. 15; see below, pp. 183, 184, 207.
28. Milton, *Treatise of Civil Power*, *CPW*, VII, p. 249, italics mine.
29. Ibid., pp. 242–3, italics mine.
30. See P. J. Donnelly, *Milton's Scriptural Reasoning*.

31. Milton, *Paradise Regained*, WJM, II.ii, I, 185; see above, p. 9.
32. See S. Goldsmith, 'The Muting of Satan'.
33. Milton, *Paradise Regained*, WJM, II.ii, IV, lines 560–1.
34. Milton, *Samson Agonistes*, WJM, I, line 16.
35. For Quaker influence in *Paradise Regained*, see Loewenstein, 'The Kingdom Within'; and P. Samuels, 'Labor in the Chambers'.
36. Fox, G., *Autobiography*: 'At last I was moved of the Lord to speak; and they were struck by the Lord's power. The Word of life reached to them, and there was a general convincement amongst them' (p. 63); and B. Blaugdone, *An Account of the Travels, Sufferings & Persecutions of Barbara Blaugdone* (1691): 'And the Power and Spirit of the Lord was so strong in me, that it set me upon my Feet, and constrained me to speak the words; for I was never hasty nor forward' (p. 8).
37. T. Weld, R. Prideaux, S. Hammond, R. Cole and W. Durant, *The Perfect Pharise*, fol. A1v.
38. Ibid., fol. A1v.
39. See above, p. 37.
40. Weld et al., *The Perfect Pharise*, p. 51.
41. S. Austin, *The Character of a Quaker*, p. 4.
42. F. Higginson, *Brief Relation*, p. 16.
43. See above, pp. 38–9, 51, 55, 110, 113–14, 138, 139.
44. D. Lupton, *The Quacking Mountebank*, pp. 16–17.
45. See above, pp. 50, 55, 110, 112–13.
46. Anon., *The Quakers Dream*, p. 6.
47. J. Gilpin, *Quakers Shaken* (1653), p. 5.
48. For additional accounts of Gilpin, see R. Blome, *The Fanatick History* (1660), pp. 71–84; and Weld et al., *The Perfect Pharise*, pp. 41–5.
49. See H. Mount, 'Egbert Van Heemskerck's *Quaker Meetings* Revisited'.
50. Ibid., p. 212. Mount includes and discusses a faithful mezzotint rendering by John Bowles of the painting. I owe special thanks to Carol Sommer of the William Andrews Clark Memorial Library for calling my attention to the painting, which had been tucked away in storage.
51. Ibid., p. 219: 'Upturned eyes appealed to satirists because they were seen as a sign of sexual as well as religious transport, and thus might be used to connote hypocrisy'; cf. Austin, *The Character of a Quaker*, p. 7.
52. Milton, *Samson Agonistes*, WJM, I, lines 1646–50.
53. 'convulsion, n.2.b.', *OED Online*, available at <http://www.oed.com.ezaccess.libraries.psu.edu/view/Entry/40905?redirectedFrom=convulsion> (last accessed 8 August 2016). '† horre, v., etym.', *OED Online*, available at <http://www.oed.com.ezaccess.libraries.psu.edu/view/Entry/88553?> (last accessed 8 August 2016).
54. Fish, 'Spectacle and Evidence', pp. 565–7.
55. M. P. Escholt, *Geologia Norvegica*, pp. 37–8.
56. H. Finch, *A True and Exact Relation of the Late Prodigious Earthquake of Mount Aetna*, pp. 14, 4, 25.
57. Fox, *Autobiography*, p. 132.
58. E. Burrough, *A Trumpet of the Lord Sounded out of Sion*.
59. Fox himself writes, 'Soon after we came to Exeter, where many Friends were in prison; and amongst the rest James Naylor. For a little before we

were set at liberty, James had run out into imaginations, and a company with him, who raised a great darkness in the nation. He came to Bristol, and made a disturbance there' (*Autobiography*, p. 124); 'I spoke to James Nayler again; and he slighted what I said, was dark, and much out; yet he would have come and kissed me. But I said that since he had turned against the power of God, I could not receive his show of kindness. The Lord moved me to slight him, and to set the power of God over him. So after I had been warring with the world, there was now a wicked spirit risen amongst Friends to war against. I admonished him and his company' (p. 125).
60. K. Peters, *Print Culture and the Early Quakers*, p. 238.
61. Collier, *A Looking-Glasse*, p. 4.
62. J. Miller, *Antichrist in Man*, pp. 6, 2.
63. J. Wigan, *Antichrists Strongest Hold Overturned*, p. 42.
64. Ibid., p. 42.
65. R. Hall, *Quakers Principles Quaking*, fol. A3.
66. J. Tombes, *True Old Light Exalted above Pretended New Light*, p. 80; cf. J. Pennyman, *Bright Shining Light* (1680), p. 35.
67. Collier, *A Looking-Glasse*, pp. 15, 18.
68. E. Dodd, *Innocents No Saints*, title page.
69. J. Deacon, *The Grand Imposter Examined* (1657), saw fit to include a subsection describing 'His Character', 'character' being a word that denotes not only physical appearance but also moral constitution or personality. The 'Character' is a brief, almost forensic description of Naylor's countenance seemingly devoid of moral judgement but placed within a text that unequivocally condemns him and his associates. What were readers supposed to divine from the description of 'this man of a ruddy complexion, brown hair, and slank, hanging a little below his jaw-bones; of an indifferent height; not very long visaged, nor very round; close-shaven; a sad down-look; and melancholy countenance [. . .] his nose neither high nor low, but rising a bit in the middle' (p. 44)? A widely circulating image depicting Naylor in a way that readily conjured Christ, but which also included the 'B' for 'blasphemer' branded upon his forehead, provoked essentially the same question: is this man an analogue for Christ or does the letter 'B' rightly mark him as Christ's blasphemer?
70. J. S. Bennett, *Reviving Liberty*, p. 199.
71. Radzinowicz, *Toward 'Samson Agonistes'*, p. 4.
72. For a compelling corrective, see Rumrich, *Milton Unbound*. 'Material indeterminacy and inconclusiveness, in the formlessness of chaos, are for Milton constitutional of the cosmos, of morality, and indeed are essential to the deity himself' (p. xii).
73. F. G. Mohamed, *Milton and the Post-Secular Present*, dismisses a 'carnal' plot: 'In order for Samson's final act to be justified, it cannot be causally related to the fleshly, rational concerns of his three major dialogues, and must instead take its impulse from the immediate divine illumination residing entirely outside of the events with which we are presented' (p. 100). Yet why, in the text, must it 'be justified'?
74. V. Neelakanta, '*Theatrum Mundi* and Milton's Theatre of the Blind in *Samson Agonistes*'.

75. Milton, *Areopagitica*, *CPW*, II, p. 514.
76. Milton, *Samson Agonistes*, *WJM*, I, lines 1605–10.
77. See Gurr, *Playgoing in Shakespeare's London*, pp. 14–26. The audience capacity of the popular English amphitheatres – between two and three thousand (pp. 20–1) – accords with the theatre as described in both Judges and *Samson Agonistes*.
78. The odd or implausible features of Milton's 'Theatre' might owe something to the implausibility of the architecture of the House of Dagon, as it is described in Judges 16:25–7, where 3,000 spectators are on the roof during the time Samson is described as pulling that roof upon him from beneath.
79. Cf. J. Arthos, 'Milton and the Passions'.
80. Milton, *Paradise Lost*, *WJM*, II.i, VII, line 27.
81. Milton, *Samson Agonistes*, *WJM*, I, lines 65, 75.
82. Ibid., line 80.
83. Ibid., lines 34, 567–8.
84. Ibid., line 41. See Fish, 'Spectacle and Evidence', p. 582: 'Self-deprived of an inward integrity that would repel alien significances, [Samson] takes on the significances projected onto him by those who behold. He becomes quite literally a "gaze", an extension of whatever glance happens to fall on him, a continually mounted spectacle, a commodified object of appropriation, always in the power of others and never in his own'.
85. See D. N. C. Wood, *Exiled from Light*, pp. 141–2.
86. Cf. above, pp. 73–5.
87. For Milton and Buchanan, see S. Kernan, 'George Buchanan and the Genre of *Samson Agonistes*'; and E. Sauer, 'Closet Drama and the Case of *Tyrannical-Government Anatomized*'.
88. See above, pp. 135–6.
89. Milton, 'Baptistes', *CPW*, VIII, p. 558.
90. Ibid., p. 558.
91. Ibid., p. 558.
92. Ibid., p. 558.
93. Ibid., p. 558.
94. Milton, *Samson Agonistes*, *WJM*, I, lines 17–22.
95. See above, pp. 39–40, 74–6.
96. Milton, *Paradise Regained*, *WJM*, II.ii, I, lines 196–200.
97. Ibid., I, lines 190–1.
98. See above, pp. 146–9.
99. Milton, *Paradise Regained*, *WJM*, II.ii, II, lines 286.
100. Ibid., II, lines 289, 291–2.
101. Ibid., II, lines 292–4.
102. See above, pp. 146–9.
103. Milton, *Paradise Regained*, *WJM*, II.ii, II, lines 296–7.
104. Ibid., II, lines 369–71.
105. Ibid., II, lines 381–2.
106. Ibid., II, lines 402–3.
107. Shakespeare, *The Tempest*, NS, III, iii, line 52ff.
108. Milton, *Samson Agonistes*, *WJM*, I, lines 111–14.
109. See above, p. 41.

110. Milton, *Samson Agonistes*, *WJM*, I, lines 610–14.
111. Ibid., lines 330–1.
112. Ibid., lines 403, 404, 423.
113. Ibid., lines 406–11.
114. Ibid., lines 457–9.
115. Ibid., line 725.
116. Ibid., lines 949–54.
117. S. Woods, 'Inviting Rival Hermeneutics'.
118. Milton, *Samson Agonistes*, *WJM*, I, lines 1003, 1005–7.
119. See, for instance, N. Flinker, *The Song of Songs in English Renaissance Literature*, pp. 120–39. Collier thoroughly defends the geneology: 'That their principles are but the principles of the old Ranters [. . .] I need not prove in this place [. . .] The Ranters would have no Christ but within; no Scripture to be a rule; no Ordinances, no Law but their lusts, no Heaven nor glorie but here, no sin but what men fancied to be'; however, the Quakers 'smooth it over with an outward austere carriage before men, but within are full of filthyness, pride and abomination, which by degrees breaketh forth' (*A Looking-Glasse*, p. 7).
120. Anon., *The Devil Turned Quaker*, p. 5.
121. Anon., *The Quaker Turn'd Jew*; see also J. Denham, *A Relation of a Quaker, That to the Shame of His Profession, Attempted to Bugger a Mare near Colchester* (1659); and the ballad 'The Four-Legg'd Quaker' (1664).
122. Blome, *The Fanatick History*, p. 41.
123. L. Damrosch, *The Sorrows of the Quaker Jesus*, p. 125.
124. Ibid., p. 131; cf. Deacon, *The Grand Imposter Examined*, pp. 38–9; and Blome, *The Fanatick History*, p. 108.
125. Samson's hostile response to Dalila's proposition to free him, to remove him to her home, and, 'With nursing diligence', to 'tend about [him] to old age' (Milton, *Samson Agonistes*, *WJM*, I, lines 924–5), finds an intriguing analogue in Simmonds's relationship with Naylor before the Bristol event. Stranger and Simmonds had ignited a broil while challenging an effort to suppress women preachers by interrupting meetings led by Francis Howgill and Edward Burrough. The women sought Naylor's intervention when expelled from the Friends. Naylor's credibility began to falter after it became known that he had remained in Simmonds's home for three days. Friends removed Naylor to Bristol by force, and Simmonds would claim that she had been thrown down a staircase in the tumult. Soon after, Naylor was jailed during a mission to Exeter. Simmonds, after serving in London as a nurse to the wife of Major-General John Desborough, sought and received an order for Naylor's release from yet another imprisonment. M. Bell, 'Simmonds, Martha (*bap.* 1624, *d.* 1665)', in Matthew and Harrison (eds), *Oxford Dictionary of National Biography*, available at <http://dx.doi.org/10.1093/ref:odnb/37959> (last accessed 12 June 2014).
126. Milton, *Samson Agonistes*, *WJM*, I, lines 1088–90.
127. Ibid., line 1091.
128. Ibid., lines 1092–3.
129. Ibid., lines 1151–5, 1168–77.
130. Ibid., line 1156.

131. N. T. Burns, '"Then Stood Up Phineas"', p. 30.
132. Milton, *Samson Agonistes*, *WJM*, I, lines 1237–9, 1266–7.
133. Ibid., line 1069.
134. Freedman suggests that the note on tragedy is not intended to provide an aesthetic framework for the drama: 'it has more to do with what others said on the subject, principally Dryden, and with the kind of works others were writing at the time' ('Waiting for Samson', p. 42); cf. Radzinowicz, *Toward 'Samson Agonistes'*, p. 5; and Rosenberg, 'Milton, Dryden, and the Ideology of Genre'.
135. Milton, 'Of That Sort of Dramatic Poem', *WJM*, I.ii, p. 332.
136. Ibid., p. 332. See Aristotle, *Poetics* V; and Sidney, *The Defense of Poesy*, p. 1078: the plays of English dramatists 'be neither right tragedies nor right comedies, mingling kings and clowns, not because the matter so carrieth it, but thrust in the clown by head and shoulders to play a part in majestical matters with neither decency nor discretion'.
137. C. A. Patrides, 'The Comic Dimension in Greek Tragedy and *Samson Agonistes*', p. 4: The note on tragedy 'is monomaniacally polemical and may not be trusted as a [. . .] definitive[ly]' proscriptive statement on the drama's aesthetics. See also Wittreich, *Shifting Contexts*, pp. 1–4.
138. Stein, *Heroic Knowledge*, p. 201.
139. G. de Brès, *Johannes Becoldus redivivus*, fol. A3v.
140. Ibid., fol. A4: 'and also [let it be considered] whether the adversary of mankind hath not in our native soil, already acted the comical part of the German enterlude represented in the sequel; and whether he watcheth not his season to bring in the Tragical part also' (fol. A4).
141. The ludic Quaker was the flipside of the morose Quaker, a different form of Quaker theatricality. The Friends, writes Damrosch, 'were given to a gravity of demeanor that struck many contemporaries as an affectation of moroseness' (*The Sorrows of the Quaker Jesus*, p. 35).
142. Blome, *The Fanatick History*, title page.
143. Ibid., p. 112.
144. G. Emmot, *Northern Blast*, title page; the title page of Lupton's *Quacking Mountebank* similarly advertises 'their Behaviours, Gestures, Aimes and Ends'.
145. Shakespeare, *The History of Henry the Fourth* (1598), title page.
146. Milton, *Samson Agonistes*, *WJM*, I, lines 318–21, 222–3.
147. Ibid., lines 324–5.
148. Ibid., lines 231–3.
149. Ibid., line 422.
150. Ibid., lines 30–2.
151. Ibid., lines 1726, 1657.
152. Ibid., lines 1385–6.
153. Ibid., lines 1626–7, italics mine throughout.
154. Ibid., lines 1640–1.
155. Ibid., lines 1643–5.
156. Ibid., lines 1388–9.
157. Ibid., argument.
158. Ibid., lines 1340–1, 1361–2.
159. Ibid., line 1448.

160. Milton, *Animadversions*, CPW, I, p. 661; cf. Ephesians 6:6 and Milton, *Of Reformation*, CPW, I, p. 520. See also Coiro, 'Fable and Old Song', p. 147.
161. Milton, *Samson Agonistes*, WJM, I, lines 202–5.
162. Ibid., lines 77–8.
163. Ibid., lines 53–5.
164. Ibid., lines 196–7.
165. Ibid., lines 201–2
166. Ibid., lines 1377–9.
167. Ibid., lines 1220, 1222–3.
168. Ibid., lines 1588–9.
169. Ibid., lines 420–1.
170. Ibid., lines 352, 355–6.
171. Ibid., line 231.
172. Ibid., lines 1318, 1323–5.
173. See above, pp. 109, 112–13.
174. Milton, *Samson Agonistes*, WJM, I, lines 1335–41.
175. Cf. Milton, 'Cupids Funeral Pile', CPW, VIII, pp. 558–9: 'the Gallantry of the town passe by in Processi[on] with musick and song to the temple of Venus Urania or Peor'; the two 'noble strangers' (angels of the Lord) are 'invite[d]' to 'thire city solemnities'.
176. A. Low, *The Blaze of Noon*, p. 80.
177. Bennett, *Reviving Liberty*, p. 152: 'Now,' she continues sardonically, 'if in response to his "rousing motions", Milton's protagonist, instead of pulling down the pillars of the Temple, had stood between them and preached reformation and reconciliation to the Philistines (suffering martyr-like their scorn and violence), then presumably the divine origin of Samson's rousing motions would be in less doubt'.
178. Loewenstein, 'Revenge of the Saint', p. 162.
179. Milton, *Paradise Lost*, WJM, II.i, V, lines 625, 620.
180. Ibid., II, line 191.
181. Milton, *Areopagitica*, CPW, II, p. 527.
182. See above, pp. 94–5.
183. Milton, *Tenure of Kings and Magistrates*, CPW, III, p. 255; cf. Milton, *Of Education*, CPW, II, p. 411; and Milton, *The History of Britain*, CPW, V, p. 341.
184. Milton, *Treatise of Civil Power*, CPW, VII, p. 261; *Paradise Lost*, WJM, II.ii, XI, line 91; cf. above, pp. 167–8.
185. Bulwer, *Chirologia*, fols. A7–A7v, p. 7.
186. Bulwer, *Pathomyotamia*, title page.
187. J. Miller, *Antichrist in Man*, p. 2.
188. Blome, *The Fanatick History*, p. 74.
189. Ibid., p. 74.
190. See Wood, *Exiled from Light*, p. xx.
191. The Tyndale, Cranmer and Geneva translations choose 'stirred up' rather than 'wrought' or 'did work' to interpret the passive *energeito*, 'enacted'. The translations and cross-references are to be found in A. Marshall and J. B. Phillips (trans.), *The Interlinear Greek–English New Testament*.
192. A facsimile of the title page is printed in WJM, I.ii, p. 330.

193. Ibid., I, ii, p. 330.
194. Milton, 'Of That Sort of Dramatic Poem', *WJM*, I.ii, p. 331.
195. See Grossman, 'Textual Ethics', pp. 95–8.
196. Burbery, *Milton the Dramatist*, pp. 151–63, extends the bizarre argument that 'visual cues' in the text of *Samson Agonistes* indicate that Milton intended the drama to be staged, at some point. It is entirely unclear why such 'cues' would seem out-of-place in a closet drama, where they would supply lacking visual information.
197. Milton, *Samson Agonistes*, *WJM*, I, line 1660.
198. Scholarly misinterpretation of catharsis is discussed in Wood, *Exiled from Light*, pp. 60–79; cf. Radzinowicz, *Toward 'Samson Agonistes'*, pp. 8–14.
199. Milton, 'Of That Sort of Dramatic Poem', *WJM*, I.ii, p. 331.
200. Kahn, 'Aesthetics as Critique'.
201. S. H. Butcher, *Aristotle's Theory of Poetry and Fine Art*, pp. 243–7; cf. F. Woerther, 'Music and Education of the Soul in Plato and Aristotle'.
202. W. S. Hett, Introduction, in Aristotle, *Problems*, pp. vii–x.
203. Aristotle, *Problems*, II, p. 163.
204. Shakespeare, *Richard II*, NS, V, vi, lines 19–21.
205. Shakespeare, *The Comedy of Errors*, NS, V, I, lines 45–8. See also *Henry VI, Part II*, NS, III, iii, line 303; and *The Taming of the Shrew*, NS, V, ii, line 161.
206. J. Marston, *The Scourge of Villeiny*, Satire XI, 'Humours', line 154.
207. Milton, *Samson Agonistes*, *WJM*, I, lines 1755–8.
208. M. Straznicky, *Privacy, Playreading, and Women's Closet Drama, 1550–1700*, especially pp. 1–2; see also K. Raber, *Gender, Class, and Genre in the Early Modern Closet Drama*, pp. 240–8.
209. W. Baldwin, *The Last Part of the Mirour for Magistrates*, title page.
210. 'Mirrors' that placed sectarians on display as cautionary figures also appeared, such as T. Nash, *A Myrror for Martinists and All Other Schismatiques* (1590); and J. Vicars, *Speculum scripturale schismaticorum* (1649), a broadsheet.
211. Milton, *Samson Agonistes*, *WJM*, I, line 290.
212. Collier, *A Looking-Glasse*, pp. 4, 15; see above, pp. 175, 183–4, 207n214.
213. R. Younge, *An Experimental Index of the Heart* (1960), title page.
214. J. Batchiler, *Christian Queries to Quaking-Christians* (1663).
215. See above, pp. 175, 183, 184.
216. Milton, *Samson Agonistes*, *WJM*, I, lines 1710–11, 1708.
217. Ibid., lines 1712, 240.
218. See above, p. 56.
219. Coiro, 'Fable and Old Song', p. 124: 'John Milton read back and then projected the future of his own poetic career in the voice of Samson and the voices that surround and remain behind after his death'.
220. See Milton, *Areopagitica*, *CPW*, II, pp. 549–50.
221. Ibid., p. 253; see above, pp. 20, 54.

Epilogue: A Systemic Corpus

Here, I hope to push just beyond the scope of the preceding chapters in order to apply the insights of a theatrical Milton to the *behaviour* of the Miltonic corpus *as a theatrical body*. In essence, this consideration offers a definition of what that corpus *is*, at least insofar as Milton had controlled and consolidated it, to the best of his ability, before his death.

First, it would be helpful to set forth some definitive aspects of Milton's theatricality as established above:

- Theatricality involves an embodied rhetorical performance intended to have an effect on an audience.
- Theatricality marks a countering response that works upon this rhetorical body. Theatricality entails a management of a communication between two bodies: that of the rhetor-actor-poet and that of the rhetorical audience-spectators-readers.
- Theatricality destabilises identity, threatening to feminise it, to queer it, to render it indecorous, or to render it foolish and risible.
- Theatricality identifies a discursive field – entailing the rhetorical strategies and effects of framing a given human action, including speech and writing – as an act of theatre. This discursive field takes its origin in classical rhetorical tradition, in the rhetoric of *actio*, and becomes richer and more expansive during the political and religious struggles of the middle seventeenth century.
- The negotiations of theatricality are negotiations of influences that work to shape the body by way of the passions, which are understood by Milton as a conflux of spiritual feeling, physiological stimulation, and emotions that, in real experience, cannot fully be differentiated.
- Theatricality marks limitations of authority by way of the visual field, in the tension between the rhetor-actor-poet's optical force

upon a focal point and the menace of an answering gaze that inhabits the periphery and cannot fully be countered; this menace threatens not only to pull upon the theatrical body, but also to disintegrate it. Theatrical experience can thus involve distinct emotions, ranging from confidence to terror, desire to antagonism, and a range of emotions simultaneously.

- The negotiations of theatricality can be based on script and understood in relation to script. Both rigid obedience to the letter of the script and a wild improvisation based in the performative, embodied ego will violate script, which is always itself and more than itself. Particularly in Milton's later works, theatricality can take scripture as its foundation. Since this foundational script contains significant ambiguities, obscurities and apparent contradictions; since any scriptural place must be understood within the fuller contexts of scripture; since any performance of script is located within a unique rhetorical situation and performed toward a unique purpose; since the Spirit plays a fundamental role in aiding this management; and since, within any performance context, the Spirit is, almost inevitably, confluent with physiology and the passions, theatricality marks a specific relationship to scripture and spirit that is open to analysis as it plays out within the text and within any given social context.

In the Restoration Milton, theatricality achieves its highest realisation as a system of authorial and textual management. It entails the strategy and effects of the author's observation of and response to his own shaping within the actor–audience dialectic. The author bears responsibility for the operations of the system and for cooperating with his audience – both in its present and in its future forms – to reproduce an evolving choreography.

A theatrical Milton is a Milton staged, a Milton continually present within a text that continually exerts its authority upon readers, even while these readers continually exert authority over the text, re-sedimenting it, as it were, from within the discursive communities that it shapes. Milton the man died in 1674; yet, as he asserts in *Areopagitica*, 'a good Booke is the pretious life-blood of a master spirit, imbalm'd and treasur'd up on purpose to a life beyond life'.[1] In each of the texts at the centre of these chapters, we have seen Milton, as it were, testing himself as a poet by theatricalising the scene of writing. Not only does he stage himself before his public, but he also analyses and offers up for analysis the poet staged, the poet who is interpreting and creatively augmenting scripture in the attempt to communicate its significance – always an exfoliating, incomplete significance – to a reading public that, ultimately, is beyond his complete control.

In the terms of the systems theoretical approach of German sociologist Niklas Luhmann, we can understand the Miltonic corpus not as a measurable, material entity but, rather, as a system in which the readership and the author inheres. If the relationship between actor and audience is embodied, to the extent that it is not two separate bodies but one dialectically co-shaping body, so too is the corpus an evolving system. As Luhmann posits, the system cannot be understood to exist without the presence of the observer, which inevitably obtrudes upon the systemic operation and thus becomes integrated into it.[2] We might borrow from Luhmann this concept of the observer and apply it, liberally, to identify the poet himself as he inheres within his own text as an observer of the author–reader dialectic.

Although it is undeniable that Milton's texts absorb and respond to the social, textual and cultural materials and forces of his immediate context, we might follow Luhmann's insistence that a system remains independent of its environment. In other words, the dynamic body of *information* constituted by poet, reader and observer that *is* the corpus operates independently of its *immediate* environment.[3] The immediate environment – whether physical, discursive or semiotic – does not simply seep into the corpus as though it were a cell with a permeable outer membrane that filters nothing. Otherwise, any communicating system would dissolve indistinguishably into its immediate environment; the agons of authority in Milton would disappear into a Barthesian fabric of textuality.[4] Of course, the evolution of a readership is not exclusive to the operations of the system in which it inheres, but is, rather, further informed by new forms and theories of knowledge, as well as by discursive communities that apply new modes of reading and interpretation. We can continue to follow Luhmann by adopting the principle of 'structural coupling', which posits that independent systems are capable of touching or connecting to each other and, thus, of feeding into their respective operations.[5] For example, discussions and debates about religious extremism and terrorism could meet with the 'rouzing motions' of *Samson Agonistes*, both altering it and being altered by it in turn. The corpus and the coupled discursive community do not impose upon each other in isolated phenomena; rather, each participates continuously in sedimenting the other.

It should be clear that the theatrical Milton explodes Fish's Milton, the poet of certainty who imposes his certainty – a certainty of which Fish is too often certain – on audiences and repeatedly checks their efforts to question it. By returning the body to Milton's understanding, use and representation of rhetoric and thus by moving beyond the strictures and implied ontology of the Ramist model, we also move beyond the limits of the Lewalskian Milton, who is an elevated teacher of the people, indeed a type of Moses who writes to raise them from chains into liberty. Yet, given the double nature of the poet – as both the author interacting with his audience and as the observer of that interaction – the system of the Miltonic corpus does not, or should not, dissolve into a producer of absolute indeterminacy, into a centre of naked writhing flesh.[6] Inversely, we would reach the same zero-level of authority if we were part of a concretised corpus of dead piety and unyielding certainty.

Given its role in a systemic corpus, the theatrical Milton offers new ways of analysing the more local forms of Milton's texts: 'Structures' or forms, writes Luhmann,

> would then be the general representation of the continuous activation of recursive orientations in a system. That is to say, structures themselves would be something that is fluid from moment to moment and which serves merely to furnish the continuation, processing, and continued operation of the system with information and directions.[7]

There is one significant way that the systemic corpus differs in its operations from systems as Luhmann defines them. The observing Milton exerts far more authority than Luhmann would allow, in that he plays an active role in both establishing significant and productive ambiguities and in placing limits upon them. For instance, Milton's use of the phrase 'rouzing motions' in *Samson Agonistes* challenges us to locate its sense anywhere between the stimulus of un-agential flesh and pure spiritual experience.[8] In this case, the form, 'rouzing motions', would be 'fluid from moment to moment' and would 'furnish the continuation, processing, and continued operation of the system with information and directions'.

Of the elements of Milton's prosody, his use of enjambment demonstrates most clearly how the system can operate at the level of poetic form. Consider the ambiguity-ridden final lines of Eve's creation narrative in book IV: 'Thy gentle hand / Seisd mine, I yielded, and from that time see / How beauty is excelld by manly grace / And wisdom, which alone is truly fair'.[9] The spatial-temporal gap of lines 488–9 at once separates and brings together senses of gentle and violently coercive touch. 'Seisd' epitomises Adam's legalistic language of property throughout the passage and further suggests Eve's status as a *feme covert*. Its Latin corollary being *rapere*, the word carries the connation of rape. These meanings directly conflict with 'gentle' and what elsewhere appears to be the genuinely loving nature of Paradisal marriage. Fish, eliding the enjambment from the text, quotes Eve's 'yield[ing]' as 'obviously' pointing to the episode's primary 'moral', namely, the right choosing between vain narcissism and the doctrinally appropriate embrace of the marriage.[10]

Yet the ironies surrounding the enjambment unsettle any certainty. The lines have also been read as further evincing the poem's challenge to a misogynistic exegetical tradition by foregrounding the tension between its seemingly authoritative affirmations of gendered hierarchy and its reiterations of the language of mirroring equality in Genesis.[11] The disturbing senses of 'seisd' invite a critique of gendered hierarchy in the Garden that seems in tension with Eve's pronouncement of the conventionally patriarchal affiliation of femininity with outer 'beauty' that is inferior to 'manly grace / And wisdom, which alone is truly fair'. Even the seemingly obvious sense of 'wisdom' as an exclusively 'manly' virtue is called into question by the second enjambment, between lines 490 and 491. While the superficial 'beauty' of woman may be 'excelled' by a 'grace' that is gendered masculine, the enjambment dislodges 'wisdom' from 'manly', leaving it potentially un-gendered, a capacity shared by either sex. There indeed seems a peculiar 'wisdom' working through Eve's narrative, a 'wisdom' that unsettles the patriarchal truisms it evidently affirms.[12]

The dance of authority becomes infinitely more complicated, of course, once form and signification begin to respond to intertexts, such as to the other uses of 'yield' in book IV, to early modern literatures about gender, to the texts of Shakespeare and Spenser, etc., and to intertexts that informed how early moderns and moderns read. 'Varietie without end', yes.[13] But not without bound.

As Adam's hand extends across the enjambment to touch Eve's hand at once lovingly and coercively, the poetic line, undulating ironically, plays upon the understanding and desire of readers: 'gentle hand' pulls us toward the ideally loving union of first man and meet help; 'seisd' repulses us, leaving us to reflect at a distance – if we are ready to accept the invitation. It is as though this entirely extra-scriptural episode were extending *its* hand, beckoning readers at once to uphold the hackneyed anti-feminism of exegetical tradition and to cooperate with the poet in the Genesis narrative's 'renovating and reingendring'.[14] As Mary Nyquist has shown, the irony opened by 'gentle hand / Seisd' rearticulates a tension between senses of the Genesis narrative traceable to conflicting scribal source texts.[15] Such disjunctions seem less intended to enforce doctrine than to lubricate, as it were, the continuing spiritual and passionate re-engendering of scriptural meaning. They allow Milton's own poem to behave like scripture as he receives it – and to behave, moreover, as a theatrical body.

Notes

1. Milton, *Areopagitica*, *CPW*, II, p. 253.
2. N. Luhmann, *Introduction to Systems Theory*, pp. 101–30.
3. Ibid., pp. 43–62.
4. Cf. R. Barthes, 'The Death of the Author', p. 223.
5. Luhmann, *Introduction to Systems Theory*, pp. 83–100.
6. See above, pp. 40–2.
7. Luhmann, *Introduction to Systems Theory*, p. 244.
8. See above, pp. 196, 200–2.
9. Milton, *Paradise Lost*, *WJM*, II.i, IV, lines 488–91.
10. Fish, *Surprised by Sin*, p. 218.
11. See S. Miller, *Engendering the Fall*; and Turner, *One Flesh*.
12. Thanks to Louis Schwartz for pointing me toward this insight.
13. Milton, *Paradise Lost*, *WJM*, II.i, VII, line 542.
14. See above, pp. 121–3.
15. Nyquist, 'The Genesis of Gendered Subjectivity in the Divorce Tracts and in *Paradise Lost*'.

Works Cited

Abbreviations

CPW *The Complete Prose Works of John Milton*, ed. D. Wolfe, 8 vols (New Haven, CT: Yale University Press, 1953–82).
NS *The Norton Shakespeare: Based on the Oxford Edition*, ed. S. Greenblatt, W. Cohen, J. E. Howard and K. E. Maus (New York: Norton, 1997).
WJM *The Works of John Milton*, ed. F. A. Patterson, 18 vols (New York: Columbia University Press, 1931–8).

Other works

Achinstein, S., *Milton and the Revolutionary Reader* (Princeton: Princeton University Press, 1994).
Achinstein, S., 'The Politics of Babel in the English Revolution', in J. Holstun (ed.), *Pamphlet Wars: Prose in the English Revolution* (London: F. Cass, 1992), pp. 14–44.
Achinstein, S., '*Samson Agonistes* and the Drama of Dissent', *Milton Studies*, 33 (1997), 133–58.
Aiton, W., *Hortus Kewensis: Or, a Catalogue of the Plants Cultivated in the Royal Botanic Garden at Kew* (London: George Nicol, 1789).
Anon., *Advice to a Parson: Or, The True Art of Preaching, in Opposition to Modern Practice* (London: Thomas Harper, 1691).
Anon., *Canterbury's Will: With a Serious Conference Betweene His Scrivener and Him* (London: [n. pub.], 1641).
Anon., *The Devil Turned Quaker* (London: John Andrews, 1656).
Anon., *A Dialogue Betwixt Three Travellers, as Acidentally They Did Meet on the High-way* ([n.p.]: [n. pub.], 1641).
Anon., *The Discontented Conference Betwixt the Two Great Associates* (London: [n. pub.], 1641).
Anon., *A Modest Confutation of a Slanderous and Scurrilous Libell* (London[?]: [n. pub.], 1642).
Anon., *News from Hell, Rome and the Innes of Court* ([n.p.]: [n. pub.], 1642).

Anon., *The Quakers Dream: Or the Devil's Pilgrimage in England* (London: G. Horton, 1655).
Anon., *The Quaker Turn'd Jew* (London: W. L., 1675).
Anon., *The Stage-Players Complaint: In a Pleasant Dialogue between Cane of the Fortune, and Reed of the Friers* (London: T. Bates, 1641).
Anselment, R. A., *'Betwixt Jest and Earnest': Marprelate, Milton, Marvell, Swift, & the Decorum of Religious Ridicule* (Toronto: University of Toronto Press, 1979).
Apollodorus, *Gods and Heroes of the Greeks: The Library of Appollodorus*, trans. M. Simpson (Amherst: University of Massachusetts Press, 1976).
Aristotle, *Poetics*, trans. S. Halliwell, in *Aristotle: Poetics. Longinus: On the Sublime Demetrius: On Style* (Cambridge, MA: Harvard University Press, [1995] 1999), pp. 1–141.
Aristotle, *Problems*, trans. W. S. Hett and H. Rackman, 2 vols (Cambridge, MA: Harvard University Press, 1936).
Arnold, M. H., 'The Platan Tree in *Paradise Lost*', *Papers in Language and Literature*, 11: 4 (1975), 411–14.
Arthos, J., 'Milton and the Passions: A Study of *Samson Agonistes*', *Modern Philology*, 69 (1972), 209–21.
Augustine, *City of God*, trans. G. E. McCracken, 7 vols (Cambridge, MA: Harvard University Press, 1957).
Austin, S., *The Character of a Quaker in His True and Proper Colours* (London: 1672).
Aylmer, G. E., *Rebellion or Revolution? England from Civil War to Restoration* (Oxford: Oxford University Press, 1983).
Bacon, F., *The Advancement of Learning*, in *The Works of Francis Bacon*, ed. J. Spedding et al., 6 vols (London: Longmans, 1887), III.
Baldwin, W., *The Last Part of the Mirour for Magistrates* (London: Thomas Marsh, 1578).
Balla, A., 'Wars of Evidence and Religious Toleration in Milton's *Samson Agonistes*', *Milton Quarterly*, 46: 2 (2012), 65–85.
Barthes, R., 'The Death of the Author', in *The Book History Reader*, ed. D. Finkelstein and A. McCleery (London: Routledge, 2002), pp. 221–4.
Batchiler, J., *Christian Queries to Quaking-Christians: Containing Thirteen Queries Modestly Propounded to Those Who Are Commonly Known by the Name of Quakers* (London: J. Batchiler, 1663).
Bell, M., 'Simmonds, Martha (*bap.* 1624, *d.* 1665)', in H. C. G. Matthew and B. Harrison (eds), *Oxford Dictionary of National Biography* (Oxford: Oxford University Press, 2004), available at <http://dx.doi.org/10.1093/ref:odnb/37959> (last accessed 12 June 2014).
Bennett, J. S., *Reviving Liberty: Radical Christian Humanism in Milton's Great Poems* (Cambridge: Cambridge University Press, 1989).
Bernard, R., *The Faithfull Shepheard* (London: John Bill, 1607).
Berry, H., 'The Miltons and the Blackfriars Playhouse', *Modern Philology*, 89 (1992), 510–14.
Bevington, D., *Action Is Eloquence: Shakespeare's Language of Gesture* (Cambridge, MA: Harvard University Press, 1985).
Beza, T., *Abraham sacrifant*, published as *A Tragedie of Abraham's Sacrifice*, trans. A. Golding (London: Vautroullier, 1577).

Black, J., 'The Rhetoric of Reaction: The Martin Marprelate Tracts (1588–89), Anti-Martinism, and the Uses of Print in Early Modern England', *The Sixteenth Century Journal*, 28: 3, 707–25.

Blake, S., *The Compleat Gardeners Practice* (London: Thomas Pierrepoint, 1664).

Blaugdone, B., *An Account of the Travels, Sufferings & Persecutions of Barbara Blaugdone* (London: T. S., 1691).

Blome, R., *The Fanatick History: Or, an Exact Relation and Account of the Old Anabaptists and New Quakers* (London: J. Sims, 1660).

Borel, P., *A New Treatise Proving a Multiplicity of Worlds* (London: Streater, 1658).

Bradburn, E., 'Theatrical Wonder, Amazement, and the Construction of Spiritual Agency in *Paradise Lost*', *Comparative Drama*, 40 (2006), 77–98.

Brady, M., 'Space and the Persistence of Place in *Paradise Lost*', *Milton Quarterly*, 41: 3 (2007), 167–78.

Brathwaite, R., *An Excellent Piece of Conceipted Poesy; Divided into Two Subjects: A Voice from the Vault; and An Age for Apes* (London: R. Hodgkinsonne, 1658).

Brathwaite, R., *Mercurius Britanicus, or The English Intelligencer* (London, 1641).

Breasted, B., '*Comus* and the Castlehaven Scandal', *Milton Studies*, 3 (1971), 201–24.

Britland, K., *Drama at the Courts of Queen Henrietta Maria* (Cambridge: Cambridge University Press, 2006).

Broaddus, J. W., *Spenser's Allegory of Love: Social Vision in Books III, IV, and V of 'The Faerie Queene'* (Madison, NJ: Fairleigh Dickinson University Press, 1995).

Brown, C. C., *John Milton's Aristocratic Entertainments* (Cambridge: Cambridge University Press, 1985).

Brown, C. C., 'Presidential Travels and Instructive Augury in Milton's Ludlow Masque', *Milton Quarterly*, 21: 4 (1987), 1–12.

Brown, E. C., '"The Melting Voice Through Mazes Running": The Dissolution of Borders in *L'Allegro* and *Il Penseroso*', *Milton Studies*, 40 (2001), 1–18.

Bulwer, J., *Chirologia; or, The Naturall Language of the Hand* (London: Thomas Harper, 1644).

Bulwer, J., *Chironomia; or, The Art of Manuall Rhetoricke* (London: Thomas Harper, 1644).

Bulwer, J., *Pathomyotamia, or, A Dissection of the Significative Muscles of the Affections of the Minde* (London: Humphrey Moseley, 1649).

Burbery, T., *Milton the Dramatist* (Pittsburgh: Duquesne University Press, 2007).

Burns, N. T., '"Then Stood Up Phineas": Milton's Antinomianism, and Samson's', *Milton Studies*, 33 (1996), 27–46.

Burrough, E., *A Trumpet of the Lord Sounded out of Sion* (London: Giles Calvert, 1656).

Butcher, S. H., *Aristotle's Theory of Poetry and Fine Art* (Mineola, NY: Courier Corporation, [1894] 1951).

Butler, J., *Bodies That Matter: On the Discursive Limits of 'Sex'* (New York: Routledge, 1993).

Butler, J., 'Performative Acts and Gender Constitution: An Essay in Phenomenology and Feminist Theory', in S. Case (ed.), *Performing Feminisms: Feminist Critical Theory and Theatre* (Baltimore: Johns Hopkins University Press, 1990), pp. 270–82.
Butler, M., 'A Provincial Masque of *Comus*, 1636', *Renaissance Drama*, 17 (1986), 149–74.
Butler, M., *Theatre and Crisis, 1632–1642* (Cambridge: Cambridge University Press, 1984).
Campbell, G., 'The Satire on Aristotelian Logic in Milton's "Vacation Exercise"', *English Language Notes*, 15 (1977), 106–10.
Campbell, G., and T. Corns, *John Milton: Life, Work, and Thought* (Oxford: Oxford University Press, 2008).
Carroll, J. D., '*Gorboduc* and *Titus Andronicus*', *Notes & Queries*, 51: 3 (2004), 267–9.
Carroll, R., and S. Prickett (eds), *The Bible: Authorized King James Version* (Oxford: Oxford University Press, 2008).
Carson, L. H., *Martin Marprelate, Gentleman: Master Job Throckmorton Laid Open in All His Colours* (San Marino, CA: Huntington Library, 1981).
Carter, R., *The Schismatick Stigmatized* (London: Francis Coles, 1641).
Champagne, C. M., 'Adam and His "Other Self" in *Paradise Lost*: A Lacanian Study in Psychic Development', *Milton Quarterly*, 25: 2 (1991), pp. 48–59.
Church of England, *The Booke of Common Prayer, and Administration of the Sacraments* (Edinburgh: Robert Young, 1637).
Cicero, *Orator*, trans. H. M. Hubbell (Cambridge, MA: Harvard University Press, 1962).
Cicero, *De oratore*, ed. E. W. Sutton and H. Rackham, trans. E. W. Sutton (Cambridge, MA: Harvard University Press, 1942), 2 vols.
Clark, S., *Vanities of the Eye: Vision in Early Modern European Culture* (Oxford: Oxford University Press, 2007).
Clay, D., 'Royal Samson', *Milton Studies*, 46 (2006), 123–48.
Coiro, A. B., 'Anonymous Milton, or, A *Maske* Masked', *ELH*, 71: 3 (2004), 609–29.
Coiro, A. B., 'Fable and Old Song: *Samson Agonistes* and the Idea of a Poetic Career', *Milton Studies*, 36 (1998), 123–52.
Collinson, P., 'Ben Jonson's *Bartholomew Fair*: The Theatre Constructs Puritanism', in D. L. Smith, R. Strier and D. Bevington (eds), *The Theatrical City: Culture Theatre and Politics in London, 1576–1649* (Cambridge: Cambridge University Press, 1995), pp. 157–69.
Collier, T., *A Looking-Glasse for the Quakers, Wherein They May Behold Themselves* (London: Thomas Brewster, 1657).
Como, D. R., 'Secret Printing, the Crisis of 1640, and the Origins of Civil War Radicalism', *Past & Present*, 196 (2007), 37–82.
Creaser, J., 'Milton's *Comus*: The Irrelevance of the Castlehaven Scandal', *Milton Quarterly*, 21: 4 (1987), 24–34.
Creaser, J., '"The Present Aid of this Occasion": The Setting of *Comus*', in D. Lindley (ed.), *The Court Masque* (Manchester: Manchester University Press, 1984), pp. 110–34.
Cressy, D., *England on Edge: Crisis and Revolution 1640–42* (Oxford: Oxford University Press, 2006).

Damrosch, L., *The Sorrows of the Quaker Jesus: James Nayler and the Puritan Crackdown on the Free Spirit* (Cambridge, MA: Harvard University Press, 1996).
D'Assigny, M., *The Art of Memory* (London: A. Bell, 1699).
de Brès, G., *Johannes Becoldus redivivus: Or, The English Quaker, the German Enthusiast Revived: Visible in This Narrative*, trans. J. Scottow (London: John Allen, 1659).
Deacon, J., *The Grand Imposter Examined, or, The Life, Tryal, and Examination of James Nayler* (London: Henry Brome, 1657).
Dell'Antonio, A., *Listening as Spiritual Practice in Early Modern Italy* (Berkeley: University of California Press, 2011).
Demaray, J. G., 'Love's Epic Revel in *Paradise Lost*: A Theatrical Vision of Marriage', *Modern Language Quarterly*, 38: 1 (1977), 3–20.
Demaray, J. G., *Milton and the Masque Tradition: The Early Poems, 'Arcades', and 'Comus'* (Cambridge, MA: Harvard University Press, 1968).
Demaray, J. G., *Milton's Theatrical Epic: The Invention and Design of 'Paradise Lost'* (Cambridge, MA: Harvard University Press, 1980).
Demaray, J. G., 'The Temple of the Mind: Cosmic Iconography in Milton's *A Mask*', *Milton Quarterly*, 21: 4 (1987), 59–76.
Denham, J., *A Relation of a Quaker, That to the Shame of His Profession, Attempted to Bugger a Mare near Colchester* (London: [n. pub.], 1659).
Descartes, R., 'Optics', in *The Philosophical Writings of Descartes*, ed. J. Cottingham, R. Stoothoff and D. Murdoch, 3 vols (Cambridge: Cambridge University Press, 1985), I, pp. 152–76.
Descartes, R., *Les Passions de l'âme* (Amsterdam: Chez Louys Elzevier, 1650).
Dobranski, S. B., 'Milton's Social Life', in D. Danielson (ed.), *The Cambridge Companion to Milton*, 5th edn (Cambridge: Cambridge University Press, 1999), pp. 1–24.
Dodd, E., *Innocents No Saints: Or, A Paire of Spectacles for a Dark-sighted Quaker* (London: Francis Tyton, 1658).
Donnelly, P. J., *Milton's Scriptural Reasoning: Narrative and Protestant Toleration* (Cambridge: Cambridge University Press, 2009).
Dubrow, H., 'The Masquing of Genre in *Comus*', *Milton Studies*, 44 (2005), 62–83.
Duran, A., *The Age of Milton in the Scientific Revolution* (Pittsburgh: Duquesne University Press, 2007).
Eastwood, B., *Astronomy and Optics from Pliny to Descartes: Texts, Diagrams, and Conceptual Structures* (London: Variorum Reprints, 1989).
Edwards, K. L., *Milton and the Natural World: Science and Poetry in 'Paradise Lost'* (Cambridge: Cambridge University Press, 1999).
Egan, J., 'Milton and the Marprelate Tradition', *Milton Studies*, 8 (1975), 103–22.
Egan, J., 'Rhetoric, Polemic, Mimetic: The Dialectic of Genres in *Tetrachordon* and *Colasterion*', *Milton Studies*, 41 (2002), 117–38.
Emmot, G., *A Northern Blast, or the Spiritual Quaker Converted* (London: R. Lambert, 1655).
Escholt, M. P., *Geologia Norvegica*, trans. D. Collins (London: S. Thomson, 1663).
Evelyn, J., *Sylva, or, A Discourse of Forest-Trees, and the Propagation of*

Timber in His Majesties Dominions (London: J. Martyn and J. Allestry, 1664).
Fallon, S. M., 'Alexander More Reads Milton: Self-Representation and Anxiety in Milton's *Defences*', in G. Parry and J. Raymond (eds), *Milton and the Terms of Liberty* (Cambridge: D. S. Brewer, 2002), pp. 111–24.
Fallon, S. M., *Milton among the Philosophers: Poetry and Materialism in Seventeenth-Century England* (Ithaca, NY: Cornell University Press, 1991).
Fallon, S. M., *Milton's Peculiar Grace: Self-Representation and Authority* (Ithaca: Cornell University Press, 2007).
Finch, C., and P. Bowen, 'The Solitary Companionship of *L'Allegro* and *Il Penseroso*', *Milton Studies*, 26 (1991), 253–70.
Finch, H., *A True and Exact Relation of the Late Prodigious Earthquake of Mount Aetna* (Savoy: Thomas Newcomb, 1669).
Fish, S., *How Milton Works* (Cambridge, MA: Harvard University Press, 2001).
Fish, S., 'Spectacle and Evidence in *Samson Agonistes*', *Critical Inquiry*, 15 (1989), 556–86.
Fish, S., *Surprised by Sin: The Reader in 'Paradise Lost'* (Cambridge, MA: Harvard University Press, [1967] 1998).
Fish, S., 'Wanting a Supplement: The Question of Interpretation in Milton's Early Prose', in J. G. Turner and D. Loewenstein (eds), *Politics, Poetics and Hermeneutics in Milton's Prose* (Cambridge: Cambridge University Press, 1990), pp. 41–68.
Fletcher, A., *Time, Space, and Motion in the Age of Shakespeare* (Cambridge, MA: Harvard University Press, 2007).
Fletcher, A., *The Transcendental Masque: An Essay on Milton's 'Comus'* (Ithaca, NY: Cornell University Press, 1972).
Flinker, N., *The Song of Songs in English Renaissance Literature: Kisses of Their Mouths* (Cambridge: Boydell and Brewer, 2000).
Fox, G., *George Fox; an Autobiography*, ed. R. Jones (Philadelphia: Ferris and Leach, 1909).
Freedman, M., 'Waiting for Samson: The Modernity of *Samson Agonistes*', *Milton Quarterly*, 13: 2 (1979), 42–5.
French, J. M. (ed.), *The Life Records of John Milton*, 5 vols (New York: Gordian Press, [1949–58] 1966).
General Assembly of the Kirk of Scotland, *A Directory for the Publike Worship of God Throughout the Three Kingdoms of Scotland, England, and Ireland* (Edinburgh: Evan Tyler, 1645).
Gerarde, J., *The Herball, or General Historie of Plants* (London: Islip, Norton and Whitakers, [1597] 1636).
Gibson, J., 'The Logic of Chastity: Women, Sex, and the History of Philosophy in the Early Modern Period', *Hypatia*, 21: 4 (2006), 1–19.
Gillum, M., 'Yet Once More, "Gumms of Glutenous Heat"', *Milton Quarterly*, 44 (2010), 47–51.
Gilpin, J., *Quakers Shaken; or, A Fire-brand Snach'd out of the Fire* (London: Simon Waterson, 1653).
Goldsmith, S., 'The Muting of Satan: Language and Redemption in *Paradise Regained*', *Studies in English Literature, 1500–1900*, 27 (1987), 125–40.
Goodman, K., '"Wasted Labor"? Milton's Eve, the Poet's Work, and the Challenge of Sympathy', *ELH*, 64 (1997), 415–46.

Gosson, S., *Plays Confuted in Five Actions*, in T. Pollard (ed.), *Shakespeare's Theater: A Sourcebook* (Malden, MA: Blackwell, 2004), pp. 84–114.
Gosson, S., *The School of Abuse*, in T. Pollard (ed.), *Shakespeare's Theater: A Sourcebook* (Malden, MA: Blackwell, 2004), pp. 19–33.
Greenblatt, S., *Renaissance Self-Fashioning: From More to Shakespeare* (Chicago: University of Chicago Press, 1980).
Greenblatt, S., *Shakespearean Negotiations: The Circulation of Social Energy in Renaissance England* (Berkeley: University of California Press, 1988).
Greene, J., *A Refutation of the Apology for Actors*, in T. Pollard (ed.), *Shakespeare's Theater: A Sourcebook* (Malden, MA: Blackwell, 2004), pp. 255–73.
Greenstadt, A., *Rape and the Rise of the Author: Gendering Intention in Early Modern England* (Farnham: Ashgate, 2009).
Greteman, B., '"Perplex't Paths": Youth and Authority in Milton's *Mask*', *Renaissance Quarterly*, 64 (2009): 410–43.
Grossman, M., *Authors to Themselves: Milton and the Revelation of History* (Cambridge: Cambridge University Press, 1987).
Grossman, M., 'The Dissemination of the King', in D. L. Smith, R. Strier and D. Bevington (eds), *The Theatrical City: Culture Theatre and Politics in London, 1576–1649* (Cambridge: Cambridge University Press, 1995), pp. 250–81.
Grossman, M., 'Textual Ethics: Reading Transference in *Samson Agonistes*', in M. Grossman (ed.), *Reading Renaissance Ethics* (New York: Routledge, 2007), pp. 85–103.
Guillory, J., 'Milton, Narcissism, Gender: On the Genealogy of Male Self-Esteem', in C. Kendrick (ed.), *Critical Essays on John Milton* (New York: G. K. Hall, 1995), pp. 194–233.
Guillory, J., *Poetic Authority: Spenser, Milton, and Literary History* (New York: Columbia University Press, 1983).
Gunderson, E., *Staging Masculinity: The Rhetoric of Performance in the Roman World* (Ann Arbor: University of Michigan Press, 2000).
Gurr, A., *Playgoing in Shakespeare's London* (Cambridge: Cambridge University Press, [1987] 2004).
Hale, J., *Milton's Cambridge Latin: Performing in the Genres, 1625–1632* (Tempe: Arizona Center for Medieval and Renaissance Studies, 2005).
Hale, J., 'Milton Plays the Fool: The Christ's College Salting, 1628', *Classical and Modern Literature: A Quarterly*, 20: 3 (2000), 51–70.
Hall, J., *A Defence of the Humble Remonstrance* (London: Nathaniel Butter, 1641).
Hall, J., *An Humble Remonstrance to the High Court of Parliament* (London: Nathaniel Butter, 1641).
Hall, R., *Quakers Principles Quaking, or, Pretended Light Proved Darkness, and Perfections Found to Be Greatest Imperfections* (London: R. I., 1656).
Hammond, P., *Milton and the People* (Oxford: Oxford University Press, 2014).
Hanford, J. H., 'The Dramatic Element in *Paradise Lost*', *Studies in Philology*, 14 (1927), 178–95.
Haskin, D., *Milton's Burden of Interpretation* (Philadelphia: University of Pennsylvania Press, 1994).
Heckscher, W., *Rembrandt's Anatomy of Dr. Nicolaas Tulp: An Iconological Study* (New York: New York University Press, 1958).

Heinemann, M., *Puritanism and Theatre: Thomas Middleton and Opposition Drama under the Early Stuarts* (Cambridge: Cambridge University Press, 1980).
Herbert, G., 'The Flower', in J. Rumrich and G. Chaplin (eds), *Seventeenth-Century British Poetry, 1603–1660* (New York: Norton, 2005), pp. 280–1.
Herbert, G., 'The Windows', in J. Rumrich and G. Chaplin (eds), *Seventeenth-Century English Poetry, 1603–1660* (New York: Norton, 2005).
Hermogenes, *Hermogenes' 'On Types of Style'*, trans. C. Wooten (Chapel Hill, NC: University of North Carolina Press, 1987).
Hett, W. S., Introduction, in Aristotle, *Problems*, trans. W. S. Hett and H. Rackham, 2 vols (Cambridge, MA: Harvard University Press, 1936), I, pp. vii–x
Higginson, F., *Brief Relation of the Irreligion of the Northern Quakers* (London: H. R., 1653).
Hill, C., *The Century of Revolution: 1603–1714* (New York: Norton, 1982).
Hill, C., *Milton and the English Revolution* (London: Faber and Faber, 1977).
Hill, C., 'Radical Prose in 17th Century England: From Marprelate to the Levellers', *Essays in Criticism*, 32: 2 (1982), 95–118.
Hinds, H., '"And the Lord's Power Was over All": Calvinist Anxiety, Sacred Confidence, and George Fox's Journal', *ELH*, 75 (2008), 841–70.
Hobbes, T., *Leviathan; or The Matter, Form, & Power of a Common-wealth* (London: Andrew Crooke, 1651).
Hobbes, T., *A Minute or First Draught of the Optiques* (1646), British Library, Harley MS.3360.
Horace, *The Art of Poetry: A Study of Habit and Experience*, trans. B. Raffel (Albany, NY: State University of New York Press, 1974).
Howard, J., *The Stage and Social Struggle in Early Modern England* (London: Routledge, 1994).
Howard-Hill, T. H., 'Milton and "The Rounded Theatre's Pomp"', in P. G. Stanwood (ed.), *Of Poetry and Politics: New Essays on Milton and His World* (Binghamton, NY: Medieval and Renaissance Textual Studies, 1995), pp. 95–120.
Hoxby, B., *Mammon's Music: Literature and Economics in the Age of Milton* (New Haven: Yale University Press, 2002).
Hughes, M., Introduction to *Paradise Lost*, in *John Milton: Complete Poems and Major Prose*, ed. Hughes (New York: Macmillan, 1957), pp. 173–205.
Hunt, J. D., 'Milton and the Making of the English Landscape Garden', *Milton Studies*, 15 (1981), 81–105.
Hunt, M., 'Managing Spenser, Managing Shakespeare in *Comus*', *Neophilologus*, 88 (2004), 315–33.
Jones, E., 'The Loyalty and Subsidy Returns of 1641 and 1642: What They Can Tell Us of Milton's Family', in K. A. Pruitt and C. H. Durham, *Milton's Legacy* (Selinsgrove: Susquehana University Press, 2005), pp. 234–47.
Jonson, B., *The Alchemist*, in D. Bevington, L. Engel and K. E. Maus (eds), *English Renaissance Drama: A Norton Anthology* (New York: Norton, 2002).
Jonson, B., *Volpone or The Fox* (London: Thomas Thorpe, 1607).
Kahn, V., 'Aesthetics as Critique: Tragedy and *Trauerspiel* in *Samson Agonistes*', in Grossman (ed.), *Reading Renaissance Ethics*, pp. 104–27.

Kahn, V., 'Allegory and Sublime in *Paradise Lost*', in A. Patterson (ed.), *John Milton* (London: Longman, 1992), pp. 185–201.
Kernan, S., 'George Buchanan and the Genre of *Samson Agonistes*', *Language and Style*, 19: 1 (1986), 21–4.
Kerrigan, W., *The Sacred Complex: On the Psychogenesis of 'Paradise Lost'* (Cambridge, MA: Harvard University Press, 1983).
Kietzman, M., 'The Fall into Conversation with Eve: Discursive Difference in *Paradise Lost*', *Criticism*, 39 (1997), 55–88.
Kilgour, M., '"Thy Perfect Image Viewing": Poetic Creation and Ovid's Narcissus in *Paradise Lost*', *Studies in Philology* 102: 3 (2005), 307–39.
Kirkconnell, W. (ed.), *The Celestial Cycle: The Theme of Paradise Lost in World Literature* (New York: Gordian Press, 1967).
Knoppers, L. L., General Introduction, in *The Complete Works of John Milton*, II: *The 1671 Poems: 'Paradise Regain'd' and 'Samson Agonistes'*, ed. L. L. Knoppers (Oxford: Oxford University Press, 2008), pp. xix–lvviv.
Kranidas, T., *Milton and the Rhetoric of Zeal* (Pittsburgh: Duquesne University Press, 2004).
Kranidas, T., 'Milton's Trinculo', *Notes & Queries*, 26 (1979), 416.
Lacan, J., *Four Fundamental Concepts of Psycho-Analysis*, ed. J. Alain-Miller, trans. A. Sheridan (New York: Norton, 1998).
Lacan, J., 'The Mirror Stage', in J. Lacan, *Ecrits: The First Complete Edition in English*, trans. B. Fink (New York: Norton, 2006), pp. 75–81.
Lares, J., *Milton and the Preaching Arts* (Pittsburgh: Duquesne University Press, 2002).
Le Faucheur, M., *An Essay upon the Action of an Orator; as to His Pronunciation and Gesture*, trans. N. Cox (London: Nicholas Cox, 1680).
Leggatt, A., *Jacobean Public Theatre* (London: Routledge, 1992).
Lehnhof, K. R., '"Impregn'd with Reason": Eve's Aural Conception in *Paradise Lost*', *Milton Studies*, 41 (2002), 38–75.
Leo, R., 'Milton's Aristotelian Experiments: Tragedy, *Lustratio*, and "Secret refreshings" in *Samson Agonistes* (1671)', *Milton Studies*, 52 (2011), 221–52.
Lewalski, B. K., *Paradise Lost and the Rhetoric of Literary Forms* (Princeton: Princeton University Press, 1985).
Liblein, L., 'Embodied Intersubjectivity and the Creation of Early Modern Character', in P. E. Yachnin and J. Slights (eds), *Shakespeare and Character: Theory, History, Performance, and Theatrical Persons* (New York: Palgrave Shakespeare Studies, 2009), pp. 117–35.
Lieb, M., *Milton and the Culture of Violence* (Ithaca, NY: Cornell University Press, 1994).
Lieb, M., 'Milton's *Of Reformation* and the Dynamics of Controversy', in M. Lieb and J. T. Shawcross, *Achievements of the Left Hand: Essays on the Prose of John Milton* (Amherst: University of Massachusetts Press, 1974), pp. 55–82.
Lieb, M., *Theological Milton: Deity, Discourse and Heresy in the Milton Canon* (Pittsburgh: Duquesne University Press, 2006).
Lieb, M., '"Two of Far Nobler Shape": Reading the Paradisal Text', in D. T. Benet and M. Lieb (eds), *Literary Milton: Text, Pretext, Context* (Pittsburgh: Duquesne University Press, 1994), pp. 114–32.

Liebert, E., 'Rendering "More Equal": Eve's Changing Discourse in *Paradise Lost*', *Milton Quarterly*, 37 (2003), 152–65.
Limouze, H. S., 'Joseph Hall and the Prose Style of John Milton', *Milton Studies*, 15 (1981), 121–41.
Lindley, D., 'The Politics of Music in the Masque', in D. Bevington and P. Holbrook (eds), *The Politics of the Stuart Court Masque* (Cambridge: Cambridge University Press, 1998), pp. 273–95.
Loewenstein, D., 'The Kingdom Within: Radical Religious Culture and the Politics of *Paradise Regained*', *Literature and History*, 3: 2 (1994), 63–89.
Loewenstein, D., *Milton and the Drama of History: Historical Vision, Iconoclasm, and the Literary Imagination* (Cambridge: Cambridge University Press, 1990).
Loewenstein, D., *Representing Revolution in Milton and His Contemporaries: Religion, Politics, and Polemics in Radical Puritanism* (Cambridge: Cambridge University Press, 2001).
Loewenstein, D., 'The Revenge of the Saint: Radical Religion and Politics in *Samson Agonistes*', *Milton Studies*, 33 (1997), 159–80.
Low, A., *The Blaze of Noon: A Reading of 'Samson Agonistes'* (New York: Columbia University Press, 1974).
Luhmann, N., *Introduction to Systems Theory*, ed. P. Gilgen (Cambridge: Polity Press, 2013).
Lupton, D., *The Quacking Mountebank: Or, The Jesuite Turn'd Quaker* (London: E. B., 1655).
McGuire, M. C., *Milton's Puritan Masque* (Athens: University of Georgia Press, 1983).
McMahon, R., *The Two Poets of Paradise Lost* (Baton Rouge: Louisiana State University Press, 1998).
Macrobius, *Saturnalia*, trans. R. A. Kaster (Cambridge, MA: Harvard University Press, 2011).
Marcus, L., 'The Earl of Bridgewater's Legal Life: Notes toward a Political Reading of *Comus*', *Milton Quarterly*, 21: 4 (1987), 13–21.
Marcus, L., *The Politics of Mirth: Jonson, Herrick, Milton, Marvell and the Defense of Old Holiday Pastimes* (Chicago: University of Chicago Press, 1986).
Marprelate, M. [pseud.], *Oh Read over D. John Bridges [The Epistle]* (Fawsley: [n. pub.], 1588).
Marshall, A., and J. B. Phillips (trans.), *The Interlinear Greek–English New Testament* (London: S. Bagster, 1958).
Marston, J., *The Scourge of Villeiny*, in *The Works of John Marston*, ed. A. H. Bullen, 3 vols (London: John C. Nimmo, 1887), III, pp. 295–382.
Martin, C. G., *Milton among the Puritans: The Case for Historical Revisionism* (Farnham: Ashgate, 2010).
Martz, L., *Poet of Exile: A Study of Milton's Poetry* (New Haven: Yale University Press, 1980).
Maus, K. E., '"Playhouse Flesh and Blood": Sexual Ideology and the Restoration Actress', *ELH*, 46 (1979), 595–617.
Marvell, A., 'On Mr. Milton's *Paradise Lost*', in *The Poems of Andrew Marvell*, ed. N. Smith (New York: Routledge, 2006), pp. 180–4.

Maximus, V., *Memorable Deeds and Sayings: One Thousand Tales from Ancient Rome*, trans. H. J. Walker (Indianapolis: Hackett, 2004).
Mayne, J., 'On Dr. Donne's Death', quoted in J. Bulwer, *Chironomia: Or, The Art of Manuall Rhetorique* (London: Thomas Harper, 1644), p. 20.
Mead, S. X., '"Thou Art Chang'd": Public Value and Personal Identity in *Troilus and Cressida*', *The Journal of Medieval and Renaissance Studies*, 22 (1993), 237–60.
Merleau-Ponty, M., *Le Visible et l'invisible; suivi de notes de travail* (Paris: Gallimard, 1964).
Miller, J., *Antichrist in Man the Quakers Idol* (London: L. Loyd, 1655).
Miller, J. A., 'Milton and the Conformable Puritanism of Richard Stock and Thomas Young', in D. Jones (ed.), *The Young Milton: The Emerging Author, 1602–1642* (Oxford: Oxford University Press), pp. 72–106.
Miller, S., *Engendering the Fall: John Milton and Seventeenth-Century Women Writers* (Philadelphia: University of Pennsylvania Press, 2008).
Milton, J., 'At a Vacation Exercise in the Colledge, Part Latin, Part English', in J. Hale, *Milton's Cambridge Latin: Performing in the Genres, 1625–1632* (Tempe: Arizona Center for Medieval and Renaissance Studies, 2005), pp. 289–93.
Milton, J., *A Maske: The Earlier Versions*, ed. S. E. Sprott (Toronto: University of Toronto Press, 1973).
Milton, J., *A Maske Presented at Ludlow Castle* [1637 version] (London: Humphrey Robinson, 1637), reprinted in *Milton: Complete Shorter Poems*, ed. and trans. J. Carey (London: Longman, 1997), pp. 173–233.
Milton, J., *Vacation Exercise*, in J. Hale, *Milton's Cambridge Latin: Performing in the Genres, 1625–1632* (Tempe: Arizona Center for Medieval and Renaissance Studies, 2005).
Mitchell, P., *The Purple Island and Anatomy in Early Seventeenth-Century Literature, Philosophy, and Theology* (Madison, NJ: Fairleigh Dickinson University Press, 2007).
Mohamed, F. G., *Milton and the Post-Secular Present: Ethics, Politics, and Terrorism* (Stanford: Stanford University Press, 2011).
Mohrmann, G. P., 'Oratorical Delivery and Other Problems in Current Scholarship on English Renaissance Rhetoric', in J. J. Murphy (ed.), *Renaissance Eloquence: Studies in the Theory and Practice of Renaissance Rhetoric* (Berkeley: University of California Press, 1983), pp. 56–83.
Moore, S. H., 'Sexing the Soul: Gender and the Rhetoric of Puritan Piety', in R. N. Swanson (ed.), *Gender and Christian Religion: Papers Read at the 1996 Summer Meeting and the 1997 Winter Meeting of the Ecclesiastical History Society* (Suffolk, NY: Boydell Press, 1998), pp. 175–86.
Mount, H., 'Egbert Van Heemskerck's *Quaker Meetings* Revisited', *Journal of the Warburg and Courtauld Institutes*, 56 (1993), 209–28.
Mullaney, S., *The Place of the Stage: License, Play, and Power in Renaissance England* (Chicago: University of Chicago Press, 1988).
Mulvey, L., 'Visual Pleasure and Narrative Cinema', *Screen*, 16: 3 (1975), 6–18.
Nardo, A. K., '"Sung and Proverb'd for a Fool": Samson as a Fool and Trickster', *Mosaic*, 22: 1 (1989), 1–16.
Nash, T., *A Myrror for Martinists and All Other Schismatiquess* (London: John Wolfe, 1590).

Neelakanta, V., 'Theatrum Mundi and Milton's Theatre of the Blind in Samson Agonistes', Journal for Early Modern Cultural Studies, 11: 1 (2011), 30–58.
Nelson, A. H., Early Cambridge Theatres: College, University and Town Stages, 1464–1720 (Cambridge: University of Cambridge Press, 1994).
Nelson, A. H. (ed.), Records of Early English Drama: Cambridge, 2 vols (Toronto: University of Toronto Press, 1989).
Norbrook, D., 'The Reformation of the Masque', in D. Lindley (ed.), The Court Masque (Manchester: Manchester University Press, 1984), pp. 94–110.
Northbrooke, J., A Treatise Against Dicing, Dancing, Plays, and Interludes, in T. Pollard (ed.), Shakespeare's Theater: A Sourcebook (Malden, MA: Blackwell, 2004), pp. 1–18.
Nyquist, M., 'The Genesis of Gendered Subjectivity in the Divorce Tracts and in Paradise Lost', in M. Nyquist and M. W. Ferguson (eds), Re-membering Milton: Essays on the Texts and Traditions (London: Methuen, 1987), pp. 99–127.
Nyquist, M., 'Reading the Fall: Discourse and Drama in Paradise Lost', English Literary Renaissance, 14 (1984), 199–229.
An Ordinance of Both Houses, for the Suppressing of Stage-Playes (London: John Wright, 1642).
Ong, W. J., Ramus, Method, and the Decay of Dialogue: From the Art of Discourse to the Art of Reason (Chicago: University of Chicago Press, [1958] 2004).
Orgel, S., 'The Case for Comus', Representations, 81 (2003), 33–45.
Overton, R. [?], The Bishops Potion: Or, A Dialogue betweene the Bishop of Canterbury, and His Phisitian (London: [n. pub.], 1641).
Overton, R. [?], A New Play Called Canterburie His Change of Diot (London: [n. pub.], 1641).
Ovid, Metamorphoses, trans. W. S. Anderson (Norman: Oklahoma University Press, 1997).
Ovid, Ovid, 'Amores': Text, Prolegomena, and Commentary, ed. J. C. McKeon, 4 vols (Wolfeboro, NH: F. Cairns, 1987).
Parkinson, J., Paradisi in sole, paradisus terrestris, or, A Choise Garden of All Sorts of Rarest Flowers (London: Lownes and Young, 1629).
Parkinson, J., Theatrum botanicum: The Theater of Plants (London: Thomas Cotes, 1640).
Patrides, C. A., 'The Comic Dimension in Greek Tragedy and Samson Agonistes', Milton Studies, 27 (1977), 3–21.
Patterson, A., Reading Between the Lines (Madison: University of Wisconsin Press, 1993).
Peacham, H., Square-caps Turned into Round-heads, or, The Bishops Vindication and the Brownists Conviction (London: Gyles and Londsey, 1642).
Pennyman, J., Bright Shining Light, Discovering the Pretenders to It. Recommended to the People Called Quakers (London: Francis Smith, 1680).
Peters, K., Print Culture and the Early Quakers (Cambridge: Cambridge University Press, 2005).
Peyton, Sir E., Divine Catastrophe of the Kingly Family of the Stuarts, in W. Scott (ed.), Secret History of the Court of James I, 2 vols (Edinburgh: J. Ballantyne and Co., 1811), II, pp. 301–466.

Picciotto, J., *Labors of Innocence in Early Modern England* (Cambridge, MA: Harvard University Press, 2010).
Pierce, H., 'Anti-Episcopacy and Graphic Satire in England, 1640–1645', *The Historical Journal*, 47: 4 (2004), 809–48.
Plett, H. F., *Rhetoric and Renaissance Culture* (Berlin: de Gruyter, 2004).
Plutarch, *Twelve Lives*, trans. J. Dryden (Cleveland: World Publishing Company, 1950), pp. 359–62.
Poole, W., *Milton and the Idea of the Fall* (Cambridge: Cambridge University Press, 2005).
Potter, L., *Secret Rites and Secret Writing: Royalist Literature, 1641–60* (Cambridge: Cambridge University Press, 2009).
Prawdzik, B., 'Similitude, Deception, and the Reader of "Upon Appleton House"', talk presented at Exploring the Renaissance, St Louis, MO, 26 March 2016.
Price, L., *A New Disputation betweene the Two Lordly Bishops* (London: [n. pub.], 1642).
Prins, J., 'Hobbes on Light and Vision', in T. Sorrel (ed.), *The Cambridge Companion to Hobbes* (Cambridge: Cambridge University Press), pp. 129–56.
Pruitt, K. A., *Gender and the Power of Relationship: 'United as One Individual Soul' in 'Paradise Lost'* (Pittsburgh: Duquesne University Press, 2003).
Prynne, W., *Histriomastix*, in T. Pollard (ed.), *Shakespeare's Theater: A Sourcebook* (Malden, MA: Blackwell, 2004), pp. 279–96.
Quilligan, M., *Milton's Spenser: The Politics of Reading* (Ithaca, NY: Cornell University Press, 1983).
Quintilian, *The Orator's Education*, trans. D. A. Russell, 5 vols (Cambridge, MA: Harvard University Press, 2002).
Quintslund, B., and A. Escobedo (eds), *Milton Quarterly*, 37 (2003).
Raber, K., *Gender, Class, and Genre in the Early Modern Closet Drama* (Newark: University of Delaware Press, 2001).
Radzinowicz, M. A., '"To Play in the Socratic Manner": Oxymoron in Milton's "At a Vacation Exercise in the College"', *University of Hartford Studies in Literature*, 17: 3 (1985), 1–11.
Radzinowicz, M. A., *Toward 'Samson Agonistes': The Growth of Milton's Mind* (Princeton: Princeton University Press, 1978).
Rapin, R., *Reflections upon the Eloquence of these Times; Particularly of the Barr and Pulpit* (London: Richard Preston, 1672).
Reichert, J., *Milton's Wisdom: Nature and Scripture in 'Paradise Lost'* (Ann Arbor: Michigan University Press, 1992).
Richek, R., 'Thomas Randolph's "Salting" (1627), Its Text, and John Milton's Sixth Prolusion as Another "Salting"', *English Literary Renaissance*, 12 (1982), 102–31.
Roche, T. P., Jr, *The Kindly Flame: A Study of the Third and Fourth Books of Spenser's 'Faerie Queene'* (Princeton: Princeton University Press, 1964).
Rogers, J., 'The Enclosure of Virginity: The Poetics of Sexual Abstinence in the English Revolution', in R. Burt and J. Michael (eds), *Enclosure Acts: Sexuality, Property, and Culture in Early Modern England* (Ithaca, NY: Cornell University Press, 1994), pp. 229–50.
Rogers, J., *The Matter of Revolution: Science, Poetry, and Politics in the Age of Milton* (Ithaca, NY: Cornell University Press, 1996).
Ronnick, M. V., 'Concerning the Dramatic Elements in Milton's *Defensiones*:

Theater without a Stage', *Classical and Modern Literature: A Quarterly*, 15 (1995): 271–9.

Rose, J., *Sexuality in the Field of Vision* (London: Verso, 1996).

Rosenberg, D. M., 'Milton, Dryden, and the Ideology of Genre', *Comparative Drama*, 21: 1 (1997), 1–18.

Rosenberg, D. M., '*Samson Agonistes*: "Proverb'd for a Fool"', *The Centennial Review*, 32: 1 (1988), 65–78.

Rumrich, J. P., *Milton Unbound: Controversy and Reinterpretation* (Cambridge: Cambridge University Press, 1996).

Samuel, I., '*Samson Agonistes* as Tragedy', in J. A. Wittreich, J. G. Taaffe and J. Cerny (eds), *Calm of Mind: Tercentenary Essays of 'Paradise Regained' and 'Samson Agonistes'.in Honor of John S. Diekhoff* (Cleveland: Press of Case Western Reserve University, 1972), pp. 235–57.

Samuels, P., 'Labor in the Chambers: *Paradise Regained* and the Discourse of Quiet', *Milton Studies*, 36 (1998), 153–76.

Sanders, J., 'Brathwaite, Richard (1587/8–1673), poet and writer', in H. C. G. Matthew and B. Harrison (eds), *Oxford Dictionary of National Biography* (Oxford: Oxford University Press, 2004), available at <http://www.oxforddnb.com.ezaccess.libraries.psu.edu/view/article/3290> (last accessed 4 August 2016).

Sauer, E., 'Closet Drama and the Case of *Tyrannical-Government Anatomized*', in M. Straznicky (ed.), *The Book of the Play* (Amherst: University of Massachusetts Press, 2006), pp. 80–98.

Sawday, J., *The Body Emblazoned: Dissection and the Human Body in Renaissance Culture* (London: Routledge, 1995).

Schoenfeldt, M., *Bodies and Selves in Early Modern England: Physiology and Inwardness in Spenser, Shakespeare, Herbert, and Milton* (Cambridge: Cambridge University Press, 1999).

Schoenfeldt, M., '"Commotion Strange": Passion in *Paradise Lost*', in G. K. Paster, K. Rowe and M. Floyd-Wilson, *Reading the Early Modern Passions: Essays in the Cultural History of Emotion* (Philadelphia: University of Pennsylvania Press, 2004), pp. 43–67.

Schwartz, R., 'Revelation and Idolatry: Holy Law and Holy Terror', *Genre*, 40: 3–4 (2007), 1–16.

Shakespeare, W., *The History of Henry the Fourth* (London: Andrew Wise, 1598).

Shawcross, J. T., *John Milton and Influence: Presence in Literature, History, and Culture* (Pittsburgh: Duquesne University Press, 1991).

Shore, D., *Milton and the Art of Rhetoric* (Cambridge: Cambridge University Press, 2012).

Shuger, D., '"Gums of Glutinous Heat" and the Stream of Consciousness: Theology in Milton's *Maske*', *Representations*, 60 (1997), 1–21.

Shuger, D., *Sacred Rhetoric: The Christian Grand Style in the English Renaissance* (Princeton: Princeton University Press, 1988).

Shullenberger, W., *The Lady in the Labyrinth: Milton's 'Comus' as Initiation* (Madison, NY: Fairleigh Dickinson University Press, 2008).

Sidney, Sir P., *Astrophel and Stella*, in S. Greenblatt, G. Logan, K. E. Maus and B. K. Lewalski (eds), *The Norton Anthology of English Literature*, 9th edn, 6 vols (New York: Norton, 2012), B, pp. 1084–101.

Sidney, Sir P., *The Defense of Poesy*, in S. Greenblatt, G. Logan, K. E. Maus and B. K. Lewalski (eds), *The Norton Anthology of English Literature*, 9th edn, 6 vols (New York: Norton, 2012), B, pp. 1044–83.

Silverman, K., *The Subject of Semiotics* (New York: Oxford University Press, 1983).

Smectymnuus, *A Vindication of the Answer to the Humble Remonstrance* (London: John Rothwell, 1641).

Smith, D. L., 'From Petition to Remonstrance', in D. L. Smith, R. Strier and D. Bevington (eds), *The Theatrical City: Culture Theatre and Politics in London, 1576–1649* (Cambridge: Cambridge University Press, 1995), pp. 209–23.

Smith, N., *Perfection Proclaimed: Language and Literature in English Radical Religion, 1640–60* (Oxford: Oxford University Press, 1994).

Smith, N., 'Richard Overton's Marpriest Tracts: Towards a History of Leveller Style', *Prose Studies*, 9: 2 (1986), 39–66.

Spenser, E., *The Faerie Queene*, in A. C. Hamilton (ed.) (London: Longman, 1997).

Stackhouse, A., 'Sleeping with the Muse: Milton and the Gender of Authorship', in T. H. Howard-Hill and P. Rolinson (eds), *Renaissance Papers: 1999* (Rochester, NY: Camden House, 1999), pp. 137–46.

Steggle, M., '"The Tragical Part": Milton's *Masque* and Euripides', *Classical and Modern Literature*, 20 (1999), 18–36.

Stein, A., *Heroic Knowledge* (Hamden: Archon Books, 1965).

Stevens, P., *Imagination and the Presence of Shakespeare in 'Paradise Lost'* (Madison: University of Wisconsin Press, 1985).

Stone, L., *Causes of the English Revolution, 1529–1642* (New York: Routledge, [1972] 2002).

Straznicky, M., *Privacy, Playreading, and Women's Closet Drama, 1550–1700* (Cambridge: Cambridge University Press, 2004).

Sugimura, N. K., *'Matter of Glorious Trial': Spiritual and Material Substance in 'Paradise Lost'* (New Haven: Yale University Press, 2009).

Tertullian, *Apology: De spectaculis, and Minucius Felix*, trans. T. R. Glover, G. H. Rendall and W. C. A. Kerr (Cambridge, MA: Harvard University Press, 1977).

Teskey, G., *Delerious Milton: The Fate of the Poet in Modernity* (Cambridge, MA: Harvard University Press, 2009).

Tombes, J., *True Old Light Exalted above Pretended New Light* (London: Thomas Underhill, 1660).

Tomlinson, S., *Women on Stage in Stuart Drama* (Cambridge: Cambridge University Press, 2005).

Townshend, A., *Tempe Restored*, in S. Orgel, *Inigo Jones*, 2 vols (Berkeley and Los Angeles: University of California Press, 1973), II, pp. 479–504.

Treip, M. A., '*Comus* as "Progress"', *Milton Quarterly*, 20 (1986), 1–13.

Turner, J. G., 'Milton among the Libertines', in C. Tournu and N. Forsyth (eds), *Milton, Rights, and Liberties* (Bern: Peter Lang, 2007), pp. 447–60.

Turner, J. G., *One Flesh: Paradisal Marriage and Sexual Relations in the Age of Milton* (Oxford: Clarendon, 1987).

Turner, J. G., *The Politics of Landscape: Rural Scenery and Society in English Poetry, 1630–60* (Cambridge, MA: Harvard University Press, 1976).

Urban, D., 'The Lady of Christ's College Himself a "Lady Wise and Pure": Parabolic Self-Reference in John Milton's "Sonnet IX"', *Milton Studies*, 47 (2008), 1–23.
Vicars, J., *Speculum scripturale schismaticorum or, A Scripture Looking-Glasse, Most Exactly Characterizing All Sorts of Schismaticks* (London: T. M., 1649).
Virgil, *The Eclogues of Virgil*, trans. D. Ferry (New York: Macmillan, 2015).
Virgil, *Virgil's Aeneid: Books I–VI, VII, IX, and Selections from the Other Books*, ed. D. Y. Comstock (Boston: Allyn and Bacon, 1896).
Waith, E. M., 'The Metamorphosis of Violence in *Titus Andronicus*', *Shakespeare Survey*, 10 (1957), 39–49.
Webster, T., '"Kiss Me with the Kisses of His Mouth": Gender Inversion and Canticles in Godly Spirituality', in T. Betteridge (ed.), *Sodomy in Early Modern Europe* (Manchester: Manchester University Press, 2002), pp. 148–63.
Weld, T., R. Prideaux, S. Hammond, R. Cole and W. Durant, *The Perfect Pharise, under Monkish Holines, Opposing the Fundamental Principles of the Doctrine of the Gospel* (London: Richard Tomlins, 1654).
Wigan, J., *Antichrist's Strongest Hold Overturned: Or, The Foundation of the Religion of the People Called QUAKERS, Bared and Razed* (London: John Wigan, 1665).
Wiseman, S., *Drama and Politics in the English Civil War* (Cambridge: Cambridge University Press, 1998).
Wittreich, J. A., *Interpreting 'Samson Agonistes'* (Princeton: Princeton University Press, 1986).
Wittreich, J. A., *Shifting Contexts: Reinterpreting 'Samson Agonistes'* (Pittsburgh: Duquesne University Press, 2002).
Woerther, F., 'Music and Education of the Soul in Plato and Aristotle', *Classical Quarterly*, 58: 1 (2008), 89–103.
Wood, D. N. C., *Exiled from Light: Divine Law, Morality, and Violence in Milton's 'Samson Agonistes'* (Toronto: University of Toronto Press, 2001).
Woods, S., 'Inviting Rival Hermeneutics: Milton's Language of Violence and the Invitation to Freedom', in R. J. DuRocher and M. O. Thickstun (eds), *Milton's Rival Hermeneutics: 'Reason Is but Choosing'* (Pittsburgh: Duquesne University Press, 2012).
Younge, R., *An Experimental Index of the Heart: Or Self-Knowledge* (London: James Crump and Henry Cripps, [1658] 1660).
Zaret, D., 'Petitions and the "Invention" of Public Opinion in the English Revolution', *The American Journal of Sociology*, 101 (1996).

Index

Abdiel, 34, 39, 41
Accademia degli Umoristi, 62
Achinstein, Sharon, 95–6
actio, 3–4, 6–10, 17–18, 20, 88, 95, 100–1, 107, 112, 114, 121, 177, 194–5, 218; *see also* gesture
actors, 3, 7–8, 10–11, 14, 16, 18–21, 23–4, 26, 29–30, 37–40, 51, 54–8, 68, 74, 110, 112–14, 116–20, 121, 138, 149, 178, 189, 199, 209; *see also* fool: stage fool
ad hominem, 88, 91, 117
Adam, 35, 38, 42, 136, 139, 144, 147, 150–62, 176, 188, 200–1, 221–2
admiring, 8, 61, 117–20, 145, 161–3
Aeschines, 21
Aesopus, 18
agency, 11, 32–3, 36–43, 54, 56–7, 62–72, 73–7, 139–41, 154, 163–4, 174, 176–8, 180, 184–5, 187–8, 198–201
allegory, 41, 70–1, 74, 133, 136–7
amazement, 39–41, 195, 196
ambiguity, 9, 21, 23, 25, 30, 32–3, 35–6, 50, 52, 78, 89, 104, 149, 170, 172–3, 177, 182–3, 185–7, 195–7, 200–6, 208–9, 212n, 213n, 218–22
ambivalence *see* ambiguity
Amoret, 73–5
amphitheatres, 5, 57, 90, 108–9, 185–6, 213n; *see also* theatre: London
Anabaptists, 194, 195, 215n
anagnorisis, 133–5
Andreini, Giambattista, 137, 146
Andronicus, 3, 18–19

anger, 38, 48n, 92, 186, 191, 192–3, 198, 204–5
Anglican Church, 5–6, 38–9, 52, 55, 56, 86–104, 107, 109–14, 121–3, 199–200; *see also* theatricality
Anselment, Raymond A., 87
antic, the, 7, 73, 110, 111, 113, 114, 121, 163, 194, 199; *see also* ludic, the
anti-feminism, 57–8, 63–4, 66, 137–8, 159, 172, 190–2, 221–2
antimasque, 63, 65, 73, 135, 199–200
antinomianism, 139, 174–6, 206; *see also* Quakers
anti-theatricality, 1–2, 7–9, 14, 18, 50–2, 54, 56–9, 63, 90, 101–2, 107, 110, 112–14, 117–21
aping, 38, 110–12
Apollodorus, 47n
apology, 38, 154
applause, 23–9, 34, 38, 41–2, 59, 68, 96–7, 111, 113–14, 117, 122–3, 185; *see also* hissing
Archimago, 69
architecture, theatre, 2, 4–5, 185–6
  Dagon's theatre, 35–6, 68, 170, 185–6
  frons scaenae, 146–7, 185–6
  galleries *see* architecture, theatre: seating
  heavens, the, 186–7
  pillars, 180–2, 185–6
  platforms, 24, 68, 186
  porch, 51–2, 76
  roof, 186, 189, 213n
  scaena, 185–6
  scaffold, 36, 68, 126n, 185–6
  seating, 146–9, 150, 155, 163, 185

stage, 7–8, 24, 29, 38, 68, 74, 83n, 102, 106, 109, 113, 121, 147, 170, 189
  tiring house, 10, 95
  wall, 60, 146–9, 150, 188–9
  Woodie Theatre, 60, 146–50, 163, 186, 188–9
  woody scene, 147, 189
Aristotle, 17, 26, 27, 30, 52, 88, 131, 132–7, 172, 202–5
arousal, 21, 37, 72, 144, 187, 202
Attendant Spirit, 60, 63–5, 67–8, 75, 77
atticism, 113–14
audience, 1–2, 4, 6, 9–11, 14, 16–17, 20–36, 38, 40–3, 52–3, 56, 59, 60–2, 67–8, 76–8, 91, 94, 95–7, 99–102, 113–14, 117–18, 119–20, 122–3, 130, 132, 134–8, 146, 164, 166n, 177, 185, 188, 208–9, 219–21; *see also* spectators
Augustine, 101
Austin, Samuel, 177–8
authenticity, 2, 5–7, 38, 87–8, 100, 102–7, 161, 173, 177–84, 191–3, 194–6, 206–7

Bacchantes, 10–11, 34, 56–7, 67–8, 72; *see also* Orpheus
Baroni, Leonora, 61–2
Bastwick, John, 92, 96
Batchiler, John, 207–8
Belial, 200
Bennett, Joan, 184, 200, 216n
Bernard, Richard, 106
Bevington, David, 12n
Beza, Theodore, 134, 194
Bible, 5, 35, 56, 118, 132, 175, 210n
  1 Corinthians, 61, 70, 71n, 81n
  Deuteronomy, 176
  Exodus, 22, 121
  Genesis, 10, 157, 222
  Hebrews, 196
  Judges, 177, 185, 208, 213n
  Leviticus, 9, 121–2
  Numbers, 196
  Proverbs, 6, 91, 107, 114–15, 123, 198–9
  Psalms, 98–9
  Revelation, 9, 50–1, 122, 134, 159
  Romans, 118, 201–3
  2 Samuel, 196–8
  Song of Songs, 192
  see also King James Version; scripture

bird-liming, 68–9, 75, 83n
Blaugdone, Barbara, 177, 211n
blindness, 1, 10, 32, 173, 183–4, 186–7, 208
Blome, Richard, 195, 201
blood circulation *see* Harvey, William
body as text / text as body, 20, 54, 97, 180, 209
bonds, collateral, 151–3, 154–8
Book of Sports and Pastimes, 119
botany, 78, 131, 138–40, 146–56, 158–60
Brathwaite, Richard, 111–13, 128n
bride of Timna, 195, 197
Britomart, 53, 72–6, 84n
Broaddus, James W., 73
Brutus, 114
Buchanan, George, 187
buffoon, 6, 107–12, 199
Bulwer, John, 18–19, 21–2, 101, 104, 106, 118–19, 201
Burbery, Timothy, 12n, 132, 217n
Burns, Norman T., 193
Burton, Henry, 92, 96
Busyrane, 53, 73–5
Butler, Martin, 115, 125n

Caeneus, 31
Calvinism, 174–5, 194
Campbell, Gordon, 15; *see also* Campbell, Gordon and Thomas Corns
Campbell, Gordon and Thomas Corns, 15, 31, 108, 117; *see also* Campbell, Gordon
canting, 109
canvassing, 116
caress, 157–8, 162–3; *see also* touch
carnality, 56, 64, 69–71, 99, 101–2, 114, 122, 172, 178, 183, 202–3
Carter, Richard, 106
Castlehaven scandal, 80–1n
castration, 30, 34–5, 191
catastrophe, 135, 170, 186–7, 193, 196–200, 203, 205–6, 208
catharsis, 43, 52, 133–7, 172–3, 202–7
Catholicism, 92, 94, 118, 119, 177
character, 2–3, 7, 26, 29, 56–7, 65, 91, 96, 109, 111, 124n, 130, 131–2, 133–8, 146, 165n, 170–1, 173, 194, 199
Charissa, 84n
charity, 70–1, 136; *see also* Charissa

Charles I, 6–7, 8, 89–90, 97, 104, 117–20, 171
chastity, 31, 33, 53–4, 57–66, 69–73, 77–8, 80–1n, 82n, 84n, 195; *see also* virginity
chorus, 121–2, 134, 136; *see also* Chorus, the
Chorus, the, 171, 177, 184–5, 189–90, 191, 193, 195, 203, 205, 206, 208
Cicero, 3–4, 7–8, 17–21, 101, 114, 208
Circe, 60, 65, 75, 80n, 109
city comedy, 109, 111
Clark, Stuart, 140–1
Cleon, 18–19
closet drama, 1, 72, 111, 172–3, 177, 187, 203–6, 217n
Coiro, Ann Baynes, 78, 217n
Coliseum, 185
Collier, Thomas, 175, 183, 184, 207, 214n
Collinson, Patrick, 91
comedic, the, 1, 4, 6, 8, 15–16, 24, 30, 91, 93, 100, 102, 104, 106–12, 114, 115, 116–17, 119, 121, 178, 194–5, 199, 215n; *see also* ludic, the
comedy, 14, 24, 59, 61, 91, 93, 100, 102, 108–9, 111, 113–14, 115–16, 121, 135, 178, 194, 215n
Comus, 56, 60, 63–9, 71–2, 74–7
conscience, 35, 101, 174–6, 191
constraint, 11, 17, 36, 52, 66, 77–8, 88, 102
contingency, 11, 139, 209
Corpus Christi plays, 132
costume, 2, 5, 8, 10, 20, 35, 37–8, 58, 65, 71, 95, 108, 118, 121, 189, 201
countenance, 6, 26, 34, 38, 41, 65, 93, 97, 104n, 106, 117, 154, 157, 194, 212n
counter-influence, 18, 33–4, 36, 40, 62, 218–19; *see also* influence
courage, 36–7, 73–4, 99
Cromwell, Oliver, 171
curtains, 97, 177

Dalila, 185, 190–2, 195–6, 197, 214n
Damrosch, Leo, 192, 227n
dance, 15, 57–9, 77, 144, 177, 197, 200
Danites *see* Chorus, the
D'Assigny, Marius, 20–2
David, King, 98–9, 197

Davus, 113–14
de Brès, Guy, 194
declamation, 3–4, 6, 15, 19–21, 110, 199
decorum, 6, 7, 9, 30, 38, 77, 87–8, 91, 93–100, 102, 104, 106–10, 113, 116–17, 121, 123, 132, 183, 195, 218
decorum personae, 87–8, 91–4
delight, 23, 43, 52, 91, 99, 139, 144, 157, 159, 166n, 203
delivery *see actio*
della Salandra, Serafino, 137, 146
Dell'Antonio, Andrew, 62
Demaray, John G., 133, 149
Demosthenes, 3–4, 18–20, 21, 208–9
deportment, 116–17, 119
derision *see* laughter
Descartes, René, 11, 36–8, 48n, 140–2, 166–7
desire, 10–11, 16, 17, 23, 29, 30, 34, 35, 37–9, 41, 43, 52, 53, 55, 57–8, 59–60, 62, 64–8, 71, 73–6, 78, 98–9, 131, 137–8, 158–9, 161–3, 191, 202, 204, 209, 219, 222
deus ex machina, 75, 135
dialogue, 17, 77, 87, 90, 92, 96, 98–100, 125n, 133, 136, 176, 190–1, 207
Diodati, Charles, 14, 59–60, 89
Directory for the Publike Worship of God, 102, 104–5
discernment, 99, 113, 120, 123, 172, 184, 200, 204–8
discovery *see anagnorisis*
disguise *see* costume
dispensation, 121, 156, 195–8, 200–1
dissonance, 10, 25, 32, 34, 53, 67–8
Dobranski, Stephen, 45n
Dodd, Edward, 184
Donne, John, 101
drama, 1–3, 51, 53–4, 56, 72, 78, 92, 99, 114, 122, 130–8, 146, 151, 160, 164, 170, 173, 176–7, 187, 200, 202–5; *see also* theatre
dramatic time, 55, 109–10, 131, 136–8, 146, 172–3, 176–7
drooping, 150, 154–5
dualism *see* Platonism
Duran, Angelica, 138

earthquakes, 71, 182
echo, 24, 34, 40–1, 67, 68, 78, 147
Echo, 76–8

economic metaphor, 63–7, 72, 76, 78, 83n, 110
Edwards, Karen, 138–9
Egerton, Alice, 56–7, 71, 80n, 80–1n
Eikon Basilike, 8, 18, 97, 117–20
Elder Brother, 64–6, 72, 75, 77, 144
Ellwood, Thomas, 174
Emmot, George, 195
empiricism, 138–9, 164
encompassing, the, 6, 10, 29, 32, 35, 39–42, 72, 90, 95, 100, 146–9, 163, 185–7, 188
energeito, 202, 216n
enjambment, 34, 39–41, 161, 199
enthusiasm, 100–1, 104–6, 114, 119, 171–4, 204–6; see also Quakers
envy, 38
Erasmus, 94
ethics see ethos
ethos, 2, 38, 40, 42–3, 54–5, 87–8, 96–9, 113, 123, 145, 150, 163, 170, 184–5
Eumenides, the, 25
Euripides, 4, 18–19, 194
Eve, 30, 38, 41, 42, 133, 136–9, 140, 144, 146, 150–2, 153–4, 156–9, 161–2, 189
Evelyn, John, 152
exegesis, 8–9, 11, 120–4, 130, 137, 151, 156, 159, 171, 176–7, 208–9, 222; see also scripture; scripture-as-script
exemplarity, 51, 132, 134–5, 136, 191, 202, 206–7l; see also theatre: as edifying
explosion see applause; hissing
exposure, 5, 10, 29–30, 34–5, 38–9, 94–100, 107–8, 186–7, 189–90; see also nakedness
extramission, 142, 144–5; see also optics
eyes see optics

Fall, the, 122, 131–3, 136–40, 142, 146, 154–6, 159–64, 189
Fallon, Stephen, 55, 62
farce, 15, 23, 26–7; see also interlude
fear, 14, 29, 36–7, 74–5, 98, 106, 130–1, 204; see also horror; terror
feminine, the, 4, 16, 30–1, 58, 64–5, 71, 74–7, 190, 222; see also anti-feminism; gender
Finch, Heneage, 182

Fish, Stanley, 120, 170, 182, 213n, 220, 221
Fletcher, Angus, 138
fool
  grim fool, 92, 100, 109, 122
  jester, 199
  Pauline fool, 92, 94, 171, 194, 197
  stage fool, 4–7, 9, 11, 38, 91–2, 107–9, 111–12, 116–18, 123, 178, 194, 198–9
  unwise fool, 88, 91, 94, 113, 115, 117, 194, 198–9
footsteps, 53, 67, 98–9, 190
form, monstrous, 53, 70, 73
form, systemic, 221
Fox, George, 174, 177, 182–3, 192, 207, 211–12n
French, J. Milton, 94

Gabriel, 136
gardening see botany
gaze, 6, 8, 34–6, 40–2, 53, 58–62, 66, 71, 97, 118–19, 144–6, 149, 158, 161–3, 176–7, 186–7, 191, 197, 213n, 218–19
gender, 4, 16, 21, 30–3, 35, 54, 59, 62–8, 71, 73–7, 161–3, 190–2, 221–2; see also anti-feminism; feminine, the
genitals, 30, 35, 202; see also nakedness
gesture, 3–4, 6–8, 10–11, 17–22, 24, 28, 30, 35, 37–9, 55, 58, 65, 71, 89, 95, 100–2, 104, 106–7, 109–10, 112–14, 122–3, 127n, 146, 155, 157–9, 163, 177–8, 180, 188, 193–5, 198–201, 208–9
Gilpin, John, 178–80, 201
God
  Hebrew, 171, 185, 192
  hermaphroditic, 32–3
  solar, 150, 155
  spectator, 35, 155, 163, 185
Goodman, Kevis, 156
Gosson, Stephen, 58, 71
Greene, John, 51
Griffith, Matthew, 83n
Grotius, Hugo, 137, 146
gumms of glutenous heat, 68–9
Gurr, Andrew, 55, 213n
gymnasts, 199

Hale, John, 15–16, 24, 29
Hall, Joseph, 3, 6, 35, 55, 86–7, 93, 96–100, 107, 113–14

Hall, Ralph, 183
Hammond, Paul, 4, 115, 131, 164
Harapha, 185, 191–3, 197
Harvey, William, 201
Haskin, Dayton, 9
hate, 34
Hausted, Peter, 110
Hebrew Law, 9, 56, 122, 146, 184, 195–8, 201–2
Heckscher, William, 97
Heinsius, Daniel, 133
Henrietta Maria, 57, 92
herbals, 147–8, 158, 160; see also botany
Herbert, George, 101, 150
Hercules, 116
Hercules Gallicus (Anglicus), 20–1, 22, 26, 28
Hermogenes, 100–2
Herod, 121, 187
Hesiod, 31
Higginson, Francis, 177–8, 180
Hill, Christopher, 171, 202
Hinds, Hilary, 174
hissing, 5, 14, 25, 34, 38, 41–2, 68, 90, 97, 99, 113, 122; see also applause
Hobbes, Thomas, 11, 140–3
Holy Spirit, 5, 6–7, 9, 32–3, 59, 60–2, 95, 113, 121–3, 138, 171–8, 180, 184–5, 189, 195–6, 200–1, 204, 206–8, 210n, 211n, 219; see also inner light
homeopathy see humours
Homer, 28, 60
Horace, 87, 124n
horror, 42, 180, 182
Hortensius, 18, 21–2, 30
horticulture see botany
Howard, Jean, 58
Hoxby, Blair, 66
Hughes, Merritt, 133
humours, 203–5
Hunt, John Dixon, 147
hypocrisy, 6, 37–8, 42, 88, 94–100, 113–14, 177, 207, 223n

iconoclasm, 88, 93; see also Milton, John: *Eikonoklastes*
identification, 33, 53, 59, 61, 70, 76, 99, 133, 135, 154, 203–5
identity, 4, 6, 16, 23, 30–1, 33, 52–3, 55, 60, 66, 89, 108, 114; see also gender; identification
idolatry, 93, 171, 183, 193, 197–8

imitation, 112, 178
improvisation, 5–6, 8–9, 11, 88, 100, 104, 107, 120–3, 155, 173, 176, 189, 196–7, 199–200, 209, 219
impulsion, 177, 183, 195–7, 201–2, 207; see also motions
indecorum see decorum
indeterminacy see ambiguity
influence, 10, 21, 34, 40, 42, 51, 144–5, 150, 161–3, 187, 191–2, 207, 218
inner light, 7, 171–6, 177, 178, 183–4, 191, 207, 211–12n; see also Holy Spirit
interlude, 1, 6, 15–16, 23, 27–31, 56, 109, 116, 132–3, 194
intromission, 140–4; see also optics
introspection, 172–3, 205–7; see also discernment
inventio, 23, 28, 39, 184
invocations of *Paradise Lost*, 10, 32–4, 123, 129n, 144–5

James I, 119
Jesus, 9, 118, 122, 147, 173, 176–7, 188–9, 196, 205
jig, 8, 77, 91, 92–3, 119, 125n
John the Baptist, 187, 196
Jones, Inigo, 75
Jonson, Ben, 2, 14–15, 60, 65, 88, 112
juggling, 69, 127n, 199

Kahn, Victoria, 70, 204
Kerrigan, William, 54
King, Edward, 89
King James Version, 201–2; see also Bible; scripture
kneeling, 8, 29, 102, 178, 180
Knoppers, Laura, 166, 172
Kranidas, Thomas, 87, 110
Kyd, Thomas, 2, 88

Lacan, Jacques, 11, 35
Lactantius, 14, 50–1
Lady, the, 26, 31, 53–4, 56–7, 63–4, 66–72, 74–80, 144
Laud, William, 5, 52, 89–90, 92, 96, 100, 101
laughter, 10, 24, 26, 86, 91–4, 96–7, 99, 100, 106, 108, 115, 119, 200
Lawes, Henry, 67, 76, 78
Levellers, 92
levity, 93, 102, 116
Lewalski, Barbara, 133, 146, 149, 221

light *see* optics
Lodge, Thomas, 206
Loewenstein, David, 171, 175, 183, 188, 200
looking-glass literature, 173, 175, 206–8
love *see* bonds, collateral
Low, Anthony, 200
ludic, the, 5, 88, 91, 94, 177, 183, 194; *see also* comedic, the
Ludlow Castle, 64–5, 71, 77–8, 82n
Lupton, Donald, 178
Luxon, Thomas, 147

Macrobius, 44
madness, 7, 37, 130, 146, 178, 183, 195, 204
Manoa, 171, 185, 190, 195–6
Marcus, Leah, 80–1n
Marprelate, Martin, 5–6, 87, 90–4, 96, 107, 109
marriage *see* bonds, collateral
Marshall, William, 18–19, 21–2, 118, 208
Marston, John, 205
Martin, Catherine, 91
Marvell, Andrew, 1, 87, 183
masque, 1, 4, 10–11, 15, 31, 35, 37, 50, 52–3, 56–61, 63–6, 68, 71–85, 89, 95, 118–19, 133, 135–6, 144, 149, 199–200
Maus, Katherine, 80n
Maximus, Valerius, 18
Mayne, Jasper, 101
mechanism, 40, 95, 139–41, 164
melancholy, 48n, 68, 102, 150, 194, 203–5, 212n; *see also* sorrow
Merleau-Ponty, Maurice, 33–5
metadrama, 2–3
metamorphosis, 60, 65–6
Michael, 133, 163
Michelangelo, 137–8
miles gloriosus, 3, 113–14
Millennium, 6, 9, 50–1, 52, 59, 71, 81n, 94, 121–2, 129n, 130, 208
Miller, Joshua, 183, 201
Milton, John
  ambivalence toward theatre, 1–2, 14, 50, 52, 78, 89
  comedian, 16, 113, 199
  death, 209, 218–20
  Domina, nickname of, 26, 30–1, 57
  fetish, as scholarly, 16, 57, 164, 171, 172
  home on Aldersgate Street, 90
  interluder, 109–10, 116
  Italy, in, 89, 185
  people, and the, 6, 8, 88, 100, 109, 115–23, 130–6, 164, 188, 208–9
  playgoer, 1–2, 14–15, 59, 108–10, 112–13
  playwright, popular, 1–2, 14, 15, 52, 78, 88, 132
  poetics, generative, 7, 9–10, 88, 107, 120–3, 130, 133, 144, 149, 164, 170, 176, 184, 196, 209, 219–22
  scholarship, 1–2, 3, 15, 16, 17, 44n, 54, 57, 61, 69, 79n, 81n, 110, 133, 138, 139, 164, 170–2, 175, 184, 193, 200, 201, 217n
  stage fool, 4, 6, 9, 107–10, 123, 199
  stage fool, disavowal of, 115–17, 123
  voyeur, 59–60
WORKS
  'Abram from Morea, or Isaack Redeemd', 133–4, 136, 165n
  Ad Leonoram Romae canentem and *Ad eandem*, 61–2
  'Adam Unparadiz'd', 133, 136, 137, 146, 167n
  Animadversions, 4, 5, 6, 35, 55, 86–8, 90–100, 107–9, 113, 114, 116, 117, 120–2, 138, 197, 205
  Apology against a Pamphlet, 3, 5–6, 14, 38–9, 54–5, 97, 108, 110, 112–13, 121, 122, 163, 199
  Arcades, 1
  Areopagitica, 20, 32, 42–3, 54–5, 64, 76, 97, 115, 129n, 132, 161, 200, 219
  Ars logica, 17
  'Baptistes', 187, 193
  Brief Notes upon a Late Sermon, 83n
  Colasterion, 114–16, 119, 120, 198
  Commonplace Book, 50–1
  'Cupids Funeral Pile. Sodom Burning', 133, 135, 136, 199–200, 216n
  De doctrina Christiana, 70, 101, 115, 132, 172, 175–6, 205–6, 222n
  'Deluge, The', 135
  Doctrine and Discipline of Divorce, 115, 132
  Eikonoklastes, 5, 6, 14–15, 97, 117–20
  Elegia prima, 59–60
  Elegia sexta, 14, 59–60, 62, 109
  Epistolarum familiarum liber, 15

Milton, John (*cont.*)
  'Golden Calfe, The', 135
  'Il Penseroso', 56, 60–2
  'L'Allegro', 14, 56, 60–2, 134
  'Lycidas', 11, 28, 56, 68, 87, 89
  'Macbeth', 134
  Maske at Ludlow Castle, 1, 11, 31, 52–4, 56–61, 63–73, 74–8, 80–1n, 82n, 89, 91n, 135, 144
  'Murmurers, The', 135
  Of True Religion, 174
  Paradise Lost, 1, 4, 5, 9–11, 16, 20, 28, 32–3, 35, 37, 40–2, 56–9, 68, 122–4, 130–1, 133, 136–9, 144–7, 149–52, 154–9, 161–4, 188–9, 200–1, 208, 221–2
  Paradise Regained, 1–2, 5, 9, 16, 110, 122–3, 136–7, 147, 173, 174, 176–7, 188–9, 205
  Prelaticall Episcopacy, Of, 5, 86, 94, 120
  Pro populo Anglicano defensio, 26, 117
  Pro populo Anglicano defensio secunda, 26, 117
  Pro se defensio, 117
  'Quails, The', 135
  Readie and Easie Way to Establish a Free Commonwealth, 26, 130–1
  Reason of Church Government, 5, 35, 51–2, 56, 87, 91, 95, 109, 113, 121, 132, 133, 135–7
  Samson Agonistes, 1, 5, 11, 16, 52, 68, 120, 123, 136–7, 170–3, 175, 176–7, 180, 182, 184, 187, 189, 195, 197, 200–9, 221–2
  'Shakespear, On', 5, 61–2
  sonnet XIII, 76
  Tenure of Kings and Magistrates, 200
  Tetrachordon, 9, 115
  'Tragedy, Of that Sort of Dramatic Poem Call'd', 43, 52, 172–3, 203–5, 215n
  Tenure of Kings and Magistrates, 200
  Treatise of Civil Power, 174, 175–6, 200–1
  Trinity Manuscript, 1, 28, 63–4, 78, 122, 130–7, 146, 167n, 187, 193, 199–200, 206
  Vacation Exercise, 1, 5, 15, 21, 26–7, 30–4, 35, 43, 50, 53, 57
Milton, John, Sr., 12
miming, 7, 94, 104, 109, 112, 177, 195, 199

mirth, 24, 102
Modest Confutation of a Slanderous and Scurrilous Libell, 6, 9, 93–4, 107–10, 112–14, 115–16, 117, 121, 127n, 199
moly, 60
monologue, 63, 188, 190, 196
More, Alexander, 117
Morris, Samuel, 207
Mosaic Law *see* Hebrew Law
Moses, 34, 146
motions, 7, 20, 95, 101, 106, 141, 144, 150, 155, 158, 163, 171–2, 176–7, 180, 182, 200–3
mountebank, 15, 68, 83n, 118n, 127n, 178
mouthing, 6–7, 9, 39, 121, 178, 180
Muggleton, Lodowicke, 207
mumming, 199
music, 10, 61–2, 67–8, 76–7, 97, 121–2, 175n
mutilation *see sparagmos*

nakedness, 27, 29–30, 34–5, 40, 70, 84n, 95, 97, 120–1, 191, 197; *see also* exposure; genitals
narcissism, 39–40, 150–1, 221–2
Nardo, Anna K., 194
Naylor, James, 172, 182–3, 191–2, 211–12n, 214n
Nazarite, 196–8
Neelakanta, Vanita, 185
Neo-Platonism *see* Platonism
New Historicism, 14, 66
Newcastle ministers, 177, 180
Newton, Isaac, 138, 166n
Northbrooke, John, 58, 71
Nyquist, Mary, 222

obedience, 8–9, 33, 94n, 104, 113, 123, 131, 134–5, 150, 151–2, 154–7, 163, 176, 184, 185, 200, 219
Officer, 170, 185, 199, 202
Ong, Walter J., 17
ontology, 21, 63–4, 75, 139–40, 142, 184
optics, 11, 33–42, 65, 75–6, 138–46, 149–50, 156–8, 163; *see also* vision, peripheral
oratory, 3–4, 15–18, 20–3, 25, 55, 114, 117
original sin *see* Fall, the
Orpheus, 10, 34, 43, 56–7, 62, 72; *see also vates*

Overton, Richard, 90, 92–3, 96
Ovid, 31, 59, 86, 150–1

paneguries, 51–2, 132–3, 136
Paraeus, Don, 121
Parkinson, John, 147–8, 153
passions, 7–8, 10–11, 20–1, 33–4, 36–40, 42–3, 52, 74, 100–1, 104, 106, 111, 119, 131, 133–5, 139–42, 144–6, 150, 156–7, 159, 161–3, 170, 172–3, 177–8, 182, 184–5, 187–93
pathos see passions
patience, 73, 110, 131
Patterson, Annabel, 72
Peacham, Henry, 86
perception, 25, 69, 141–2
peripeteia, 75, 133–4, 135, 203, 206
periwig, 7, 35, 97, 108; *see also* costume
personation, 94, 96
perspective, 37, 64, 72, 74–5, 141, 189
Peters, Katie, 183
petitions, 93
Petrarchism, 63–4, 66, 73–4
Peyton, Edward, 58
Philips, Edward, 108
physiology, 36, 187, 190, 201; *see also* passions
Picciotto, Joanna, 138–9
Pierce, Helen, 90
pity, 135–6, 203–4
Plato, 17, 151
Platonism, 63–4, 70–1, 77, 151, 184
Plautus, 3, 113–14
playacting, 8, 102, 111
players *see* actors
playlets, 4–5, 90–4, 96, 111, 125n, 127n
pliancy, 38, 113, 199
Pliny, 31, 152
Plutarch, 3–4, 17–18, 20, 44
poetasters, 56, 71, 132
polyscmy *see* ambiguity
pranks, 195
prayer, 8–9, 100, 102–5, 118–19, 121–2, 155–6, 201
preachers, women, 192, 214n
preaching, 5, 14, 17, 100–6, 114
prelacy, 5, 87–8, 89–100, 112–15, 121–2, 127n, 199; *see also* Hall, Joseph; Laud, William
pride, 34, 42, 73, 92, 98, 193, 198, 207

privacy, 53, 55–61, 66–7, 72, 188, 205–6
prologue, 38, 74, 98, 146, 154–5
prompting, 24, 38, 102, 112, 154, 190, 195, 197, 200
pronunciation, 4, 7, 17–18, 20, 38, 100, 106, 113–14; *see also actio*
properties, stage, 2, 5, 8, 37, 95, 108, 189; *see also* costume
proposals, 51–2, 59, 132
prospect, 37, 144, 147, 149, 188–9
prostitution, 38, 57–8, 71, 110, 111–13, 138
Prynne, William, 14, 30, 57–71, 92, 96
public sphere, 90
puppet shows, 15, 95, 177, 200

Quakers, 7, 9, 16, 77, 100, 171–8, 180, 182–4, 191–2, 194–6, 200–1, 207–8, 211–12n, 214n, 215n
Quintilian, 3, 17–18, 101, 104–5

rabble, 8, 40, 84n, 118, 120, 177; *see also* throng
Radzinowicz, Mary Ann, 184
Ramism, 17
Randolph, Thomas, 14, 27, 111
Ranters, 171, 191–2, 214n
Raphael, 144, 150, 154–5, 157–9, 200
rationalisation, 43, 141, 160–1, 177, 183–4, 187, 190, 195–6, 198
reason, 36–7, 43, 65, 69, 70, 101, 140–1, 150, 161, 171–2, 173, 180, 184–5, 187–8, 190, 193, 198, 200–1, 212n; *see also* rationalisation
recognition *see anagnorisis*
recursion, 40–2, 221–2
regeneration, 131, 136, 155–6, 185, 189–90, 197, 200–2, 208
Reichert, John, 156
remorse, 36, 157, 191
reversal *see peripeteia*
ridicule *see* laughter
Roche, Thomas P., 73
Rogers, John, 71, 139, 166n
Root and Branch Petition, 94, 107, 127n
Roscius, 4, 18–19, 208–9
roundedness *see* encompassing, the
Rumrich, John P., 224n

Sabrina, 53, 63, 71, 75–8
sadness *see* melancholy; sorrow

Salmasius, 26
salt, 108, 203–5
salting, 1, 15, 23–4, 27, 57, 68, 110
Samson, 1, 35, 122, 137, 170–3, 175–7, 180, 182, 184–200, 202–6, 208
Satan, 4, 10, 20–1, 28, 32, 34, 37–41, 71, 122, 131, 145–7, 149, 156, 158–9, 161–2, 176–8, 188–9, 207
Satyrus, 18, 20
Sawday, Jonathan, 97, 138n
scepticism, 140, 172, 176, 200, 206, 208
Schoenfeldt, Michael, 42
Scottow, Joshua, 194, 215n
script, 5, 7–9, 11, 23, 30, 94–5, 100, 102, 103–6, 114, 121–3, 155, 176, 189, 196–7, 208, 219; see also scripture-as-script
scripture, 1, 5–6, 9, 10, 11, 100–4, 114, 120–2, 130, 132–3, 170, 173–7, 183–4, 196–7, 201, 205, 206–7, 214n, 219–20, 222; see also Bible; King James Version
scripture-as-script, 4, 9, 11, 121, 176, 197; see also script
scurrility, 6, 94, 107–9, 112, 113–14, 117, 199, 127n
Second Bishops' War, 89
Second Brother, 65, 72, 75, 77
self-creation, 39, 40–1
sermons see preaching
Shakespeare, William, 5, 7–8, 14, 61–2, 64, 72, 77, 86, 88, 110, 118, 138, 222
  Comedy of Errors, 205
  Coriolanus, 8, 12
  Hamlet, 3, 7–8, 39, 88, 121, 135
  Henry IV, part 1, 14–15, 195
  Julius Caesar, 118
  Macbeth, 134
  Measure for Measure, 77
  Midsummer Night's Dream, 61
  Richard II, 118, 205
  Richard III, 15, 118
  Tempest, The, 189
  Titus Andronicus, 86, 88
  Twelfth Night, 83n
shame, 35–6, 42, 97, 99, 110, 119–20, 190, 198, 203
shape-shifting, 37, 114
Shore, Daniel, 117–18
Shuger, Debora, 100–1
Shullenberger, William, 54, 57, 72–3, 77
Sidney, Philip, 119, 134, 144, 158, 215n
sighing, 122, 154–5
Simmonds, Martha, 183, 191–2, 214n
Sin, 40, 42
Smectymnuus, 4, 86–7, 91, 93, 98, 109
Smith, David L., 93
Socrates, 17, 151
solemnity, 9, 18, 24, 51, 78, 93, 100–2, 104, 106, 108–10, 113, 116–17, 119, 121, 123, 132, 135, 194, 215n
song see music
Sophocles, 4, 18–19, 25, 194
sorrow, 93, 134, 149, 150, 190, 198–9; see also melancholy
soul, the, 17, 36, 65–6, 77
sparagmos, 11, 34, 43, 92
spectacle, 15, 37–8, 40–1, 50–1, 53, 58, 61, 63, 64–7, 72, 73–7, 96, 99–100, 102, 122, 135–6, 149, 155, 158, 161–3, 186–7, 192, 197, 203–4, 208
spectators, 2, 4–5, 7–8, 10–11, 14, 16, 24, 27–30, 34–6, 37–8, 38–42, 53, 55, 58, 63, 66, 71, 72, 73–7, 84n, 87, 90, 94, 95–7, 99, 110–11, 113, 117, 121, 122, 127n, 131, 135, 137–8, 139, 146, 149, 155, 161–3, 176–8, 185–6, 193, 196, 202, 205–6, 213n, 218
Spenser, Edmund, 53, 63, 69, 72–5, 84n, 133, 222
springing, 39–40, 150–2, 154–5, 158, 176
Stackhouse, Amy, 33
stage directions, 30, 90, 110, 189; see also prompting
stage-players see actors
standing, 41, 102, 113, 155, 157, 176, 178, 180
Stein, Arnold, 194
stirring, 43, 51, 122, 146, 202–3, 216n
Stranger, Hannah, 183, 191–2, 214n
Straznicky, Marta, 205
suburbs, of London, 108–9, 115–16
Sugimura, N. K., 44n, 46n, 63
sword-players, 199
sympathy, 23, 26, 42, 56, 72, 76, 118, 131, 156
system, 32, 33, 40–2, 170, 209, 219–22

Tarlton, Richard, 5, 91
Teatro Olimpico, 185–6
tempering, 7–8, 43, 52, 132, 134, 162–3, 172–3, 177, 190, 198, 203–6, 208
Terence, 113–14
terror, 40, 42, 135, 142, 182, 203–4; *see also* horror
Tertullian, 14, 50–1
theatre
  anatomy, 15, 97, 126n
  chaste, 53, 78
  corruptive, as, 51, 56–9, 132, 166n
  coterie, 53, 61, 62, 77–8
  destruction of, God's, 50–1, 186
  as edifying, 51–3, 59, 122, 132, 135, 166n, 187, 204
  Elizabethan, 7, 92–3, 125n
  Interregnum, 136
  London, 14, 51, 59, 64, 90, 102, 107–8, 186
  medicinal, as, 172, 204–5
  microcosm, as, 33, 64, 93, 131
  popular, 2, 15, 52, 78, 88, 132
  print, of, 90
  Quaker, 177, 194–5
  Roman, 59, 108, 135, 147, 185
  Satanic, 40–1, 146–7, 149, 189
  spaces of, implied, 5, 29, 33, 35, 53, 54, 59, 62–3, 162
  visual field, as, 60, 62, 65, 141, 149, 163
theatricality, 2–11, 14–16, 20–1, 31, 34, 37–9, 42–3, 50, 54–6, 66, 87–8, 90–1, 94–100, 102–7, 109–14, 116–23, 131–2, 139–40, 146–9, 155–6, 161–4, 170, 176–80, 183, 185, 187, 188–9, 194–200, 203, 208–9, 219–22
theatrum mundi, 155–6, 185
Thraso, 3, 106, 113–14
Throckmorton, Job, 6
throng, 21, 36, 40–1, 68, 74–6, 93, 118, 120, 131, 185–6, 188; *see also* rabble
Thyrsis *see* Attendant Spirit
Tiresias, 31–2
toleration, 172–4, 176, 183, 207
Tombes, John, 183–4
touch, 65, 75, 157, 191, 221–2; *see also* caress
Townshend, Aurelian, 65, 74, 75, 80n

tragedy, 4, 18, 20, 43, 51–2, 109–10, 115–17, 119, 121, 134–7, 172, 194, 202–5, 215n; *see also* tragic, the
tragic, the, 93, 109–10, 115–17, 119, 137, 194; *see also* tragedy
tragi-comedic, the, 93, 108, 111, 116–17, 119, 194–5, 215n
transsexuality, 30–3
trembling, 104–5, 177–8, 180, 182, 207; *see also* horror
Trinculo, source of, 110–12
Turner, James Grantham, 146, 149

uncasing, 35, 94, 96–9, 113
Uriel, 10, 37, 146, 149, 177

van Dyck, Anthony, 158–60
van Heemskerck, Egbert, 178, 180, 181, 211n
vates, 53–6, 59, 78, 89; *see also* Orpheus
vehemence, 72, 91–2, 154, 171
Virgil, 16, 31, 33, 43, 60, 68, 78, 131, 147
virginity, 33, 59–60, 69–70, 72; *see also* chastity
visage *see* countenance
visards, 35, 95, 97, 108; *see also* costume
vision, peripheral, 10–11, 35–6, 142, 145–6, 150, 161, 186, 193; *see also* optics
vitalism, 139, 154, 164
Vitruvius, 185–6
vocation, poetic, 1, 16, 33, 53, 59, 67–8, 78, 89, 123, 219n

Waith, Eugene, 86
Wentworth, Thomas, Earl of Strafford, 90, 96
Whitehall Palace, 58, 118–19
Wigan, John, 183
wiliness, 135
Woods, Susan, 191
wreathing *see* mouthing
wrestlers, 199

yawling, 178
Younge, Richard, 207

Zaret, David, 95
zeal, 10, 20, 34, 91–3, 100–2, 106, 121–3, 128n, 130, 173, 208

EU representative:
Easy Access System Europe
Mustamäe tee 50, 10621 Tallinn, Estonia
Gpsr.requests@easproject.com